STALIN'S WORLD

STALIN'S WORLD

Dictating the Soviet Order

Sarah Davies and
James Harris

Yale UNIVERSITY PRESS
New Haven & London

Published with assistance from the foundation established in memory of Philip Hamilton McMillan of the Class of 1894, Yale College.

Yale University Press books may be purchased in quantity for educational, business, or promotional use. For information, please e-mail sales.press@yale.edu (U.S. office) or sales@yaleup.co.uk (U.K. office).

Set in Galliard and Copperplate type by IDS Infotech, Ltd. Printed in the United States of America.

Library of Congress Cataloging-in-Publication Data

Davies, Sarah (Sarah Rosemary)
    Stalin's world: dictating the Soviet order / Sarah Davies and James Harris.
      pages cm
    Includes bibliographical references and index.
    ISBN 978-0-300-18281-1 (hardback : alkaline paper)
1. Stalin, Joseph, 1879–1953—Political and social views. 2. Stalin, Joseph, 1879–1953—Language. 3. Political leadership—Soviet Union—History. 4. Communism—Soviet Union—Philosophy. 5. Political culture—Soviet Union—History. 6. Heads of state—Soviet Union—Biography. 7. Dictators—Soviet Union—Biography. 8. Soviet Union—Politics and government—1917–1936. 9. Soviet Union—Politics and government—1936–1953. I. Harris, James R., 1964– II. Title.
    DK268.S8D375 2014
    947.084'2092—dc23

                                                2014011490

A catalogue record for this book is available from the British Library.

This paper meets the requirements of ANSI/NISO Z39.48–1992 (Permanence of Paper).

10 9 8 7 6 5 4 3 2 1

FOR LOUIS AND ALICE

CONTENTS

ACKNOWLEDGMENTS

This project has been aided by many individuals and organizations over the course of its long gestation. The original research was supported by grants from the Arts and Humanities Research Council and research leave funded by Durham University and the University of Leeds. We received invaluable research assistance from Larissa Malashenko of the Russian State Archive for Social and Political History (RGASPI) and Vladimir Nevezhin of the Institute of Russian History of the Russian Academy of Sciences (IRI RAN). The staff of RGASPI, RGVA, and AVP RF went to great lengths to facilitate the research process. A number of colleagues have generously offered various forms of assistance, from commenting on written drafts and conference papers to supplying us with copies of their forthcoming publications. We are particularly grateful to Jorg Baberowski, David Brandenberger, William Chase, R. W. Davies, Sheila Fitzpatrick, Arch Getty, Wendy Goldman, Yoram Gorlizki, Paul Hagenloh, Mark Harrison, Oleg Khlevniuk, Matthew Lenoe, Joe Maiolo, Jan Plamper, David Priestland, Arfon Rees, Alfred Rieber, Gabor Rittersporn, David Shearer, Ronald Suny, Lynne Viola, and the anonymous readers for Yale University Press. The criticisms, comments, and advice have improved the volume. Errors, omissions, and other faults remain the responsibility of the authors. Finally, we would like to thank Vadim Staklo, Christina Tucker, and Mary Pasti of Yale University Press for their unflagging support for this project.

An abridged version of chapter 3 was published as "Encircled by Enemies: Stalin's Perceptions of the Capitalist World, 1918–1941" in the *Journal of Strategic Studies* 3 (2007). It is reprinted here with permission of the journal. Some sections of chapter 4 were published in Balazs Apor, Jan C. Behrends, Polly Jones, and E. A. Rees, eds., *The Leader Cult in Communist Dictatorships: Stalin and the Eastern Bloc* (Basingstoke, England, 2004). They are reprinted here with the permission of Palgrave Macmillan.

TERMS AND ABBREVIATIONS

Abwehr	German military intelligence
Agitprop	Department of Agitation and Propaganda of the CC
APRF	Archive of the President of the Russian Federation
ARCOS	All-Russian Cooperative Society
AVP RF	Archive of Foreign Policy of the Russian Federation
Basmachi	group fighting Soviet power in Central Asia during and after the Revolution
batrak	farm laborer
bedniak	poor peasant
byvshie liudy	"former people," typically members of the pre-revolutionary elite
CC	Central Committee of the Communist Party
CCC	Central Control Commission
Comintern	Communist International
Donbas	Don Basin
Donugol'	Donbas Coal Trust
dvurushnichestvo	"double-dealing" (praising policy in public and working to undermine it in private)

dvurushnik	"double-dealer"
edinolichnik	independent farmer
fond	archival collection
FOSP	Federation of Organizations of Soviet Writers
FSB	Federal Security Service
gorkom	city committee of the Communist Party
Glavlit	Main Directorate for Literary and Publishing Affairs (state censorship)
Gosizdat	State Publishing House
Gosplan	State Planning Commission
GPU	State Political Administration
gubkom	regional committee of the Communist Party (until the late 1920s)
GUKF	Main Directorate for Cinematography and Photography Industry
Gulag	Chief Administration of Camps
Hetman	Ukrainian Cossack leader
IMEL	Institute of Marx-Engels-Lenin
INO OGPU	Foreign Department of the OGPU
intelligent	member of the intelligentsia
ITR	engineering and technical workers
Izvestiia	national state newspaper
Kadet	member of the Constitutional Democratic Party
khoziaistvenniki	leading economic officials
kolkhoz	collective farm
kolkhoznik	collective farmer
komitety sodeistviia (OGPU)	committees for cooperation with the OGPU
Komsomol (VLKSM)	All-Union Leninist Young Communist League
KPK	Party Control Commission
KR	counterrevolutionary
krai	territory
kraikom	territorial party committee

KRO (OGPU)	Counterintelligence Unit of the OGPU
KSK	Commission for State Control
kulak	wealthy peasant
Kul'tprop	Department of Culture and Propaganda of the CC
kul'turnost'	culturedness
kustar'	craftsman
KVZhD	Chinese Far Eastern Railway
Litfront	extreme left faction of RAPP
Lubianka	building containing the offices of the political police in Moscow
MKhAT	Moscow Art Theater
Narkompros	People's Commissariat of Enlightenment
Narkomzdrav	People's Commissariat of Health
NEP	New Economic Policy
NKID	People's Commissariat of Foreign Affairs
NKVD	People's Commissariat of Internal Affairs
obkom	regional committee of the Communist Party
oblast'	region
oblispolkom	regional executive committee
OGPU	Consolidated State Political Directorate
Orgburo	Organizational Bureau of the CC
Orgkomitet	Organizational Committee of the Writers' Union
Osoaviakhim	Union of Societies of Assistance in Defense and Aviation-Chemical Construction in the USSR
opis'	inventory (of an archive collection)
ORPO	Department of Leading Party Organs of the CC
otkhod	seasonal departure of peasants to cities
partiinost'	party spirit
peredyshka	breathing space
perestroika	reconstruction

Petliurovite	supporter of Simon Petliura's movement for Ukrainian independence
piatiletka	five-year plan
Pioneers	Soviet mass organization for children
Politburo	Political Bureau of the CC
polpredstvo	Soviet equivalent of an embassy in the early years after the Revolution
polpred	ambassador
Pravda	the Communist Party's national newspaper
Profintern	Trade Unions International
Proletkul't	Proletarian Culture Movement
Rabkrin (RKI)	Workers' and Peasants' Inspectorate
raion	district
RAPP	Russian Association of Proletarian Writers
revoliutsionnoe chut'ye	revolutionary instinct
RGASPI	Russian State Archive for Social and Political History
RGVA	Russian State Military Archive
RSDWP	Russian Social Democratic Workers' Party
RSFSR	Russian Soviet Federated Socialist Republic
samokritika	self-criticism
Secretariat	Secretariat of the CC
seredniak	middle peasant
skloki	squabbles; factional infighting
sluzhashchii	white-collar worker
Smena vekh, smenovekhovstvo	"Change of Landmarks" movement
smychka	link
sovkhoz	state farm
Sovnarkom	Council of People's Commissars
SR	member of the Socialist Revolutionary Party
stazh	length of service
TASS	Telegraph Agency of the Soviet Union

USSR	Union of Soviet Socialist Republics
VChK (Cheka)	All-Russian Extraordinary Commission for Combating Counterrevolution and Sabotage.
VAPP	All-Union Association of Proletarian Writers
VKP(b)	All-Union Communist Party (Bolshevik)
vozhd'	leader, chief
VSNKh	Supreme Council of the National Economy
VTsSPS	All-Union Central Council of Trade Unions
White Guard	White forces during and after the civil war

STALIN'S WORLD

INTRODUCTION: STALIN'S VISION

Over the past twenty-five years, historians of the Stalin era have gained access to millions of archival files generated by the Communist Party and its leaders. It will take many years to digest this material, although we have made considerable progress. We have learned that Iosif Stalin was not a weak dictator, that he was not embattled or buffeted by factions, that he steadily accumulated personal power and exercised it vigorously. Few decisions of any importance were made without his consent or knowledge. No one would now contest that Stalinism—the set of policies, practices, and ideas associated with the period from the late 1920s to 1953—was at least in some measure a product of his influence: economy, society, culture, and politics all bear his imprint. The purpose of this book is simple: by drawing on little-known documentation we hope to broaden our understanding of the dictator's vision of the world, of how he interpreted the Soviet system he was trying to build and its wider international context.

We investigate Stalin's vision from two different but complementary angles.

We begin by addressing the question of how he interpreted information concerning matters of state. Stalin inhabited a world composed largely of written texts. Since he rarely left his offices, particularly after the mid-1920s, he comprehended Soviet and international affairs primarily through the prism of the documents that crossed his desk.[1] When we compare the material that he read from week to week with the decisions he subsequently shaped, it is possible to draw conclusions about the way he understood and interpreted that information. By looking at information flows and the way information was processed, we can understand not only how he perceived the world but also how he *mis*perceived it and the sometimes far-reaching consequences of those misperceptions.

After reviewing Stalin's interpretation of information, we then examine Stalin's efforts to establish what Pierre Bourdieu terms "a legitimate vision of the social world." Although Stalin was by no means solely responsible for this undertaking, his personal contributions did play a critically important role. In particular, he had to devote a vast amount of time to the whole business of generating authoritative *words*. This was necessary because, as Bourdieu puts it, "the categories of perception, the systems of classification, that is, essentially, the words, the names which construct social reality as much as they express it, are the crucial stakes of political struggle, which is a struggle to impose the legitimate principle of vision and division."[2] We argue, therefore, that Stalin's words deserve as much scholarly attention as his deeds; in a sense, his words *were* his deeds.[3] John Lewis Gaddis is surely right when he contends that "it would be easy to make too much of Stalin's words, for reality always separates what people say from what they do. What is striking about Stalin, though, is how small that separation was. To a degree we are only now coming to realize, Stalin *literally* imposed his rhetoric upon the country he ran."[4] To understand the nature of the dictator's power, we need to be attentive to the various ways in which he deployed words in the struggle to create and impose a compelling vision of the world.

We consider Stalin's vision through an examination of several important themes, all of which were at the forefront of the leader's attention and which continue to occupy the attention of scholars: Bolshevik leadership, spymania, capitalist encirclement, the leader cult, the working class, and Soviet culture.[5] Since the archival material is richest for 1924–41, the era in which the Stalinist system was formed and consolidated, the primary chronological focus of the volume is on these formative years, although where feasible and appropriate, comparisons are drawn with earlier and later periods.

The study is based on extensive research in Stalin's personal archive, *fond* 558, particularly *opis'* 11, which was transferred to the Russian State

Archive for Social and Political History (RGASPI) from the Archive of the President of the Russian Federation (APRF) in 1999. *Opis'* 11 comprises a large number of files taken from the office of the General Secretary at the time of his death. Stalin evidently kept vast quantities of documentation to hand, some of which appears to have been transferred to other archives, with the remainder located in *opis'* 11. Probably only the staff of APRF know on what principle certain files were selected for retention in Stalin's personal archive. We cannot exclude the possibility that materials were chosen to present Stalin in a certain light, but the archive is of immense value to historians in any case, containing as it does a wealth of material, including the leader's unpublished correspondence, speeches, articles, and reports he received.[6] In addition, we have examined unpublished materials from the Politburo, Secretariat, Orgburo, and Central Committee (CC), the personal archives of other party leaders, and various state archives. Recently published document collections and memoirs have also been an invaluable resource.

When the archives first opened, scholars expected that the previously unpublished, confidential papers—the "hidden transcripts"—would reveal Stalin's inner world, what he *really* believed. The consensus now is that the Bolsheviks' "public" and "private" materials actually differ very little from each other; for example, the latter are as saturated with Marxist-Leninist categories as the former.[7] Although we would largely concur with this important finding, it would be a mistake to conclude that the unpublished materials are not revealing. They may not yield revelations of the sensational variety, but they certainly offer a fuller and more nuanced understanding of Stalin's vision of the world.

Information and Interpretation

Leaders faced with ambiguous or contradictory information tend to favor those interpretations that reinforce their preexisting assumptions. Some are better than others at reflecting on their assumptions. "Facts are stubborn things," as John Adams, the second president of the United States, wrote in 1770. "Whatever may be our wishes, our inclinations, or the dictates of our passion, they cannot alter the state of facts and evidence." Ronald Reagan raised this dictum from its relative obscurity by misquoting it at the 1988 Republican National Convention: "Facts," he declared, "are *stupid* things."[8] Though this makes an amusing political anecdote, there is a weighty issue underlying it that deserves serious consideration. What was Stalin's relationship with "facts"?

Stalin was exceptionally well informed about events both at home and abroad. He received regular reports from a vast array of agencies, including the information departments of the Central Committee, the political police, the Commissariat of Foreign Affairs, Comintern, and the agencies checking the fulfillment of decisions. He also received many thousands of letters from Soviet citizens. Stalin had an extraordinary appetite for reading this material, as we can see in the *opisi* of documents he received while he was on vacation. Even then, he was reading hundreds of pages of material every day.[9] How he interpreted that material is a crucial, though underdeveloped, subject in our field. There is an old and rather artificial debate about whether Stalin was driven by ideology or power-political considerations; the middle ground is to observe that both came into play.[10] This answer does not address more than superficially the question of how Stalin interpreted the information he received. Ours is a question of perception and misperception. At the risk of sounding positivistic, let us state the question this way: How did Stalin interpret, or misinterpret, his world?

David Priestland has recently offered an intriguing approach to the question.[11] He observed a tension in Bolshevik, and indeed Marxist, thought between its scientistic and voluntarist strands. Stalin, like many of his Bolshevik contemporaries, was determined to employ the latest technologies and techniques in order to build socialism according to rational, albeit noncapitalist, principles. But he was also prone to think of Marxism-Leninism as a system of thought, a clear understanding of which opened almost limitless possibilities. Priestland shows how the tension contributed to a deepening misperception of events that played a significant role in the Terror, the political violence of 1936–38. Stalin never quite grasped that the Marxism-Leninism did not cause basic problems of administration and governance to melt away. As his industrialization plans clattered into the fortress walls they were meant to storm, he was more inclined to assess blame than to reassess the principles underpinning his policies.

Andrea Graziosi provides another interpretation in a perceptive article on archival sources and the political history of the Stalin period. Writing at a time when historians were gaining access to an ever wider range of documents from the locus of Soviet power under Stalin, Graziosi warns that the documents should not be read at face value: "Even in its bona fide, pre-1917 version, Marxism was an ideology in the Marxian sense, i.e. a fictitious, reassuring, self-gratifying and self-explanatory construction and, at the same time, a deceptive lens reproducing a distorted image of reality of such an atypical country from classical Marxism's point of view, as the former tsarist empire."[12] Graziosi is particularly interested in the ways the regime was drawn in by its own deliberate myth-building. Especially after 1917, the Soviet leadership applied labels to, and imposed ways of understanding on, certain phenomena that did not square nicely with Marxist categories. For example, it divided peasant society into classes according to a crude scheme (poor, middle, kulak) that merely served to obscure the complexities of social relations. The crude categorization was replicated in reports from local officials, thus serving further to convince the center of the objectivity of its scheme. Graziosi's point is that the leadership wanted to understand what was happening in the country, but it tended to get drawn into the categories of its own propaganda as they were repeated by a deeply conformist bureaucracy:

> [Stalin] did want the truth. Obviously, however, nobody was going to risk annoying or irritating him with unexpected news, so that the degree of falsity increased even more, thereby fuelling the despot's rage, which in turn made people even more afraid, subservient and false in the most classic vicious cycle . . . The Soviet top leadership thus ended up feeding on its own propaganda . . . Inevitably, the system grew more and more inefficient. Nor could it be otherwise since its centre became blinder and blinder, gradually losing its capacity to see in a more or less objective way and thus to act in a more or less rational way. We are not far from the truth when we say that the Soviet state was the victim of its own lies and built its own trap.[13]

Graziosi's warning has not been heeded consistently, nor have the dimensions and implications of the trap been adequately explored.

Understanding the trap is not easy. Stalin never left documents outlining how he interpreted his sources of information, let alone how he misinterpreted what he read. Our approach to this thorny problem involves analyzing known streams of Stalin's sources of information available from the Stalin archive in the context of other documents, particularly the decisions and resolutions of upper party and state bodies. By analyzing information received in the context of decisions subsequently taken, we can build a picture of how that information was interpreted. In some cases, it is possible to add to that analysis Stalin's instructions on what information should be collected and how it should be prioritized, as well as correspondence and memoirs from those who supplied the leadership with information. In these cases we can clearly see how Stalin privileged certain types of information and dismissed others in a way that reinforced his prejudicial reading and made it difficult for information gatherers to support alternative viewpoints, as Graziosi has observed.

Understanding Stalin's interpretation and misinterpretation of information needs a further context beyond a reading of information and decisions. In most ways, Stalin was like other Bolshevik leaders. Broadly speaking, he shared their experiences, their aspirations, and their fears. He faced the same dilemmas of power, though they did not always share the same view of how to resolve them. When the Bolsheviks seized power in November 1917, they shared the aspiration to contribute to the spread of communism, both domestically and internationally. In the context of peasant Russia, this aim was ambitious in the extreme. Their hopes to trigger an international revolution were disappointed, and they were almost immediately faced with a struggle to survive a civil war and foreign intervention that was more ferociously violent than the world war that had immediately preceded it. Bolshevik ideology in part explains why. The Bolsheviks' prevalent understanding of the history of revolution and reaction dictated that they must not shrink from any means to preserve the Revolution. Against the odds, they emerged victorious from the civil war but considerably weakened and changed. The working class in whose name they had seized power had all but melted away amid economic collapse. The Bolsheviks could no longer rely on the benign neutrality of a peasantry angered by grain seizures and in the midst of a famine. The army was mutinous, and the apparatus of government and economic administration of necessity remained under the influence of a pre-revolutionary officialdom doubtful of, when not hostile to, Soviet power. This context is critical to an understanding of the information-gathering systems the Bolsheviks created, which Stalin inherited and made his own.

Because the Bolsheviks aspired to a withering away of the state under communism, they never coherently engaged in state-building in the sense of establishing permanent, regular institutions with clearly defined powers. The implications are explored in chapter 1. Lenin, in his last writings at the end of the civil war, insisted that Soviet Communists had to learn about leadership and administration from Europe and America and not rashly plow forward without adequate skills and knowledge. His warnings went unheeded. Stalin was inhibited by Leon Trotsky's accusation that he was a mere bureaucrat. He could not have focused his energies on regularizing state structures without appearing to justify Trotsky's portrayal of him. And yet, again to borrow from Priestland, rather than study and apply the lessons of state-building in the developed world as the scientistic vein of Bolshevik thought might dictate, Stalin was drawn to its more revivalist strand. His experience as General Secretary was convincing him that institutions in themselves, in the form of committees, councils, and commissariats, were prone to be dead weights of bureaucratism. But if the right person was put in the right position, officials could be made to work together such that any obstacle could be overcome.

Directly contradicting Lenin's injunction not to move forward rashly without developing an adequate machinery of state, Stalin insisted that "there are no fortresses that Bolsheviks cannot storm."[14] At the end of the 1920s, he oversaw the confirmation of ever more ambitious economic plans, well beyond what could be achieved with every sinew strained. He made matters considerably worse for himself and the state when he declared in 1930 that officials could not cite "objective reasons" for any failure to achieve targets: "The party does not simply adapt to objective conditions. The party has the power to influence them, to change them, to find itself a more advantageous combination of objective conditions."[15] Three years later, in the face of massive underfulfillment of quotas, production bottlenecks, and general confusion, plans were reduced, but Stalin never acknowledged that he had been wrong. Plans continued to be ambitious, and he continued to insist that they were realistic, that there could be no discussion of objective reasons for not fulfilling them. Put in an impossible position, officials at all levels adapted variously by misleading the center about the real state of affairs locally, by degrading the quality of production, by hiding production capacity, and by otherwise subverting central directives that made it harder for them to meet the all-important targets.[16] Stalin had a good sense that much of officialdom was engaging in corrupt and counterproductive practices, but he never seemed to grasp that these practices were largely a consequence of his policies. Rather, through the 1930s, Stalin railed against the "*dvurushnik*," the "two-faced" officials who supported central policies in public and worked to subvert them in practice. Despite three years of solid economic growth between 1934 and 1937, Stalin ripped the heart out of the economic apparatus to wipe out the practices that his policies had engendered.

Chapters 2 and 3 examine other perceived threats to the Soviet system: spies, saboteurs, wreckers, and hostile capitalist states. In chapter 2, on spymania, we observe that Stalin was not alone in thinking that victory in the civil war did not mean that domestic and internal enemies of the Revolution would stop their efforts to undermine the new Soviet order. It was the head of the Cheka-GPU, Feliks Dzerzhinskii, who originally pressed this case, though Stalin shared his concerns from the start without apparent hesitation. Chapter 2 shows how early GPU operations such as Trest and Sindikat-2 generated an exaggerated picture of the threat posed by spies and saboteurs, but GPU leaders were not inclined to cast a critical eye on the evidence, because it helped them protect their organization from cuts to their budgets and efforts to restrict their powers. Stalin firmly defended them from both and rarely challenged the quality of the intelligence that the political police generated. He was not alone in thinking that enemies of the USSR were, as the Bolsheviks themselves had been before 1917, "experienced conspirators." The GPU could not be expected to base its investigations on material evidence of counterrevolutionary crime, because the conspirators would not leave any behind. The political police were instructed to rely on "revolutionary instinct." As in the darkest days of the civil war, they were told that they should be able look a suspect in the eye and see if he or she was an enemy of the regime. They tended to rely heavily on circumstantial evidence and confessions obtained under torture. The unreliability of such evidence, combined with the self-interest of the political police in playing up threats and the conspiratorial mentality of the Bolsheviks, induced a fundamental misperception of the threat posed by wreckers and saboteurs. Stalin was not the sole author of this institutional paranoia, but he contributed greatly to its spread and influence.

Chapter 3, on capitalist encirclement, presents a similar story. At the end of the civil war, Bolshevik leaders prudently assumed that even though the Whites and foreign armies had withdrawn, neither had surrendered the ambition to put an end to communism. Well before Stalin took power, the highest priority of intelligence-gathering agencies was the identification of threats to Soviet sovereignty. Once again, the sense of threat was exaggerated. Unlike in the story of spymania, though, there was not, at least initially, a strong institutional interest in the exaggeration of the threat. Rather, it was the intensity of the reaction against revolutionary events in the early 1920s, the strength of anti-communist sentiment in ruling circles, right-wing revanchism, and a fundamental misreading of diplomatic activity that contributed to this exaggeration. Most obviously, in the 1920s and into the 1930s, Soviet intelligence gatherers time and again misread measures to contain Germany as measures to build an anti-communist alliance. There were some dissenters, like Commissar for Foreign Affairs Georgii Chicherin, who was scathing in his criticism of this sort of conspiratorial viewpoint, but as in the spymania case, Stalin, as he confirmed his monopoly of power, made it ever more difficult for information gatherers to present evidence that contradicted his vision of the USSR as surrounded by capitalist powers bent on a new invasion. The materials in the Stalin archive indicate that there was not just one war scare in 1927 but a continuous fear, more intense at some moments than others, that the Soviet Union faced a new invasion. The view was almost wholly misguided, but information gatherers collected a steady stream of material that seemed to justify Stalin's view. By 1936, in the midst of an arms race and in the face of resurgent, fascist, passionately anti-communist revanchist states and the beginning of the Spanish Civil War, which locked communists and fascists in a struggle for supremacy, Stalin could be forgiven for thinking he had been right all along. There really was an imminent threat of invasion, and it came to pass in 1941.

Stalin appeared deeply troubled by the specter of an enemy, not realizing that it was ultimately the product of a faulty system of information gathering. The flaws in that system, particularly its excessive focus on identifying threats to the Revolution, pre-dated Stalin. Those flaws became more pronounced as his personal dictatorship emerged. All of this is not to say that Stalin was paranoid, or that his misperception was pervasive. Even less is it our intention to argue that Stalin would not have murdered millions if he had just had accurate information. Stalin's vision of the world was shaped by Marxism-Leninism, by his personal experience, including his time with the revolutionary underground, by war, and by political struggle within the party. He was far from alone among Bolshevik leaders in taking a conspiratorial view of the world, in defending the Revolution with ruthless single-mindedness. The information-gathering system he inherited should have kept him extremely well informed and confident of the security of his position and the growing strength of the USSR. Instead, it gave him a consistent, detailed, and compelling picture of pervasive threat and vulnerability. Understanding how Stalin received and processed information is critical for our evaluation of the Stalin era more broadly.

The Power of Stalin's Words

Equally important is an understanding of Stalin's contribution to the process of creating and imposing an authoritative vision of the world. As the written and spoken utterances of the *vozhd'* were central to this process, Stalin was expected to pay particularly close attention to his choice of words and phrases. Whereas others have written at length about Stalin's "ideology," "beliefs," or "political thought," we focus more closely on his *words*.[17]

Words always mattered a great deal in the USSR. Natalia Kozlova goes so far as to claim that "Soviet society is often referred to as a society of ideas, but it is, rather, a society of words and word games."[18] Soviet power was, or at least aspired to be, a dictatorship over words, and the establishment and enforcement of verbal orthodoxy was a high priority for Bolshevik "verbal imperialists" from the outset.[19] R. V. Daniels, who identifies this early "concern for verbal correctness," observes that in the 1920s "party leaders manifested habits of thought not usually associated with the metaphysical materialism which they formally acknowledged. The word, the slogan, the formula, were in practice treated as the real thing."[20] Invented categories such as "kulak" or "middle peasant" acquired a "real" existence thanks to Bolshevik linguistic conjuring.[21]

This logocentrism—the privileging of the word—intensified in the 1930s in tandem with Stalin's burgeoning dictatorship. Eric Naiman makes a persuasive case that Stalinist culture and Soviet ideology should be viewed as verbal phenomena. He points to the metadiscursive qualities of the leader's own speeches and writings, such his notorious article "Dizzy with Success," where he writes: "Everyone is *talking* about the successes of Soviet power in the area of the kolkhoz movement . . . What does this all *say?*" Naiman proposes that for Stalin, "events were primarily discursive and metadiscursive," citing the preoccupation with slogans in his speech to the April 1929 party plenum: "Remember the latest events in our Party. Remember the latest *slogans,* which the Party has put forward lately in connection with the new class shifts in the country. I am *speaking* about *slogans,* such as the *slogan* of self-*criticism,* the *slogan* of heightened struggle with bureaucracy and the purge of the Soviet apparatus, the *slogan* of organization, etc."[22] As Naiman puts it, "The transition from slogans to events is almost a matter of synonymity in Stalin's representation of Soviet realia."[23]

Katerina Clark and Evgenii Dobrenko also highlight the significance of the word in their reflections on the importance of authoritative written texts in the Stalin-era USSR, when "writing was a means for promulgating the Party's ultimate authorship of Soviet reality." The 1930s, a period of "textual obsession," saw the publication of a succession of authoritative works, including the Stalin Constitution (1936) and the canonical *History of the All-Union Communist Party (Bolsheviks): Short Course* (1938). Hierarchies of power developed on the basis of who had access to texts, who had the right to author them, and who had the power to censor and edit them. Stalin stood at the apex of all these hierarchies as the supreme "guardian of the texts."[24] Alexei Yurchak, drawing on Claude Lefort's work, describes Stalin as the "master," as the editorial voice that evaluated and legitimized Marxist-Leninist discourse from an ostensibly "external" position. The master was able to obscure the paradox that any modern ideology, including Marxism-Leninism, is based on claims about objective truths, which supposedly have an existence external to the terms of the ideological discourse itself. Without the external voice of Stalin, the legitimacy of the dominant ideology was bound to be undermined.[25]

One particularly vivid illustration of the significance accorded to words in the 1930s, and the importance of Stalin as master of the word, is a conflict in May 1934 centered on Nikolai Bukharin's choice of terminology in an article for *Izvestiia*, "The Economics of the Soviet Land."[26] Two prominent figures in the ideological establishment, the head of Kul'tprop (the culture and propaganda department of the Central Committee), Aleksei Stetskii, and the *Pravda* editor Lev Mekhlis, pounced on this article, flagging its supposedly unorthodox vocabulary for Stalin himself. Bukharin's use of the term "agrarian revolution" to describe collectivization and his description of one phase of the New Economic Policy (NEP) as "classical" were regarded as particularly suspect by Stetskii, who accused Bukharin of trying to be original (*On original'nichaet*) and "to say 'new words.' " Stalin evidently took the matter seriously, forwarding Stetskii's note and a similar letter from Mekhlis to the Politburo. Bukharin, in his reply to Stalin, defended himself by rebutting Stetskii's points and questioning the latter's desire for verbal uniformity: "Maybe com. Stetskii wants *generally* to forbid the words 'agrarian revolution'?" He suggested that Stetskii was displeased because "I do not always use the *words* that he likes." He continued: "Stetskii is training for *words* instead of *thoughts,* and later the CC has to issue directives even for Pioneers against cramming *words*. From 'philology' and verbalistics, which are *worse* than scholastics (the latter had *concepts,* while Stetskii only has *words*), people's brains dry up and they become mentally sterile."

Stetskii retaliated with a further letter to Stalin accusing Bukharin, among other things, of excessive abstraction. One of the points that Bukharin had made in his own defense was that Marx had used the term "agrarian revolution," but clearly this appeal to the authority of Marx did not carry much weight with Stetskii at this stage. Observing that Marx was writing long ago, he argued that now they could use more precise terms: "'collectivization' and 'liquidation of the kulaks as a class'—these 'words,' as Bukharin says scornfully, are close and accessible to every toiler because they express the essence of the party's policy. Com. Bukharin evidently 'does not recognize' these new words: he prefers to speak of agrarian revolution and the expropriation of the kulaks." Stetskii proceeded to question Bukharin's use of the term "classical" before concluding: "He asserts that the arguments are about 'words.' But it's a matter of big words, which express the essence of policy . . . when characterizing the party's policies, com. Bukharin operates with such gutta-percha [rubbery] 'words,' which can contain much, including com. Bukharin's former opportunistic views, or these gutta-percha formulations might be a loophole for further attempts by Bukharin to justify his former errors . . . Isn't it time for com. Bukharin . . . to speak the language of the party?"

Stetskii's point was clear: words mattered, and Bolsheviks were obliged to use the orthodox (Stalinist) lexicon, the language of the party, rather than invoke their own slippery terms. Stalin confirmed this in his own letter to the Politburo of 14 July, asserting categorically that "com. Stetskii is right, and not com. Bukharin," and reiterating many of Stetskii's points. He agreed that the term "agrarian revolution" was incorrect because it ignored the specifics of collectivization, explaining that "this is, of course, not an argument about 'words.' It's a question of clarity and definition in formulations. The Bolsheviks are strong because they do not ignore the demands of clarity and definition." Stalin also objected to Bukharin's misleading use of the term "classical": "It's wrong to speak of 'classical' and 'non-classical' NEP. It's wrong because it confuses the issues and might confuse people. 'New' words are necessary if they arise through necessity, create clarity, offer obvious advantages. They are harmful if they do not arise through necessity and create confusions. The Bolsheviks do not need a game of 'new little words' [*slovechik*]."[27]

We have dwelled on this incident because it reveals much about the significance of words in the eyes of the Stalinist leadership. The criticism of Bukharin was not simply another attempt to put the former oppositionist firmly in his place; it was also designed to convey a strong message about the need for verbal uniformity, for all to communicate in the authorized Bolshevik idiom, whose anointed custodian in chief at this point was Stalin.[28]

As the period unfolded, Stalin's utterances came to be surrounded by a growing aura of sanctity and received correspondingly reverential treatment. The media were increasingly saturated with quotations from his speeches and writings; importantly, however, such quotations could be published only with official sanction, for his words were jealously guarded, and anyone daring to cite his unpublished pronouncements in print without permission was liable to be severely reprimanded. In 1929, for example, Ukraine's agitprop chief, A. Khvylia, was admonished for publishing excerpts from Stalin's speech to Ukrainian writers without the authorization of the top party leadership. Even previously published speeches and writings were monitored: Lavrentii Beria's decision to republish some of Stalin's early writings in 1935 elicited a furious response from their author, who claimed that this had been done without proper care and insisted that he alone had the right to sanction the republication of his own work. The affair culminated in a Politburo resolution to publish a full edition of Stalin's *Works*, a complex undertaking that did not reach fruition until after the war.[29]

As this episode suggests, Stalin himself took his responsibilities as master of the word extremely seriously.[30] Dmitrii Shepilov observed at firsthand how Stalin was "well aware of the significance that was attached not only to his every word but to his every nuance."[31] Stalin was also comfortable handling the written word: like other leading Bolsheviks, he had notched up many years of experience as a writer, a journalist, and an editor before the Revolution. We now have at our disposal a large corpus of his hitherto unpublished writings, ranging from lengthy letters to laconic resolutions, and it is evident just how much time he devoted to the wording and structuring of these texts, writing for the most part, it seems, without much assistance.[32]

Also available for the first time are the written records of many of his unpublished speeches and oral remarks. Although it is generally acknowledged that Stalin was no great orator, a number of witnesses attest to the scrupulous care he took over the formulation of his spoken as well as his written words.[33] Reflecting on his considered manner of speaking, Shepilov was impressed by "his extraordinarily keen sense of responsibility for his every word."[34] The German writer Lion Feuchtwanger was similarly struck: "Stalin speaks slowly in a low, rather colourless voice. He has no liking for a dialogue of short, excited questions, answers and interruptions, but prefers to string together slow, considered sentences. Often, what he says sounds ready for the press, as if he were dictating."[35] (Feuchtwanger's impression was quite accurate, for such utterances were indeed regularly reproduced almost verbatim in the form of articles, decrees, or resolutions.) Stalin was attentive to the wording of both his less formal remarks (conversations, interjections, and so on) and his more formal speeches. He prepared thoroughly for the latter, and the archival material shows how he edited the transcripts prior to their publication.

Finally, the archives contain abundant evidence of Stalin's role as editor in chief of the documents generated by others, ranging from decrees and party slogans to film scripts and works of history. Editing consumed Stalin's time right up to the final months of his life as he sought to ensure that others' words aligned with his dominant vision. As Leonid Maksimenkov puts it: "Stalin as a politician was above all the editor of a text prepared for confirmation . . . He perceived Russian [*rossiiskuiu*] political culture through the written text."[36]

We draw on all these newly available sources, as well as Stalin's previously published *Works,* to analyze his words on three subjects that were the source of particular tension and uncertainty for the party in power: the place of leader cults within a Marxist polity, the status of the Soviet working class, and the relationship between the party-state and the arts.

As Stalin developed his vision, he had to balance Bolshevik ideological desiderata with the imperatives of Soviet state-building. Following the confrontational and destabilizing "class war" fervor of 1928–31, he sought to project a more inclusive vision designed to foster a sense of a unified "Soviet" political community.[37] At the core of the community was the burgeoning cult of Stalin, which is considered in chapter 4. Its existence in a nominally Marxist collectivist state created the potential for considerable tension, and although Stalin tacitly promoted the cult, he made a point of describing it as a concession to popular tradition, criticizing its excesses and insisting that cultic texts remained within acceptable parameters.

The heterogeneity inherent in Stalin's approach to the cult was also evident in his interpretations of class and Soviet culture. In chapter 5 we explore how Stalin dealt with the long-standing Bolshevik ambivalence toward the working class, and indeed the whole concept of class itself. Without ever abandoning the language of class, Stalin moved steadily toward a more inclusive vision of the Soviet people. Our primary focus is on his attempts to divert attention from a central Bolshevik symbol, the manual laborer, toward a newly legitimized "Soviet" or "people's" intelligentsia. The final chapter turns to the subject of the arts, another sphere in which Stalin strove to find words to unite instead of divide. We examine his efforts to justify a "Soviet" rather than a narrowly "proletarian" culture and to promote a heterogeneous vision of the USSR as a place where artists served the party-state yet also enjoyed creative freedom.

Stalin's interventions, clad in the mandatory yet reasonably flexible framework of Marxism-Leninism, aimed to provide authoritative interpretations and to smooth over the many tensions and ambiguities surrounding these issues. While some of his utterances were designed for more limited audiences and others were targeted at a wider public, all were intended, in various ways and with varying degrees of success, to produce and impose a distinctive vision of the world: Stalin's world.

INFORMATION AND INTERPRETATION

1

"BOLSHEVIK" LEADERSHIP

The opening of the Soviet archives told us more about the way the state worked than anything else. The archives confirmed much that we already knew, but it has been possible to add considerable nuance to the picture. For all that progress, though, scholars are still locked in a debate about whether the Soviet state under Stalin was "weak" or "strong."[1] Does the big picture show us that Stalin gradually built an unassailable personal dictatorship in the 1930s, or that he was embattled, frustrated, and angered by the unresponsiveness of officialdom to the will of the center?

Some of the best work on the subject has suggested a sort of middle ground. Paul Gregory, R. W. Davies, and others have argued convincingly that although Stalin was the final arbiter in all significant matters of policy, he "was not immune to pressure and persuasion from Politburo members, or from society at large."[2] Gregory emphasizes the role of "bargaining" between the center and "lower levels" in shaping policy.[3] The most obvious manifestation of this came after the persistent crises of the first five-year plan, when targets were reduced to more sustainable levels in the second plan.

The suggestion is that neither the "weak state" nor the "strong state" perspective accounted adequately for the process of bargaining that underlay the evolution of policy. But one needs to be careful, because the process of bargaining was not stable and its "rules," to the extent that there were any, were far from clear. Davies and Gregory account for changes in policy such as the moderation of plan targets and the relatively stable growth of 1934–37, but neither accounts for the devastating purge of state and party officialdom at the end of those "three good years." Davies has argued emphatically that economic problems did not contribute to the purge.[4] But if the economy was doing well, and the process of bargaining was having its effect, why did Stalin see fit to decimate officialdom in 1937 and 1938? Is the notion of bargaining a useful middle ground for understanding the weak-state/strong-state conundrum?

This chapter examines Stalin's conception of "Bolshevik" leadership and administration from his early years as General Secretary to the Great Terror of 1936–38 as a way of addressing the conundrum. It argues that Stalin's experience as de facto head of state convinced him that he, and perhaps his inner circle, were alone in upholding the interests of the state as a whole.[5] When he declared in the early 1930s that officials were not permitted to cite "objective" reasons for failing to meet targets, he effectively closed off a key source of information about the situation in the country. Often asked to do the impossible, officials learned the fine arts of expectation management, evasion, and even the subversion of central directives.[6] Stalin did manage to build a state apparatus capable of extraordinary feats of mass mobilization, but it was never as responsive as he thought it should be. He knew about the "coping behaviors" of Soviet officialdom from the work of agencies checking the fulfillment of decisions, but he never grasped that these behaviors were products of the excessive demands issued by the center.[7] In forbidding any attribution of underfulfillment to the demands of the plan, Stalin inhibited his capacity to understand and resolve economic problems. The reduction of plan targets by 1933 powerfully reinforced his determination to obtain complete plan fulfillment, though plans remained taut and local officials continued to exhibit coping behaviors that Stalin was ever less willing to tolerate.

By the mid-1930s, he showed a growing concern for the "*dvurushnik*," the "two-faced" official who praised policy in public and worked to subvert it behind closed doors. He increasingly argued that officialdom was littered with enemies of the Revolution. Though the economy grew stably for three years from 1934, by 1937 Stalin felt compelled to root out the "*dvurushnik*." Because the coping behaviors were so pervasive, the political violence directed against economic officials was doomed to be devastating. The mechanism of "bargaining" had failed in this instance. So how can we resolve the strong-state/weak-state conundrum? In short, the state *was* strong, but Stalin and his inner circle *perceived* it to be weak.

Lenin, Stalin, Trotsky

To understand the origins of the purge of economic officials, it is important to understand the evolution of Stalin's views on leadership and administration. As the tide of the civil war was turning in the Bolsheviks' favor, Lenin turned his attention to new demands that would be placed on the state apparatus in the post-war era. At first he calculated that a network of inspectors (Rabkrin—the "Workers' and Peasants' Inspectorate") could be a guarantor of an efficient and effective state apparatus. Stalin was the first head of the Inspectorate and his two years in charge did not reinforce his reputation as a skilled administrator. Rabkrin proved only to be "an additional source of muddle, corruption, and bureaucratic intrigue."[8] As Lenin reflected on this failure, he warned against building communism by means of the mass mobilization characteristic of the civil war period and accepted that the Bolsheviks lacked a solid grasp of how to organize the state:

> We must show sound skepticism for too rapid progress, for boast-fulness, etc. We must give thought to testing the steps forward we proclaim every hour, take every minute and then prove every second that they are flimsy, superficial, and misunderstood. The most harmful thing here would be haste . . . [W]e must not forget that we are too prone to compensate (or imagine that we can compensate) our lack of knowledge by zeal, haste, etc.
>
> In order to renovate our state apparatus we must at all costs set out, first, to learn, second, to learn, and third, to learn, and then see to it that learning shall not remain a dead letter, or a fashionable catchphrase (and we should admit in all frankness that this happens very often with us), that learning shall really become part of our very being, that it shall actually and fully become a constituent element of our social life. In short, we must not make the demands that were made by bourgeois Western Europe, but demands that are fit and proper for a country that has set out to develop into a

socialist country . . . We ought to at once announce a contest in the compilation of two or more textbooks on the organization of labor in general, and on management in particular . . . We ought to send several qualified and conscientious people to Germany, or to Britain, to collect literature and to study this question.

And yet at the same time, he was not proposing that the Soviet state be organized and run like Germany or England. Rather, he insisted that the knowledge of administration obtained through careful study be applied in such a way that bureaucratic practice would not be a drag on revolutionary change: "In all spheres of social, economic, and political relationships we are 'frightfully' revolutionary. But as regards precedence, the observance of the forms and rites of office management, our 'revolutionariness' often gives way to the mustiest routine. On more than one occasion, we have witnessed the very interesting phenomenon of a great leap forward in social life being accompanied by amazing timidity whenever the slightest changes are proposed."[9]

Lenin never clarified how the best of European administrative practices could be employed to underpin revolutionary change. Shortly after publishing these reflections in *Pravda,* he suffered the stroke that permanently removed him from politics and initiated the struggle to succeed him. In that struggle, Stalin and Trotsky were the key figures; the issue of how the state should function was one of the key debating points between them, and their contributions to that debate were substantially influenced by the political struggle, with each contribution a carefully crafted exercise in self-promotion and character assassination.

What were Stalin's views on the Soviet state? From the time of the Revolution, no one apart from Lenin was as involved as Stalin in the task of making the machinery of the Soviet state work. After his rather inglorious years as Commissar of State Control and chief of Rabkrin, fighting "bureaucratism" and improving the quality of Soviet administration, Stalin was appointed the General Secretary of the party. There, he looked at the same problem from only a slightly different perspective. As General Secretary, he was responsible for assigning party officials to the most important posts in the capital and the regions. His focus shifted from the question of what made effective institutions to that of the qualities of intellect and temperament that made a Bolshevik a good leader. This seems to have suited him much better. As we shall see, Stalin never had a particularly sophisticated grasp of how institutions function and what makes them effective. Stalin was always more interested in individual cadres. From within the Secretariat, Stalin developed the view that cadres need considerable training in general education, in Marxism-Leninism, and especially in the actual practice of running an organization. Not everyone could rise to the challenge and become a proper Bolshevik leader, and if they did not, they should be replaced with someone who had that potential. Stalin was convinced that the right person, in charge of the right team, could have a transformative effect on the work of any organization.

In the emerging political struggle, Stalin knew he was vulnerable to the accusation that he was not a sophisticated thinker. He was a capable administrator but he was shaken by the Rabkrin experience, and it left him vulnerable to the accusation that he was a mere bureaucrat. Yet Trotsky was perhaps in an even more disadvantageous position. He was head of the Red Army as the civil war was coming to a close. His position could only remain relevant if the Soviet Union remained at war with the capitalist world. Most of Stalin's few published speeches and articles from the time are calculated to stress that his role had become the more important one. For example, in the summer of 1921, he argued that since the civil war had been won, the central task had shifted "from all for the war to all for the economy." The future of the regime was not in further revolutionary wars abroad. On the contrary, "our domestic successes make us the avant-garde of the world revolution." Now was the time for cooperation with the capitalist powers, rather than confrontation: "The proletariat must hold firmly the power it has won, skillfully employ the wealth and knowledge of the bourgeoisie for the economic regeneration of the country."[10] Trotsky responded by observing the parlous state of the apparatus. Not only was it full of corrupt and class-alien elements, but it also lacked clear organizational principles. He argued that Stalin had done little to bring order out of the chaos. Stalin replied by reasserting the consensus view among Bolshevik leaders that periodic purges were necessary to remove corrupt, careerist, and class-alien elements from the party and state structures, but he insisted that Trotsky was insulting the CC, which had done much to correct the situation.[11] He took no credit for his work in Rabkrin on the fulfillment of decisions, which was going nowhere. Rather, he emphasized his efforts within the CC to create a unified and centralized system of decision making at the top and bring a basic order to the system.

In his first year as General Secretary, Stalin said and wrote little about his work, but in the course of 1923, he began to express his views on leadership and administration with some regularity. As his struggle with Trotsky had not diminished, these views continued to be colored by the political imperatives of the Lenin succession. While Trotsky warned about incompetence, corruption, and the "embourgeoisement" of the apparatus, Stalin understood that such criticisms were insulting to officials and that Trotsky risked alienating a key constituency whose support could play a decisive role in the leadership struggle. In April 1924, Stalin addressed that very constituency when he gave the "Organization Report" to the twelfth party congress. His speech was modest and conciliatory. He observed that the role of the party was not only to give the correct political line, but also to ensure that the right people are in place to realize it. Regional party officials were the key in that strategy, "lead[ing] the economic and political life of the region." Stalin acknowledged that producing good leaders was not easy. Few members of regional party committees had experience in running a large organization. The most capable officials were concentrated in regional centers and the quality of officialdom tapered off dramatically from there. Stalin discussed the challenge of producing new leaders, while taking another swipe at Trotsky the military leader: "It takes five to ten years and more. It is easier to conquer a country with the help of comrade Budennyi's cavalry than to draw two or three cadres from below who can in time become real leaders of the country." Those five to ten years were not to be spent in study. You can't teach cadres with books, he insisted, only on the job. He complimented the regional officials for learning on the job in the past year,[12] and he repeated the compliments at subsequent meetings with leading (*otvetstvennye*) workers.[13]

Leading officials were indeed learning on the job, and the double-digit growth rates generated by the NEP economy in these years appeared to be proof of that, but the apparatus was not functioning smoothly by any measure. Stalin could not be boundlessly patient with leading Soviet officials; he had to make the system work. Perhaps the biggest problem for Stalin was that the apparatus was riven with factional infighting (*skloki*).

Lines of authority remained foggy, and in the absence of a clear and univer-
sally agreed hierarchy of power, infighting was inevitable. Officials preferred
to give orders rather than to take them. Regular meetings of leading workers
were meant to "build mutual understanding between those who develop
policy and those who implement it,"[14] but they were not enough. Stalin
decided to reinforce the powers of existing "bosses," and particularly the
local party secretaries. In effect, the bosses became the main arbiters of
the struggles, with the power to remove officials who did not submit to
their decisions.[15]

    In time, the creation of powerful bosses dealt with the problem of
bureaucratic infighting and the lack of clarity in the administrative hierarchy,
but Stalin had failed to anticipate that the move would create other problems. Stalin soon found himself criticizing those bosses who exercised their
powers too aggressively and without regard to the attitudes and opinions
of those they led. This was a "habit of civil-war days," Stalin warned. He
demanded that they combine an active encouragement of the broadest
expression of opinion and the criticism of "mistakes" with "iron discipline"
and a "unity of will." It was not enough just to exercise their power. Leaders
had to carry their organizations with them.[16] In a letter to a leading official
of the German Communist Party, Stalin wrote: "I am decidedly against
simply removing comrades who hold opinions different from one's own.
I am against it not because I want to preserve those differences, but because
that sort of approach leads to a regime of fear, a regime that undermines
the spirit of self-criticism and initiative [from below]. It is not good when
the leaders of the party are feared but not respected. Leaders are real leaders
only if they are not only feared, but also respected, if they have authority
in the party."[17]

    In this respect, Lenin was the obvious model. Stalin observed that, by
force of argument, Lenin had carried the Bolsheviks with him. He had
respected the opinion of the majority, but never became its hostage. At
times, he took principled positions against the majority and brought it
around to his point of view with his clarity of vision and force of argument.[18] This model remained something of an ideal for party officials in
leadership posts. Stalin had given them dictatorial powers to sort out the
skloki and they were not about to renounce their use. Besides which,
carrying an organization with "clarity of vision and force of argument"

was a lot to expect of officials with little more than a primary education and often with only the crudest understanding of Marxism-Leninism.

Yet this did not lead Stalin to downplay the importance of ideology to leadership. On the contrary, Stalin observed that ideology underpinned everything the Bolsheviks did. Marxism-Leninism was not just about explaining how the world works, it was a guide to changing the world. The Bolshevik Party was an avant-garde organization. Bolshevik leaders did not merely respond to events, they shaped them. Like Lenin, they had to be both thinkers and doers, theoreticians and practical politicians. The "Leninist style of work," Stalin asserted, combined "Russian revolutionary sweep [*razmakh*]" and an "American managerial efficiency [*delovitost'*]."[19] He contrasted his ideal of the Bolshevik leader to the "gaping intellectual"[20] (the "thinker" who cannot "do") and to the "bureaucrat" (the "doer" who cannot "do"). And he remained convinced that a cadre who combined a firm grasp of Marxism-Leninism and good managerial skills could overcome any obstacle, could always achieve whatever target he was set.

Senior officials were persistently encouraged to deepen their understanding of Marxism-Leninism. Indeed they risked being purged from the party if they could not establish a basic knowledge of the canon. But they were equally encouraged to develop their managerial skills. Perhaps because of Trotsky's persistent and trenchant criticism of Stalin for the rise of Soviet "bureaucratism" and perhaps because Stalin was himself frustrated with the lack of "*delovitost'* (business-like manner)" among Soviet officials, he frequently provided practical advice to officials in his speeches and publications. Given that Stalin was the head of what was in essence the party's personnel department (the CC Secretariat), it should perhaps not come as a surprise that he considered personnel issues to be of crucial importance to the efficient function of an organization. As he explained in an article printed in the journal *Proletarskaia revoliutsiia* in November 1924:

> What does it mean to be a leader-organizer [*vozhdem-organiza-torom*] in our conditions, with the proletariat in power? It doesn't simply mean choosing assistants, creating an administrative apparatus and issuing instructions through it. A leader-organizer in our conditions must know the abilities and shortcomings of officials, and assign them places such that:

(1) each was comfortable with his work
(2) each was capable of giving to the revolution the maximum he
     could
(3) the given assignment of cadres maximized agreement, unity,
     and results.[21]

In the early 1920s, as the state apparatus was expanding rapidly and the
basic institutional structure of the Soviet state was coming into being, the
advice was rather obvious. But for decades afterward Stalin continued to
return to two of the ideas in this passage. First, he argued that the right
person in the right position could have a transformative effect on an institution that was otherwise failing to function efficiently. Second, when an
organization was failing, he tended to blame leaders and their "assistants"
who were merely "issuing instructions." This was what Stalin called "leadership on paper" [*bumazhnoe rukovodstvo*]: "The substance of leadership
lies not in the formulation of directives, but in their implementation, in
their realization."[22] This was a sensible principle, but it was not at all clear
how to apply it in practice. In Soviet conditions, the realities of implementation could be pretty messy.

New Challenges, New Demands

In the course of the 1920s and into the 1930s, the demands placed
on Soviet officials were growing dramatically both in their volume and
complexity. Making sure decisions were implemented also involved technical
skills, an understanding of an organization and what it did. In the summer
of 1925, Stalin explained to students at Sverdlov University: "In order to
properly lead [a given organization] you must understand what it does.
You must study it conscientiously, patiently, and with determination. You
can't lead in the countryside without an understanding of the cooperative
system, without an understanding of pricing policy, without having studied
the laws relating directly to the countryside. You can't lead in urban areas
without a knowledge of industry, without studying the needs and demands
of workers, the cooperative system, trades unions, and workers' clubs."
    This was reasonable to ask of the small cohort of students preparing for
careers in the party, but what of the greater mass of officials with little or

no education? Stalin knew it would take a long time to build the necessary skills among the many hundreds of thousands of officials populating the colossal state apparatus, but could the regime afford to wait for those skills? The speech betrayed that Stalin's patience was wearing thin:

> Can we achieve [these technical skills and knowledge] in one stroke? Unfortunately that is not possible. In order to make the necessary improvements to the quality of party leadership, we must improve the education [*kvalifikatsiiu*] of party leaders. Now, improving the quality of our officials is a task of the highest priority. But to raise the quality of the party official with a wave of the hand is not so simple. It is still common for officials to apply the old habits of unthinking rule by decree [*toroplivogo administrirovanie*] in place of a proper knowledge of affairs. So-called party leadership occasionally degenerates into a sorry conglomeration of useless directives, into empty and glib "leadership" which accomplishes nothing. There is a very serious danger that this sort of thing will weaken party leadership and cause it to decline.[23]

But in the context of the leadership struggle, the time was not yet right for Stalin to confront, or to make extraordinary demands of, leading officials whose support was crucial to his chances. Theoretically, weak officials could be demoted, or party leaders purged. The periodic party purge (*chistka*, or "cleansing") was meant to be the guarantor of the quality of party officialdom, but there was not yet a new generation to take its place.[24] Perhaps more important, Stalin needed the support of leading officials as Politburo members Lev Kamenev and Grigorii Zinoviev were distancing themselves from the majority and threatening to join Trotsky. In his speech to the fourteenth party congress in December 1925, Stalin pointedly contrasted his praise of the apparatus with his opponents' criticisms of "bureaucratic degeneration" and pessimistic assessments of the current situation: "Our cadres, young and old, are deepening their grasp of Marxism-Leninism [*rastut v ideinom otnoshenii*] . . . Now they read, study, and begin to understand. Not only the leaders, but the middle levels [*seredniaki*] of the party have begun to understand and think for themselves . . . [T]he successes of foreign and domestic policy, in the context of the threats posed by capitalist encirclement abroad and the promise of socialist construction at home, would not have been possible if the party were not in command of the challenges it faces, if it were not growing and becoming stronger."

As he concluded his speech Stalin introduced a subtle ambiguity. On the surface, he continued to attack the "pessimism" of his opponents, but he was also warning those senior officials in the audience who were not up to the tasks ahead: "Without help from abroad we won't lose heart, we won't cry for help, we won't abandon our work, we won't fear new challenges. Let he who is tired, he who is nervous and afraid of difficulties, make way for those who remain firm and brave. We are not among those who are afraid of difficulties. That is what makes us Bolsheviks. Because we have been forged in the Leninist school, we will not shrink from difficulties, but meet them head-on and overcome them."[25]

In more private settings, Stalin expressed more openly his concerns that leading officials were not ready to meet the tasks ahead let alone overcome them. In the mid-1920s, as economic growth increasingly relied on new construction rather than the restoration of existing capital stock, sustaining growth became increasingly difficult. In order to generate the funds for investment in new plants, the center demanded that all enterprises improve the efficiency of production by simultaneously increasing output and lowering costs. American production efficiency was held up as the standard, implausible as that was in the context of Soviet backwardness.[26] Many enterprise directors and other leading economic officials (*khoziaistvenniki*) sensibly had grave doubts that the targets set by the center could be achieved, doubts that were generally reinforced by the technical specialists they worked with. In some cases, regional party leaders sympathized with the *khoziaistvenniki* and sought to protect them from the demands imposed by the center by sending misleading reports or simply ignoring central directives. In others, regional leaders used their dictatorial powers and fired, or threatened to fire, those *khoziastvenniki* and technical specialists who resisted targets.

Both approaches concerned Stalin. In the spring of 1927, the information department of the CC warned Stalin that some regional party organizations were "systematically misleading" Moscow about their activities.[27] He received similar information in the form of denunciations directly from regional party organizations.[28] In the midst of the struggle with the United Opposition, he did not want to confront senior party leaders, and instead he spoke publicly in general terms of the need for an increase in the verification of fulfillment.[29] But Stalin did not express such moderate views in private. When he discovered that some procurement agencies were violating central directives, he wrote to his deputy, Molotov: "They are mocking us. Turn them over to the courts, and publish articles in the press about how they are enemies of the working class."[30] He did not like it, however, when party leaders in the regions took similar actions. Stalin was critical of those who created "an atmosphere of terror and harassment," and those who sacked subordinates wantonly. He told them they needed to train and promote new cadres, support them, and "surround them with an atmosphere of trust." He accepted that there probably were "enemies" among the *khozi-aistvenniki* but he told party leaders to distinguish mistakes from wrecking.[31]

More broadly, there was no shortage of advice on how a Bolshevik leader should behave and act, but it was virtually impossible to follow because of the gulf between the center's idealized vision of politics on the ground and the messy realities. Stalin and others in the party Secretariat continued to recognize that educational levels even among senior officials remained low and they knew that there was little that could be done about it in the short term. They also knew that the exceptional power of party secretaries discouraged "collective leadership," and that the lack of participation in the decision-making process discouraged initiative and inhibited the development of a new generation of leaders.[32] This they thought they could change. Party committees at all levels were told not only to draw all committee members as well as the *aktiv* (an honorary group of the most "active" party members) into decision making, but also to encourage them to criticize the "shortcomings" of the organization (*samokritika*, or "self-criticism"). Further, party committees were meant to engage the participation of the population, to show sensitivity to their needs, and to act on problems they identified (*signaly* or "signals").[33] Stalin does not seem to have grasped adequately that the increasing complexity of decisions and growing pressure from the center to meet targets made that sort of participatory decision making not only difficult but also counter-productive.

The challenges faced by party committees were not getting any easier. Because of crop failures in Ukraine and the North Caucasus, the grain procurement campaign of 1927 fell well short of its targets, and by the late autumn the shortfall threatened to undermine plans for industry, defense, and even the country's ability to feed itself.[34] Stalin knew that collections would be extremely difficult but saw no alternative than to compel regional officials to make up the shortfall. Despite the obvious signs of trouble, Stalin did little until December. It is possible that he held fire through the autumn because the battle with the United Opposition was in its final stages and he was concerned not to weaken his support within the party.

At a CC plenum on 14 November 1927, Trotsky and Zinoviev were expelled from the party. The decision was ratified by the fifteenth party congress a month later. In opening the congress with his "political report" of the CC, Stalin, following the common practice of party leaders, reviewed the successes of the party in foreign and domestic policy. He praised leading officials for those successes and contrasted that praise with Trotsky's purported criticisms: "I would like to say a few words about the rise, the qualitative improvement, in the work of leading party officials, in both the economy and politics. There was a time, comrades, two or three years ago, when a group of comrades, perhaps headed by Trotsky (laughter, voices: 'perhaps?'), criticized our provincial party committees, our CC, asserting that party committees were not competent and should not be involved in the economic affairs of the country. Yes, there was such a time, but now no one would dare to suggest such a thing. It is obvious to everyone that provincial committees, party organizations generally, have developed a mastery of economic leadership, have taken command of economic construction, and drive events rather than being driven by them."

He observed that this improvement in their leadership skills was what made possible the transition to a planned economy, letting it drop in a sentence that "our plans are not prognoses, not guesses, but directives that must be fulfilled by all leading organs." Delegates might have missed this if they were not paying close attention, but in the coming weeks and years, failure to meet those directives was increasingly met not merely with reproaches but also threats and punishments.

Stalin's speech was not without criticism of party officialdom. Indeed he described their three "shortcomings" at some length:

> Let me say a few words about these shortcomings.
> Take for example the party's leadership of economic and other organizations. Is everything going well here? No not everything.

Both in the center and in the localities, decisions are made, not infrequently, in a familial way, as in the home, so to speak. Ivan Ivanovich [the Russian equivalent of John Smith], a member of the leadership group of such and such an organization, has made a terrible mistake and made a mess of things. But Ivan Fedorovich [Joe Bloggs, as it were] does not want to criticize him, to expose his mistakes, correct his mistakes. He doesn't want to because he doesn't want to "make himself enemies." Made mistakes, made a mess of things—so what! Who doesn't make mistakes? Today, I, Ivan Fedorovich, will let him get away with it. Later, Ivan Ivanovich will let me get away with it, for there is no guarantee that at some point I will not make mistakes. Decorous and calm. Peace and goodwill. Who says that a mistake overlooked will undermine our great mission. No way! We'll find a way out somehow.

These, comrades, are common judgments for some of our leading workers. What does it mean? Can we, Bolsheviks, who criticize the whole world, who storm the heavens, to use the words of Marx, shy away from self-criticism for the sake of the peace of one or other of our comrades? Is it not clear that this will lead to nothing other than disaster for our great mission . . . Is it not clear that in shrinking from open and direct self-criticism, shrinking from the honest and open correction of our mistakes, we make forward movement impossible, we make impossible further improvements and new successes.

The second shortcoming concerns the use of compulsion in place of persuasion, rule by administrative fiat instead of by conviction. This shortcoming is no less dangerous than the first. Why? Because it threatens to turn our resourceful, autonomous [*samodeiatel'nye*] party organizations into useless pen-pushing, bureaucratic [*kantseliarskie*] offices. You have to remember that we have no less than sixty thousand of the most active [party] workers struggling against bureaucratism in economic, cooperative, and state institutions. It must be admitted that in the course of their struggle some become infected with bureaucratism and carry it into the party organization . . . particularly because of this, we need to arm ourselves in the struggle against this shortcoming, to raise the activity of the party masses, to draw them into the resolution of issues before party leaders, rooting systematic inner-party democracy and not permitting the use of compulsion in place of persuasion.

The third shortcoming consists of the desire of some comrades to swim with the current, smoothly and quietly, without planning, looking to the future, such that everywhere there should be a triumphal mood, that every day there should be a celebratory meeting and applause all round, and so that every one of us should have the chance to be included among the honorary members of all sorts of presidia . . . A desire to swim with the current leads to work without foresight, without direction, without a drive . . . And the consequence of this? The consequences are clear. First, (cadres) come to be covered with mould, then they go dull, gray, and are swallowed up in the slime of philistinism and themselves become run-of-the-mill philistines.[35]

Stalin had told delegates that they (1) protected one another and hid their mistakes, (2) resorted too quickly to dictatorial methods, and (3) wanted to make life easy for themselves. But he did not explore what gave rise to these shortcomings, nor did he consider whether the shortcomings were the product of pressures he imposed. The coming weeks should have given him food for thought.

As the congress broke up, regional officials were sent directives demanding "strict discipline and immediate action" to combat the fall in grain collections. Further instructions at the end of December forcefully restated that grain procurement targets had to be met in full and accounts of actions taken and their results sent to Moscow fortnightly.[36] When these failed to achieve the desired result, the tone of communication from the center grew markedly harsher. Stalin personally signed the following letter to regional organizations on 5 January 1928: "Despite repeated firm directives from the CC, there has been no improvement in grain collections. Local organizations are still working unacceptably slowly . . . All this speaks of a completely unacceptable forgetting of your revolutionary responsibilities before the party and proletariat . . . The CC warns you that any delay in the fulfillment of this directive and the failure to achieve concrete results in one week in the form of a decisive improvement in grain collections may force the CC to change the current leaders of party organizations."[37] Five days later, OGPU, the political police, were put in charge of checking on the fulfillment of these targets. It was no wonder that regional officials wanted to cover up one another's mistakes, felt they had no choice but to resort to dictatorial methods, and dreamt of a quiet life. It is unclear whether or not Stalin saw that his directives were the source of the bureaucratic behavior he criticized.

In one respect, Stalin showed himself to be capable of taking his own advice. He had long told leaders they should know their subordinates, and their work, well. In January 1928, members of the Politburo and CC traveled to the regions to see the process of grain procurements up close. Stalin himself spent two weeks in Siberia developing and promoting a series of repressive policies ("extraordinary measures," including the arrest of private traders and confiscation of grain from better-off peasants) that would ensure that targets were met. Stalin witnessed local resistance to the new measures, but he (not surprisingly) won over a majority in the Siberian kraikom. He appeared to be magnanimous and conciliatory in victory:

> What do you have to hide? You have doubts. We all have doubts . . . about many questions. Issues don't become 100 percent clear straightaway. Let there be doubts, and when we work things out all will be better in the end . . . Locally, you need to verify not only the implementation of directives, but also whether they are correct. You check this in the course of practical work. If you discover that practice shows that the law is not correct, then you need to correct the mistakes of the center, insofar as the directives of the center are not 100 percent correct. You can't say that in the center sit wise men who never make mistakes. While the general line is correct, there may be mistakes in the details, and if there is something to correct, you need to say so quickly and directly. Do you really not consider yourselves fit to correct the directives of the center?[38]

Here Stalin appeared explicitly to be referring to the sort of "bargaining" about which Davies and Gregory have written.[39] But these comments were more than slightly disingenuous. They were also out of step with Stalin's letter of 6 January. Instances in which Stalin accepted that he, or the center generally, was wrong were extremely rare and this was not one of them. If one looks at the bigger picture of the procurements campaign of winter 1928, senior officials understood that they had no choice but to meet the targets. The measures that Stalin developed for Siberia, and Molotov for the Urals, were applied to the rest of the country. Stalin sent a congratulatory letter to party organizations a few weeks later when procurement levels started to look up, but he concluded the letter demanding that all organizations be purged of those who would resist the new policies.[40] Many local state and party officials were indeed fired in February and March.[41]

Senior officials in the regions were given several other signals in the coming months that life was not going to get any easier. At the beginning of March 1928, the Shakhty affair hit the papers. Technical specialists in the southern mining industry had been arrested for committing acts of sabotage on behalf of hostile foreign powers. The arrests returned attention to the problem of leadership in industry, highlighting the extent to which the regime was dependent on the technical skills and knowledge of a group whose political loyalties were unclear. Most specialists had been trained before the Revolution and were from the middle class ("bourgeoisie"), assumed to be hostile to Soviet power. As far as the center was concerned, the affair demonstrated that plant and mine directors and other *khoziaistvenniki* (mostly Communists) were too beholden to the bourgeois specialists, too reliant on them, not sufficiently vigilant in their oversight of them. In the aftermath of the affair, the center not only stressed the importance of training and promoting "Red" specialists, but also demanded more personal responsibility among bosses for the detailed oversight of the work of bourgeois specialists for the fulfillment of targets and a further encouragement of "self-criticism," particularly insofar as that meant encouraging the workers to criticize the way things were done and to suggest improvements.[42] These substantially deepened the already burdensome demands placed on party bosses and *khoziaistvenniki.*

The other signal at this time was substantially closer to home. In the spring and summer of 1928, the results of investigations of regional organizations by party "instructors" reporting to the Central Control Commission (CCC) were published in the national press as "scandals."

The best known of these, the "Smolensk scandal," held up for public vilification the behavior of some regional party leaders.[43] The main charge against them was related to the experience of grain procurements in the preceding autumn and winter: they had become agents of the peasantry in government rather than agents of Soviet power among the peasants. In particular, they were accused of being infected with the petit bourgeois values of the kulak, the well-to-do Russian peasant, the class enemy who threatened plans for industrialization by withholding grain. Instructors had supposedly identified cases in which kulaks had been promoted to positions of authority in the region. This had led to regional leaders protecting the class enemy from the thrust of central policy—the application of extraordinary measures in the grain procurements campaign of the preceding autumn and winter. In this way, the scandal was played out on the pages of the central press in order to make clear not just to the public, but perhaps particularly to regional leaders, the costs of resisting central policy.[44] The scandal also marked the beginning of open conflict in the leadership. While Stalin, Molotov, Kaganovich, and others had developed and imposed the idea of emergency measures to overcome the grain crisis threatening industrialization, others around Nikolai Bukharin were worried that a confrontation with the peasantry might provoke an even deeper crisis. Stalin was using the "kulak sympathizers" of the Smolensk organization as a symbol for what he would later label the "Right danger" (or "Right deviation," or "Right opposition") in the party. There was also a further subtext. The Smolensk organization was punished for more than resisting state policy. It was also being punished for failing to live up to the ideal of Bolshevik leadership that Stalin had been laying out in the previous year. The Smolensk organization had suppressed self-criticism and inner-party democracy. Leaders were promoting friends and cronies whom they could trust and covering up one another's mistakes. They had sought a quiet life instead of facing challenges head-on.

In a speech to the eighth congress of the Komsomol on 16 May 1928, Stalin returned yet again to the issue of political leadership. Too many leaders were carried away with talk of successes, he explained. The Shakhty affair had demonstrated that there was no opportunity for a quiet life, for letting things simply take their course (*samotek*). The enemies of the USSR were active both within and outside Soviet borders, and this meant that cadres had always to be prepared as if for war. Then in a thinly veiled reference to the Smolensk scandal, he spoke of the very real presence of "Communist bureaucratism" and the need to organize mass criticism of "shortcomings," of bureaucrats among their bosses.[45] This speech was followed up with articles in the press and party directives pushing "self-criticism" (criticism of organizations and their leaders from below).[46]

The reactions of leading Bolshevik officials are difficult to gauge because they were not inclined publicly to voice their opinions, particularly if they were not consonant with central policy. The experience of Trotsky and the United Opposition had made the costs of open dissent quite clear. By the summer of 1928 it had become clear to Bukharin that he was about to receive the same treatment he and Stalin had dished out to Trotsky and company. In a letter to Stalin written shortly after the July 1928 CC plenum, Bukharin expressed a concern that it was becoming impossible to express independent views. In essence, he was accusing Stalin of dictatorial methods and of suppressing inner party democracy and self-criticism at the highest level:

> [About the procurements] campaign for the autumn, we have neither a [political] line nor a common opinion. Does that not worry you? We have stopped speaking on these issues: people are afraid to speak, to criticize. If the central intellectual laboratory has been destroyed, if we can't discuss the most important political questions openly and without fear, then the country is in danger. The economy is not an executive director. You can't shout at it and threaten to arrest it. We are not thinking things through enough. Self-criticism and so on—and the lack of communication about ideas [the phrase "*otsutstvie ideinoi sviazi* " can also mean "lack of ideological coherence"] in the leadership—is a paradox of paradoxes, which is extremely dangerous.
>
> As you know, I wrote the draft resolution on grain collections [for the July plenum]. I didn't object when it was modified after it had been confirmed by the Politburo. I did not orchestrate any "blocs" [at the plenum]. I restricted my comments to the minimum of what I considered correct (though I was deeply upset by the people who clearly lied about the state of affairs in the localities, and "sniffed the air" instead of speaking the truth.)[47]

Certainly Bukharin did not see any kind of "bargaining" between the center and local officials. Rather, he concluded that the opponents of extraordinary measures had been intimidated into silence. Bukharin was not alone in thinking that the confiscation of grain, and more generally a confrontational policy toward the countryside, would hinder and not help the prospects of Soviet industrialization. Many leading party officials, particularly in agricultural regions, were worried by the turn in policy. Studies of regional politics in Moscow and Siberia at this time have shown that while the party first secretary had serious doubts about extraordinary measures, others in the regional buros opted to support Stalin's line.[48] In essence, the conflict at the top of the party leadership was mirrored in the regional buros. That is not surprising given the unpleasant choice the regime faced: risk confronting the peasantry or accept that the pace of industrialization was going to fall. It is not surprising either that the supporters of Stalin and the extraordinary measures should have won the day. The Bolsheviks were a movement of the working class, not known for their sympathetic views on the peasantry. And many regions stood to benefit substantially from the proposed investment.[49] But intimidation also played an important role in Stalin's victory. The Smolensk scandal was the most prominent example. The organization was thoroughly gutted and senior figures replaced as a punishment for their "kulak sympathies."[50] A. A. Sol'ts of the CCC (the organization that directed the purge) wrote to Sergo Ordzhonikidze, Politburo member and commissar of heavy industry, at the beginning of July complaining that Stalin and Molotov were being "bloodthirsty" in their policy toward Smolensk. Bukharin's supporters were certainly intimidated from expressing their views, but even those who supported Stalin's policies must have begun to suspect that expressing any kind of opposition to central policy could stop one's career short.

In the autumn of 1928 and into 1929, Stalin sharpened his attack on Bukharin and opposition to central policy by very publicly warning of a "Right deviation" in the party. In October 1928 he made a speech to the still-divided Moscow party committee, with the ostensible purpose of sorting out the conflicts. The speech was then published in *Pravda,* from which Bukharin had only recently been removed as chief editor. Stalin did not limit himself to the previous jibes about "kulak sympathies," but spoke of the Right deviation as a "petit bourgeois infection," a departure from

Marxism, that threatened the very foundations of the Soviet state. The "deviationists" wanted to slow down "socialist construction" just as acceleration was needed. Rapid industrialization was needed in order to meet the threat presented by the regime's enemies within and abroad. They wanted to strengthen capitalist elements, partially to restore capitalism, and thus aid the enemy. Stalin then demanded that those who supported his policies take more aggressive action against those who opposed them: "We have in the party those who are not opposed to call for a struggle against the Right danger much like the popes pronounce their halleluiahs, to cleanse their consciences, but then they take no concrete action to set the struggle firmly in motion and overcome the Right danger. This conciliatory approach to the Right is an openly opportunist deviation and we must fight it in order to fight the Right."[51]

Stalin's public attack on the "Right deviation" was relentless and carefully orchestrated. He ratcheted up his rhetoric, characterizing the Right as an anti-party "faction" on the eve of the party purge in spring 1929.[52] Much as Bukharin had warned, Stalin was making it very difficult to express any political views other than full-blooded support for his line. There was no opportunity for senior party officials to express doubts or concerns about central policy.

At the same time, the practical tasks senior officials faced were becoming ever more challenging. They were in the midst of a violent confrontation with the peasantry and the perceived threat from the capitalist world was deepening. Stalin meanwhile was pushing them harder still, repeatedly voicing the ambition to overtake the advanced capitalist countries economically:

> Is it possible to get by without demanding [economic] plans? Is it possible to work with slower tempos in more "calm" conditions? Can we explain the rapid tempos for the development of industry in terms of the restless character of the members of the Politburo and Sovnarkom? Of course not! They are calm and sober people in the Politburo and Sovnarkom. Speaking abstractly, ignoring internal and external circumstances, we could, of course, move at a slower pace. But we can't lose sight of external and internal circumstances, and we must admit that these circumstances dictate

> the necessity of the rapid development of industry . . . We are
> surrounded by capitalist countries with a much more technically
> developed industry. So we have the more advanced political system,
> but with an extremely backward industrial base. Can we achieve
> the decisive victory of socialism given that contradiction . . . In
> order to achieve the decisive victory of socialism in our country,
> we must catch up to and overtake these countries technologically.
> Either we do that or they will wipe us out [*nas zatrut*].[53]

As ever, Stalin was rather light on the details as to how rapid industrialization could be achieved. At the July 1928 CC plenum he had given a
sympathetic portrait of the challenges facing officials in meeting tough
grain requisition targets while increasing rates of growth of industry, but
gave little concrete advice to officials, expressing only his confidence that
overcoming these difficulties would "firm up the Bolsheviks' ranks" and
"open the path to the socialist transformation of our country."[54] More
privately, he was equally vague. When his commissar of trade, Anastas
Mikoian, expressed worries about the tasks the Commissariat faced, Stalin
replied that "[you] must have restraint, not be afraid of difficulties, because
panic will only make the problem greater."[55] Behind the scenes, the CCC,
the body charged more than any other with the smooth functioning of
the apparatus, was only slightly more penetrating in its analysis of the
problems senior officialdom faced. The August 1928 plenum of the
Commission considered the importance of improvements to efficiency in
industry ("rationalization"), to the task of catching up to and overtaking
the advanced capitalist countries. It blamed enterprises, trusts, and the
state organs that supervised them for "weak leadership" and a "lack of
system and planning" in implementing cost-cutting measures. Self-criticism
in this context had generated much heat and little light: "a hunt for scandal,
an irresponsible discrediting of *khoziaistvenniki*, and a pervasive failure
to investigate what problems had been uncovered."[56] Stalin returned to
this question himself at the end of December 1928 when a Politburo
meeting discussed the work of Donugol' (the Donbas Coal Trust). He
asked why costs continued to rise *after* an efficiency drive that included
sweeping mechanization of key mining processes. He observed that the
Shakhty affair had resulted in the purge of some experienced technical

experts, but he denied that current problems lay in the lack of the necessary skills. Rather, he blamed "mismanagement" characterized by the failure to spend enough time understanding the miners and the mines, the failure to verify the fulfillment of instructions and targets, and the failure, simply, to work hard enough: "Workers need to know it's not idiots organizing production, but people who know what they're doing and who are prepared not to sleep in order to resolve the tasks before them." Party organizations, trades unions, *khoziastvenniki,* and workers should be working together instead of blaming one another for problems, verifying the fulfillment of instructions instead of just issuing orders. "Sitting around arguing about who is to blame is a serious bureaucratic perversion."[57] But for all Stalin's specific denials, the fact remained that in Donugol', as in most other trusts and enterprises, undereducated and inexperienced officials were driven to achieve demanding and complex targets. Where those targets could not be achieved, blame shifting and scapegoating were logical strategies. The regime was training new "Red" specialists at a ferocious pace, but Stalin was not prepared to slow the rate of industrialization until the necessary technical skills were present. The campaign against the "Right deviation" made any public challenge to the rate of industrialization politically impossible.

This is not to say that there was any sort of political consensus behind the slowing of tempos. On the contrary, among leading economic officials, indeed among party and state officialdom generally, there was a broad impatience, if not hostility, toward the New Economic Policy and its compromises with capitalist elements. There was an enthusiasm for the industrialization drive, for the promise of the first five-year plan, for "socialist construction," as it was commonly labeled. That enthusiasm was, of course, by no means uniform. Rural officials were not so happy about the assault on the peasantry. And in industry, the farther down the administrative hierarchy one went, down the spectrum of order issuers to order implementers, the more the practical implications of "socialist construction" gave pause for thought.

While Stalin and his immediate lieutenants set the targets, the second tier of Bolshevik leaders at the heads of the commissariats and regional party organizations relayed them to trusts and enterprises, which in turn relayed them to engineers, shop-floor heads, and ultimately to the workers.

The lowest tiers of officialdom faced the gravest challenge in the emerging order, caught between demanding targets and vague instructions from above, and workers, who were not only unenthusiastic about rising targets and stagnating living standards but who were at the same time aggressively encouraged from the center to criticize their "bosses" and to look for "wreckers" and "class enemies" among them. Back toward the top of the leadership hierarchy, the second tier by no means had it easy. Stalin had made it clear in the spring and summer of 1928 that they would lose their jobs if they failed to ensure that central directives were implemented. But his relations with the regional leaders and the heads of commissariats remained largely cordial and business-like in the late 1920s. Their regular reports to the center, often addressed directly to Stalin, could and did discuss obstacles to the fulfillment of central targets and they often contained specific requests for help. When Syrtsov explained in the winter of 1928–29 that grain collections were under target because of the slow deliveries of consumer goods, Stalin assured him that "we'll do everything we can to supply you with goods." Similarly when Nikolai Shvernik, first secretary of the Urals Provincial Committee, outlined the causes of under-fulfillment in his region, Stalin replied that "there are no grounds to complain, you did all you could." He often issued new targets and directives to them with the very polite phrase "I strongly request" (*Ia ochen' proshu vas*) and signed them under the equally polite and collegial "I shake your hand" (*Zhmu ruku*).[58]

Nevertheless, as the targets of the first five-year plan spiraled higher and higher in 1929 and 1930, and the center's control of the economy became increasingly dictatorial, Stalin's relationship with the second tier became strained. Particularly after the defeat of Bukharin and the so-called Right opposition, Stalin's demands of them grew at the same time as their scope for raising concerns and doubts narrowed. The campaign against the Right was only part of this tightening control. Most obviously, Bukharin and others associated with the Right were accused of trying to slow the rate of "socialist construction," of shrinking from challenges, of not understanding the vast potential of the planned economy.[59] But Stalin was also going beyond this economic critique to limit the scope of political discussion. In mid-June 1929, Lazar Shatskin published an article in *Komsomol'skaia pravda* encouraging Komsomol members to question central policy and debate issues of the day from a Marxist-Leninist perspective. A month later, the deputy director of the Institute of Marx and Engels, Ia. Sten, published an article in the same paper asserting that it was "careerism" to submit unthinkingly to party directives. V. V. Lominadze, a Comintern official, expressed the same thought in a letter to the Institute of Red Professors, complaining about the large number of officials who were making decisions only on the basis of their sense of the prevailing winds. Without being aware of it, these three, all critics of the Right, were expressing the same concerns as Bukharin had done in his letter to Stalin a year before, that when Communists were afraid to express their views, it posed a danger to the party in the longer term. Stalin was not pleased, and complained in a letter to Molotov: "To call the subordination of the Komsomols (and that means party members as well) to the general party line 'careerism' as Sten does, means to call for a review of the general party line, for the undermining of the iron discipline of the party, for the turning of the party into a discussion club. That is precisely how any opposition group has begun its anti-party work."[60]

The three, and others who had expressed similar views, were very publicly taken to task in the national press and party journals. Stalin was convinced that "iron discipline" was required to face immediate challenges. Of particular concern in the summer of 1929 was the beginning of the new grain procurement campaign. On 10 August he wrote to Molotov complaining that the Politburo was not taking a hard enough line. He insisted that the OGPU had to be brought in to ensure that peasant resistance to collections was broken. He was well aware too that there was a strain of resistance within party and state organizations as well. Less than two weeks later, he wrote to Molotov that no discussion of the targets could be tolerated: "the danger of missing the targets will grow if you don't enforce the complete fulfillment of the decisions of the CC savagely and implacably [*nalegat' . . . so vsei zhestokost'iu i neumolimost'iu*]."[61] Following his instructions, relentless pressure was exerted on regional organizations through the autumn, and it appeared to produce the necessary results. Not only were grain collection targets being met, but the collectivization of agriculture was also accelerating and industry was growing rapidly, all as if to spite the Right's warnings of impending crisis.

"Objective Conditions"

The atmosphere of the autumn and winter of 1929–30 was heady with excitement and confidence, drowning out the voices of the doubters. Stalin famously called 1929 the "Year of the Great Break" as he listed the regime's economic successes on the twelfth anniversary of the Revolution.[62] The projected targets of the five-year plan were raised and raised again, a fact generally celebrated by leading party and state officials who were being promised ever larger state investment in their regions and enterprises.[63] Stalin poured scorn on the Right and its sympathizers for their defense of the idea that sectors of the planned economy needed to be in balance. He was delighted when Gosplan officials gave up their persistent efforts to restrain the more extreme production and investment targets.[64] It was not economic balance that led to socialism, he insisted, but the victory of the proletariat over capitalist elements in the economy, the victory of large over small-scale production. For that, they needed to maintain their momentum, to maintain the relentless drive forward through mass mobilization.[65]

The extraordinary ambitions of the plans and the relentless pressure on officials to meet ever more challenging targets naturally produced unintended consequences. In early 1930, the pressure to collectivize agriculture at a breakneck pace generated such resistance in the countryside that the ensuing violence threatened to undermine the spring sowing campaign. Stalin was not inclined to see such problems as a product of central policy, and this was no exception. He disingenuously accused local officials of violating the "voluntary principle" of collectivization and of committing "excesses." Whereas the pressure led some officials to do whatever they felt was necessary to meet targets up to and including acts of extra-judicial violence, other simply failed to meet them. When Stalin signaled the temporary halt to the collectivization drive in his 2 March 1930 *Pravda* article "Dizziness with Success," he warned both leading officials who "ran too far ahead" and those who "lagged behind."[66] The party press picked up on and elaborated his ideas.

In the middle of March, an article in the party journal *Bol'shevik* further explored the ideas Stalin had presented. In what was essentially a clarification of Stalin's position, the article made it clear that the General Secretary was not calling for any kind of moderation in economic policy. Both "deviations from correct leadership" made poor use of the "colossal reserves of the economy waiting to be exploited." Those who moved too slowly, who "cited 'objective reasons' for their failure to fulfill plan targets," were told: "the party does not simply adapt to objective conditions. The party has the power to influence them, to change them, to find itself a more advantageous combination of objective conditions."

In other words, no plan target was too ambitious or poorly formulated that it could not be met. Excessive zeal made a mockery of the other "deviation"; those officials who pushed too far and too fast, applied "naked force," and committed "excesses" were guilty of the now rather improbable-sounding sin of "overestimating the strength of the party."[67] Nevertheless, both faults of leadership were demonized. At the sixteenth party congress in July, Stalin associated the commission of excesses with Trotskyism or "Leftism," and "passivity" with Bukharin and the Right, implying that they were a form of opposition to party policy. He demanded a "merciless struggle against them" by means of party purges, campaigns of "self-criticism," worker oversight from below, the ruthless exposure of inefficiency, and the strictest verification of the fulfillment of central directives.[68]

The formulation did not leave leading officials with much flexibility in the way they could deal with central directives, and even less so given that they were told it was their responsibility to "prove the correctness of party policy in practice"! Stalin and the party press repeatedly asserted that central policy was correct a priori: "The [political] line of our party is clearly the uniquely correct line. Its correctness is obvious and indisputable . . . The party must, as ever, watch its own ranks with unwavering attention, exposing and targeting all manifestations of both Rightist and Trotskyist deviations . . . [The party] must defend itself against all those who attack its line, the correctness of which is being proven by experience every day. This is why deviationists rarely risk coming out in the open. Now they are more inclined to support the party line in public in order to make it easier to undermine it in practice."[69]

The center put officials in a bind. The fulfillment of the overambitious targets of the first five-year plan was going badly, but it had become politically very awkward to report openly and objectively on local conditions.

It was difficult publicly to be anything less than enthusiastic about high targets and it was more difficult to discuss openly the problems of target fulfillment even with colleagues for fear of being denounced as a "deviationist." Even more serious denunciations were in circulation at the time. In the summer of 1930, while Stalin was in the midst of directing the investigation and prosecution of several "counterrevolutionary conspiracies" including what was known as the Industrial Party and the Toiling Peasants' Party, he linked their actions to other economic problems in the absence of clear trails of evidence. On the basis of Stalin's assumptions, dozens of officials were accused of wrecking and were executed. The executions were prominently reported in the central press.[70] As such, to draw attention to problems in one's own organization was to invite dire consequences.

Stalin seemed convinced that plan targets could be met. But to do so, it was necessary to mobilize and direct "the enthusiasm of the masses," to ensure the effective use of existing resources, to have energetic leadership and strict verification of the fulfillment of directives, and to sustain momentum and be intolerant of anything less than total commitment. Perhaps the most important of the targets was grain collections. Without the income from grain exports, the plan as a whole would fail. Stalin watched the progress of the collections closely, and from the beginning he did not like what he saw. A 5 September Politburo resolution on the first phase of the collections declared that they were "absolutely unsatisfactory" and characterized by complacency, inadequate measures against kulak and anti-collective farm sentiment, and insufficient work to strengthen the kolkhoz organizationally and create new collectives. Stalin ordered that "leading regional officials" should be brought back from vacation and set to work.[71] A week later, the regional party first secretaries were called to Moscow to discuss the plan for collections. Molotov subsequently wrote to Stalin, who himself was on vacation at the time, that he told the secretaries that "[we need] a merciless struggle against those with hesitations about whether the plan can be fulfilled. Any thought that the plan cannot be fulfilled would be the purest opportunism."[72] He told Stalin that "for the first time" no one complained about the plan for collections, though this was not entirely true. A few party secretaries were brave or foolish enough to express their doubts, but Molotov chose not to relay these to Stalin.[73]

Underfulfillment of plan targets in industry was also a major concern. In early September, a letter from the CC to local organizations insisted that officials could only blame themselves for failures: "The most important reasons for the underfulfillment of production tasks of industry, especially in its main branches, are the lack of the necessary energy and initiative in the mobilization of internal resources; insufficient use of existing equipment; poor application of the shift system; lack of energy in overcoming bottlenecks; frequent idle time of equipment due to breakdowns and the poor organization of material-technical supply; many accidents due to a criminal lack of care and poor technical oversight; the lack of systematic rationalization and thoroughly unsatisfactory in-factory planning."[74]

The center was not in a mood to let leading officials evade the plan targets they had been set. They referred to the common habit of underestimating production capacity and the exaggeration of inputs needed as "examples of opportunist lack of faith in the potential of socialist industry . . . baseless attempts to justify the underfulfillment of industrial targets in terms of the lack of imported equipment (when existing equipment is sufficient) are rife." Rather than surrender to those who hinted that the plan was unrealistic, the letter called for the party to help "overcome technical conservatism."[75] Three weeks later Stalin proposed to Molotov the creation of a "Fulfillment Commission of the Council of Peoples' Commissars exclusively charged with the systematic verification of the decisions of the center, with the power quickly and directly to prosecute party and non-party officials for bureaucratism, non-fulfillment or the evasion of central decisions." Stalin suggested that the commission should have direct access to the services of the RKI, OGPU, the Procuracy, and the press. "Without such an authoritative and fast-acting commission, we will not break the wall of bureaucratism and the shoddy work of our apparatus. Without such a reform, our directives will remain unrealized everywhere."[76]

Stalin did not pause for reflection and contemplate the extent to which underfulfillment was the product not of "bureaucratism" or of a "lack of faith" but rather of unrealistic targets. Nor did he or those around him consider the consequences of telling leading officials that they could no longer explain their shortcomings in terms of "objective conditions." Stalin did not see that his directive would close down channels of communication between himself and his leading officials. He had ignored Bukharin's warning in 1929 that if senior officials were afraid to speak out, the "intellectual machinery" of the state would be broken. Rather, the center proceeded to break it down even further by demonizing those who questioned central policy. When two senior party officials, S. I. Syrtsov (a candidate member of the Politburo) and V. V. Lominadze (a leading official in the Nizhnyi Novgorod party organization), chose to swim against the current and express their doubts about the direction of central policy, Stalin responded ferociously, accusing them of forming a "Right-Left bloc" against the party.[77] His private correspondence suggests he was convinced that Syrtsov and Lominadze were trying to gather the support of those who were unhappy with party policy in order to orchestrate a coup d'etat.[78] Stalin was clearly worried about disaffected officials, because the party press was ordered to warn officials of "hidden rightist elements" who praised policy in public while quietly working to undermine it. They were warned that "anyone who challenges the iron will of the party will be crushed."[79]

The ferocity of Stalin's response is striking given that the economic situation was still relatively healthy. There were, however, dark clouds on the horizon. The spring sowing had been successful, and a good harvest was anticipated, though peasant resistance had knocked back the process of collectivization and led to serious losses of livestock. The industrial economy continued to grow at an impressive pace, though as targets for industrialization were getting more ambitious, bottlenecks and breakdowns were becoming more frequent. The party leadership did not perceive any imminent threat of invasion from capitalist powers, though the investigation of the so-called Industrial Party convinced Stalin that the capitalist states were still trying to orchestrate one by employing specialists as "wreckers" to undermine Soviet industry.

At the beginning of February 1931, the relatively moderate tone of Stalin's speech to the first All-Union Conference of Industrial Workers might have reassured some senior party officials. Stalin warned against making empty promises to fulfill the plan. He insisted that there was "incontestable evidence" of the potential to meet plan targets, but he also recognized the necessity of making sure that the necessary material resources were made available to meet those targets. And he admitted that the center had been slow to improve the level of technical skills in production. It was time to turn that around, he observed. In the early 1930s, the most advanced technologies in the world were being introduced to the Soviet economy on an unprecedented scale, so Stalin encouraged workers and specialists to "master technology." "In all things, technology is decisive," he told his audience. Technology would allow the Soviet economy to continue to move ahead in "seven mile steps."[80] There was plenty of promise and some optimism, but it was also clear that Stalin expected them to "strain every nerve" to meet targets and many of the targets were not realistic. Bottlenecks and shortages made it inevitable that key plan targets could not be met, and as enterprises and entire industries slipped ever further behind their plan targets, Stalin and the other members of the Politburo took a harder line. At a conference of economic managers in June 1931, Stalin told delegates that the plan "is realistic because fulfillment now depends exclusively on ourselves, on our ability and our will to use the very rich possibilities we have. . ." Similarly, Molotov and Kuibyshev (then the head of Gosplan) insisted that industrial plans were realistic and told managers that they could not blame the failure to meet targets on shortages of inputs, on the problems of the transportation system, or on other "objective reasons." They could only blame failures in the organization of labor and production, which was to say that they could only blame one another. And this is precisely what was happening. Commonly, factory directors and regional party officials targeted technical specialists when plan targets were not met. According to one rapporteur at the same conference, "up to one half of all engineers at the Donbas coal mines had been sentenced to . . . forced labour."[81] This worried Stalin and the party leadership, but not as much as the spirit of "opportunism," the questioning of the realism of the plan, the lack of will to rise to the challenges ahead.

"Break the Sabotage"

By July 1931, the focus of Stalin's attention shifted from industry back to agriculture. He was determined that the upcoming grain collections should be undertaken in a properly Bolshevik spirit. The Politburo sent regional leaders letters to the effect that "their targets were final, and that they should forbid any discussion of its revision." Where regional leaders did any more than simply pass directives down to local officials, they were reprimanded. M. M. Khataevich and R. I. Eikhe, first secretaries of the Middle Volga and West Siberian regional party committees, respectively, managed to convince Stalin to reduce their targets for areas affected by drought, though they were not reduced nearly as far as they had requested.[82] They and others raised the issue again at the October CC plenum, not to ask for reductions of the plan, but to blame district-level officials and even some central plenipotentiaries for the failure to meet regional targets. Many district officials were, they said, held "hostage" by the kulak's "spirit of resistance" to collections.[83] Stalin sustained the pressure to meet regional collection targets despite the growing evidence that resistance to the collections could only be overcome through violence: the arrest and exile of peasants and the local officials who were found to be protecting them.[84]

Stalin was even less open to compromise in 1932. As regions fell behind in the sowing campaign, their requests for extra seed grain were almost without exception rudely rejected. Through the summer of 1932, he bristled at any questioning of the quality of the harvest. The Politburo was primed to see anything short of enthusiasm for meeting grain collection targets as a "rotten" (*gniloe*) and "totally unacceptable" attempt to "reduce targets and get more grain out of Moscow."[85] As the country descended toward famine, Stalin remained convinced that the problem lay in the weakness of leadership and the lack of will to confront the kulaks who were hiding grain from the state. Stalin, on vacation at the time, ordered Kaganovich and Molotov to organize a conference of regional party secretaries to discuss the upcoming grain collections and told them that "the center of the decisions of the conference of secretaries must be the organization of the collections with 100 percent fulfillment of the plan." After the opening of the conference, Kaganovich wrote to Stalin:

> At the beginning of the conference we exposed the hesitation to admit mistakes and the effort to hide shortcomings. There were a good number of business-like suggestions, but clearly not enough criticism. We had to help them along, particularly by leaning on the Ukrainians and by pointing out that the CC demands that they stop repeating, in a dressed-up form, the chatter of

undesirable elements in the countryside unwilling to part with their grain, and that they must decisively rid themselves of capitulationist attitudes to the collections . . .

Stalin's reply pushed Kaganovich to be tougher still, particularly on republican and other top-level regional officials who did not unreservedly drive the collections forward: "Take all measures to break the current mood of officials, isolate the whiners and rotten diplomats (no matter who!) and ensure genuinely Bolshevik decisions."[86]

Millions of peasants would die in the course of the following year and a half because Stalin and his inner circle were not prepared to accept that the overambitious collection targets left the countryside without the food necessary for survival. When, despite unrelenting pressure, targets were not met, the Politburo began to contemplate reductions. Not because they accepted that there was a shortage of grain, but because they had failed to break the "opportunist mood in party organizations." In early November, Kaganovich wrote to Stalin from the North Caucasus where he had been sent to shake up the party organization:

> People speak as if begging for crumbs, others dissipated, others still in an anti-party manner. If one were to sack them, one would have to sack half. We'll have to remove some, and work on others. At the stanitsa [village level] no one pushed [our campaigns]. Judges passed sentence, but no one carried them out. Clearly, in such a situation, they're making fun of us . . . Counterrevolutionaries occupy their places without a worry. The situation and our unsatisfactory work, that is, the work of local organizations, liberalism, inaction, and opportunism, have made fertile soil for the emergence of anti-Soviet organizations. Now we have to make up for this and it will necessarily lead to excesses . . . But most important is to break the sabotage that is doubtlessly being organized and lead from some unified center.[87]

Stalin's assessment was the same, focused on putative "anti-Soviet elements." Addressing a joint session of the Politburo and Presidium of the Central Control Commission at the end of November 1932, he asked: "How do we explain the difficulties [in the collection of grain] this year?

They follow from two factors: (1) the infiltration of kolkhozy and sovkhozy by anti-Soviet elements and organizations . . . (2) the incorrect un-Marxist approach of a significant part of our rural Communists to kolkhozy and sovkhozy . . . The main task now is to promote experienced, honest, and devoted comrades, but there are few of them and this creates opportunities for anti-Soviet elements."[88] Regional and local officials who had done anything to mitigate the effects of the center's catastrophically misguided grain collections policy faced being labeled as anti-Soviet. The center had narrowly prescribed the language they could use to describe the situation in the countryside, so of necessity, regional and local officials adopted the center's terms.[89]

The first five-year plan formally came to a close in December 1932. The regime had good reason to be proud of what it had achieved, but many of the successes Soviet leaders claimed were consciously exaggerated or misleading. The show of strength and dynamism to the capitalist world was driven largely by considerations of foreign policy. In fact, Stalin and the rest of the Politburo had drawn the conclusion months before this that it was counterproductive to project for the second five-year plan the rates of growth characteristic of the first. Despite repeated edicts banning the utterance of any doubts about the realism of the plan, Stalin knew well that these doubts existed.[90] But were the more modest growth rates projected in the second five-year plan a product of "bargaining" with lower-level organizations? We should not lose sight of the fact that Stalin never acknowledged in public or in private that the targets set in the first five-year plan had been unrealistic.[91] Rather, he concluded that leading officials had not risen to the challenge. He did not blame the failure on the low level of education or weak technical skills of leading officials. Hundreds of thousands had undergone, or were undergoing, courses to build technical skills, but for Stalin that was almost beside the point. He insisted that: "You can't just train leading officials [*kadry*] . . . they emerge in the process of work."[92] The technical skills were less important that the "Bolshevik spirit" with which they approached their work. The more modest targets of the second five-year plan were an acknowledgement of the gravity of the task ahead in forging a party capable of leading in a truly Bolshevik manner.

Stalin asserted that the successes and failures of the plans were a matter of personal responsibility. "What made our successes possible?" he asked the delegates to the January 1933 joint plenum of the CC and Central Control Committee. He told them that "it was the dynamism, self-sacrifice, enthusiasm and initiative of millions of workers and kolkhozniki, releasing, together with engineers and specialists, the colossal energy of socialist competition and shock work."[93] A few days later, his description of the failures of the most recent grain collection campaign listed the reverse of those personal qualities: the lack of enthusiasm, initiative, and self-sacrifice [*samotek*], as well as the failure to understand central policy and "the tactics of the class enemy." He forcefully denied any shortfall in the harvest itself and never raised the possibility of any errors in central policy.[94] One can infer from this that, for Stalin, the single most important factor in achieving plan targets was the identification and removal of officials who had doubts about the plan, "opportunists" and other "anti-state elements," and their replacement with officials imbued with a Bolshevik spirit. One could see this approach in the resolutions of the January 1933 plenum. They created a new layer of political oversight in the countryside, whose primary roles were (1) to promote state policy; (2) to isolate and exclude anti-social and anti-state elements, wreckers, and opportunists; and (3) to improve the Marxist-Leninist education of party members.[95] This was followed up with articles in the party press insisting on the need for "a monolithic, centralized [party] organization [and] an uncompromising struggle against rotten liberalism, double-dealing, and opportunism." The articles were preparing the ground for the announcement, in April 1933, of a party purge. The purge commissions were instructed to target first and foremost "class-alien and hostile elements," "double-dealers," and "open and hidden violators of party discipline [who are] not fulfilling the decisions of the party and government [and are] casting doubt on them and discrediting them as 'unrealistic' and 'unachievable.'" [96] In the following weeks the party press observed that "those passing the purge are firm fighters for the party line and Bolshevik tempos in production."[97] The center made it explicit that doubting the realism of the plan would cost you your job. Given the determined insistence that central policy was correct and plan targets could be met, any failure to achieve targets or implement policy could only be associated with incompetence or, more likely, some form of anti-state thought or action. In either case he made it clear that no one should be spared. In his report to the seventeenth party congress in January 1934,

Stalin made it clear yet again that explaining difficulties "in terms of so-called 'objective conditions' cannot be justified . . . The responsibility for our failures and shortcomings rests in nine cases out of ten not on 'objective conditions,' but on ourselves alone." Even officials "with a well-known record of services in the past" should be held to account. Among them, Stalin observed, "there were those who think that party and Soviet laws are written not for them but for idiots. These are the same people who don't consider it their responsibility to conform to the foundations of party and state discipline . . . We must not hesitate to remove them from their leading posts regardless of their services in the past."[98] Efforts to identify these undesirable elements were stepped up. The congress resolutions included a thorough reform of the institutions verifying the fulfillment of central decisions, creating two new and more powerful bodies, the Commissions for State Control (KSK) and Party Control (KPK).

The second five-year plan was more moderate, but production targets would be enforced more ferociously and consistently. At the same time, the center's impatience was making life more difficult for leading officials from the top to the bottom of the apparat. Back in August 1933 Sergo Ordzhonikidze objected when the directors of a combine plant were threatened with prosecution for delivering unfinished goods. Ordzhonikidze tried to protect them on the grounds that finishing them had not been possible. The first instinct of Kaganovich, who was chairing Politburo meetings while Stalin was on vacation, was to defend Ordzhonikidze and the plant directors, but Stalin insisted that "Sergo's behavior can only be characterized as anti-party, because its obvious goal is to protect reactionary elements of the party against the CC."[99] Ordzhonikidze was reprimanded, but others in a similar situation did not get off so lightly. In September, Kaganovich reported to Stalin a rise in the output of defective goods in the textile industry, blaming weak administration and poor organization of labor. Stalin insisted that the guilty parties be punished regardless of their "Communist" rank. To reports of corruption in the Urals regional organization, Stalin insisted that "the accused should be sacked and punished." His approach to sorting out problems on the railway network was to send threatening telegrams and to order the arrest of "those guilty of upsetting traffic plans."[100] In discussing the high accident rate on the railroad network around Khabarovsk, he told regional officials to "purge the railroads of the 'nests of wreckers.'" Any delay in doing so, he warned ominously, "might end badly for you."[101] The message was even more blatant in the grain collections campaign of the summer and autumn of 1934. Regional officials were told: "Either fulfill the plan or you will be removed from your post."[102] Stalin agreed with Molotov that resistance to the collections should be characterized as "counterrevolutionary sabotage."[103] Several local trials were organized and executions followed that were publicized in the press.[104] Lest there was any doubt about the center's uncompromising attitude to the fulfillment of directives, the central party press repeatedly asserted the importance of "iron discipline" in work and relentlessly directed purge commissions to expel "open and hidden violators" of it.[105]

As things stood toward the mid-1930s, Soviet officials were without the narrowest opportunity to explain shortcomings in their work though plan targets continued to be extremely demanding. They were unable to justify anything short of the total implementation of central directives. They were not so much unable as unwilling, because they had a clear sense of the consequences of admitting to any problems, and if they did not identify problems there was a raft of organizations devoted to exposing them if their subordinates did not expose them first. The state and party apparatus was consequently riven with tensions as officials blamed one another for problems in order to escape blame themselves.[106] Stalin was aware of these tensions and resultant conflicts. He received regular reports of leading officials taking repressive action against subordinates who criticized them, and of regional organizations so badly divided by infighting that normal work had become impossible.[107] And yet Stalin seemed not to see that the tensions and conflict were an inevitable consequence of the plan targets he was imposing. He saw the manifestations of the problem, but did not appear to understand its underlying causes. Rather, he saw the conflicts as a healthy and necessary process in which the "Bolshevik" leaders should be encouraged to win out over the "opportunists,"[108] as if flushing out the opportunists would make it possible to meet exaggerated plan targets. He sometimes gave one side of a dispute a "mandate" to arrest its opponents, but he increasingly found it necessary to intervene in order to restrain this sort of judicial violence as it got out of hand. The way the press described it, in such cases, "administrative methods" were taking the place of proper "Bolshevik" leadership.

As the conflicts deepened and violence worsened, Stalin appeared blind to the roots of the problem. This is not surprising. He had, after all, specifically prohibited officials from questioning the realism of plans. He had prohibited them from mentioning this source of the conflicts. Rather than act to limit the conflicts, Stalin introduced further initiatives that only exacerbated them. For example, the Stakhanovite movement was intended to encourage innovation in the organization of production, but in practice it was terribly disruptive.[109] Stakhanovite records were often achieved by concentrating resources in one shift, starving those that preceded and followed it. The movement drove up labor costs. It led to increases in damage to equipment, accidents, and defective production. It pitted non-Stakhanovites against Stakhanovites, and would-be Stakhanovites against managers holding them back. Little wonder that many managers did what they could quietly to subvert the movement.

This sort of resistance was more dangerous than ever. The murder of Politburo member Sergei Kirov in December 1934, and the subsequent investigations, had deepened Stalin's conviction that enemies of the regime were at work.[110] Calls for vigilance were getting louder in 1935 and 1936. The verification and exchange of party cards at this time ensured that every organization was brought into the hunt for enemies. Organizations were told that finding two or three enemies per district was not enough. If that was all they got, they were clearly not "taking to heart the many directives of the CC and Comrade Stalin that as our successes grow, the class enemy resorts to ever more sophisticated methods of struggle, making use in the first instance of the opportunist complacency and daydreaming of Communists."[111] The calls for vigilance did not let up. A secret CC letter to regional organizations in July 1936 insisted that the "single most important characteristic of every Bolshevik in the current situation ought to be his ability to recognize and identify enemies of the party no matter how well they have camouflaged their identity."[112] This sort of pressure inevitably led the party and Soviet apparatus to turn on itself in a downward spiral of denunciation and counterdenunciation.

Few leading officials could believe that they were blameless in the eyes of the regime. Few were safe from denunciation. Few officials could claim to embody Stalin's ideal of "Bolshevik leadership," because it demanded the impossible. Who was not an "opportunist," if an opportunist attempted to shield himself from the regime's impossible demands? Who was not a "Leftist" (or Trotskyist/Zinovievite), if a Leftist was one who lacked faith in the construction of socialism? Who was not a "Rightist," if a Rightist wanted to slow the tempo of socialist construction? The apparat was full of officials who could be described as "double-dealers," praising central policy in public but trying to escape its impossible demands in less public settings. They had achieved three years of relatively stable growth, but not without engaging in practices that Stalin considered wholly unacceptable and, worse, counterrevolutionary. Campaigns of vigilance in the summer of 1936 provoked a trickle of denunciations that became a flood. Through the winter and into the spring of 1936–37, Stalin received a stream of reports about the misdeeds of local officialdom. He had been aware of their "coping behaviors" before, but he did not grasp how deep and pervasive they were.[113] His shocked reactions to news of their "misdeeds" is perhaps the most compelling evidence that he never grasped how the pressures of taut planning and how the threat of sacking or worse at any failure to meet the plan engendered those behaviors. His steadfast refusal to accept any report asserting that plans were unrealistic meant that even those organizations designed specifically to verify the fulfillment of central decisions were not given the opportunity to explain the underlying problems of the Stalinist command economy. Stalin himself had inhibited the flow of accurate information on the economy. By 1937, Stalin thought the party and state apparatus was full of wreckers, saboteurs, and counter-revolutionaries. They were largely "enemies" of Stalin's creation.

It is beyond the scope of this chapter to explore Stalin's views on leadership and administration after the Terror. The documentary record is rather thin in the immediate aftermath of the Terror, and with the onset of the war, the state structure and function of the party and state apparatus changed dramatically. A detailed history of that period remains to be written. The late Stalin period, though, is covered brilliantly by Yoram Gorlizki and Oleg Khlevniuk, who argue that Stalin continued to battle with the dilemmas of the 1930s, trying to promote efficient and professional "Bolshevik" leadership and administration that was, at the same time, responsive to his will.[114] "Bargaining," in the sense that Gregory describes as a regular interaction between the center and lower level officials, only emerged in this later period.

The 1920s and early to mid-1930s were different. Then, the regime did not yet have a stable working relationship with the nomenklatura. While the Lenin succession was ongoing, Stalin had to be careful with this group because it could influence the outcome. When Trotsky and others on the Left accused Stalin of "bureaucratism," he benefitted from publicly drawing the inference that the accusation applied similarly to the nomenklatura. But as administrative challenges grew sharply in the late 1920s and early 1930s, and particularly after Stalin had decisively won the succession struggle, he put immense pressure on officialdom to meet production plans and other targets. Stalin never entirely grasped that it was the pressure exerted by the center that generated the phenomena he labeled "double-dealing." By 1933, Stalin understood that targets had to be restrained from the extremes of the previous four years, but only in a very limited sense can that "restraint" be understood as the product of "bargaining." The so-called three good years of stable growth masked a deepening crisis of Stalin's confidence in officialdom. The economic crisis that contributed to the Terror of 1936–38 was not a crisis of production. It was a crisis of leadership and administration.

The notion of "bargaining" is thus not a particularly fruitful way to resolve the strong-state/weak-state conundrum in the history of Stalinism in the 1930s. One subtle distinction is needed. While the overwhelming predominance of political power was in the hands of the center, Stalin and his inner circle convinced themselves that their power rested on a knife's edge as they were surrounded by enemies. The state *was* strong, but leaders *perceived* it was weak.

2

SPYMANIA

How were Stalin's interests served by the execution and exile of millions of Soviet citizens in the 1930s? A new consensus is emerging in the scholarly literature. In the last twenty years, scholarly work on the subject has increasingly viewed Stalin's Terror[1] as a response to growing anxieties rather than a drive to achieve totalitarian control. Research in Russian archives has been revealing the substantial resistance to the regime. Stalin was nagged by doubts that central directives were being fulfilled. The problem was not his immediate subordinates, but rather the greater mass of the party and state bureaucracy that responded to impossible demands from the center with foot-dragging and deception. Meanwhile, workers were upset, in no small part because Stalin's industrialization program was funded largely by the suppression of their living standards. There were new opportunities for advancement and an end to unemployment, but enthusiasm was tempered in the early 1930s as work norms were raised, the food situation deteriorated, and pressure on housing increased.[2] Worker unrest occasionally spilled into strikes and other forms of protest.[3] The peasantry would not soon forgive the regime for forced collectivization and grain collections that ultimately led to the loss of hundreds of thousands, if not millions, of lives in the famine of 1932–33. Living standards were much better for the mass of officialdom, but they were disturbed at being landed with the impossible task of fulfilling the overambitious targets of the plan while stuck between resentful subordinates and threatening bosses. Amidst crisis and chaos, those party officials who had supported

Stalin at party congresses and CC plena may have wondered whether they had made the wrong choice.[4] Of course, the promise of building a socialist society did generate plenty of enthusiasm, but Stalin could have had few illusions about the level of resistance and disaffection to his rule. The prospect of an imminent war made this resistance and disaffection more disturbing still. As war with Nazi Germany came to appear inevitable, Stalin perceived the threat to his leadership in the form of a fifth column.[5]

At the time of the Terror, the press was full of stories of the agents of foreign powers recruiting "unstable elements" in Soviet government and society with the express aim of destroying the regime from within.[6] From the summer of 1936, the press also asserted that the former oppositions from the leadership struggles of the 1920s had themselves become agents of fascism. Indeed, this was the central charge against the accused in the infamous Moscow trials of 1936–38. Was there any substance to these charges? Did Stalin believe them? Although it is very difficult to know with any certainty what Stalin believed, we now have access to some of the foreign and domestic intelligence that Stalin received and that helped shape his views of the threat of subversion. We also have substantial parts of his correspondence with the political police and organs of justice, from which it is possible to see not only how he acted on these reports, but also how he shaped the collection of intelligence.

It is clear not only from Soviet sources, but also from sources originating in the "bourgeois" governments surrounding the USSR, that there were foreign spies and saboteurs at work in the Soviet Union. Just how many it is impossible to say.[7] The political police (Cheka/GPU/OGPU/NKVD) relied heavily on a network of unpaid informants to identify them, and lacked the inclination and the resources to verify the testimony of these informants. They trusted their agents' "revolutionary instincts" (*revoliutsionnoe chut'ye*) rather than rely on material evidence of subversive acts, despite repeated directives to the contrary. Once suspects were arrested, the political police relied largely on forced confessions not only to "prove" the guilt of the accused, but also to identify those with whom they worked. Stalin understood that the political police tended to exaggerate the threat of subversion,[8] but he preferred that they arrest, and even execute, the innocent rather than let spies and saboteurs get away. Stalin often relied on his own "revolutionary instinct" and on many occasions directed the political police to draw conclusions before an investigation had begun. In short, the whole apparatus for the collection and interpretation of intelligence lacked a reliable system of verification. In the course of the 1920s and 1930s, Stalin received some very disturbing reports of subversive activities, but particularly under the influence of Nikolai Ezhov, the actual threat of subversion came to be grossly exaggerated. This chapter explores the origins of Stalin's mistaken perception that by the middle of the 1930s, the national security of the USSR had been thoroughly compromised by multiple, interlocking networks of foreign spies and subversives.

Foreign Spies and Saboteurs in the Soviet Union

Spying and sabotage were common facts of political life in the first half of the twentieth century. The arms race that culminated in World War II hugely intensified not only the need to know one's enemies' military capabilities and war plans, but also the fear that information of one's own military capabilities and war plans was vulnerable to espionage or sabotage. The unstable peace that followed World War I, challenged by the constant threat of revisionism, meant that these fears and desires were hardly tempered in the interwar years. Meanwhile the ever increasing political tensions of the interwar, the pitched battles between Left and Right, between revolutionaries and counterrevolutionaries, created new opportunities to destabilize the political order of neighbors and foes.

That states spy on one another is well known. That they had particularly good reason to engage in espionage and subversion in the profoundly unstable interwar is also not controversial. But because the archives of the agencies of espionage and subversion are closed, our knowledge of their activities is sketchy. We know that the Balkans was a hotbed of terrorism between the wars. Bulgaria, Hungary, and Italy variously supported Macedonian and Croatian terrorists in order to destabilize Yugoslav politics. Italy was similarly involved in Greece, Albania, and Ethiopia. During the Spanish Civil War, the Italians initiated a bombing campaign in southern France in the hopes that it might further destabilize the Third Republic and hinder arms shipments to the Republicans. The Germans did their best to unsettle affairs in Czechoslovakia, Romania, and the Baltic states,[9] among others. By the mid–1930s, the Abwehr had an entire department devoted to sabotage and the orchestration of uprisings.[10] Meanwhile, in realizing its imperial ambitions, Japan not only invaded China, but also undertook to undermine the interests of those countries, notably the United States, Britain, and the Soviet Union, competing for spheres of influence in south and east Asia.[11] In these fields of international espionage and terrorism, the Soviets were probably the most active practitioners, doing their best to unsettle affairs in Poland, Bulgaria, China, and Manchuria, to murder and harass their critics, and to obtain any information that would reveal the nature of the threat posed by the capitalist states that surrounded them.

Spying and sabotage were objects of fear and fascination not only among political leaders, but also among the broader public. Perhaps most famously, the British public obsessively feared an infiltration of German spies before World War I.[12] The fascination with and fear of spies brought with it a proliferation of literature about spies and saboteurs across Europe.[13] The huge numbers of people displaced by the war peppered urban centers with foreign nationals. That not only deepened the impression that spies were everywhere, but it underpinned the reality of it. The poverty of the displaced, the lives and careers interrupted, left many more than willing to engage in espionage or subversion. Governments and political movements were happy to recruit them.

The Bolshevik government had more reason to worry about spies and saboteurs than most other governments in the interwar. The seizure of power in November 1917 met an extremely fierce resistance, and although the official historiography broadly painted the struggle to retain power as a battle between the working class and their enemies among the old elites and bourgeoisie, the reality was considerably murkier. If they were to ensure the survival of the Revolution, the Bolsheviks had little choice but to co-opt the tsarist officer corps into the new Red Army and to rely on officials of the tsarist bureaucracy and so-called bourgeois specialists in order to keep the new state and economy functioning effectively. They were perhaps too suspicious of these "class aliens" in their midst, many of whom were happy to contribute to the new state the Bolsheviks were building, but there many who seized the opportunity to undermine this new state from within. Stalin had immediate experience of this sabotage as a Red Army commander on the southern front. At times, it was clear that the enemy knew in advance of troop movements and battle plans. The front was full of characters that passed from one side to the other out of conviction, for adventure, or for money, and a commanding officer had to be extremely careful to watch and judge the loyalty of his officers at all times.[14]

On the home front, the Soviet political police, the Cheka, kept a careful watch on those they deemed "class enemies," and they found no shortage of evidence, much real, but probably even more imagined, of underground counterrevolutionary organizations. In the course of the civil war, most counterrevolutionaries were shot on suspicion without much evidence, if any, but Soviet efforts to infiltrate such organizations, as well as the armies and foreign governments that supported them, produced considerable evidence of a very real threat. It should come as no surprise that the "White" armies and foreign armed forces fighting the Bolsheviks should have attempted to make use of those individuals and groups who shared their desire to see the end of this revolution in Russia. There is no shortage of evidence of their efforts to spread anti-Soviet propaganda, to blow up rail lines, to disrupt military and civilian production, and to assassinate leading Soviet officials.[15]

As the tide of the war turned in the Bolsheviks' favor, their enemies' use of espionage, sabotage, and terror does not appear to have lessened meaningfully. On the contrary, as the likelihood of an outright military victory faded, reliance on the "fifth column" was likely to grow. Boris Savinkov, Robert Bruce Lockhart, Sidney Reilly, and other agents of the Whites and foreign forces of the intervention were focused on the potential of the assassination of Bolshevik leaders to disorganize the Soviet state, provoke a popular uprising, and reverse the fortunes of the war.[16] Fortunately for the Bolsheviks, the Cheka was able to infiltrate the anti-Bolshevik underground. Savinkov and Reilly were both ultimately captured and shot. But no intelligence agency can ever be sure that it has all subversive organizations under control. Well after the end of the civil war, most of the states sharing borders with the Soviet Union—Japan, Poland, Romania, the Baltic states, Finland, Persia, Afghanistan, and others—had good reason to continue to engage in spying, sabotage, and subversion against the Soviet Union: some had territorial disputes with the Soviet regime; some felt threatened by their neighbor, or concerned about her military capabilities; some, like Japan, saw an opportunity to seize Soviet territory. Most simply shared the hatred for communism common in the developed world and wished to see the earliest possible end to the Soviet experiment. At the same time, although the defeated White armies had ultimately retreated beyond the borders of the Soviet Union, they did not entirely disband, leaving a substantial military force ready to re-enter the Soviet Union when a suitable opportunity arose. And tens of thousands of other citizens of the Russian Empire who had retreated with the Whites were ready, out of a sense of patriotic duty, boredom with exile, a desire for adventure, or the promise of money, to return to their homeland to help subvert the new regime.

One might assume that subversive activity would be desperately difficult in a brutal, authoritarian state, but it was, on the contrary, rather simple. In the first instance, Soviet borders were porous. Preventing cross-border traffic across thousands of kilometers of borders was desperately difficult if not impossible. Through the 1920s and 1930s, the issue was raised regularly in the Politburo without ever resolving the issue to anyone's satisfaction. More and more troops, horses, cars, and other equipment were assigned to secure the border. Entire populations were moved from border zones, new forms of personal identification were introduced, but reports of border incursions continued unabated. At the same time, reports of attacks on transport infrastructure and enterprises both military and civilian continued as well.

Recruiting spies and saboteurs was also easy. Among the millions of Russians who had left at the time of the Revolution, there were always those willing to risk their lives for a few dollars and the opportunity to contribute practically to the downfall of the hated regime. Inside the country, further recruitment was not especially difficult either. There were plenty of disaffected citizens (workers, peasants, soldiers, white-collar workers, *byvshie liudy* [ci-devants], etc.) to target among Russians and non-Russians and those for whom a few extra rubles were critical for survival. The Polish government had little trouble recruiting among the populations along their borders with Belorussia and Ukraine. Most illegal traffic between Poland and the USSR consisted in contraband goods and among families divided by the borders, but it was not difficult for Polish intelligence agencies to use this traffic and contribute to it in order to gather information on, among other things, Soviet troop locations and military capabilities. More worrying for the Soviet leadership were Polish efforts to destabilize border areas politically in the 1920s and 1930s. Small groups of armed Poles and White Russians would murder officials and destroy infrastructure, generally within a relatively short distance of the border.[17] Particularly during the famine of 1932–33, Polish attempts to organize anger with the regime were sufficiently successful for Stalin to express the concern that they might "lose Ukraine."[18] This sort of danger receded not only with the end of the famine but also with the stabilization of Soviet-Polish relations in the mid–1930s in the face of the growing threat to them both posed by Nazi Germany. In the process of negotiating a non-aggression pact in the mid–1930s, the Soviet ambassador to Poland, V. A. Antonov-Ovseenko, was assured that Marshal Pilsudski had issued a directive to stop raids on Ukraine and Belorussia.[19] It is unclear whether they stopped or not, but Polish espionage against the Soviet Union continued to have notable successes. Polish intelligence took advantage of the Soviets' willingness to give refuge to persecuted Communists from abroad by sending agents posing as persecuted Communists. Given the Soviet habit of then deploying these émigrés in the business of spying on Poland, it was a matter of time before the Soviet agent network in Poland was betrayed. By the time the Soviet network had collapsed, the entire Polish émigré community was held in suspicion of spying.[20]

There is also considerable evidence in the archives of the spying and sabotage of Japanese agents in the Soviet Union. Japan had considerable budgets for recruiting and running an agent network. In one relatively minor case, in April 1932, the Japanese general staff sent 6,000 yen to Torashiro Kawabe, their military attaché in Moscow, to pay for agents who could gather information on military equipment being shipped from Samara and Sverdlovsk.[21] When the Japanese ambassador Koki Hirota was recalled to Tokyo in 1932, rumors circulated in diplomatic circles that the move was necessitated by the imminent exposure of his agent network.[22] The rumors had a basis in fact, for in November 1932, the OGPU reported to Stalin that it had uncovered the "main" spying/sabotage organization of the Japanese general staff.[23] The OGPU clearly did not think it had the whole network; signals intelligence from other sources indicated otherwise, and efforts to infiltrate and uncover further Japanese agent networks in the Soviet Union continued unabated.[24] Most Japanese agents were in the

Soviet Far East monitoring military capabilities in the region and preparing the ground for a possible invasion.[25] The preparations included the accumulation of hidden supplies of guns and explosives along the far eastern coast,[26] the sabotage of infrastructure and military and civilian production, and plans to contact and organize opponents of the regime among peasants, workers, national minorities, and members of the former oppositions.[27] The Japanese military was especially interested in recruiting the followers of the "Left opposition" because, it was argued, they too sought to overthrow the regime.[28]

Although the Whites, the Poles, and the Japanese seem to have been the most active sponsors of spying and sabotage in the USSR, they were not the only ones. Although other states that shared a border with the USSR, including Finland, the Baltic states, Romania, Turkey, Persia, and Afghanistan, were generally either less hostile or too weak to pose a substantial threat on their own, they were used at times with or without their knowledge as conduits for the agents of other states, including Britain, France, and Germany. Successful Soviet efforts to infiltrate anti-Soviet organizations abroad confirmed their suspicions that major European powers were willing financially to support efforts to destabilize the regime. Other sources, such as the transcripts of the Nuremburg trials, confirm that Nazis sent armed teams of White Russians across Soviet borders on missions to kill Soviet leaders.[29] From signals intelligence they also understood that information obtained by foreign intelligence agencies in the Soviet Union was widely shared. There was every appearance of a conspiracy of "bourgeois" governments, including major and minor powers surrounding the Soviet Union, to build an effective agent network that could expose state secrets, destroy infrastructure and civilian and military production, and destabilize the country, not least by assassinating Soviet leaders.

Through the 1920s and 1930s, the GPU provided Soviet leaders with a steady stream of reports of the terrorist activities of foreign agents.[30] Several times a month, the Politburo discussed a GPU report on an act of terrorism, took measures to combat it, or decided on a punishment for captured spies and saboteurs.[31] Members of the Politburo and a few other leading Soviet officials regularly received a range of White Russian periodicals, many of which discussed tactics of struggle against the USSR. Although the GPU was looking for spying and sabotage across a broad front, it paid close attention to foreign nationals and foreign companies in the USSR. Commissar of Defense Kliment Voroshilov received weekly intelligence reports that included a special section on acts of sabotage at plants producing for the military. And Stalin appears to have had the most direct communication with the main intelligence services including the GPU/NKVD and military intelligence. He was immediately informed of illegal border crossings, incidents of sabotage, and evidence of spying. He received transcripts of interrogations and all raw intelligence suggestive of the hostile intentions of foreign governments toward the USSR.

Not only did Stalin receive the most intelligence, but he also had a very direct and unmitigated influence over the direction of intelligence operations and over the interpretation of the information obtained. Because Stalin had extraordinary power over the collection of intelligence, the interpretation of intelligence reports, and the actions taken in response to them, and because there were no checks on the quality of intelligence beyond Stalin's judgment, the prevalent image of the threat from spies and saboteurs could and did become detached from the underlying reality.

The Rise and Fall—Twice—of the Cheka-GPU-OGPU

Soviet intelligence services were not entirely under Stalin's control until the end of the 1920s. In the ten or so years between the Revolution and the confirmation of Stalin's uncontested grip on the Soviet political order, the Soviet intelligence services grew and evolved considerably. They were shaped, perhaps even more than other Soviet institutions, by the experience of civil war.[32] The Cheka, in particular, played a critical role in the survival of the Bolshevik regime. This "glorious" period in its history was also among its most violent. The Cheka had almost certainly infiltrated, uncovered, and eliminated many serious threats to the Revolution. It developed a reputation as the "eyes and ears of the regime" as well as its "shield and sword," and these two metaphors encapsulate its essential position in the civil war. The Cheka was responsible for both investigation and punishment. It combined the roles of policeman, judge, and executioner, and in the context of the civil war it did not get bogged down in the niceties of investigation. Though the Cheka did conduct some serious investigations, it lacked the qualified staff and the time to build cases on the basis of material evidence. Rather, Chekisty were told to rely on their "revolutionary instincts," and this largely amounted to identifying an enemy by class origin, a foreign-sounding name, or proximity to the scene of some crime. Those suspected of spying, sabotage, or other counterrevolutionary crimes were generally shot without trial, and often on the spot.

These powers were granted only with some hesitation in the weeks after the creation of the Cheka, and they were subsequently challenged on a fairly regular basis until Stalin's death.[33] At issue was always the danger of "excesses." The lack of any check meant that large numbers of innocent people were being executed. The challenge to Cheka powers came from emerging legal institutions seeking to uphold basic standards of justice and from the diplomatic service, which viewed with grave concern the outrage of foreign governments at the Bolshevik Red Terror. It was worse still for the diplomats when they were unable to explain what happened to individual foreigners who were caught up in the Terror because the Cheka refused to offer such information. The diplomats were left to deal with the damage this would do to Soviet foreign relations. And yet, because Bolshevik leaders perceived the regime to be in grave danger, attempts to place limits on the Cheka rarely lasted for long.

The best chance for restraining the Cheka was at the end of the civil war, when the immediate threat to the regime appeared to be receding.[34] The Ninth Congress of Soviets in December 1921 decided on a fundamental reorganization of the structure and function of the organization. Stalin co-chaired (with L. B. Kamenev) the commission that oversaw the process.[35] Obscurely renamed the State Political Administration or GPU, the new structure had much more carefully circumscribed rights to investigate and try political cases on its own, and the Commissariat of Justice was granted its demand to review GPU verdicts. Furthermore, in the subsequent three years, the staff of the new organization was allowed to decline by 50 percent.

Feliks Dzerzhinskii, candidate member of the Politburo and the head of the OGPU (and Cheka before it), was by no means indifferent to the weakening of his organization. He tried to resist and limit the supervision by the legal organs of its activities.[36] He pushed several times, unsuccessfully, to focus all intelligence-gathering activity in the hands of the GPU.[37] He fought to ensure that the GPU could continue to conduct major operations and that it did not shrink further due to an inability to provide a decent standard of living for its workers. Among party leaders, Trotsky and Kamenev were proponents of further cuts to the OGPU budget, whereas Stalin was inclined to defend the organization before the Politburo.[38] Stalin did so perhaps because he understood the role that the political police could play in the struggle for power after Lenin's death, but he also appears to have been sympathetic to Dzerzhinskii's claims that the work of the OGPU was critically important to the security of the Soviet state. Dzerzhinskii repeatedly complained to him that that security would be compromised both by budget cuts and the limits imposed on it by the Commissariat of Justice.[39]

The best case he could make for strengthening the OGPU was rooted in the results of its investigations. If his fellow Politburo members shared his sense of the grave threats that the Soviet Union faced, they would be more inclined to accept his case for more powers, staff, and financing. The Politburo membership was kept well informed of ongoing OGPU operations and investigations. In the first half of the 1920s, there were operations against "banditism" and currency counterfeiting, against "anti-Soviet elements" in the Russian Orthodox Church, and against intellectuals, among others. But none of these operations of itself would have commanded the attention of the Politburo as critically important to national security. There had to be a threat to the Soviet state itself. For Dzerzhinskii, the breakthrough came with "Trest" and "Sindikat–2" and other similar operations in which OGPU agents posed as representatives of anti-Soviet organizations in search of material assistance abroad. The agents contacted and ultimately infiltrated various White Russian organizations and obtained information about their plans for anti-Soviet activity, their hopes to organize and unite opposition to the Soviet Union from within, and the support that they had, supposedly, been promised by the French, British, Polish, Romanian, and other "bourgeois" governments. Dzerzhinskii now had "evidence" of the plans and combined efforts of foreign governments and anti-Soviet groups to undermine the Soviet state.[40]

This "evidence" suggested that while some groups still threatened to orchestrate a coup by means of the assassination of Soviet leaders and the organization of mass uprisings,[41] the graver threat to Soviet security came in the form of efforts to undermine the Soviet economic recovery by means of sabotage: the destruction of plants and infrastructure by anti-Soviet organizations funded by foreign powers. This danger was sufficiently credible to the party leadership that, despite the continuing strain on the national budget, the OGPU was given further funding and staff to support the collection of intelligence abroad.[42] Meanwhile, on 10 March 1922 regional GPU organs were instructed to focus their attention on "transport and enterprises especially important to the economy and strengthen operations to uncover and prevent sabotage by SRs, Kadets, and monarchists; secure these enterprises from the bombs and arson of counterrevolutionary elements; . . . [and] take further measures to uncover the espionage activities of foreigners and those with links to foreign diplomatic institutions and counterrevolutionary organizations."[43] The instruction made sense, insofar as the regional organs were best placed to secure local enterprises facing this supposed threat. And yet the regional OGPU organs did not have the staff, expertise, or funding to undertake successful operations to infiltrate anti-Soviet organizations as their counterparts in the Foreign Department (INO OGPU) did. At best, they maintained a crude surveillance of known SRs, Kadets, monarchists, "class aliens," and other individuals and groups suspected of being hostile to the regime and arrested suspects on the basis of "revolutionary instinct."[44] In one sense, they had no choice. Central party and OGPU organs tended to demand that investigations of sabotage result in the prosecution of those responsible. But the situation also presented opportunities for ambitious regional OGPU officials. *Preventing* sabotage by "uncovering" anti-Soviet organizations often won high praise and promotion even if the evidence supporting arrests and prosecutions was largely circumstantial. Either way, the OGPU, and in turn the party leadership, received a steady stream of reports from the regions detailing successful operations against saboteurs with links to foreign governments.[45]

By the mid–1920s, the growing and increasingly confident Foreign Department of the OGPU was passing to the party leadership reports indicating a heightened danger of war. White Russian military forces, the Polish and Romanian governments, backed by the British and French, were meant to be increasing espionage and sabotage in anticipation of an invasion.[46] In July 1925, the OGPU was given almost 4 million rubles to improve the guarding of borders.[47] In October 1925, Dzerzhinskii insisted on a tightening of security in the Kremlin in response to reports of assassination plots. At the same time he was pushing the Politburo hard to free the OGPU from further oversight of the Commissariat of Justice: "Now is not the time, politically, to take from us the right to deal with cases involving terrorists, monarchists, White Guard groups, and otherwise restrict our ability to fight counterrevolution."[48] Through 1926 and into 1927, reports of fires and explosions on the transport system and at major enterprises rose sharply.[49] In the autumn of 1926, VSNKh and OGPU were working out measures to fight sabotage.[50] On 13 January 1927, Stalin ordered the OGPU to report to the Politburo on the measures it had come up with "to combat fires and explosions and other deliberate attacks on enterprises."[51] Viacheslav Menzhinskii pleaded that it did not have the resources adequately to defend enterprises from the current threats and subsequently got more money, more troops, a new department to deal specifically with the threat of sabotage, and so-called committees for cooperation with the OGPU (*komitety sodeistviia*) in every enterprise under its surveillance.[52] In the summer of 1927, OGPU lecturers toured regional, city, and district party organizations as well as factory committees and general factory meetings in order to draw attention to the new security risks posed by the hidden agents of hostile powers.[53] Significantly, the OGPU was also given the right to try cases of sabotage without having to consult the Commissariat of Justice or the Politburo Commission on Political Affairs.[54] With the perceived increasing danger of war, this right was "temporarily" extended in June to include cases involving White Russians, spies, and bandits.[55]

By the time Dzerzhinskii died, suddenly, in July 1926, the OGPU was well on its way to recovering from the cutbacks it had faced at the end of the civil war and the limits placed on it by the Commissariat of Justice. It is likely that concrete acts of sabotage and espionage uncovered by the organization, as well as the worsening international situation, put it in a better position to plead its case before the Politburo. When asked about the extraordinary powers of the OGPU by foreign delegations on the tenth anniversary of the Revolution, Stalin publicly declared they would be suspended and the OGPU disbanded "when the capitalists of all countries stopped organizing and financing counterrevolutionary groups, conspirators, terrorists, and saboteurs."[56] But as the OGPU received more resources and broadened its investigations and intelligence collection, as it eased its way out of the control of the Commissariat of Justice and the publicity given to the danger presented by foreign agents increased, ever more spies and saboteurs were found. Dzerzhinskii and his successor Menzhinskii passionately believed that they were protecting the regime from very real dangers, but the general lack of rigorous skepticism of the evidence of that threat contributed significantly to the belief. When the Commissariat of Justice accused them of "excesses," of prosecuting cases on the basis of flimsy evidence, they reacted with scorn, insisting, as Dzerzhinskii did in 1925, that such complaints only helped the regime's enemies.[57]

Stalin was sympathetic to the OGPU. He did not ignore the concerns of the Commissariat of Justice, and he understood the propensity of the OGPU to exaggerate dangers and the necessary response to them, but he had seen enough evidence to convince him that that there were real threats to the Soviet state and that the first priority had to be the survival of the Revolution.[58] A close relationship with the OGPU also served his political interests. The political police played a critical role in his rise to power, harassing and limiting the freedom of action of his opponents within the Bolshevik Party. A perception of the domestic and foreign threats to the Soviet Union promised to reinforced support among the public and the party rank and file for his patriotic commitment to "build socialism in one country." Toward the end of the 1920s, the fear of war played an important role in his struggle with the Right. It underpinned his calls for radically increased tempos of industrial construction and for party unity under his leadership.

The Shakhty affair of 1928 shaped and deepened Stalin's relationship with the OGPU. As we have seen, growing concern about sabotage had brought, in January 1927, a more thorough surveillance of key Soviet enterprises and particularly the "class aliens" (in this case, "bourgeois" specialists) who worked there. Local OGPU officials relied, as ever, on their revolutionary instincts to sniff out hidden enemies of the state. The discovery of a "plot" was made almost inevitable by the combination of shop-floor politics, generational conflict among specialists, prejudices bred by longstanding OGPU operations against intellectuals and those with connections abroad, and a genuine hostility toward the Soviet regime and its methods among specialists.

Local OGPU organizations had rich material for their regular reports to the center on the progress of fulfilling the January 1927 directive, but it was in the coal industry of the North Caucasus region that one OGPU plenipotentiary, E. G. Evdokimov, and the economic department of the OGPU began to build a case suggesting a broader conspiracy against the regime. It was, as ever, based on circumstantial evidence. The accused Shakhty specialists did not always work well with party authorities or enterprise directors. They were resented and distrusted by the workers since civil war days.[59] They were treated with hostility by Soviet-trained specialists. They were critical of the plan and of enterprise directors. They had plenty of contacts abroad in Poland, Britain, and other countries thought to be preparing an invasion of the Soviet Union. But the material evidence of sabotage that appeared to justify the hostility of those they worked with, that made the contacts with foreigners seem sinister, and that spurred on the investigation came from the assessments of decisions the specialists had made: the flooding of certain mines, the purchase of certain equipment, the use of certain construction methods. K. I. Zonov of the OGPU economic department, whose personal file lists his educational level as "lower," concluded that these decisions were so counterproductive of the efficient functioning of the enterprises for which they worked that they could only be characterized as deliberate sabotage.[60] Armed with Zonov's conclusions, Evdokimov took the materials of the investigation to Menzhinskii, who told him to stop the investigation. Menzhinskii's decision may have been a rare assertion of skepticism, particularly in the light of Zonov's qualifications, but it is more likely to have been rooted in his assessment of the importance of the "bourgeois" specialists to the success of the Soviet economy in general and the Donbas in particular. Evdokimov was not put off, though, and he took the risky step of going over his boss's head directly to Stalin. Like Menzhinkii, Stalin saw the dangers in such a move, but he gave Evdokimov his approval to continue the investigation. Scores of specialists were arrested, subject to lengthy interrogations, and pressured to confess to their crimes.[61] The Politburo first discussed the Shakhty sabotage at the end of February 1928. In a week, a Politburo commission had been established to review the OGPU materials, and a few days later news of the "plot" was splashed across the national press.[62] This publicity was uncharacteristic. Most spy rings and conspiracies to commit sabotage were dealt with quietly and without significant press coverage by the Politburo Commission on Political Affairs.[63] Why organize a show trial for the Shakhty affair?

The affair served Stalin's political purposes at the time. The threat of war was rather abstract, but the possibility of enemies in every enterprise working to undermine the Soviet state brought home the importance of vigilance, of party unity behind his leadership, of further raising the tempo of industrialization, and of the hard work necessary to achieve them. A trial also promised to demonize those who would question ambitious plans for construction, like his emerging opponents on the Right. There were dangers for Stalin in such a course of action, not only in the loss of the technical skills to the economy, but also in the danger that he might not carry the party leadership with him. Some Politburo members, notably Aleksei Rykov, argued that the accusations against the specialists were blown out of proportion. Others, like Valerian Kuibyshev, simply shared Menzhinskii's assessment that it was not the right time to attack specialists. But the correspondence of most other Politburo members, including the moderates Nikolai Bukharin and Mikhail Tomskii, suggests that they genuinely believed that economic sabotage had become a key weapon of hostile capitalist powers in their struggle against the Soviet Union and that that sabotage extended well beyond Shakhty and the Donets Basin.[64] Even Trotsky supported the trial.[65] And what about Nikolai Krylenko? He had consistently criticized the OGPU for conducting arrests on the basis of flimsy evidence, and here the case almost entirely lacked material proof of guilt. It rested on the technical assessments of someone who was manifestly unqualified and on confessions that had been obtained under duress. Still Krylenko acted as chief prosecutor, defending the use of confessions in evidence and soldiering on when some of the defendants began to retract their confessions.[66] Perhaps Krylenko had no choice but to act as he did in his role as chief prosecutor, but he and the others appear to have acquiesced to Stalin's promotion of the Shakhty trial not so much because they were convinced of the legal case against the accused, but because they accepted the political case for a show trial, convinced that wrecking was going on, that "bourgeois" specialists in general were hostile to Soviet power, that they were inclined to resist the plan, that they had suspicious contacts with Western powers, that a public trial portraying the dangers posed by the specialists was necessary. Of course, rather than reducing the incidence of wrecking, the calls for vigilance generated by the trial resulted in an increase in denunciations and reports of wrecking. In the weeks and months that followed, the Politburo discussed further OGPU investigations of the sabotage committed by specialists in the defense industry, transport, and metallurgy.[67] Each appeared to be part of a growing conspiracy to destabilize the economy in advance of a new foreign intervention. The investigations served as the basis for a new show trial, of the so-called Industrial Party, in late 1930. In turn, this trial implicated a number of prominent members of the Academy of Sciences, who were in the dock for a further show trial. Like Shakhty, these further cases rested on forced confessions, circumstantial evidence, and little if any physical evidence of a crime.

This period of show trials provides revealing glimpses of Stalin's attitude to evidence in judicial matters. For example, we can see how Stalin directed the investigation of the so-called Industrial Party. In an October 1930 letter, he dictated to Menzhinskii the conclusions he should draw from the testimony of the engineer L. K. Ramzin, the only arrested specialist to openly "confess" to committing acts of sabotage on instructions from abroad in preparation for a foreign intervention. Rather than wait to see if the testimony of others reinforced Ramzin's, he encouraged the OGPU to make the other's testimony conform: "Run Messrs. Kondratiev, Yurovskii, Chaianov, etc. through the mill; they have cleverly tried to evade [the charge of having a] 'tendency toward intervention' but are (indisputably!) interventionist . . . If Ramzin's testimonies are confirmed and corroborated in the depositions of other persons accused . . . that will be a serious victory for the OGPU . . ." In the letter, Stalin also dictated to Menzhinskii, without reference to any evidence, which of the figures abroad—the wealthiest émigrés and capitalists with contacts in the British and French governments—were "directing" the accused specialists in the Soviet Union: "It might seem as if the 'TPP' or the 'Promparty' or Miliukov's 'party' represents the main force. But that's not true. The main force is the Riabushinskii-Denisov-Nobel group and the like—that is, Torgprom.

The TPP, the Promparty, and Miliukov's 'party' are errand boys for Torgprom."[68]

Like the rank and file OGPU investigator, Stalin relied on his "revolutionary instincts," rather than on strong material evidence, to identify the enemies of the regime. The OGPU subsequently obtained the "confessions" and shaped the testimony according to his wishes, and Stalin was subsequently prepared to put his judgments before an international court of public opinion: "Are we ready for this?" he asked Molotov, his second in command, of the "Industrial Party" show trial. After answering his own question in the affirmative, he added: "By the way, how about Messrs. Defendants admitting their mistakes and disgracing themselves politically, while simultaneously acknowledging the strength of the Soviet government and the correctness of the method of collectivization? It wouldn't be a bad thing if they did."

Here Stalin showed he was aware that the OGPU could obtain confessions to order. Perhaps by requesting such further "confessions" he was acknowledging that the case against the "Industrial Party" was not as strong as he had hoped, but he never doubted that saboteurs in the pay of foreign powers were preparing the ground for an invasion. As he concluded his October 1930 letter to Menzhinskii with a statement of his hopes for a successful show trial: "we'll make the material available in some form to the Comintern sections and the workers of the world, and we'll make the broadest campaign possible against the interventionists and will succeed in paralyzing them and in heading off interventionist attempts for the next one or two years, which is of great significance for us."[69]

Two years on, Stalin had every reason to conclude that this judgment was overoptimistic. As the depression deepened in the early 1930s, Stalin increasingly worried that European powers would use a war against the Soviet Union to distract their angry working classes. Campaigns against Soviet "dumping" were viewed as part of an effort to whip up anti-Soviet sentiment. Pope Pius was contributing to the danger of intervention with a campaign against communist ideology. Chiang Kai-shek was leading attacks on the Soviet-controlled Chinese Far Eastern Railway in what appeared to be an attempt to provoke war. Governments were conspicuously unwilling to criticize the Chinese. More disturbing though was the evidence that an ever broader range of countries was sharing intelligence useful for an attack on the Soviet Union.[70] OGPU moles among the White Russians noted an activization of plans for terrorist activities in the Soviet Union.[71] In 1931 alone, the OGPU arrested 15,670 people for terrorist activity. Surveillance of Japanese diplomatic personnel appeared to be revealing disturbing dimensions of Japanese sabotage and spying in the Soviet Union.[72] Networks of Polish and Czech spies were uncovered in Kiev, Leningrad, and Moscow, and the Poles were taking advantage of the response to collectivization and famine in order to provoke peasant uprisings.[73]

For Stalin, the danger of war, in the context of bitter resistance to, and sabotage of, state policies, was sufficiently grave to warrant a further relaxation of legal safeguards on OGPU powers to act as investigator, judge, and executioner. This was particularly the case in the countryside, where they played a key role in breaking resistance to collectivization and overcoming resistance to grain collections. Summary justice was meted out on a grand scale and the Soviet labor-camp system, the Gulag, came into its own.

This return to tactics characteristic of the civil war period was not limited to the countryside. Concerns about the loyalty of the military, heightened by the revelation of an apparent conspiracy among officers in Kharkov in 1931, provoked the arrest of thousands of soldiers and officers in "Operation Spring" led by Genrikh Iagoda.[74] These mass operations, and the "excesses" they inevitably generated, drew criticism. That criticism had been seething under the surface of Soviet political life for some time. Georgii Chicherin, who had been left putting out diplomatic fires provoked by the implication of foreigners in the show trials, had complained in a private letter to Maxim Litvinov in July 1930 about the total failure to control the baseless arrests of the OGPU: "The leaders of the OGPU have a blind faith in the words of every idiot and cretin they make their agent."[75]

The Commissariat of Justice was concerned not only about the quality of evidence underlying OGPU operations but also more broadly about the weakening of elementary standards of justice. A review of the investigative apparatus of the OGPU both in the center and the regions begun in 1931 found, not unexpectedly, a cavalier attitude to evidence in its operations. In the midst of the review, Iagoda was compelled to issue a letter to all OGPU officials condemning the use of torture to obtain confessions.[76]

In essence, the OGPU was forced to acknowledge the widespread arrest and execution of innocent people. It is a measure of the sense of the general crisis of the regime in these years that such an admission did not have more serious consequences for the OGPU and its leadership. It was only a year later, in the summer of 1932, that a decree of the Central Executive Committee and the Council of Peoples' Commissars "On Socialist Legality" reasserted the importance of the law. Even then, the summary justice meted out in the countryside by the OGPU was not brought to an end until 1934, and in the case of "Operation Spring," criticism of baseless arrests from within the OGPU resulted in the sacking not of Iagoda, but rather of his critics.[77] Nevertheless, behind the scenes, there was a sharp restraining of repression from 1931. Arrests for terrorist activity fell from 15,670 in 1931 to 8,544 in 1932. Arrests for counterrevolutionary activity fell from 343,734 in 1931 to 195,540 in 1932 and 90,417 in 1932.[78]

The restraining of repression should not be interpreted as a "neo-NEP" or as evidence of some kind of growing political liberalism. Rather, the restraint of repression can in its early phase be attributed to a loss of control over the work of the political police. The huge numbers of arrests and executions conducted by the OGPU were deemed to be counterproductive of state security. Neither prisons nor the Gulag could accommodate the influx. Besides which, by 1933, the restraint of repression was sustained by gradual lessening of the sense of immediate crisis. The first five-year plan considerably strengthened the Soviet economy and capacity for self-defense. Peasant resistance to collectivization had been crushed. A new generation of "Red" had replaced the old technical intelligentsia.

The threat of war continued, however, as did the danger posed by foreign spies and saboteurs, as well as banditism and other counterrevolutionary crime. The Commissariat of Justice renewed its efforts to limit the powers of the political police, though they did not meet with much success. A meeting of OGPU plenipotentiaries in May 1933 discussed the need to restrain repression and observe the law. Five days later, a CC decree forbad the conduct of mass arrests in the countryside. In August, that decree was reinforced by a directive of the CC and the Council of Peoples' Commissars that the Procuracy should supervise OGPU arrests. But even before the directive was issued Iagoda insisted on the necessity of a range of exceptions to that general supervision to Stalin, and by early 1934 the Procuracy was complaining that the directive was being ignored.[79] The battle over the judicial independence continued well after the OGPU was absorbed into the Peoples' Commissariat of Internal Affairs.

The battle was hard fought, but not especially meaningful because Stalin regularly assented to "exceptional" extensions to OGPU powers where he perceived the situation demanded it. For example, in May 1933, the suspension of mass arrests was not applied to the Far Eastern Region, where anger with collectivization and grain collections was affecting the "political mood" among soldiers and the commanders and the party. It was reported to Stalin that twenty-four counterrevolutionary groups engaged in espionage and sabotage were uncovered in the previous six months.[80] Similar organs of summary justice continued to work in Leningrad *oblast'* and Central Asia as well.[81] By 1934, the OGPU/NKVD was permitted to apply summary justice to cases of banditism and violent crime.

Stalin also continued to demonstrate his own preference for revolutionary instinct over material evidence in judging counterrevolutionary crimes. In August 1934, Kaganovich reported to Stalin, who was on vacation at the time, that a certain A. S. Nakhaev, the commander of a division of *Osoaviakhim* in Moscow, attempted to get his men to take arms against Soviet power. They did not follow him and Nakhaev was arrested immediately. The political police, and Kaganovich, assumed he was suffering some kind of breakdown, but Stalin insisted that Nakhaev was a spy in the pay of a foreign power: "Of course (of course!) he's not working alone. We have to hold him to the wall and force him to tell the whole truth—and then punish him severely. He must be a Polish-German agent (or Japanese). The Chekisty make a mockery of themselves when they discuss his 'political views' with him. (This is called an *interrogation!*) Hired thugs do not have their own political views, or else he wouldn't be an agent of a foreign power."[82]

Three weeks later, Stalin received his "whole truth," when Nakhaev "confessed" that he had been recruited by Estonian agents.[83] In essence, through Kaganovich, Stalin had ordered the NKVD to torture Nakhaev until he confessed along lines that suited his revolutionary instincts. Four months later, Stalin again directed the NKVD in such a way as to prejudice the investigation and guarantee that it would confirm his suspicions. When

Politburo member Sergei Kirov was murdered in Leningrad, Stalin told the NKVD to "look for the perpetrators among the Zinovievites."[84]

Connecting the Former Oppositions to Foreign Powers

By 1936, Stalin had become convinced that the former Left and Right oppositions were in league with hostile foreign powers. To understand how that happened, one must return to the details of their defeat in the late 1920s. The intelligence Stalin received from the OGPU in the late 1920s and into the 1930s indicated that the expulsion of oppositionists from the party did not put an end to their hostility to his leadership, and in some cases, on the contrary, it radicalized opposition. Only days after Zinoviev, Kamenev, and Trotsky had been expelled from the CC by a joint CC-Central Control Commission plenum, Menzhinskii warned Stalin that unnamed members of the opposition planned to murder Soviet leaders in a coup d'état timed to coincide with the celebrations of the tenth anniversary of the Revolution in November 1927. He observed that opposition propaganda in the army was threatening to undermine its loyalty to the regime and that top-secret information about activities and decisions at the highest levels was being leaked to foreign powers by the "opposition and its agents." The idea that the oppositions would collude with foreign powers was in circulation ten years before the accusation became a central feature of the Moscow trials. The threat this supposed collusion posed was taken very seriously. Menzhinskii warned that the survival of the regime was at stake: "We must steel ourselves for energetic action, even if we have to arrest them all overnight. For now we have the forces and resources to do that, but there is a question as to whether three or four months from now we will still be able to do that."[85]

In a subsequent letter to the members of the CC and Central Control Commission, Stalin did not agree with Menzhinskii's assessment that the regime was under an immediate threat, but he did agree that the activities of the opposition would be treated as high treason "in the capitalist states and therefore punishable by death, and I see no reason why we should not protect the dictatorship of the proletariat with the strictest measures." He insisted that "they . . . are spies and accomplices of our internal and external enemies," and he defended a plan proposed by the Collegium of the GPU for the infiltration of "hostile elements" inside the party, the party leadership, and the government apparatus. "The apparatus of the party and state has to be purged of all unreliable elements immediately and the apparatus has to become again what it used to be."[86]

We have little evidence of the work of the GPU "cells" set up among oppositionists, but we know that GPU arrested hundreds of oppositionists in the course of 1928. The information Stalin received on the activities of oppositionists in the process of these arrests provoked him to write a further letter—a memorandum to the members of the Politburo—in which he argued that the opposition had completed a transformation "from an underground anti-party group into an underground anti-Soviet organization." The letter was later published as a *Pravda* editorial under the title "They Have Sunk to This."[87] Stalin had reason to believe that Trotsky had been able to control and lead this subversive organization despite the effort to isolate him in Alma Ata, and so the decision was taken to expel him from the Soviet Union. Trotsky's interviews in the Western press upon his arrival in Turkey in February 1929, collected by the Soviet telegraph agency (TASS) and translated and distributed among members of the Politburo and Central Control Commission, immediately indicated that the fact of exile would have little effect. Western journalists, sensing a dramatic story, emphasized Trotsky's assertions that he would maintain contact with his underground network in the USSR and the danger that his network posed to the Soviet leadership. The interviews and reports painted a picture of Trotsky's substantial support in the party, the Red Army, and foreign Communist Parties, and hinted that Trotsky's struggle against Stalin would have the support of capitalist governments.[88]

The hopes Stalin expressed for a sense of discipline and unity of purpose in the party could only have been fading. As the surveillance of the Trotskyists and other opponents of Stalin on the left was continuing in 1929, Stalin's battle with the opponents on the right was heating up. He orchestrated the exclusion of Bukharin, Rykov, and Tomskii from the Politburo in due course, but as with opposition on the left, it was much easier to deal with leaders than followers. Stalin demanded that his opponents should publicly confess that they were wrong and he was right before they would be allowed to have any further role in the party, but he never trusted these confessions.[89] Rather, he relied on the GPU and the system of surveillance that Menzhinskii had developed to root out "double-dealers": those who supported Stalin and the "CC line" in public and worked to undermine it in private.

Stalin was not inclined to see a middle ground. Either you were with him or against him, and in the context of the first five-year plan, a period of "crisis and progress," to use R. W. Davies's phrase, attitudes tended to lie between the two absolutes. There a great enthusiasm for the revolutionary changes being wrought, but there was a lot of grumbling about the overwhelming pressures of plan fulfillment, shortages of consumer goods and housing, the violence of collectivization and dekulakization, and the imposition of conformity in all spheres of public life, among other things. Most leading party members were solidly behind Stalin, but it is unclear how many were so out of conviction or out of consideration for their careers. If anyone was in doubt of the consequences of criticizing state policy, S. I. Syrtsov (head of the RSFSR government) and V. V. Lominadze (a party official from the North Caucasus) had clearly demonstrated the consequence of public criticism of central policy. Both were reported to think Stalin should be "removed."[90] They were expelled from the party and given minor posts in the provinces. But that was not enough. Stalin wanted to know with whom Lominadze and Syrtsov had shared their political ideas. How did they propose to remove him? What measures were they taking to achieve their goals? Through the summer and autumn of 1930, OGPU investigations again reinforced Stalin's sense of a conspiracy against him. At a joint meeting of the Politburo and Central Control Commission Presidium in November, Stalin asserted that Syrtsov and Lominadze were both building "factional groups" in Moscow and the regions with the aim of installing rightists in power.[91] This was unfortunate for Bukharin because OGPU investigations were also revealing that he had continued to meet his "disciples" (from the Institute of Red Professors) and discuss Stalin and current policy in disparaging terms. Stalin accused Bukharin of "cultivating terrorists among Right deviationists."[92] The OGPU did not have to dig deep to find evidence of quite virulent criticism of current Soviet policies and of Stalin's leadership, and Stalin was receptive of their efforts to present that criticism in a conspiratorial light. Faced with so many challenges in domestic policy and threats from abroad, Stalin was determined to destroy anyone who criticized the regime either publicly or privately:

Double-dealing [*dvurushnichestvo*] is dangerous because it culti-
vates in the party a rotten diplomacy that undermines the very
foundations of the mutual comradely trust of party members. We
must exterminate double-dealing and mete out exemplary punishments to double-dealers. This applies even more so to factional
activity at the present time. Factional activity of even the smallest
groups is water on the mill of the enemies of the working class
from Kondrat'ev and Ramzin to the imperialists of the world.[93]

While the cost of criticizing the regime was clear, further policy crises—
particularly the terrible famine in the countryside—inevitably provoked
conversations that caught the attention of the OGPU. The most prominent
officials to be reported for this were A. P. Smirnov, N. B. Eismont, and
V. N. Tolmachev, all heads of major institutions, who met and discussed
the problems of Soviet policy over vodka.[94] OGPU qualified them as
"counterrevolutionary." At approximately the same time, M. N. Riutin, a
member of the Presidium of VSNKh, wrote a virulent critique of the regime
in a 167-page tract entitled "Stalin and the Crisis of the Proletarian
Dictatorship," calling for, among other things, Stalin's dictatorship to be
overthrown.[95] This was rather more serious not only for its content, but
also because it was unclear who else was involved in drafting the document
and who had read it. Zinoviev and Kamenev were summoned to the Central
Control Commission to explain if they had any link to Riutin.[96] They were
accused of having known of the tract without informing the CC. It is
possible that Stalin may have suspected worse. Stalin may already have
known about Trotsky's ongoing efforts to build a coalition of opponents
to the regime, thanks to Menzhinskii's efforts to organize the infiltration
of his inner circle.[97] Pierre Broue makes a compelling argument that
Zinoviev and Kamenev were in contact with Trotsky and agreed in principle
to join his coalition, though he does not think Stalin knew about it until
1935.[98] Stalin seems at least to have had an inkling of it, because many of
the figures Trotsky had recruited were rounded up in the aftermath of the
Riutin affair and sent to jail or into exile. Arch Getty's work in the Trotsky
archive at Harvard indicates that Trotsky was undaunted and a few months
later taunted Stalin that he would continue to promote his ideas within
the party. If this promised only the further distribution of tracts like Riutin's,

there was good reason for Stalin to worry, but when Kirov was shot at point-blank range by an ex-party member, Leonid Nikolaev, Stalin may have assumed that the members of the coalition still at large had changed their tactics from discussion to terrorist action. They had only recently been given new opportunities in Leningrad, for Kirov had since 1933 lowered barriers to preventing former oppositionists from finding work in the city and region.[99]

Despite Stalin's unambiguous instruction, for three weeks the NKVD investigators refused to exclude the possibility that Nikolaev was an agent of a foreign power. Indeed, in the days after the assassination, his interrogators had him admit to visiting both the Latvian and German consulates in Leningrad in the summer and autumn of 1934. From the latter, he apparently received deutsche marks that he subsequently spent in a hard-currency shop. By the end of December, after almost four weeks of interrogations, he "confessed" that he asked the Latvian consul to help his counterrevolutionary "group" get in contact with Trotsky. But the "foreign agent" strain of the investigation was fading by then, not only because of Stalin's instruction, but also because already on the fourth of December, the "Zinovievite" approach was proving productive.[100] Nikolaev "confessed" that his decision to assassinate Kirov had been influenced by the Trotskyists Shatskii and Kotolynov, with whom he had worked ten years before. In his report to Stalin, Agranov referred to the three as "best friends." Nine days later, he confessed that Shatskii and Kotolynov had ordered the assassination.[101] From there, this small circle widened. For one who worked in the Leningrad organization—headed by Zinoviev until 1927—for as long as Nikolaev did, it was impossible not to have come into contact with a raft of "Zinovievites" and sympathizers of the Left opposition[102] His colleagues, acquaintances, and relatives, and those of Kotolynov and Shatskii, were quickly rounded up.

The arrests then spread to the Leningrad Komsomol, which had had strong ties to Zinoviev's Leningrad opposition. The Leningrad NKVD alone arrested 843 "former Zinovievites" in the ten weeks after the murder.[103] From the first hours after the assassination, Stalin had lifted legal safeguards in this case and given the NKVD carte blanche in the conduct of the investigation. As ever, the conditions of the interrogations ensured that those arrested would denounce others and ever widen the scope of the inquiry. A picture of a widespread "Trotskyist-Zinovievite" organization began to emerge with "centers" in Moscow and Leningrad. The investigators' "revolutionary instinct" was soon reinforced by "material evidence" in the form of guns and oppositionist literature, including copies of the Riutin tract found in house searches at the time of arrest. By the end of December, the testimony of those under interrogation suggested that the Trotskyist-Zinovievite group calculated that the Stalin leadership would not be able to cope in the event of war against the USSR, and that in such an event Kamenev and Zinoviev would inevitably come to power.[104] After the trial of those supposedly directly involved in the murder, a further trial of those who had "inspired" the murderers took place. It concluded that the "Leningrad counterrevolutionary Zinovievite group was systematically cultivating a hatred of the party leadership and particularly Stalin" and bore a "moral and political responsibility for the Kirov murder." But the evidence of the NKVD investigation suggested to Stalin that Zinoviev and Kamenev were planning more serious crimes.

Almost immediately, further evidence of threats to Soviet leaders was found. In the weeks after the Kirov murder, Stalin had ordered a review of security in the Kremlin. This was entirely sensible given that the investigation in Leningrad had appeared to have uncovered a large number of "hostile elements"—not least Nikolaev—with access to party institutions and, consequently, party leaders. The review of the Kremlin, undertaken by Nikolai Ezhov, revealed that security vetting had been lax. Former Mensheviks, Socialist Revolutionaries, and "class aliens" had Kremlin passes, as did, significantly, Lev Kamenev's brother N. B. Rozenfel'd. At first, the investigation only uncovered evidence of conversations (among cleaners, couriers, and other minor personnel) critical of Soviet policy and of Stalin—the sort of private conversations that were taking place up and down the country. But in the now well-established pattern of the NKVD, arrests and interrogations, and the investigation of friends, relatives, and acquaintances of the accused, inevitably produced the appearance of a counterrevolutionary conspiracy to assassinate Soviet leaders.[105] Lev Kamenev was himself interrogated and admitted that his brother had been in his flat at times when he and Zinoviev were having conversations critical of Soviet policy and of Stalin. He categorically denied any link to events in the Kremlin and any knowledge of the political views of his brother, but his protests were not entirely convincing. Yet again, Stalin was presented with circumstantial evidence that members of the Left opposition were conspiring against his regime.

The Conspiracy Grows

From the spring of 1935, Iagoda and the NKVD broadened their surveillance of former oppositionists, but they did not identify any other centers of conspiracy for over a year. This was not a matter of Iagoda displaying a "conciliatory attitude" toward oppositionists, as Nikolai Ezhov later asserted before replacing him as NKVD chief. Rather, in the course of 1935 and 1936, aggressive measures were being taken at all levels to "verify" cadres and purge, exile, and otherwise keep at a safe distance those whose political loyalties were in any doubt. Ezhov was in charge of a "verification" of all party cards, which had been mooted in October 1934 and began in earnest in May 1935.[106] It uncovered a few small Trotskyist and Zinovievite organizations through the autumn. The CC department in charge of cadres (ORPO), also headed by Ezhov, was compiling lists of party members who had previously been expelled, or those whose lesser punishments might call into question their loyalty to the party. These were to be reviewed in the course of a later purge. Meanwhile, the NKVD was devoting considerable energy and resources to deporting "alien elements" from cities.[107] This approach to identifying and "disarming" those who posed a danger to the regime was at once active and restrained (for the NKVD). Iagoda thought that the Trotskyist-Zinovievite underground was dangerous, but not particularly large or widespread. While the "verification" was doing its work to identify enemies, he took a longer-term perspective, insisting that the NKVD's ability to capture the regime's hidden enemies depended on improvements in the training of agents and in the organization's ability to run successful counterterrorism operations.[108] In part, this approach was influenced by external constraints. The Commissariat of Justice was arguing once again that too many people had been arrested without sufficient incriminating evidence, and, with Kamenev and Zinoviev once again behind bars and the Kremlin Affair exposed, the party leadership assented to its request that the NKVD be allowed to conduct arrests only with the consent of the Procuracy.[109]

The forces of restraint were, however, not very strong. While Iagoda presided over the continuing surveillance of oppositionists and followed up the results of the Verification of Party Cards, Ezhov was adopting a different approach. His recent, dramatic rise through the party apparatus had followed from his reputation for identifying enemies, and he sought to reinforce that reputation, particularly with Stalin, by presenting a unified theory of opposition activity. In May 1935, he asked Stalin to read his manuscript "From Factional Activity to Open Counterrevolution," in which he brought together materials from previous investigations to argue that Zinovievites, Trotskyists, and the followers of the Right opposition were now combining forces in an unprincipled struggle to overthrow the regime. The struggle was no longer about differing visions of Soviet socialism, but rather about putting an end to Stalin's regime. In this sense, Ezhov had begun to equate the former oppositionists with agents of foreign powers—though not yet explicitly. While he continued to revise his manuscript, he took a growing interest in Soviet citizens who had lived abroad, political émigrés and other Soviet citizens with contacts abroad. To assist him in the collection of information on political émigrés, Stalin arranged for him to be elected to the Comintern Executive Committee in the summer. From that position, he requested reports from foreign Communist Parties on the measures being taken to expose spies. By September, he had concluded that the community of political émigrés in the USSR was full of spies. In March 1936, new measures were introduced to limit the intake of political émigrés and to inhibit the free movement of émigrés within the USSR.[110]

Concern about foreign spies and saboteurs had increased since the Hitler had come to power in Germany. While the Poles had continued their efforts to subvert Soviet power, particularly in Belorussia and Ukraine, and the Japanese had continued their aggression in the Far East and along Soviet borderlands in the southeast, Soviet intelligence reports suggested that the Nazis were not only using the substantial population of Soviet Germans to their subversive ends, but were also able to employ the substantial communities of German workers and specialists who had come to the Soviet Union when relations with the Weimar Republic were close and cooperative. Between 1934 and 1936, NKVD investigations had uncovered German espionage and subversive activities in the military industry, communications, transport, gas and shipping, and new German agents and their contacts among Soviet citizens were being uncovered regularly.[111] If capitalist governments and the former oppositions were both working to overthrow the Stalin regime, why should they not work together? As Stalin had read from his signals intelligence, the Japanese had explicitly expressed a desire to work with the oppositionists remaining in the Soviet Union. Surely their German allies would want to do so as well.

At the beginning of 1936, Ezhov found an opportunity to answer this question. On 5 January the NKVD arrested V. P. Ol'berg, who had recently arrived in Gorky from Germany, on suspicion that he was an emissary of Trotsky. Stalin asked Ezhov to direct the NKVD investigation, though he was not formally a part of the political police. Iagoda's star was now clearly on the wane. Stalin may have blamed him for failing to prevent the Kirov assassination, or for failing to take more aggressive measures to detect hidden enemies. What is clear is that Ezhov was successfully undermining Iagoda's reputation by convincing Stalin that the leader of the NKVD underestimated the threat to the regime posed by terrorists. Within a month, Ol'berg "confessed" to counterrevolutionary activity and began to name scores of "co-conspirators." With the approval of the Procuracy,[112] the circle of arrests began to widen such that by April over five hundred "Trotskyists" had been arrested. Zinoviev, Kamenev, Trotsky, and other prominent Left oppositionists were implicated as the leaders of a terrorist counterrevolutionary organization. As the investigation progressed, "evidence" of Trotsky's links with fascist governments emerged. Ol'berg and others with links in Germany and to the Left opposition testified to the cooperation between Trotskyists and the Gestapo in the organization of acts of terrorism against Soviet leaders.[113] Stalin demanded that the investigation should, as a matter of urgency, "expose and obliterate all Trotskyist forces, their organizational centers and connections."[114]

While Ezhov's influence in the NKVD was growing, Iagoda remained in charge, and perhaps for tactical reasons, kept to his line that there was only a handful of active counterrevolutionary Trotskyists in the USSR and that Ezhov was exaggerating the threat. It would not serve his career prospects to agree with Ezhov and thus admit that he had bungled the investigation of the Kirov murder. Besides which, he was well aware that Stalin had rejected NKVD "panic mongering" in the past. But Ezhov pushed on relentlessly and in the summer of 1936, transcripts of NKVD interrogations were painting a portrait of an ever growing and dangerous counterrevolutionary conspiracy. They had also implicated members of the Right opposition as well as several leading figures in the party and state apparatus and in the army.[115] Against this background, the Foreign Department of the NKVD and the Comintern Cadres Department were revealing that communities of political émigrés (particularly German and Polish) in the Soviet Union had been more thoroughly infiltrated by Trotskyists, Pilsudskiites, and Nazi agents than had previously been thought.[116] A further Foreign Department operation in Paris is purported to have captured a packet of documents revealing the names and activities of Trotsky's supporters in the Soviet Union.[117] The image of a widespread network of counterrevolutionaries, spies, and subversives that was a driving force of the Great Terror was beginning to take a very concrete form.

The trial of the "Trotskyist-Zinovievite center" in August 1936 put the seal of Stalin's approval on Ezhov's investigations by making many (though by no means all) of the findings public. It brought with it a fresh wave of calls for vigilance and new pressure on NKVD agents to "unmask" hidden enemies of the regime, and consequently, further revelations. At the end of September 1936, Stalin had seen enough to side firmly with Ezhov against Iagoda. In a letter to the members of the Politburo, he wrote that "Iagoda has clearly turned out not to be up to his task in the matter of exposing the Trotskyist-Zinovievite bloc. The OGPU was four years late in this matter."[118] Indeed, once Ezhov took over, he behaved as though he was making up for lost time. He immediately drafted a resolution, which Stalin signed, redefining the official position on "Trotskyist-Zinovievite elements": Until very recently, the CC of the VKP(b) considered the Trotskyist-Zinovievite scoundrels as the leading political and organizational detachment of the international bourgeoisie. The latest facts tell us that these gentlemen have fallen further. They must therefore now be considered foreign agents, spies, subversives and wreckers representing the fascist bourgeoisie of Europe.[119]

The two major subversive threats faced by the regime were now officially merged into one. Those who, like Iagoda, played down the threat of subversion were silenced. Ezhov purged the NKVD apparatus and ratcheted up the pressure to find enemies. Ezhov gave Stalin a steady stream of interrogation transcripts and translations of foreign studies of espionage and subversion. Under Stalin's editorial supervision, the Soviet press regularly published articles suggesting that spies and saboteurs were everywhere, even among those with apparently unblemished work or party records. More than ever before, NKVD agents, party members, and Soviet citizens were asked to exercise their "revolutionary instinct" to unmask enemies. For the next two years, material evidence almost ceased to play a role in investigations of counterrevolutionary activity.

Stalin did not make a secret of this. In a conversation with the German writer Lion Feuchtwanger at the beginning of January 1937, he argued that the reliance on confession was within the Anglo-Saxon legal tradition and that the regime was fighting "experienced conspirators . . . they don't leave behind a trail of documents in their work. When exposed by their own people, face-to-face, they are forced to admit their guilt."[120] Ezhov also acknowledged that material evidence played a small role in NKVD investigations. He even made it a point of pride. Addressing a group of young Communists and Komsomol members drafted into NKVD work in March 1937, he contrasted intelligence collection in the capitalist states and the Soviet Union. The capitalists were a few spying on many in order to stamp out the smallest signs of resistance, but Soviet intelligence collection relied on material collected from the population at large. "The people are our collective agent," he said. Denunciations, rather than investigation, drove arrests. He acknowledged that the collection of evidence should play a bigger role, but only in order to speed the process by which "confessions" were obtained from those denounced by the "collective agent." He also acknowledged that in the absence of material evidence the investigator "has no objective criteria on which to check the veracity of a confession." One might think this was a damning indictment of the whole NKVD system of investigation. But no. Rather, Ezhov observed that in the absence of material evidence, the accused would only confirm or deny the scenario presented to him. The presence of material evidence would ensure a fuller, more detailed confession. In short, he told his new recruits that collecting material evidence of counterrevolutionary activity was desirable, but not necessary.[121]

As long as Stalin and Ezhov believed the confessions that were obtained under torture, the dimensions of the conspiracy would expand until it began to strain their imaginations. Given the core of truth in the accusations—Trotsky's network of contacts in the USSR, widespread dissatisfaction with the regime and Stalin's leadership, foreign spies and saboteurs—their imaginations accommodated a great deal. Stalin knew that thousands of innocent people were being arrested and sent to the Gulag or summarily executed, but to him, the preservation of the Soviet state was paramount. At the beginning of the devastating purge of the Soviet military in the summer of 1937, Stalin ominously complained to leading military figures about the lack of denunciations from the lower ranks: "if even 5 percent of these denunciations are true, then it helps."[122] Even as the Terror came to a close and the methods of the NKVD were subject to criticism, Stalin never expressed any doubt that there had been a grave conspiracy against the regime. In his account of the Terror to the eighteenth party congress in 1939, he told delegates that, on the contrary, they had "underestimated the . . . bourgeois governments and their intelligence organs encircling us, trying to use peoples' weaknesses, their conceit, in order to draw them into their fascist network."[123]

Since the Moscow trials, scholars have tended to assume that the prosecution case against the former oppositionists and other defendants was a pure invention, or at least a gross exaggeration of events, intended to destroy politically and physically those who had dared to challenge Stalin's leadership, or whose presence could prove a rallying point for those who might.[124] The domestic and foreign intelligence in Stalin's archive suggests a different story. In the two decades after the Revolution, Stalin and other Soviet leaders received a steady stream of reports on the activities of foreign spies and saboteurs and their recruitment of domestic agents. The systems for the collection and interpretation of intelligence, the reliance on revolutionary instinct and on testimony obtained under torture, combined to underpin an exaggerated sense of the threat to the regime. At the same time, Stalin was informed of plans and attempts by the oppositions and other disaffected party members to remove him from power. Trotsky made no secret of his desire to do so. It would appear that Stalin believed, and had good reason to believe, the essence of the prosecution case as it was presented at the Moscow trials.

3

CAPITALIST ENCIRCLEMENT

When the Bolsheviks came to power they had only a weak sense of the value of diplomacy. They hoped that the Revolution in Russia would lead to revolutions in Europe and the rest of the world, obviating the need for a foreign ministry. There is a well-worn anecdote that once Leon Trotsky was appointed as the first Commissar of Foreign Affairs, he joked that he would "issue a few revolutionary proclamations and close up shop."[1] Of course, when the Revolution failed to spread to Europe, Trotsky and his successors had plenty of work to do, and they found that diplomacy could be a useful instrument for the Bolsheviks. One of the early initiatives of the Commissariat (NKID) was a sort of "anti-diplomacy," sorting through the papers of their pre-revolutionary counterparts and publishing those that exposed the backroom machinations of the European powers. The exposure of the "nefarious" activities of the enemies of the Soviet Union by publishing diplomatic documents remained a favored tactic of Soviet leaders not only in the interwar, but right up to the collapse of the USSR itself. The Ministry of Foreign Affairs published an impressive quantity of documents that put Soviet diplomacy and diplomats in the best possible light. Over the years, the documents allowed historians to undertake some impressive (and careful) research at a time when historians of other aspects of Soviet history had little in the way of primary sources to work with. At the time, diplomatic historians understood that critical parts of the story of foreign policymaking were missing. In particular, the collections of diplomatic documents almost entirely overlooked the role of the party leadership in the formulation of foreign policy. Some historians were tempted to argue that Stalin did not play a decisive role in the formulation of foreign policy,[2] but particularly since the opening of the "Stalin archive," we have seen clearly for the first time evidence of Stalin's constant and detailed supervision of Soviet foreign policy from the mid–1920s. We have also begun to see that NKID was not the only Soviet institution influencing the formulation of Soviet foreign policy.

Stalin's vision of international politics was informed largely by his reading of intelligence. The NKID was only one of the agencies providing him with intelligence. The others included principally military intelligence, the foreign intelligence units of the political police, and the Soviet telegraph agency TASS, which surveyed the foreign press. The influence of NKID was occasionally heightened by the presence of the commissar or his deputies in Stalin's office when key issues of foreign policy were being decided, but these invitations were relatively rare. In the course of the 1930s, Commissar of Foreign Affairs Maxim Litvinov was invited to Stalin's office an average of less than thirty times a year. By contrast, in the same period, Kliment Voroshilov, the head of the Red Army, saw Stalin more than three times as often.[3] Because the NKID was directed to negotiate with foreign powers, its officials necessarily harbored the measure of professional empathy for capitalist powers that is necessary to negotiating successfully. Stalin occasionally berated NKID officials for "swimming in their wake."[4] Agencies collecting intelligence on the international situation were under orders to identify the threat they posed to Soviet security, and as such the material they collected projected a much starker image of a world divided between "us" (the Soviet Union, communist movements, and the beleaguered international proletariat) and "them" (the forces of international capital). In the cases of military intelligence, and the intelligence departments of the political police, they justified their existence by finding those threats.[5]

Soviet leaders were predisposed to see a grave danger posed by the capitalist world. In perhaps his most famous work, "Imperialism: The Highest Stage of Capitalism" (1915–16), Lenin argued that the concentration of capital and production characteristic of late nineteenth- and early twentieth-century capitalism created an ever increasing need to export capital and acquire colonies. Since the world had already been carved up by the imperial powers, the further development of capitalism inevitably led to war. There was good reason to believe that war would be directed at them. Russia offered rich pickings for the export of capital and the exploitation of resources, but more significantly, the Bolsheviks thought that the new Soviet state presented a direct threat to the capitalist powers. The Bolsheviks used the apparatus of the state not only to overthrow the Russian bourgeoisie but also to promote similar revolutions abroad as well as the liberation of colonial peoples. Bolshevik leaders doubted that the capitalists would tolerate so direct a challenge to their interests.

The Bolsheviks' sense that they were surrounded by hostile capitalist states was rooted in Lenin's thought, but nurtured by the accumulation of information on the actions and intentions of those states. By establishing the identification of threats against the regime as the first priority of the intelligence services, a bias was built into the information collected. Deepening this bias was the predisposition of Soviet leaders, not least among them Stalin, to disregard, or at least to discount, counterevidence. Indeed, there is anecdotal evidence that, by the 1930s, agencies were afraid to pass such counterevidence to the leadership. At the same time, there was no shortage of evidence of anti-communism in the capitalist world, anti-communist activity, and genuinely hostile intent toward the USSR.[6] Very little of it escaped the Soviet intelligence services, and much of it was passed to Stalin and the Politburo. As such, Stalin received a steady stream of "evidence" suggesting that capitalist powers were bent on the organization of a new invasion. The picture Stalin was given was clear and consistent. His analysis of it was logical and entirely pragmatic in its own terms. But the picture was wrong. Ideological preconceptions played an important role in Soviet misperceptions of the capitalist world, but the ways in which intelligence was collected and processed were equally important.

The literature on Stalin's perception of "capitalist encirclement" tends to focus either on 1927 or on the late 1930s. It tends to downplay Stalin's sense of threat before 1936 because, to state the obvious, no real threat existed between 1921 and the mid–1930s. But the failure adequately to distinguish the reality from the perception has meant that one of the enduring features of the Stalin era, and indeed of Soviet and post-Soviet foreign policy, has been missed. This chapter argues that from the end of the civil war to the end of the 1930s, there were not one, but three major war scares: 1927, 1931–32, and 1934–35, and little calm in between them. Stalin's intelligence left him and other Soviet leaders with the mistaken impression that they were almost constantly under siege, vulnerable to coalitions of capitalist states bent on the destruction of Soviet socialism. Britain, France, and Poland, joined somewhat later by Japan, were perceived to be the main enemies until well into the 1930s. Germany did not enter that list immediately with the rise of the Nazis, but only as they built what appeared to be anti-Soviet alliances with Poland, Japan, and other states along Soviet western borders. In the mid–1930s, an increasingly confident, revanchist Germany, building a close relationship with Poland, had upset the system that guaranteed French security and pushed her into a rapprochement with the Soviet Union. Soviet Commissar of Foreign Affairs Maxim Litvinov explored the opportunities for some structure of collective security involving France and Britain. Stalin did not discourage him, but he remained suspicious. Stalin's decisive foreign-policy choices at the end of the 1930s, not least his decision to enter a non-aggression pact with the Nazis, were substantially informed by the weight of the intelligence accumulated over the two decades since the Revolution. The war itself, the Nazi invasion, the long-delayed second front, and the subsequent fifty years of cold war deepened and hardened the Soviet, and post-Soviet, Russian vision that the powers on their eastern, southern, and especially western flanks were bent on her destruction.

The War Scare of 1927–28

The war scare of 1927–28 was very real for the Bolsheviks, and not, as some have argued, an invention serving Stalin's aims in the struggle for power.[7] The context necessary to understand the Soviet response to the events of 1927 starts with the civil war. This is not to say that the scare was simply an overreaction to the rupture of diplomatic relations with Britain conditioned by the Soviet experience of foreign "intervention," though it is useful to begin with such a trope. The Bolsheviks correctly assumed that their victory in the civil war did not end the hostility European powers harbored toward Soviet communism. One need not spend a great deal of time reading the minutes of European parliaments in session, or newspapers of the Right and even many of the Left, to divine that anti-communism in general, and hostility toward the Soviet government in particular, was an enduring feature of European politics in the interwar. The Bolsheviks understood this anti-communism and anti-bolshevism in class terms: the success of the Revolution, of the dictatorship of the proletariat, presented a concrete threat to the hegemony of the bourgeoisie in the capitalist states. While the Soviet Union existed, thrived, and rallied communist movements abroad, the likelihood of a successful revolution in Europe was substantially greater.

This was not entirely out of step with what the "bourgeois" governments of Europe thought. There was, particularly in the first five or six years after the end of World War I, a fear of communist revolution, and an awareness that the Soviet Union and its proxies were doing their utmost to provoke it. But what the Bolsheviks appear not to have adequately understood was that in the aftermath of World War I, it was Germany and not Soviet Russia that was the gravest source of concern and attention. The intervention of 1918–20 itself had a strong anti-communist element, but it began as an attempt to reopen the eastern front. After the war, European foreign policymakers were most concerned not with the supposed threat of bolshevism, but with the question of what to do with Germany. Why was the Soviet government inclined to exaggerate its place in the mental map of Europe? Some historians have argued that Soviet leaders' obsession with the danger of military confrontation with the capitalist states was rooted in catechism, in a so-called doctrine of inevitable war.[8] Contemporary Bolsheviks would have disagreed fiercely and insisted that they were supreme realists, for their foreign intelligence was probably better than any of their rivals and their assessments of threat were based on copious concrete evidence. The Soviet leadership drew the conclusion from the experience of the intervention that many European and Asian governments wanted to see an end to the Bolshevik regime. They similarly concluded that the withdrawal of foreign troops from Soviet Russia had nothing to do with a change in attitude toward them. The press in Britain and France had been against the intervention and the general public needed no convincing that troops should be brought home. Most troops had little will to fight. Morale was low and discipline had long been in decline. Mutinies among the French troops in particular engendered the hope among Soviet leaders that invading forces could be convinced to turn against their commanders and potentially turn subsequent action against Soviet Russia into a revolution at home. But in the course of 1920 as the foreign forces in the Soviet Union were in disarray, Soviet intelligence agencies thought they had detected a shift in the tactics employed against them. They perceived that British and French governments were increasingly relying on others to do their work for them. The very successful Soviet efforts to infiltrate the anti-Soviet organizations of the White Russians in exile served to convince them not only that the White Russians were taking a growing interest in the use of terrorism to overthrow the Soviet state by means of the assassination of Soviet leaders, but also that the British government and prominent figures close to the government were willing to finance these terrorist actions. At the same time, the intelligence agencies and party officials along Soviet southern borders warned Moscow that the British were trying to destabilize the regime by supporting opposition groups such as the Basmachi, and were supporting and arming anti-Soviet forces in Turkey, Persia, Afghanistan, and China.[9]

Stalin was convinced that the Entente stood financially and militarily behind the Polish forces that attacked Soviet Russia in the spring of 1920.[10] When the campaign suddenly went badly wrong for the Poles, and Soviet forces were on the outskirts of Warsaw, a large contingent of French military advisers under General Maxime Weygand made the difference in chasing the Red Army out of Poland. After a peace was negotiated, the Bolsheviks were satisfied that their enemies were now too weak to risk any further direct military action,[11] though they watched carefully as the French continued to contribute money and arms to the Polish and Romanian armies. For the French, close ties with strong and stable regimes in eastern and southern Europe was a critical part of her strategy to contain Germany. Soviet leaders continued nevertheless to see the diplomatic and military ties among Britain, France, the Balkan states, Romania, Poland, the Baltic states, and Finland as evidence of a longer-term plan to prepare a new assault on them. This sort of caution was sensible, given that these countries had given refuge to the bulk of the White armies as they had retreated from Russia. Soviet intelligence agencies warned that these states kept the hundreds of thousands of White soldiers in arms and ready for war.[12]

The difficulty for Soviet leaders of distinguishing between policy toward them and toward Germany was deepened by the Treaty of Rapallo

(April 1922), which set the basis for close Soviet-German relations until the early 1930s. Following Rapallo, any French action against Germany was seen by Soviet leaders as a precursor of action against the Soviet Union. The occupation of the Ruhr in early 1923 was one such example. French and Belgian troops occupied the Ruhr to enforce delinquent reparations payments. The Weimar government responded by ordering Ruhr workers to go on strike. Over the next eight months industrial unrest and violence convinced some Soviet leaders that Germany was on the verge of revolution. They did everything they could to set the German Communist Party at the head of events, even though they were convinced that neither France nor Poland[13] would tolerate a communist revolution in Germany. Soviet leaders shared the assumption that the military force used to crush a revolution in Germany would subsequently be turned on Soviet Russia. Soviet military intelligence suggested that the invasion of Russia was already being prepared. In February 1923, S. S. Kamenev, the commander in chief of the Red Army, wrote to P. P. Lebedev, the commander of the Western Army group, that the White Army was being reorganized by the Entente and was supported by a substantial (largely British) fleet that could make an independent landing on the Black Sea coast or be transported to Soviet western frontiers. Kamenev further warned that in the event of an invasion, all or any of the states along the Soviet western border, from Finland to Turkey, might enter a state of war with Soviet Russia.[14]

The Curzon ultimatum raised the heat higher still. In May, Lord Curzon, the British foreign minister, demanded that the Soviet government withdraw its "agents" operating against British interests in Asia or face the rupture of diplomatic relations. The action corresponded with reports of a sharp increase in anti-Soviet terrorist activities along Soviet borders.[15] A Soviet diplomat, Vatslav Vorovskii, was assassinated by a White Guard officer and monarchist in the same month.[16] The United States and France firmly supported Britain in what seemed to Soviet leaders to be an attempt to justify an invasion before a European and American public still thoroughly sick of war. Articles on the imminence of a new invasion were published in the national press in order to prepare the public for a general conscription. In Trotsky's words, "we need to tell people what's going on firmly and loudly, so that if we need to draft large numbers into the army we won't be caught out."[17]

The hopes for the German revolution were, of course, never realized, and as the political situation in Germany stabilized, the fear of invasion calmed. The German Communist Party was roundly criticized for its failure to take the lead of the labor unrest, but the German Social Democrats and European social democrats generally were accused of having betrayed the cause of revolution. Their "pacifism" was perceived to have undercut the revolutionary momentum and played into the hands of the bourgeoisie. The failure of the revolution was no surprise to Stalin. While he publicly supported the Politburo line on the events in Germany,[18] in his private correspondence he argued that neither the German working class nor the Communist Party were ready to seize power. It was not worth bringing the Entente down on their heads, he argued. He wrote to fellow Politburo member Nikolai Bukharin in August, "Let the fascists take power in Germany first, and let them fail."[19] However, once it was clear that *Stalin* could not carry the *Politburo* majority and that they were committed to the revolution and whatever consequences it would bring, Stalin kept his counsel.[20]

By early 1924, the international situation appeared to improve for the Soviets. Rather than face an invasion from the Entente powers, relations unexpectedly improved as the conservative and anti-Soviet governments of Stanley Baldwin in Britain and Raymond Poincaré in France fell and were replaced by (short-lived) governments on the Left. The new Labor government of Ramsay MacDonald even risked, foolishly, the public reaction to the diplomatic recognition of Soviet Russia. Stalin, having been proved right over Germany, continued to make and develop his main line of argument against forcing events in Europe. He insisted that the shift to the left in European politics followed from the growing sympathy the European working class felt for the Soviet Union. The stronger and more successful the Soviet Union became, the deeper will be the hatred of the bourgeois order and the desire to follow the Russian path.[21]

Stalin also insisted, however, that the growing respect for Soviet Russia did not mean that the danger of war had passed. Unresolved tensions from World War I, the continued competition over scarce resources, economic problems exemplified by high inflation, and the European bourgeoisie's continued "animal hatred" of the Soviet system meant the danger of a new imperialist war was great and the chance that it would be directed against them high.²² Though Stalin's many public statements on the continued danger of war strictly adhered to the logic of Lenin's writings on imperialism, they were not merely an expression of his faith in some kind of Bolshevik catechism. His public statements tended to be rather abstract, but they were underpinned by a wealth of concrete detail provided by the Soviet intelligence agencies. They told him that the British government and wealthy Britons were supporting counterrevolutionary terrorist groups (mostly Whites) in Ukraine, Belorussia, and Georgia, as well as anti-Soviet elements in China and Afghanistan.²³ They told him that Sidney Reilly, whom Soviet intelligence took for a British agent, was proposing a campaign of terrorist acts against party and state leaders.²⁴ Military intelligence warned him that the British were gaining a disturbing "military-political and military-economic" influence in the countries along the Soviet western border, especially Poland, Romania, and the Baltic states.²⁵ It became apparent that senior military officers of these countries were meeting on a regular basis. Given the perception that the Poles were already hard at work trying to destabilize Belorussia and Ukraine, the Soviet leadership worried about the emergence of an anti-Soviet bloc with Britain and Poland at its core. No such bloc existed, but the perception that it did continued to inform Soviet conduct. In March 1925, the Politburo ordered the army intelligence, the Foreign Department of OGPU, and the Commissariat of Foreign Affairs to "gather and systematize our existing knowledge on the preparatory actions (i.e., plans for war) of countries on our western border, including the conference of General Staffs and England's role in that conference."²⁶ In the summer of 1925, military intelligence produced outline estimates of the armed forces these countries could muster in the event of war.²⁷ In discussing plans for the industrialization of the Soviet Union, Stalin told Molotov that new factories would have to be built in the east because traditional industrial centers such as Rostov-on-Don and Leningrad were too vulnerable in the event of war.²⁸

Against this background of worrying signs, the Soviet leadership witnessed the negotiation of the Treaty of Locarno in the autumn of 1925. The treaty was meant to address unresolved issues in European security, most important, by ending the isolation of Germany since World War I. To the Soviets, Locarno was all about drawing Germany away from the USSR and eliminating the remaining obstacles to the emergence of an effective anti-Soviet bloc. Stalin sensibly assumed that Poland, Romania, and the Baltic states were much less likely to wage war on the Soviet Union if there remained a threat to their security from Germany. So the treaty had grave implications for Soviet security. In November, Feliks Dzerzhinskii asked Artur Artuzov, the head of the Foreign Department (INO) of OGPU, to report on the efforts of England and Germany through the Finns and Estonians to commit acts of sabotage and espionage in Leningrad.[29] In the case of the critical Polish-German relationship, there was the further twist of an ongoing trade war, though in November 1925, Dzerzhinskii passed to Stalin reports to the effect that Britain was trying to broker a deal between the two sides that would end the trade war and resolve tensions over disputed borders.[30]

In his speech to the fourteenth party congress in December 1925, Stalin chose to emphasize remaining "contradictions" among the "capitalist countries" that inhibited aggressive military action against the USSR: tensions between the working class and bourgeoisie, between imperialism and national liberation movements in Asia and Africa, remaining tensions with Germany about reparations payments, conflicts between England and America over oil resources, tensions between England and France over the domination of the European continent and overseas colonies. In language that would be much more familiar a generation later, Stalin asserted that the world was divided between two camps, capitalist and communist. Our camp is united and theirs is divided, and the attraction of the working class of the world to the USSR is a fast-growing source of our strength and authority.[31] While these tensions were very real, and would have made an assault on the USSR more difficult, Stalin's reassuring tone was not justified by his intelligence. In the week after the congress closed, Stalin was informed by Dzerzhinskii that the British were canvasing Whites in Prague, Paris, and Constantinople on the possibility of cooperation in an invasion of the USSR. Now there was evidence that the Japanese might join the coalition, supported by Chang Tso-lin in China.[32] The "coalition" was apparently already increasing subversion and espionage in Soviet borderlands in anticipation of military action.[33]

It seems likely that Stalin's purpose in reassuring his audience at the fourteenth congress was connected to the ongoing struggle of party factions. The labor unrest in capitalist countries to which Stalin had alluded in his speech was becoming particularly acute in Britain. The United Opposition (Leon Trotsky, Grigorii Zinoviev, et al.) was insisting that a revolutionary situation was emerging in Britain and that the Politburo majority was betraying it with inaction. They were demanding radical action in foreign policy just as they were demanding it in domestic policy over the issue of industrialization. Zinoviev pushed to abandon cooperation with the "reactionary" (read: reformist) trades unions while the majority favored radicalizing trade union action from within. But the heart of the issue for Stalin was the danger of war. Class tensions might make it difficult for Britain to wage war on the USSR, but class warfare driven by British Communists linked to Moscow might encourage the British to accelerate their plans for the anti-Soviet bloc. Stalin insisted that the British bourgeoisie were not victims of the unrest, but rather had provoked it in order to break the back of organized labor and win further concessions. When the British general strike began in May, the United Opposition attacked the weak response of Stalin and the Politburo majority.[34] Stalin was not about to risk a war and abandon the moderate policies on which the New Economic Policy was based. He again tried to take the heat out of the situation. At the beginning of June he wrote to Viacheslav Molotov, who was framing the response to Zinoviev's theses on the international situation: "Don't let them rush you. We must think this through and not let them use this to their advantage." And two days later: "We still need the united front [with British trades unions] to gather forces in defense against further attacks of capital."[35] The time was not right for a confrontation with Britain or the demands that mass mobilization for war would place on the economy.

The flow of intelligence continued to emphasize a very real danger of war. In May 1926, the democratic government of Poland was overthrown by Josef Pilsudski in a military coup d'état. While the Polish Communist Party was inclined to celebrate the coup as evidence of an emerging revolutionary situation in Poland, Stalin's foreign intelligence told him otherwise. Dzerzhinskii wrote to Stalin that he thought England was behind the coup and Pilsudski in the interests of accelerating plans for an attack on the Soviet Union.[36] Commissar of Foreign Affairs Georgii Chicherin, who was by no means an alarmist in these matters, agreed with the assessment of the threat.[37] The signing of a Polish-Romanian military convention, and frequent visits of French military attaches to the two countries, deepened the impression that an effective anti-Soviet bloc was emerging. France was now also understood to be a major player in the purported bloc. At the time, the French were beginning to realize an ambition to build political and economic influence in eastern Europe, not least in order to contain Germany and Soviet Russia. French investment, French arms sales and other military assistance to the Poles and the Romanians, and French diplomacy including the Little Entente and alliances with Poland and Czechoslovakia gave Soviet leaders the impression of the strengthening of bonds for aggressive anti-communist ends.

Soviet leaders had failed to see that British and French aims in eastern Europe were fundamentally in conflict; that neither harbored aggressive intentions and that neither had nearly as much influence in eastern Europe as they would have liked. Instead, Stalin was consistently warned that the British and French were gathering forces in eastern Europe to orchestrate an attack on the USSR that would be spearheaded by Poland. Dzerzhinskii told him that the frequent visits of French military attachés to Poland and Romania were responsible for the signing of a military convention that was one further step in the organization of a concerted attack on the USSR. In early July, Dzerzhinskii wrote to Stalin asserting that "there is an accumulation of evidence that indicates with doubtless (for me) clarity that Poland is preparing a military assault on us with the goal of seizing Belorussia and Ukraine."[38] Armed raids on the Chinese Far Eastern Railway launched by the Chinese warlord Chang Tso-lin, with the apparent support of the Japanese, created the further concern that a war in the west would encourage further aggressive action in the east.[39]

The situation was certainly fraught, but the Soviet leadership knew that an attack was not yet imminent. Military intelligence exaggerated the size and might of the Polish armed forces, but they were reasonably confident that Pilsudski would not attempt an assault without other major allies. Despite earlier intelligence to the contrary, the Polish coup had done little if anything to settle conflicts with Germany. In this context, Stalin wanted state and society to remain vigilant, but not overreact. Through the autumn and winter of 1926–27 the Politburo majority continued to emphasize publicly that tensions ("contradictions," to use the Marxist terminology) among the "imperialists" were extending the period of peace ("breathing space" or *peredyshka*) enjoyed by the USSR. At the same time, national newspapers continued, as Stalin had publicly instructed them, to "expose all efforts hidden and open to prepare for a new war."[40] These articles seem to have been targeted in the first instance at a foreign audience as a means to convey that these "efforts" were known and that an adequate response was being prepared. But the message was also intended, as in 1923, to prepare the public for the possibility of mass mobilization, should it be required. This sort of agitation had unintended consequences. From the beginning of 1927, the public was so convinced of the imminence of war that the hoarding of foodstuffs became a serious economic problem. This did not stop the Politburo from issuing stark slogans for party organizations in the front line of defense against Poland. For example, the Belorussian people were warned: "By means of fascist coups along the Soviet border, England is preparing an attack on the USSR. Be vigilant."[41] But this sort of move naturally only deepened the problem of hoarding, and at the beginning of March Stalin felt compelled to issue another, even stronger reassurance that war was not imminent. In a speech to railway workers subsequently published in *Pravda*, Stalin asserted that "there will not be war this spring or autumn because our enemies fear the results of war more than anybody, because the workers of the West do not want to fight with the USSR and they can't fight without the workers, and because we stand firmly for a policy of peace [and] it makes it more difficult to fight with us."[42] Stalin's assessment seems to have been sincere, for when the British government orchestrated the raid on the London offices of the All-Russian Cooperative Society (ARCOS) in May 1927 and claimed to have uncovered documents proving that the Soviet government was engaged in subversive activity, the Soviet leadership saw the action in terms of a new, bolder, and more aggressive effort of the British bourgeoisie to convince the working class not only in England, but also on the Continent, to support military action against the USSR.

It was far from clear at first what effect the raid, and the subsequent rupture of diplomatic relations, would have on the international situation. Within a few weeks of the ARCOS raid, an OGPU investigation into British espionage activities in Leningrad, ongoing since November 1925, revealed a British spy ring and some unspecified evidence that the British and Poles were recruiting small groups of saboteurs to help prepare for and contribute to the invasion.[43] In the first week of June, as Stalin was digesting the report of the Leningrad OGPU plenipotentiary, he was informed that Petr Voikov, the Soviet ambassador to Poland, had been assassinated. He sent a telegram to Molotov: "I received the news of the murder of Voikov by a monarchist. I feel the hand of England. They want to provoke a conflict with Poland. They want to repeat Sarajevo . . . This demands a maximum of circumspection . . . The press should publish articles to the effect that the English Conservative Party instigated this murder in an attempt to create a new Sarajevo. We need to take measures against White Guards and monarchists in the USSR. Execute six or ten."[44] Within twenty-four hours, *Pravda* announced the execution of twenty Whites accused of spying and sabotage for the British.[45] Once again, Stalin believed he was sending a clear message to the British that Soviet intelligence knew what they were up to, and their tactics would not work. Of course the message was lost on the British because they had no connection to Voikov's assassination. In fact, the action only deepened the anti-Soviet sentiments of British conservatives and much of the British press.

Various other approaches were considered. The Anglo-Russian Trade Union Committee was directed to focus on measures to "confront the impending war."[46] Maxim Litvinov presented a proposal of total disarmament to the League of Nations. A month later at the International Congress of Cooperatives, a body dominated by European social democrats, the representatives of Profintern[47] were instructed to rally participants to the cause of preventing war against the USSR.[48] TASS, the agency responsible for keeping Soviet leaders informed about the content of the world press, were instructed to look for evidence of preparations for war.[49] Meanwhile, Stalin told Menzhinskii that the contacts of British spies in the Soviet Union were "hidden deeper than it seems" and that "mass arrests were necessary to upset the British espionage network . . . We should hold one or two show trials of English spies and have official materials for use in Europe and England."[50] On a related theme, Voroshilov proposed to the Politburo that if war with Britain was imminent, "we should be establishing terrorist groups in England." The potential of working with the Irish was raised.[51]

The substance of this traffic of secret letters and directives set against the background of the previous seven years of intelligence makes it clear that the Soviet leadership feared that war with a "united imperialist front" was a very real possibility. This is not to say that Stalin did not use the fear of war for his political ends. Indeed he did not hesitate to beat the United Opposition with the accusation that they were attacking the party majority at a time when unity was desperately needed. A week after the ARCOS raid he insisted that the new anti-communist united front stretched "from Chamberlain to Trotsky."[52] But this sort of rhetorical flourish, this sort of politically motivated hyperbole, has mistakenly led many historians to assume that Stalin grossly exaggerated the threat of war for the same political ends.

From the ARCOS Raid to the Japanese Invasion of Manchuria, 1927–32

The war with the "united imperialist front" did not materialize in 1927, though Stalin assumed this was not for want of trying. In his speech to the fifteenth congress in early December 1927, he returned to the theme of "contradictions." Britain and America were still fighting over oil production. Britain, France, and Italy were in conflict over control of the Mediterranean. The rising success of the USSR and the growing authority of the Comintern among the working class were making it more difficult to orchestrate military action against the USSR. Even within the bourgeoisie there were those too attached to trade arrangements with the Soviets to agree to war. But that did not mean that the Soviet Union no longer faced a threat. France, Britain, Italy, Japan, and America continued to increase spending on arms. The spread of right-wing coalitions in Europe was stifling the voice of the working class. Britain continued to take the leading role in building an anti-Soviet coalition, but her attempts had yet to meet any success.[53]

So how would the European bourgeoisie now pursue its campaign against the USSR? A few days after Stalin's speech to the congress, the Foreign Department of the OGPU received information to the effect that Hetman (Ukrainian Cossack leader) P. P. Skoropadskii had met with Stanley Baldwin and Winston Churchill to negotiate a plan for the liquidation of Bolshevism in 1929 by means of a concerted attack of European powers reinforced by groups within the USSR. In the weeks that followed, the Ukrainian OGPU arrested large numbers of suspected counterrevolutionaries in Odessa, Umani, Kremenchug, Lugansk, Krivoi Rog, and Dnepopetrovsk.[54] This flurry of activity in Ukraine might have encouraged A. G. Evdokimov, the OGPU plenipotentiary in the neighboring North Caucasus region, to bring his investigation of counterrevolutionary activity in the local mining industry to the attention of the party leadership in Moscow. The further investigation seems to have confirmed for Stalin that the tactics of the European bourgeoisie were shifting.[55] The focus on sabotage constituted an acknowledgement that the tensions among European powers and the growing sympathy of the European working class for the USSR meant it was not yet possible to gather military forces for a war against Soviet communism. Perhaps more significant, the investigation suggested that the European sponsors of the sabotage believed that it would now be necessary to weaken Soviet industry for the intervention to succeed.

In the months that followed, Stalin addressed these issues in both domestic and foreign policy. It was not obvious how the USSR could sustain tensions among the capitalist states, but they could, and did, appeal to the European proletariat. Litvinov's proposal for total disarmament had not been taken up at the League of Nations in 1927, but this was better for the Soviets because they could then portray the European powers as the obstacles to a lasting peace. Among the slogans the Politburo agreed for the 1 May 1928 celebrations was: "The League of Nations babble about peace masks the arms race and preparations for new wars. Down with the League of Nations. Hail the struggle of the Soviets for peace, for universal and complete disarmament."[56] In August 1928, when fifteen governments signed the Kellogg-Briand Pact renouncing war as an instrument for the resolution of international disputes, the Soviets were quick to portray it as an instrument to ensure the passivity of the working class amid the general preparation for war.[57] Stalin was not about to cede the public relations advantage that the Soviet "policy of peace" brought them.

Stalin saw the Comintern as another crucial instrument for the manipulation of foreign popular opinion. While Bukharin was writing the new Comintern program in the spring and summer of 1928, Stalin frequently commented on drafts of his work. Much of what he wrote reiterated and deepened his earlier position on the critical importance of the success of

the Revolution in the USSR to the world revolution. The existence of the
Soviet Union, Stalin insisted, had "prevented a period of dark reaction,
White terror, and war." The program had to outline not only the respon-
sibilities of the working class of the USSR to the working class of the world,
but also the responsibilities of the working class of the world to the USSR.[58]
In short, the Comintern was instructed to make its priority the defense of
the USSR internationally rather than promotion of revolution at home.[59]
More concretely, having ordered it to organize a "Congress of Friends of
the USSR" to coincide with the tenth anniversary of the Revolution, the
Politburo directed the organization of a "World Anti-Fascist Congress."[60]
In the late 1920s and 1930s, the Comintern was working harder to promote
the image of the USSR abroad than to promote revolution at home.

The most significant conclusion Stalin drew from the Shakhty affair,
however, was that economic growth and the success of Soviet socialism
promised not only further to attract the working class of the world to it,
but also to make a war against the USSR too costly to contemplate. The
importance of accelerated economic development to the construction of
socialism and to the independence of the Soviet Union was a common
theme in Stalin's speeches after Shakhty.[61] His opinions on the needed
tempo of industrialization were not shared by Bukharin and his determination to force the pace of industrial growth brought these two leading
members of the Politburo into conflict. By the end of 1928, Stalin was
preparing the ground to oust Bukharin over the issue. In a speech entitled
"The Industrialization of the Country and the Right Deviation in the
Party" to the November CC plenum, Stalin declared: "We came to power
in a technologically awfully backward country . . . And we have around us
many capitalist countries with more developed and advanced industrial
technologies . . . We need to catch up to and overtake these advanced
capitalist countries . . . Either we do it or they will bury us." Without
openly saying so, he made it clear that Bukharin's opposition to rapid
industrialization was not only a threat to the independence of the Soviet
Union, but also that it was petit bourgeois and contrary to the spirit of
Leninism.[62]

Was Stalin exaggerating the threat of war to serve his interests in
a struggle for power? From the perspective of his foreign intelligence,
he was somewhat exaggerating the urgency of the matter. A slower,

more steady pace of industrialization could have been justified given that the threat of war was present but not immediate. In July 1928, military intelligence had produced an assessment of the military capabilities of the enemies of the USSR concluding that a major assault on the Soviet Union by combined forces of Poland, Romania, and the Baltic states, actively supported by England and France, would be a grave risk for the attackers because they would not have an obvious superiority over the Red Army. Such a war could end with the sovietization of eastern Europe.[63] In December, an OGPU report based on material produced by the Counterintelligence Unit (KRO) concluded that the Polish and Romanians, together with the Whites, could muster an invasion force of two million soldiers, but even if Japan agreed to open a second front in the Far East, it would not be enough to ensure victory.[64] The unexpectedly rapid advance of Soviet industry and the further growth projected in the first five-year plan would only increase Soviet security. Two months later, Litvinov, the deputy foreign minister, won a significant, if perhaps symbolic, diplomatic victory when Poland, Romania, Latvia, and other states agreed to sign a Kellogg-Briand-type pact renouncing war as an instrument for the resolution of disputes with the USSR.[65]

With these advances, the tone of public statements on foreign policy gradually gained in confidence. For example, in March 1929 *Pravda* published excerpts from a speech of Voroshilov in which he set out a vision of the capitalist states on the road to war. He outlined the growing military expenditures of the Soviet Union's main enemies—Poland and Romania remaining at the top of the list—while calmly expressing the confidence that they would be ready for whatever the capitalists threw at them.[66] When they met at a session of the Politburo, Stalin sent Voroshilov a note expressing his approval in pithy language.[67] A few months later, after the government of Stanley Baldwin—the government that had orchestrated the ARCOS raid and severed relations with the USSR—fell in the British general election, and Labor sought to reestablish relations with the Soviets, Stalin further showed his confidence in the international situation by refusing to accept any conditions.[68] Privately, he insisted that Soviet prestige and power were growing and that Britain needed the diplomatic recognition more than they did.[69] Perhaps the strongest sign of Soviet confidence, though, was the increasing radicalism of the Comintern.

This did not mean, however, that Stalin thought the foreign threat had faded into the past. In the late 1920s and early 1930s, there was a growing sense of vulnerability in the Far East. In the first instance, this came from the unpredictable behavior of the warlord Chang Tso-lin and the Chinese armies linked to the Mukden and Nanking governments, which Soviet intelligence[70] understood to be in the pay of the British, the Japanese, the Americans, or all three. The Chinese forces directed against the Soviet Union were also linked with the remnants of the White armies that had retreated east and settled in and around Harbin in north China. In the summer of 1929, the Soviet Union had its first serious meetings with them along the Chinese Far Eastern Railway (KVZhD), which despite its name was a Soviet possession. The Chinese forces were harassing, threatening, and even killing Soviet railway workers, Soviet officials, and local residents. In July, they seized parts of the KVZhD by force of arms. Stalin's response was characteristic of the left radicalism of the Comintern and his general confidence in the international situation.[71] Diplomatic relations with China were severed, Soviet forces were concentrated in the area, and Chinese forces were repelled, though it was not until December that all parts of the railway were restored to Soviet control. It appears as though Stalin perceived that the show of strength in China was necessary not only to show the capitalist powers that the Soviets were ready to defend themselves, but also to demonstrate to other countries on the Soviet border the costs of siding with these "imperialists." The Soviets had the impression that the leaders of Afghanistan, Iraq, Persia, and Turkey were then under pressure to agree to assist the British in their plans to run anti-Soviet military operations from their territory.[72]

The onset of the Great Depression did nothing to ease the concerns raised by events in China. It seemed not to occur to Stalin or Soviet intelligence agencies that the Depression had a devastating impact on the ability of the capitalist economies to wage war. Rather, Stalin saw the Depression as confirmation of his earlier assessment that capitalism was enduring a crisis of overproduction, and following the logic of Lenin's theory of imperialism, he concluded that conflicts over markets, over sources of primary production, over the export of capital, and over colonies would only increase. The Depression, he argued, brought war closer and not further away. The only industry unaffected by depression, he argued, was the armaments industry. "Bourgeois governments arm and rearm them-selves. Why? Not for negotiation (*ne dlia razgovora*), but for war." And war against the Soviet Union would solve many of their problems, not least by providing new markets for excess production and getting rid of the evil of communism exacerbating class tensions at home.[73]

The Soviet leadership watched the political events in Europe with concern. The collapse of the Grand Coalition in Weimar Germany brought a sharp shift of politics to the right under Heinrich Brüning and the onset of emergency rule. They interpreted the rise of the Lapua movement and the fall of the Social Democratic government of Finland in June 1930 as a fascist coup.[74] They had similar concerns about the rise of the Far Right in Austria and Romania.[75] According to the party journal *Bol'shevik*, the Depression was deepening the dependence of Poland, Finland, and the Baltic states on the imperialist powers and making them a solid base for imperialist aggressive plans against the USSR.[76] Following a flurry of Polish diplomatic activity in the Baltic states through the late summer of 1930, Stalin wrote to Molotov that the Poles "were establishing (if they haven't already established) a bloc of Baltic states with the goal of waging war on the USSR. I don't think they'll attempt anything without the bloc, but as soon as they have it they'll go to war."[77] Meanwhile OGPU inves-tigations into the subversive activities of the capitalist states produced a steady stream of "evidence" suggesting that they remained dedicated to destabilizing the Soviet borderlands and undermining the first five-year plan. At the end of September 1930, OGPU boss Menzhinskii informed Stalin of British espionage and economic sabotage through the Metro-Vickers Company, but Stalin took a much greater interest in the transcripts of interrogations of the defendants in the case of the so-called Industrial Party. In particular, Stalin latched onto the testimony of Professor Leonid Ramzin, to the effect that a Franco-Polish-Romanian army was preparing to invade the USSR. He demanded further testimony from the other defendants as to why the attack was delayed. He wanted Menzhinskii to ensure that future statements clarified: "(1) Why was the intervention in 1930 put back? (2) Is it because Poland was not ready? (3) Perhaps because Romania is not ready? (4) Perhaps because the Baltic states and Romania haven't yet come to terms with Poland? (5) Why have they put off the attack to 1931? (6) Why might they put it off to 1932?"[78] Stalin was already convinced that the threat of war was once again rearing its head.

Stalin told Menzhinskii that material from the interrogations would be made available to sections of the Comintern, and that a public campaign against these plans "would succeed in paralyzing and subverting attempts to attack us for the next year or two, which is very important to us."[79] He was not taking chances though. Already at the beginning of September he had told Molotov: "If we are going to be able to defend ourselves against the Romanians, Poles, and Balts, we need to create the conditions. [We need] no less than 150–160 infantry divisions, that is, 40–50 divisions more than we have now . . . This means that the size of the army in peacetime has to be raised from 640 to 700,000. Otherwise, we aren't going to be able to defend Leningrad or the right bank of Ukraine . . . Raise the money through an increase in the production of vodka."[80] In the following weeks, he issued further instructions for the expansion of tank production.[81]

The military had been pushing for more than this. The Chiefs of Staff of the Red Army had used previous war scares to press for further investment in armed forces.[82] In early 1930, as other institutions were gaining massive increases in their investment in the context of the first five-year plan, they pressed their case again, but at the time Stalin still retained some confidence in the international situation. In March, he rejected their requests as a threat to the development of the civilian economy.[83] His order, only six months later, to give the army forty to fifty new divisions and increase tank production was a sharp change of tack for Stalin. Particularly given that he had declined any substantial new investment in the army through the war scares of the mid- to late 1920s, it seems clear that he took very seriously the "evidence" of the threat of war presented at the Industrial Party trial.[84] Meanwhile the military began optimistically to revisit their most ambitious plans.

As he had done in the late 1920s, Stalin publicized the growing danger of war to motivate the workforce. When the Industrial Party trial opened, he ordered a press campaign focused on the plans for invasion of the USSR. He told Molotov that the slogans surrounding the trial had to be about achievements in socialist construction as the response to Soviet enemies.[85] His own public statements pushed home the point in even more dramatic fashion. In his often quoted speech of February 1931, he told a conference of industrial managers: "To restrain tempos is to fall behind. And those who fall behind are beaten. We don't want to be beaten. We've been beaten by the Khans, by the Turkish beks, by the Swedish feudal lords, by the Polish-Lithuanian pans, beaten by the English and French capitalists, beaten by the Japanese barons. They all beat us because of our backwardness—military, cultural, political, industrial, and agricultural backwardness. They beat us because they could do so profitably and without punishment."[86]

A month later, Molotov's speech to the Sixth Congress of Soviets described the leadership's image of the constellation of capitalist forces aligning against them: the French supporting and directing the armies of Poland, Romania, and the Whites; the British and French preparing the Baltic states and Finland; the efforts to prepare domestic opinion for the coming war; the acts of industrial sabotage and other forms of terrorism; the Vatican's efforts to rally opinion in favor of an anti-communist crusade. As with Stalin's speech, the immediate object was to motivate Soviet workers to meet the extraordinary demands of the plan, but this did not mean that they presented an exaggerated vision of the threat for effect. The steady flow of intelligence reports on foreign threats ever deepened Soviet leaders' conviction that a large-scale attack by a coalition of capitalist powers was a very real possibility. Molotov's notes for the speech to the congress consisted of the latest Soviet intelligence, and his speech was vetted and subtly edited in order to protect sources.[87]

In the spring and summer of 1931, diplomacy was the front line of Soviet efforts to forestall the war. Litvinov, now the Commissar of Foreign Affairs, had succeeded in obtaining a non-aggression pact with Afghanistan; the extension of pacts with Germany, Turkey, and Lithuania; and more significantly, the promise of a non-aggression pact with France. The French would have preferred some kind of agreement with Germany at the expense of the USSR, but the rising tide of German nationalism and anti-Versailles sentiment made that impossible. The French offered the pact with the USSR in July, but a few weeks later had second thoughts in the face of an angry domestic reaction to it. They informed the Soviets that they would proceed with the pact only when the Soviet Union had negotiated a similar deal with the Poles. The opportunity seemed to arise almost immediately, for the Polish ambassador in Moscow presented Lev Karakhan, Litvinov's assistant, with a proposal for a non-aggression pact. The Soviet response was confused and divided. Kaganovich and Litvinov were opposed to the Polish proposal, seeing it as concerted effort of Polish and French "reactionaries" to scare the Germans into their camp.[88] Berlin would certainly have perceived any pact involving the three as anti-German. Their first instinct was to deny reports in the Polish press that negotiations were taking place. Stalin was livid. As far as he was concerned, German perceptions did not matter when non-aggression pacts with these two countries could ease the threat of war "for two or three years." Litvinov was ordered to abandon his opposition to a pact with Poland and present proposals for a response to the Polish initiative, but after the initial rebuff it proved very difficult to get Poland back to the negotiating table.[89]

Just as those crucial non-aggression pacts seemed to have slipped from their grasp, events in the Far East wiped away any sense the Soviet leadership may have had that the threat of war was receding. On 18 September 1931, the Japanese launched an invasion of Manchuria. Stalin immediately concluded that the Japanese would not have acted without consulting the other capitalist powers and agreeing to some kind of division of China. He thought that some of the Chinese warlords had to be involved as well, making further attacks on the KVZhD likely.[90] As the invasion progressed, Stalin's predictions grew more pessimistic. At the end of November he wrote to Voroshilov:

> Japan plans to seize not only Manchuria but also Beijing. It's not impossible and even likely that they will try to seize the Soviet Far East and even Mongolia to soothe the feelings of the Chinese clients with land captured at our expense. It is not likely to attack this winter, but it might try next year. Japan is driven by the desire to safeguard Manchuria, which it can only do if it turns the USSR against China. To this end it can help the Chinese warlords seize the KVZhD, seize Mongolia and our Pacific coast and put their puppets in power there. They want (1) to protect themselves from the Bolshevik infection, (2) to make a rapprochement between China and Russia impossible, (3) to establish a military and economic base on the mainland, (4) to use this base to wage war on the USSR. Unless they had done that, they would have been

faced with a revolutionary China, a rapidly growing USSR, and a rapidly militarizing USA. They had to do it then, because in another two years, Soviet military expenditure would have made it impossible.[91]

Stalin's suspicions were confirmed by intelligence he received in the middle of December 1931. A letter from Yukio Kasahara, the Japanese military attaché to the General Staff in Tokyo, intercepted by the OGPU, advocated a war against the USSR and the annexation of the Soviet Far East and western Siberia essentially for the reasons Stalin had expected. It was not clear how much influence the attaché had in the General Staff, or how much influence the General Staff had in the government, but Stalin did know that Kasahara was not a lone voice in the military and that many others outside the military were also advocating this sort of war of aggression. To make matters worse, Kasahara observed that "the countries on Soviet western borders (i.e., at a minimum Poland and Romania) are in a position to act with us."[92] A month later, Voroshilov wrote to his deputy Ian Gamarnik informing him of further (unconfirmed) reports to the effect that the Japanese "were in the midst of intensive preparations for war this spring. We also have evidence of the preparations of the White Guards, who boast that they can contribute 130,000 troops to an invasion force. They are proposing the creation of a 'Russian' government in the Far East and other such nonsense. All this is for now just rumor, but symptomatic [of the general situation]. We must get working and in a Bolshevik manner in order to make up for lost time."[93]

Indeed the military was making up for lost time. Defense spending had been steadily increasing in the course of the five-year plan, but leapt forward in 1932, nearly tripling from 845 million rubles to over 2.2 billion rubles.[94] In part, this reflected the perception that war was imminent and that for the first time since the civil war the Soviet Union was threatened with a war on two fronts. But it also reflected the triumph of ideas the General Staff had been pressing for many years. It was no longer enough for the Red Army to possess superiority in numbers. Soviet security demanded that the Red Army not fall behind its enemies technologically. In May 1932, Stalin apologized to Tukhachevskii for his criticism of the ambitious 1930 plan for the Red Army.[95] Unfortunately, the sudden increase of financing proved very difficult to digest and it was a long while before it had a measurable effect on the Red Army as a fighting force.[96]

Stalin continued to receive intelligence that indicated the imminence of a war on two fronts. At the end of February 1932 he received a further (intercepted) letter of Kasahara to the Japanese General Staff which indicated that the negotiation of a combined military operation against the USSR was progressing, though he acknowledged that political and economic tensions were holding things up. Nevertheless, he asserted that "if we were to attack the USSR, Poland, Romania, and the Baltic states would join (but not immediately), supported actively by the French and the not inconsiderable force of White Russians along the borderlands. Other powers would remain favorable."[97] The gist of that Japanese letter was confirmed from the Polish side two weeks later when the OGPU passed Stalin the report of a conversation between a trusted source and the chief of the Polish General Staff. Plans for an attack were apparently well developed, and the French and Poles were trying to convince the British to take an active part in the attack. The Romanians were preparing slowly, but there was still time. The invasion was planned for harvest time in order maximally to complicate the process of conscription and to take advantage of peasant hostility to the regime.[98]

The "evidence" of an active anti-Soviet bloc must have seemed compelling to Stalin, but it certainly does not conform to what we now know about British and French plans at the very least. It is quite possible that Kasahara and his Polish counterparts were engaging in some wishful thinking, if not outright fabrications, but it is also not inconceivable that the OGPU was creatively translating the materials it had in order to exaggerate the danger of war.

Reports from the Commissariat of Foreign Affairs suggested that the situation was not quite as bad as the OGPU evidence suggested. They observed that Japan was restrained by the war in China and by reports of the strengthening of Soviet defenses in the Far East, and that Poland was unlikely to fight the USSR while the revanchist Far Right in Germany was gaining strength.[99] Officials in the Commissariat did not, however, dismiss the threat of war, and events in the spring and summer of 1932 were far from reinforcing their relative optimism. TASS summaries of the Far Right press in Japan indicated that Britain had agreed to join France and Poland in a war against the USSR, and that certain unnamed American businessmen had agreed to help finance the war.[100] Japanese and pro-Japanese forces along the borders of the Far East were trying to provoke a conflict with border skirmishes and violations of Soviet airspace. Stalin gave strict orders not to respond to such "provocations." Stalin and Kaganovich agreed that the groups that favored war with the USSR would blame any confrontation on Soviet "aggression." General Bliukher, head of the Far Eastern Military District, was raked over the coals by Stalin after shots had been fired at Japanese overflights without the permission of the Politburo.[101] These "provocations" reached a new height in June when these same groups were apparently threatening to topple the pro-Soviet government of Mongolia. Stalin was not prepared to risk sending in Soviet armed forces, though pro-Soviet forces were kept well supplied.[102]

On the western front, things were also going from bad to worse. In early 1932, the Western press published reports of a Franco-Japanese pact, and the Soviet embassy (*polpredstvo*) in Paris received information to the effect that France was supplying Japan with arms on a grand scale.[103] Elections in Germany had brought further setbacks for the Communists and signs of deepening nationalism and anti-communism. In particular, the Soviet leadership began to worry that German anti-communism was sufficient common ground for a rapprochement with Poland and participation in the war with the USSR.[104] A Franco-German rapprochement seemed already to be on its way. While the possibility of German participation in the anti-Soviet coalition hung in the air, Poland gave every indication that preparations were underway for an autumn invasion. Grain collections in Ukraine were more difficult than the Polish military had anticipated—they were leading to a devastating, man-made famine—and the Poles were attempting to capitalize, sending many small groups across the border with the aim of organizing peasant resistance and ultimately a rebellion. Stalin told Kaganovich in mid-August that the Ukrainian party and OGPU had to break resistance to the grain collections immediately:

> If we don't take measures to correct the situation, we could lose Ukraine. Keep in mind that Pilsudski [the Polish leader] is not daydreaming and his agent network in Ukraine is much stronger

than [S. F.] Redens [chief of the republican OGPU] or [S. V.] Kosior [first secretary of the Ukrainian Party] think. Also keep in mind that the Ukrainian Communist Party (500,000 members, ha-ha) has many (yes, many!) rotten elements, conscious and unconscious Petliurovites and direct agents of Pilsudski. If things get worse, these elements will not hesitate to open a front inside (and outside) the party, against the party . . . Without . . . the economic and political strengthening of Ukraine, and its *border districts* in the first instance . . . I repeat, we could lose Ukraine.[105]

Stalin had an encompassing vision of how to prevent war that stretched from the big issues, like the political situation in Ukraine and restraining the response to "provocations" in the Far East,[106] to other relatively fine details, like the tone and content of articles in the national press. He criticized the poet Dem'ian Bednyi for writing—however lyrically—that the Soviet population was ready to fight with Japan. Any aggressive posturing would play into the hands of the enemy.[107] He criticized Emelian Iaroslavskii, one of the editors of *Pravda*, for reporting labor unrest in June 1932. The resulting talk about "a new Kronstadt" (a reference to an uprising against Soviet power in 1921) would be "obviously advantageous to our enemies." Signs of internal dissent only encouraged those who proposed to invade. He also criticized the portrayal of political events in Germany as signaling a revolution, insofar as that was "advantageous to those who are trying to orchestrate the rupture of Soviet-German relations."[108] At the same time, he directed the Comintern and prominent friends of the USSR to influence public opinion against war generally and against an invasion of the USSR in particular.[109] With the encouragement of the Politburo, an anti-war congress held in Amsterdam in August 1932 set itself the task of creating a mass movement against "imperialist" war. One of its first steps was to join with the separate but related (through the Comintern) anti-fascist movement to hold an international conference of youth against war and fascism in September.[110] In Geneva, Commissar of Foreign Affairs Maxim Litvinov was reinforcing this public campaign against war by loudly proclaiming Soviet support for total disarmament. At the time, the massive increase in Soviet expenditure on the Red Army was hidden behind a smoke screen of false figures.[111]

Of course Litvinov and his Commissariat were doing much more than that to help forestall a war against the USSR. In the immediate aftermath of the Japanese invasion of Manchuria, Stalin relied on diplomacy to stabilize the situation. A restrained response to the invasion was crucially important, he thought, because conflict, or even exposed tensions, would be taken as an encouraging sign to would-be invaders in the West. He agreed to open "friendly" negotiations with the Japanese on fishing rights, as he wrote to Voroshilov, so as to "trump the Poles with our 'normal' relations with the Japanese."[112] At the same time, the Commissariat began to step up efforts to achieve diplomatic recognition from the single power challenging Japan's power in the Pacific—the United States—and to reestablish relations with the nationalists in Nanking, Japan's main enemy in China.[113] Negotiations with America, China, and with Japan itself moved slowly, but Stalin understood that the fact of negotiation would play a psychological role in restraining the Japanese.[114] Stalin made as many concessions, such as the recognition of Manchuria, as were necessary to keep negotiations going, but was not inclined to agree to conclude agreements that disadvantaged the Soviet side. He kept a close eye on his diplomats and acted quickly to pull them back if he felt they were straining too hard at the tight leash he kept them on.[115]

While negotiations with the Japanese progressed, Soviet diplomats continued to pursue pacts with Poland and France as well. In early 1932, as they were apparently in the midst of preparations for war, the Poles agreed to a draft of a non-aggression pact. After further months of difficult negotiations, the pact was formally signed at the end of July, by which time the negotiation of a similar pact with the French seemed likely. On the surface of it, Germany was the key to these agreements. The French had turned toward the USSR after Briand's attempts at a rapprochement with Germany had failed, and Poland did so in anticipation of the French but also out of concern at the anti-Polish sentiment of the nascent Far Right in Germany. But Stalin thought it was easy to exaggerate the significance of the pacts. They made aggression more difficult only insofar as the violation of a treaty upset public opinion. He doubted their commitment to non-aggression, and for good reason. At the time the pact was being signed, the Poles were actively trying to destabilize Ukraine. The national press continued to present Poland as the likely base for an imperialist invasion of the USSR.[116] Negotiations with the French were hardly more encouraging. As Jonathan Haslam observed, "when negotiating the . . . pact in August 1932, the French government attempted to insert a clause in the draft agreement stipulating its abrogation in the event 'of an attack on a third Power' (a reference to Japan in all but name), and one month later, it advised the Japanese against signing a similar pact against the Soviet Union—difficult to explain except in terms of a French attempt to turn Japanese forces northwards."[117] The conclusion of the French pact at the end of November 1932 was perhaps not as reassuring for Stalin as were the French elections of January 1933, when the Socialist Edouard Daladier came to power and the new foreign minister Joseph Paul-Boncour seemed committed to a rapprochement with the USSR in word and deed.

The War Scare of 1934–35

While Soviet leaders did not think either the French or the Poles had committed themselves to peaceful relations with the USSR, there was reason to be optimistic that the immediate danger of war had passed. Further pacts had been signed with Finland, Latvia, and Estonia in the course of 1932, and diplomatic relations with China had been reestablished in December. Signals from America suggested that diplomatic recognition of the USSR was on its way. The diplomatic activity of 1932 had made the formation of an anti-Soviet coalition seem significantly less probable than it had at the beginning of the year.

The conclusion of the first five-year plan also contributed to the sense of Soviet security. The concrete achievements of the plan, in terms of the increases in civilian and military production, had left the regime better able to defend itself from attack, though the increase in spending on the military was only just starting to have an impact. But it was even more important to project that impression of achievement to the capitalist world. The CC plenum that reviewed the results of the plan in January 1933 did not dwell on the problems of the fulfillment of many key targets or on the famine then raging in the countryside. Rather, Stalin's speech contrasted the growth of the Soviet economy with the steep decline in production that the Depression was causing in the capitalist states. He asserted that the success of the plan was winning respect for the Soviet Union not only among the working class but also among the bourgeoisie. It was winning respect, and fear too, for military spending meant that the Soviet Union was ready to defend itself from all threats, he insisted, stretching the facts more than a little.[118] The stronger the impression among the capitalist states that the USSR could defend itself against the broadest coalition, the less likely it was to be attacked.[119] The confidence of the leadership in the international situation was reflected in public statements taunting the capitalist states. Addressing the Central Executive Committee on 24 January 1933, Molotov reminded his audience of the growing number of capitalist states that had established diplomatic ties with the Soviet Union. "Some clever ones still consider further 'study' of the USSR necessary . . . The Soviet power has existed for fifteen years . . . It should have been clear already what the USSR is, especially after the fulfillment of the five-year plan. It should not be difficult to guess how Soviet might has increased, how our economy is expanding, how much the international weight of the USSR has grown. Those who are full of useless and empty phrases about further study of the USSR are the ones who have the most to lose from the absence of diplomatic ties."[120] Stalin complimented Molotov on the tone: "It's a well-placed spit in the bucket of the swaggering (*khorokho-riashchikhsia*) powers. Let them eat it . . ."[121] The mood was not upset even by the appointment of Hitler as German chancellor on 30 January. The instinct in Comintern was to interpret the success of the Nazis as further evidence of the crisis of German capitalism and the maturing of a revolutionary situation.[122] They did not, at first, take the Nazis especially seriously. Germany was too weak politically and economically for the Nazis' anti-communism to be converted into action. Or could it?

Much hinged on Hitler's diplomacy. Would Hitler enter the sort of anti-Soviet coalition that previous German governments had refused to do? Soviet leaders believed that Poland and France had not gone to war with the USSR in the previous year because they had not come to suitable terms with Germany. Soviet assessments of Hitler's intentions varied widely in the spring of 1933 largely because of the French reaction to the new German leader, exploring first a preventive war against Germany and then rapprochement involving German participation in common security arrangements. The former was almost certainly intended to push the Germans into the latter. But Hitler did not encourage the French.

A year earlier, this German caution would have signified that no deal with the Poles was possible either, but Poland was now running a more independent foreign policy. The alliance with France had failed to provide security for Poland, stuck as it was between Germany and the USSR. Now a more nationalistic and revanchist regime had come to power in Germany, while the (perceived) Soviet threat was growing exponentially. The Poles wanted to explore the possibility that a more independent foreign policy would serve them better, and indeed, they immediately found themselves courted by all. Hitler saw the opportunity immediately. The Polish-French axis had always been directed first against Germany, and not the USSR, whatever Stalin might have thought, and separating Poland from France promised substantially to increase German freedom of action. The French tried to draw the Poles back into further schemes for collective security that would include Germany, and the Soviets explored the possibility of closer relations with the Poles in order to keep them out of a new anti-Soviet alliance.[123] The advantage for the Poles would last only as long as they could keep their suitors interested. Stalin watched the situation closely.

The situation in the East was similarly mixed. As ever, Soviet intelligence indicated that the Japanese decision to wage war on the USSR rested in a fine balance in which a slim majority in government was, with difficulty, restraining pro-war forces in the Japanese military and in Manchuria. Stalin understood that to aid the forces opposed to war, he had to make war seem costly by improving Soviet defense capabilities; avoiding conflict along the borders with Manchuria, particularly skirmishes over control of the KVZhD; smoothing tensions with Japan over fishing rights; building a working relationship with the United States; and keeping Japan bogged down in its war with China. The day after diplomatic relations with the Chinese had been reestablished, the Japanese sought to diminish its significance by formally rejecting the Soviet offer of a non-aggression pact.[124] Whether or not this was a bluff, it signaled that close relations between China and the Soviet Union would not have the effect of containing Japanese ambitions. Five months later, in the spring of 1933, the diplomatic momentum appeared to be slipping the other way. On 31 May 1933 the Tangku truce ended hostilities between the nationalist Kuomintang and the Kwantung army. More disturbing still for the Soviets, there were reports to the effect that the Kuomintang were making overtures to the Japanese

about negotiating an end to the war in China.[125] Of course an end to
the war would free up Japanese forces to attack the USSR. Military and
other conservative circles in Japan continued to advocate war with the
Soviet Union, and Stalin's intelligence told him that the Japanese military
build-up proceeded at an undiminished pace and that Japanese spies and
saboteurs—most sponsored by the Kwantung army in Manchuria—
continued to operate on Soviet territory.[126] Stalin received intercepted
correspondence between the British ambassador in Tokyo and the Foreign
Office in London that reinforced the picture. The ambassador observed
that the Japanese military build-up was too great to be directed solely at
China. He speculated that it was probably evidence of preparations for war
against the USSR. He went on to observe that Japanese military officers
considered war with the USSR inevitable in the next few years.[127] In this
context, Stalin sought to strengthen the hand of those who opposed war
by means of negotiations over the sale of the KVZhD to the Japanese, thus
removing a constant source of tension. Initial reports from Japan suggested
that the military were livid about the negotiations and would try to inter-
fere, but would not be able to stop them.[128] But the reports were subject
to revision in the autumn of 1933. Negotiations had broken down because
the Japanese were not prepared to pay a price acceptable to the Soviet side,
and Stalin received reports to the effect that the Kwantung army was
preparing to seize the KVZhD by force of arms. The Politburo ordered
Pravda and *Izvestiia* to "expose" the plans by publishing, in a disguised
form, the intelligence they had been receiving.[129] Meanwhile, the Americans
finally agreed to recognize the USSR in November 1933. Stalin attempted
to deepen the rapprochement by granting an interview with the *New York
Times* correspondent Walter Duranty in which he discussed the common
interests of the two countries, not least in the Pacific.[130]

Things nevertheless began to take a turn for the worse. In the autumn
of 1933, Koki Hirota, the former Japanese ambassador to the USSR and
well known to Stalin as an advocate of war with the Soviet Union, was
named Foreign Minister after the resignation of Yasuya Uchida. In late
November, Stalin received an intercepted letter from the American ambassador in Japan to the State Department confirming the Soviet assessment
that the promotion of Hirota represented a shift of opinion in Japanese
government. He predicted a more aggressive Japanese foreign policy, and

specifically war with the USSR in the spring, if, as he anticipated, China could be "pacified."[131] This was followed, less than two months later, by the news that Poland had signed a non-aggression pact with Germany. Although the pact was not obviously incompatible with previous Polish efforts to find a balance between its main enemies, it significantly lessened the tensions between Poland and Germany that had been a steady source of Soviet security in the past. The Soviet leadership became convinced that Polish foreign policy was developing a pro-German orientation and that there were secret protocols in the pact that set the terms of joint German and Polish military action against the USSR.[132] Subsequent reports from various sources suggested that British "ruling circles" had been encouraging Japanese aggression against the USSR for over a year.[133]

Public statements on the issue amplified this impression, suggesting that a broad coalition of capitalist states including Britain was once again preparing a counterrevolutionary war against the USSR.[134] Although there were deep concerns about anti-Soviet elements in the French government,[135] the French were not generally included in portrayals of that coalition because they were pushing in the spring and summer of 1934 for an "eastern pact" in which central and eastern European states including Poland, Germany, and the USSR would guarantee one another's security. However, French Foreign Minister Louis Barthou had little success, and the resistance of Poland and Germany to the notion of common security arrangements deepened the general pessimism among Soviet leaders. At the end of June 1934, Stalin received intelligence from a mole in the Polish Foreign Ministry to the effect that the Polish leader Josef Pilsudski and his foreign minister Josef Beck had tried (unsuccessfully) to convince French Foreign Minister Louis Barthou of the benefits of joining a Polish-German alliance against the USSR, but Pilsudski and Beck did not think they had long to wait before a more conservative government replaced that of the Socialist Daladier. Apparently, the well-placed conservatives Andre Tardieu (a former prime minister) and General Maxime Weygand advised the Poles that following a change in government, France would join a military alliance against the USSR. They had already canvassed senior figures in the British government who promised their support for an anti-Soviet war. The report went on to assert that the Poles and Germans were now more openly negotiating a military pact with the Japanese. The support of the Romanians was likely, and there were hopes that Italy, Austria, and Hungary might join. The conclusion of the report was that "war against the Soviet Union was never as realistic a possibility as now."[136] And yet none of the findings conforms to what we currently know of the intentions of any of the countries that figured in the report.[137]

In July and August, intelligence reports from the Foreign Department of the political police (now NKVD) and the Commissariat of Foreign Affairs delivered much the same message. The Poles, Germans, and Japanese were in the midst of military and diplomatic preparations for a 1935 invasion.[138] Their plans also appeared to involve subversive activities to weaken Soviet defenses and exacerbate disaffection with the regime. The Commissariat of Foreign Affairs ordered the Soviet embassies (*polpredstva*) in the Baltic states and eastern Europe to confirm reports that White Russians were being recruited in large numbers to organize sabotage in the Soviet Union in the event of war in the Far East.[139] Stalin received a long series of intercepted communications, particularly from the Japanese military attaché, on the importance of subversion to an invasion.[140] Nevertheless, the rapid rise in the number of foreign spies and saboteurs arrested in this period was probably generated less by the actual proliferation of subversives than by the pressure the Politburo exerted on the political police to find them. A verification of the credentials of foreigners living in the USSR begun in 1935 was turning up further disturbing evidence of the widespread infiltration of the USSR by enemy agents.[141]

Events in the autumn and winter did nothing to dissuade Soviet leaders that a war was coming sometime in 1935. Stalin had been warned that the Japanese would use tensions over the KVZhD to justify war on the Soviet Union, and while talks on the sale of the railroad to Japan made no progress, Manchurian forces continued to attack Soviet workers and blame the USSR for the tensions.[142] As the Japanese appeared to be preparing public opinion for war, Stalin was informed of a scandal whipping up anti-Soviet opinion in Poland. The Soviet military attaché in Poland was accused of trying to recruit spies. Stalin was informed that he was probably trying to do just that, but the treatment of the attaché and press coverage in Poland indicated to him that the incident was being used to provoke the USSR. On Stalin's orders, it was categorically denied that the attaché was involved in espionage.[143]

The gathering clouds seemed to have one silver lining. The Polish-German rapprochement had worrying implications for French security.

Although Soviet intelligence agencies were concerned that the French might join the two in a war against the USSR, they also calculated that Germany might want to expand west first, particularly in order to be in a position to use French heavy industry and raw materials production in a prolonged campaign of expansion. Soviet diplomats made the most of this vulnerability to sustain the relationship with France and to convince the Daladier government and its successors to continue to put pressure on Poland and Germany to join an "eastern pact."[144] This strategy was realized on a broader scale when the Soviet Union agreed to join the League of Nations in September. However, hopes that sustained diplomatic pressure might forestall war received two serious blows later in the autumn. On 9 October 1934, Daladier's foreign minister, Louis Barthou, was assassinated together with King Alexander of Yugoslavia while on a visit to Croatia. The Soviets were convinced that this was the work of the Nazi secret police, intended not only to destabilize Yugoslavia but also to eliminate Barthou, a key figure sustaining the French relationship with the USSR.[145] A month later, Daladier's left-of-center government fell. No sustained turn to the right followed, but the instability of French politics made her a far from reliable partner. There was guarded optimism at first. In November 1934, Stalin received intelligence to the effect that Hitler had proposed a non-aggression pact with the French, but had been rebuffed. Three weeks later, French and Soviet diplomats signed a protocol reopening the negotiation of an eastern pact, but only a short time later, Stalin was told that the French were once again flirting with the appeasement of Germany, including permission for significant German rearmament.[146] In this case, the intelligence was reasonably accurate.

At the end of December, Stalin received further intelligence from the NKVD Foreign Department indicating that a Franco-German rapprochement was being negotiated. This could be, he was told, the beginning of the Franco-German-Polish bloc that Pilsudski had been pushing for so long. The December protocol had been a tactical maneuver, and the British, who were publicly in favor of an eastern pact, were privately pushing the French toward a rapprochement with Germany. Finland was being drawn into the bloc, as was Hungary, and there were hopes that Romania and Italy would contribute. Joint Polish-German military preparations were well underway and meetings between German and Polish leaders were no longer kept secret.[147] The meetings, which Stalin interpreted as part of a preparation for war, were indeed attempts by the Germans to draw the Poles into an anti-Soviet pact. What Stalin did not know was that the Poles consistently refused the German offers. Once again Stalin thought he faced an elaborate and extensive anti-Soviet bloc, whereas nothing of the sort existed.

But to be fair to Stalin, war was a constant subject of diplomatic rumor and newspaper editorial at the time and further Soviet intelligence seemed to confirm the most pessimistic assessments. At the beginning of 1935, the Western press was reporting that the German military was on high alert and all leave was cancelled. Universal military conscription was announced in March, while the military build-up continued at a breakneck pace, now openly violating the restrictions set by the Versailles Treaty.[148] Intelligence from Japan was only slightly less bleak. The Japanese were also rapidly building up their own armed forces, though they were still substantially committed to fighting in China. In January, Japanese Foreign Minister Hirota announced to the Japanese parliament yet another effort to nego-tiate peace in China. The Soviet ambassador (*polpred*) in Britain sent Moscow a report of his conversation with the nationalists' representative in London suggesting they would take the Japanese offer seriously, not least because the British and Americans were hesitating to continue financing the purchase of arms, potentially leaving them unable fight.[149] American recognition of the Soviet Union did not help Soviet security in the Pacific. Not only did the Americans seem ready to starve the national-ists of financing at a crucial moment, but Stalin also received intelligence in January, confirmed by further intelligence in May, that the Japanese and Americans were in the process of negotiating a non-aggression pact that would have put Japan into a better position to fight the USSR.[150] Meanwhile links between East and West were growing. Soviet diplomats observed that the French bourgeoisie had started to invest heavily in Manchuria,[151] and that the Japanese were busy training the Finnish army.[152] The Commissariat of Foreign Affairs assumed that Japanese military advisers were at work elsewhere in eastern Europe.[153]

In the midst of what seemed to be a determined march to war, Soviet intelligence started to show things heading the other way. The German military build-up appeared to be turning the British and French away from the idea of supporting an anti-Soviet bloc. Anthony Eden's visit to Moscow (after seeing Hitler in Berlin) at the end March reassured Stalin that Britain was nervous about the growth of German military might. The French had even more reason to be worried. If Germany and Poland managed to conquer the USSR with the help of Japan, they might well turn on France next, and with the heart of Soviet industry and its natural resources to back them up, they would pose a serious threat. Stalin's warnings to the French had finally fallen on fertile ground. This time, however, rather than push for a multilateral pact in which the inclusion of Germany and Poland would remain a sticking point, Stalin directed Litvinov to explore French interest in a bilateral mutual assistance pact. With unusual speed, a pact was drawn up and signed on 2 May 1935. Two weeks later, a similar pact was signed with Czechoslovakia.

From Stalin's perspective, Soviet diplomacy had once again saved the USSR from imminent disaster. It was an important victory, but how long would it last? French politics was extremely unstable, and while Barthou's successor Pierre Laval had, contrary to expectation, demonstrated his willingness to work with the Soviet Union, there remained a suspicion that his commitment to collective security was superficial, that the pact was yet another bluff to secure a deal with Germany on French terms. They suspected that the British thought in similar terms, that they did not want to go to war and would try to balance Germany against the USSR, but if Germany was intent on expanding, then a deal would be struck to let her expand to the east.[154] There was little reason to assume that Germany (or Poland, or Japan) had given up ambitions for territorial expansion at the expense of the Soviet Union. The Kwantung army continued to harass and threaten the Soviets along the border with Mongolia. An attempted military coup in Japan indicated to the Soviet leadership that the Japanese army was trying to eliminate those political forces that resisted the idea of a war against the USSR.[155] Germany had signed a series of trade and credit agreements with the USSR in 1934 and 1935, and although Stalin saw them as a disincentive to war, he did not think they would prevent it. The National Socialists did not in any way tone down their anti-communist and anti-Soviet rhetoric or restrain their use of saboteurs and spies in the USSR. The same can be said of Poland and Japan. Once plans for a hot war had to be put on hold, it appeared as though efforts to subvert the USSR from within were increased. In the autumn of 1935, and through

1936, Stalin received a steady stream of reports from Genrikh Iagoda, head of the NKVD, of the terrorist and espionage activities of these three countries.[156] The regime also became convinced that the system it had used to grant asylum to political refugees had been used by their enemies to settle large numbers of spies and subversives in the Soviet Union.[157] The war was being conducted by other means.

Stalin had good reason to believe that the war had been delayed, though not for long. The start of the Spanish Civil War in July 1936 was interpreted as the unfolding of a world war "meticulously" planned by European fascists.[158] The hot war had begun. In October, the Germans established a military alliance with Italians, and a month later signed the Anti-Comintern Pact with Japan. Soviet leaders understood that the pact was not about a struggle with Communist Parties and movements generally, but about continuing and deepening the effort to build a coalition to wage war on the Soviet Union. As the whole of Europe was arming itself to the teeth, Stalin had only Britain and France to stand between it and war with Japan and Germany, and he watched as Chamberlain proceeded with a policy of concessions to Germany, and as France turned again to the right after the collapse of the Popular Front. Neither showed much interest in entering a mutual assistance pact with the Soviet Union. There was nothing in that to surprise to Stalin. For most of the more than two decades since the October Revolution, Stalin had seen the two countries as leaders and organizers of anti-Soviet coalitions. The common fear of Germany had drawn them toward the USSR, but Stalin seems to have been inclined to assume that the primary motivation of the Franco-Soviet rapprochements was to convince Germany to agree to security arrangements set by France, if necessary, at the expense of the USSR. Stalin continued to direct his diplomats to explore the potential of collective security, but a deal without a guarantee that Britain and France would come to the defense of the Soviet Union in the event of a German invasion was worse than no deal at all. It would not deter German expansion to the east.[159] A non-aggression pact with Germany made more sense than collective security, because if war was inevitable, it made more sense to push Hitler west than to rely on two enemies of longstanding to come to the aid of the Soviet Union.[160]

Without these streams of intelligence materials examined here, historians have been unable to explore in detail Stalin's perception and misperception of the world outside his borders, though it was the most decisive factor shaping Soviet foreign policy from the late 1920s.[161] Indeed, Stalin's striking misperception of the international situation has important implications for Soviet domestic policy as well. Although some studies have considered the importance of the fear of war in shaping the struggle for the Lenin succession, in Stalin's "revolution from above" and in the Great Terror, among other issues,[162] the implications of that fear have not been studied in depth because until recently historians generally assumed that Stalin understood there was no basis for it.[163] Stalin's misperceptions constitute an important field of inquiry ripe for exploration.

In the case of Stalin's misperception of the capitalist world, the ramifications extend well beyond the Stalin period. Across the 1920s and 1930s, Stalin had developed a predisposition to see the USSR as surrounded by hostile powers bent on its destruction. These fears were grossly exaggerated but reinforced by Lenin's theory of imperialism, by the Bolsheviks' experience of civil war, by the anti-communism of governments and elites in Europe and Asia, by a system of intelligence gathering designed to find evidence of anti-Soviet coalitions, by a bureaucratic self-interest among intelligence gatherers to confirm the leader's predispositions, by Stalin's inclination to dismiss counterevidence. But the experience of World War II appeared amply to justify the fears of the preceding two decades. The subsequent experience of fifty years of cold war reinforced Soviet fears further still.

It should surprise no one that the collapse of the USSR in 1991 did not suddenly change Moscow's foreign-policy orientation, so deep was the well of suspicion. And since 1999, the tenor and direction of Russian foreign policy under Vladimir Putin suggests that the fear of hostile foreign powers is largely undiminished. Scholars have no access to Putin's foreign intelligence sources, but one would be rather surprised if they were not focused in the FSB—the successor to the NKVD: Stalin's most trusted source on the international situation and the source most responsible for his exaggerated fears.

PART

THE POWER OF STALIN'S WORDS

4

THE LEADER CULT

     Stimulated by developments in mass communications as well as broader sociopolitical changes, quasi-religious "cults" of political leaders flourished in a great range of authoritarian societies in the twentieth century. In terms of their monumental scale and ambition, Soviet leader cults were particularly striking examples of the phenomenon, especially when set against the backdrop of Marxism's emphasis on the importance of anonymous social forces in history. The question of why the cults of Lenin, Stalin, and others were able to take root and thrive in Soviet soil has attracted much attention. Explanations usually focus on the general susceptibility of political life to sacralization in the secular modern age, the legacy of the cult of the tsar and Orthodox Church, the paternalism of Russian and Soviet political culture, and the inherently charismatic nature of the Bolshevik Party.[1]

The more specific question of Stalin's relationship with his own cult has also been the subject of some debate. Whereas the cult has traditionally been regarded as a means by which the leader bolstered his power and authority within the party,[2] Robert Tucker claims that it fulfilled an important psychological as well as political function: "Abundant evidence indicates that Stalin needed a cult as a prop for his psyche as well as for his power. He craved the hero worship that Lenin found repugnant."[3] More recently, David Brandenberger has proposed that Stalin valued the cult, in conjunction with "national bolshevism," as an instrument for enhancing the legitimacy of the regime in the eyes of the Soviet population as a whole.[4]

According to Erik Van Ree, Stalin's willingness to countenance the veneration of outstanding individuals (himself included) may be interpreted as a
quite legitimate expression of his genuine Marxist beliefs: "For Marxists,
the discovery that history answered to laws did not show the futility of
individual heroism but, on the contrary, provided real scope for it for the
first time . . . A cult of genius and heroism is precisely what one would
expect in a movement combining violent struggle for socialism with scientific insight into the process leading to that goal." Van Ree observes that
Stalin endeavored to keep his own cult within acceptable ideological
parameters and to demarcate the Bolshevik approach from that of the
Socialist Revolutionaries (SRs), who were criticized for exaggerating the
significance of heroic personalities.[5]

Stalin's inner thoughts and motivations concerning the cult will always
remain a matter for conjecture. Rather than dwelling explicitly on these,
our aim is to explore what Stalin said and wrote about his persona in the
hope that this will, at the very least, permit a fuller understanding of how
he wanted his image to be projected. Although a great many individuals
and institutions were involved in the production of the cult, Stalin's
personal contribution to this vast enterprise was particularly important:
his words (and his silences) helped to shape the cult in fundamental ways.

Memoir material indicates that Stalin often spoke about the cult in
ambivalent or critical terms. Molotov recalled that "at first he resisted the
cult of personality, but then he came to like it a bit." He also observed
how Stalin frequently associated the adulation with the ideas and practices
of the SRs: "Stalin used to say, 'Molotov can still restrain himself, so can
Malenkov, but others, Socialist Revolutionaries, cry openly: "Stalin, Stalin!"
You see, only Socialist Revolutionaries talk this way!' " Molotov went on
to imply that it would have been difficult for Stalin to extinguish the cult
even if he had wanted to.[6] Mikoian claimed that he and Ordzhonikidze
were displeased when Kaganovich began to extol Stalin at meetings of the
Moscow party organization at the start of the 1930s. According to Mikoian,
Stalin enjoyed the veneration, but in a narrow circle once rebuked
Kaganovich: "What is this, why do you praise me alone, as if one man can
decide everything? It's SR-ism, the SRs exaggerate the role of *vozhdi*."
They assumed that Stalin's rebuke would signal the end of the practice,
but in fact it only increased and "became the lexicon for the whole party":

if you refused to go along with it, it was assumed that you were against Stalin and the party.[7] In the rather different context of the June 1953 CC plenum, at a time when Stalin's own words were being invoked to undermine the "cult of personality," Mikoian suggested that Stalin had been unequivocally opposed to the phenomenon: "Comrade Stalin severely criticized us. He would say, 'the SRs are creating a cult around me.' At the time we couldn't correct the matter and so it went on."[8]

Even Khrushchev testified that Stalin himself frequently liked to deride the worship of an individual as an SR practice.[9] Khrushchev's stance was typically contradictory: in his "Secret Speech," for example, he argued that the cult grew to extremes "chiefly because Stalin himself, using all conceivable methods, supported the glorification of his own person."[10] However he was somewhat less categorical at the June 1957 CC plenum that denounced the "anti-party group" of Molotov, Malenkov, and Kaganovich. When discussion turned to the cult, Voroshilov insisted that Stalin was irritated by Kaganovich and others who praised him and tried to elevate him above Lenin: "He berated us several times: 'Aren't you ashamed, why do you cry—Stalin. Who is Stalin?' Moreover he spoke sincerely, with indignation. 'That,' he said, 'Stalin is shit, but Lenin is Ivan the Terrible's bell tower.' He said it several times, honestly, sincerely. The toadying (*podkhalimazh*) was so energetic that in the end . . ." Khrushchev interjected at that point, accused Voroshilov of lying, and claimed: "Stalin did not want to be venerated, but he could not cope with the situation because he did not have the opportunity. If he'd said the word, everyone would have stopped praising him." The wording of Khrushchev's intervention was rather more ambiguous in this version than in the corrected stenogram, which reads: "If Stalin had seriously wanted to stop the stream of praise and unrestrained flattery addressed to him, then he had enough power to do this. He only had to sneeze (*tsyknul by*) and everyone would have stopped the excessive praise."[11] The first version may have simply been a case of mistaken transcription, but it is equally possible that Khrushchev altered it because it did not align with his earlier unequivocal interpretation in the "Secret Speech."

The evaluations of Khrushchev and other members of the inner circle were necessarily colored by political considerations. What about the recollections of Stalin's relatives? Several of these also implied that Stalin's stance was far from straightforward: Yuri Zhdanov, for example, claimed that his father-in-law, "a modest person," was rather intolerant of the adulation. He remembered that while they were on holiday after the war, when somebody brought over a copy of *Pravda* containing a report from an international congress, Stalin asked, "What are they writing there? Is it again, 'Long live the great leader of the peoples of the world, comrade Stalin'?" He "screwed up the newspaper and threw it in the bushes. This was his real attitude to the cult of personality."[12] Artem Sergeev highlighted what appeared to be Stalin's sense of detachment from his persona: When his son Vasilii asserted, "But I'm a Stalin too," Stalin shouted, "No you're not . . . You're not Stalin and I'm not Stalin. Stalin is Soviet power. Stalin is what he is in the newspapers and portraits, not you, no not even me!"[13] Leaving aside the question of whether such views represented Stalin's "real attitude to the cult of personality," this was certainly the impression he sought to cultivate, evidently with some success.

While the recollections of both relatives and close colleagues should be approached with a degree of skepticism, in many respects this evidence does accord with the contemporary archival record. Materials from his personal papers and the Politburo archive reveal that whereas Stalin rarely reflected publicly on the subject of the cult (a silence that was itself telling), he was more forthcoming behind the scenes, where he liked to convey an impression ranging from disapproval to reluctant acceptance of the adulation. In particular, he often made a point of intervening demonstratively to restrain the cult-building zeal of others. In his recent monograph, Jan Plamper describes this pattern as Stalin's "immodest modesty," which "was affected in order to overcome the contradiction of a personality cult in a polity that claimed to be implementing a collectivist ideology, Marxism," and which resonated with the culture of modesty prevailing within the Bolshevik Party and the Russian intelligentsia more broadly.[14] Although it is difficult to judge to what extent this modesty was "affected" (or "feigned," as Arfon Rees puts it), it is certainly true that it was the central and constant characteristic of Stalin's approach.[15]

Whereas Plamper concentrates on Stalin's handling of visual expressions of the cult, our focus is primarily on how this "modesty" was projected in relation to verbal material of various kinds. We begin by considering Stalin's responses to early attempts to revere him in the period before the cult was well established (1924–30). We then turn to his pronouncements about the fully fledged cult before examining his efforts to manage the projection of his image in some of the domains that seem to have particularly concerned him: biographical writings and core political rituals and ceremonies.

The Cult in Embryo: Early Initiatives, 1924–30

A culture of venerating Stalin and other Bolshevik figures long pre-dated the emergence of an officially orchestrated Stalin cult in the 1930s. The party had a tradition of lauding heroic and exceptional individuals who had served the revolutionary cause. However, in theory at least, these individuals were extolled as outstanding representatives of the working class and party, and not purely because they possessed innately superior personal qualities. *Cults of personality*, supposedly alien to the party's collectivist, class-based ethos, were denigrated as a bad habit of the wrong-headed SRs.[16] In practice, of course, it proved difficult to maintain these theoretical distinctions. It was never entirely clear just how much weight should be attributed to the role of an individual leader as opposed to other factors (the working class, the party, the CC, the Politburo), or how much attention should be devoted to a leader's personal attributes.

This lack of clarity was due in part to the complexities and ambiguities of Marxist thought. While historical materialism privileged the role of socioeconomic factors, there remained tensions in Marx's interpretation of the relationship between "objective" forces and "subjective" factors, such as consciousness and individual agency. G. V. Plekhanov went some way toward reconciling these tensions in his essay "The Role of the Individual in History" (1898), arguing that exceptional figures could influence the individual features of particular historical events, but not alter their overall direction, which was determined by the development of productive forces and social relations.[17] Invoking the terminology of heroism, he maintained that a great man "is a hero, not in the sense that he can halt or change the natural course of things, but in the sense that his activities are the conscious and free expression of that necessary and unconscious course."[18]

Plekhanov's partial legitimization of the concept of individual agency was particularly relevant in Russia, where Marxism was never completely isolated from other intellectual influences, notably the legacy of the Populists. At the end of the 1860s, in a work that became a key text of the populist movement, P. Lavrov attributed great significance to "solitary fighting personalities" who could shape history by banding together to lead the less enlightened masses. This conception of heroes and crowds strongly influenced the theories of the SRs, however it also appears to have left some mark on Lenin, whose *What Is to Be Done?* alluded to the "miracles" that the energy of "even an individual person is able to perform in the revolutionary cause" and called for the emergence of "heroes" like those of the 1870s.[19] This vision of heroic revolutionaries and a tightly organized party attracted many to Lenin's cause, including Stalin, and it strongly defined the subsequent direction of Bolshevism.

Yet the party's recognition of the crucial importance of individual leaders did not, in theory, extend to support for the creation of actual *personality cults* around these figures. Marx and Engels had frowned on the "cults of personality" that proliferated within the socialist movement, including those focused on themselves and Ferdinand Lasalle.[20] Both scholars and Lenin's contemporaries have claimed that he too resisted the glorification of his own person, which intensified following Fanya Kaplan's attempt on his life in 1918.[21] According to V. Bonch-Bruevich, Lenin complained, "They exaggerate everything, call me a genius, some kind of special person . . . All our lives we have waged an ideological struggle against the glorification of the personality, of the individual; long ago we settled the problem of heroes. And suddenly here again is a glorification of the individual!"[22] He insisted that the press put a stop to the adulation, but it re-emerged with new vigor on the occasion of his fiftieth birthday in 1920. He himself adopted a low profile at the Moscow party committee's birthday celebrations, arriving after the speeches and suggesting that in future the party should find more appropriate ways to mark anniversaries. Nevertheless, as Nina Tumarkin has emphasized, Lenin's stance was equivocal: while projecting an image of modesty and simplicity, he did not make a particularly concerted effort to restrain the veneration.[23]

Lenin's death and the many ensuing initiatives to immortalize him, from the Mausoleum project to "Lenin corners," when combined with the power struggles following his demise, simply had the effect of intensifying cult-building tendencies centered on living leaders, such as Trotsky,

Zinoviev, and Stalin.[24] Although Stalin's public profile remained relatively low in the second half of the twenties, he emerged as the focus of various proto-cult practices, including individual and collective outpourings of praise and devotion addressed to him, the persecution of those deemed insufficiently respectful of his image, and campaigns to rename places in his honor. Reluctant to be seen to be encouraging such measures too enthusiastically, he made a point of distancing himself from some, but not all, of them. Upholding the conventions established by Lenin, Stalin made statements criticizing cult manifestations and presented himself as the modest and unexceptional representative of wider forces (the working class, the party). At the same time, he was prone to describing himself as the follower of Lenin and to extolling Lenin's leadership in the strongest possible terms.

Stalin was on the receiving end of a number of speeches and letters containing expressions of praise and devotion. The evidence suggests that he endeavored to restrain this adulatory discourse when it surfaced, or threatened to surface, in both public and private arenas. In June 1926, when workers' representatives from the Tiflis railway workshops greeted him too effusively, Stalin responded with a self-deprecatory speech, which was reported in the press at the time. He insisted that he did not deserve all their praise: "it turns out that I am a hero of October, and leader of the Communist Party of the Soviet Union, and leader of the Comintern, a hero (*chudo-bogatyr'*) and anything you like. This is all nonsense, comrades, and absolutely unnecessary exaggeration. That's the tone that's usually used over the grave of a deceased revolutionary. But I don't intend to die just yet." He went on to explain that his emergence as a leader was due not to any particularly outstanding personal qualities, but to his close relationship with key social forces, the workers of Russia and Transcaucasia, as well as the guidance of the "great teacher of the proletarians of all countries, com. Lenin."[25] In 1930 he issued a warning to the editor of *Pravda*, Lev Mekhlis, about the use of adulatory language in the press, observing that he had deleted words "about Stalin as '*vozhd'* of the party,' 'leader of the party,' and so on" from a forthcoming publication in the newspaper. He warned that "such eulogistic adornments do not bring (and cannot bring) anything but harm. The letter should be published without such epithets."[26]

Stalin appeared equally determined to rebuke those who used unaccept-able language in their personal correspondence with him. Some of his replies to these letters remained private, whereas others were only published much later in his *Works*. In 1926 he admonished the theoretician F. A. Ksenofontov for describing himself as a "pupil of Lenin and Stalin": "I don't have pupils. Call yourself Lenin's pupil, you have that right . . . But you don't have any grounds to call yourself a pupil of a pupil of Lenin. That's incorrect. That's excessive." Whereas the deceased Lenin could be referred to as a "teacher," at this stage Stalin could not allow himself to be represented as on a par with Lenin.[27] In the same year, he objected to the salutation "Helmsman of the Communist Party" applied to him by a certain V. Kurgavov. Stalin concluded his reply to Kurgavov's letter with a plea: "do not praise me in letters, and do not give me all sorts of titles,—it's all unnecessary and not good,—write, if you have the desire, simple letters without embellishment."[28] Responding to the letter of party member I. Shatunovskii in 1930, Stalin was very careful to distinguish between personal loyalty to the leader and loyalty to the cause he repre-sented. Shatunovskii had questioned some of the Stalin's recent pronounce-ments, while simultaneously proclaiming his complete personal devotion (*predannost'*) to him. Stalin recommended that he abandon this "un-Bolshevik" principle of devotion to individuals—"an empty and unnecessary intelligentsia trinket" (*intelligentskaia pobriakushka*)—and direct his devotion instead toward the working class, its party and state.[29]

This period also saw the emergence of a practice that would become more pronounced in the 1930s: the persecution of individuals who were disrespectful of Stalin. Stalin himself appeared anxious to counteract this tendency, writing letters in defense of various young people accused of insufficient reverence. In 1924, a twenty-two-year-old Komsomol member named Rokhel'man informed Stalin that he had been charged with disre-spect for the *vozhdi* after joking about whether the General Secretary might have traded lemons when he was an underground revolutionary. Although Stalin was allegedly intolerant of jokes about himself,[30] on this occasion he responded: "I think that the comrades are wrong to accuse you of disrespect toward so-called *vozhdi*." Purporting to find the comment inoffensive, he advised the Komsomol to desist from its persecution of Rokhel'man. In a similar incident in 1930, he defended a Leningrad student who faced a court case and exclusion from technical college on the grounds that he had used a Stalin portrait as a target in a shooting game. Stalin resolved that the other students had been wrong to punish him, and that on the contrary he deserved praise for his accurate aim![31]

Yet another practice that intensified in the second half of the 1920s was the naming of places after Stalin. This came to be regarded as a central attribute of Stalin's "cult of personality." Khrushchev highlighted it in his "Secret Speech" as an important example of how Stalin's own thirst for self-glorification boosted the cult, asking rhetorically, "and was it without Stalin's knowledge that many of the largest enterprises and towns were named after him?" Khrushchev also acknowledged that many other party leaders had participated in the practice of assigning their names to locations, which had the effect of making them seem like "private property." Noting that a leader's authority and importance was judged on the basis of how many places bore his name, he called for the elimination of such "private property."[32]

Although Khrushchev avoided mentioning the roots of this practice in the early Bolshevik period, it is clear that the naming of locations (and people) in honor of party leaders, both living and dead, was widely practiced after the October Revolution.[33] Graeme Gill argues that such toponymical changes are central to a new regime's quest for legitimacy, serving to anchor a fresh set of symbols in everyday life in a way that is perhaps more immediately effective than the obvious examples of flags, anthems, and so on.[34] In Russia, the principle that revolutionary leaders should be immortalized by means of place names was already visible after the February Revolution; for example, as early as 3 March 1917 the city Duma of Ekaterinoslav decreed that the central town square be named in honor of the chairman of the State Duma, Mikhail Rodzianko.[35] In the early years after October, it was more common for smaller locations to be renamed in this manner rather than towns or cities. Naturally, Lenin emerged as the most popular choice, and pressure to name places after him developed as early as 1918. He himself appears to have expressed disdain for the practice: when the Michelson factory took his name to commemorate the attempt on his life at the factory, he declined an invitation to attend a rally to mark both the renaming and the anniversary of the October Revolution, pointedly referring to it as the "former Michelson Factory" rather than the "Lenin Factory."[36]

Lenin's death generated a flurry of requests to name places in his honor, including major towns and cities, most notably Petrograd. The demand was so great that the government was forced to issue a ruling that such name changes could not proceed without its preliminary approval.[37] Lenin was not the only Bolshevik leader to be feted in this way in the 1920s: Gatchina became Trotsk, Iuzovka—Stalino, Elizavetgrad—Zinovievsk, and Enakievo—Rykovo. Sverdlov, Dzerzhinskii, Kalinin, and others all had their names assigned to various locations in this period.[38] According to Khrushchev's memoirs, Stalin expressed some unease about the potentially proprietorial connotations of this practice, responding negatively to a request that he send a letter of greeting to Stalino workers: "I'm not some big landowner, and the workers in the factories there are not my serfs."[39] However, in the second half of the 1920s he certainly did not turn down requests to name several factory workers' clubs in his honor, while in 1929 he informed his secretary Aleksandr Poskrebyshev that he had no objections to a large sugar plant, Sakhstroi, assuming his name, and that Poskrebyshev should respond positively to all such requests in future.[40]

The proposal to change the name of a major city, Tsaritsyn, to Stalingrad in 1925 was a rather more controversial matter. Stalin seemed particularly concerned to avoid any impression that he had either initiated the change or was anxious for it to proceed. He informed the secretary of the Tsaritsyn gubkom, Boris Sheboldaev, that he was aware of the intention to rename the city after him, but that he had also heard that Sergei Minin, one of the other leaders of the southern front during the civil war, wanted it to be called Miningrad. Underlining that he himself did not seek the change to Stalingrad, and that the whole matter had been instigated without his knowledge, Stalin suggested that if it was necessary to rename the city, it should be called Miningrad or something else. He insisted that if there had already been so much fuss about Stalingrad that it was impossible to back down over the issue, he would not wish to be drawn into it or attend the local Congress of Soviets since this might give the impression that he was actively seeking the name change. He concluded his letter, "Believe me, comrade, I do not seek glory or honor and would not like to give the opposite impression." Sheboldaev's response was suitably sensitive to Stalin's concerns, furnishing appropriate political justifications for the choice of Stalingrad: he argued that the name Miningrad would encourage "regionalism" (*mestnichestvo*) and "anarchist deviations," which were already strong in Tsaritsyn, and that whereas Stalingrad had been officially selected at party and workers' meetings, the name of Minin had only arisen informally. The choice of Stalingrad had already been approved by the CC's Nikolai Antipov, and had been confirmed by the local soviet, so the gubkom was not really in a position to back down. Sheboldaev also linked the choice of Stalingrad to the intraparty struggle, portraying it as a demonstration of their firm anti-Trotsky stance. He reassured Stalin that there was no expectation that he should turn up for the congress.[41] These justifications evidently proved satisfactory, and Tsaritsyn duly became Stalingrad.

Stalin's words vis-à-vis the Tsaritsyn/Stalingrad question were fairly typical of his approach to many of the emerging cult practices of the 1920s. Following the convention established by Lenin, he registered his verbal protest against some of the initiatives, while not actually doing a great deal to stop them. While criticizing the use of cult language, he himself used not dissimilar language to describe Lenin. In many ways, his rather contradictory approach simply mirrored the tensions within Bolshevik discourse itself. This discourse contained conflicting elements—a tendency to revere outstanding leaders on the one hand, and a countervailing anti-cult tradition on the other. To what extent did Stalin's stance change in the 1930s when the cult-building tendency became increasingly predominant?

The Cult in Maturity

Whereas the embryonic cult of Stalin was restricted to low-level and individual initiatives until roughly 1930, from then on an institutionalized and centrally orchestrated cult began to emerge. The contours of this are pretty familiar. In December 1929, Stalin's fiftieth birthday served as the occasion for great public celebration, including greetings from workers and hyperbole from close colleagues in *Pravda*.[42] Theoretical legitimation of Stalin's elevation to primus inter pares was offered in January 1930 in the form of an authoritative article in *Partiinoe stroitel'stvo*, "The Party and the Role of the *Vozhd'*," which designated Stalin "first among equals." The article highlighted the importance of outstanding leaders in the party's history, quoting Lenin's praise of the "exceptionally talented organizer"

Sverdlov as evidence of this. Stalin was described as holding "first place" within the collective leadership after the death of Lenin, while the latter's assertion that the "will of hundreds and tens of thousands of people can be expressed in a single person" was cited to support the principle of Stalin's dominance.[43]

For quite some time after this, the cult developed slowly and in a rather sporadic fashion.[44] Initially it was confined primarily to the sphere of the party. Stalin's 1931 letter to the editors of *Proletarskaia revoliutsiia* acted as an important stimulus, according to some scholars.[45] The contributions of figures such as Kaganovich should also not be underestimated.[46] From 1933 the cult acquired a new, more systematic direction, and, as Mikoian observed, veneration of Stalin increasingly came to be equated with loyalty to the party line.[47] In the midthirties, the cult underwent both qualitative and quantitative transformations, becoming both larger in scale and more populist. Stalin became "father of the peoples" as well as *vozhd'* of the party, the recipient of lavish displays of public affection and acclaim. The adulation subsided somewhat toward 1937 before reaching a new pinnacle of intensity in connection with the extravagant sixtieth birthday celebrations in 1939. The cult was muted during the first half of the war, accelerated again after victory at Stalingrad, and remained immense in the post-war years, when it also acquired major international dimensions. In short, the cult was neither static nor monolithic. Moreover, for much of the period, the cult of Stalin stood at the apex of a whole series of lesser cults focused on exceptional Soviet individuals ranging from leading Bolsheviks to film stars, record-breaking pilots, and Stakhanovite workers.

Stalin himself rarely reflected publicly on his burgeoning cult, thereby appearing to distance himself from it. However in front of select audiences he did occasionally discuss the phenomenon. He continued to promote Plekhanov's understanding of the role of the individual in history, and to voice criticisms of personality cults within the party, while at the same time justifying the persistence of ruler worship in the Soviet Union in terms of the "backwardness" of society.

Stalin never deviated from the orthodox party line, which maintained that great individuals were only important insofar as they reflected wider social forces. This was the gist of his conversation with the German writer Emil Ludwig, which took place in December 1931 and was published the following year. Having rejected Ludwig's comparison between Peter the Great and himself, Stalin proceeded to compare "his teacher" Lenin with Peter, describing the latter as a mere drop in the sea in relation to Lenin, who was the entire ocean. When Ludwig dared to suggest that he was contradicting the materialist understanding of history by acknowledging the role of outstanding individuals, Stalin countered with the argument that Marx did not deny the significance of heroic individuals—he simply maintained that they could operate only within a given set of conditions and that the great individuals were those who understood these conditions and how to change them.[48]

Cults of party leaders were another matter altogether. Stalin occasionally expressed disquiet at the proliferation of mini cults of regional party leaders in the thirties. His speech to the CC plenum on 3 March 1937 warned of the dangers of complacency within the party, the atmosphere of "showy ceremonies and mutual salutations," of "noisy self-congratulations," which were blunting vigilance.[49] The following day Mekhlis echoed this line, criticizing toadying (*podkhalimstvo*) in the press and pointing to specific examples such as the newspaper of Gor'kovskii krai, which was briefly entitled *For the Fulfillment of Com. Pramnek's Instructions*, and the *Cheliabinsk Worker*, which ended one report with the words "Long live the leader of the Cheliabinsk Bolsheviks, com. Ryndin!" He observed that a single edition of Kiev's *Proletarskaia pravda* quoted the name of the leader of the regional party organization, Postyshev, about sixty times, joking that this type of toadying was known as "*lizatoterapiia*" (boot-licking therapy). Mekhlis reminded delegates of the dictum that "modesty decorates a Bolshevik" and raised concerns about "*vozhdizm*" in the local party organizations. He then proceeded to quote Stalin's aforementioned note of 1930 calling for the removal of adulatory language from a piece in *Pravda*.[50] The message seemed to be that Stalin's own modesty should serve as the model for lesser Bolshevik leaders.

While he gave the impression of wanting to minimize cults within the party, including his own, Stalin appeared less concerned by cult tendencies within the wider Soviet population, suggesting to various audiences that these were an unavoidable symptom of cultural backwardness. To close relatives he explained that they were a necessary, if temporary, evil, to be tolerated for the sake of the "masses," who were accustomed to worshipping the tsar. In her diary, Maria Svanidze describes an impromptu visit by Stalin, accompanied by members of his family and entourage, to the new Moscow metro on 22 April 1935. Stalin was greeted by a crowd of delighted members of the public, and according to Svanidze, appeared genuinely moved by their spontaneous enthusiasm. Svanidze continued: "He once said about the ovations in his honor that the people need a tsar, that is, someone whom they can worship and in whose name they can live and work." Later, on 9 May, when they returned to the subject of the metro excursion and the popular enthusiasm it had elicited, Stalin again mentioned the "fetishism" of the popular psyche and the desire to have a tsar.[51]

Stalin offered similar interpretations to the writers Mikhail Sholokhov and Lion Feuchtwanger. When the former questioned why he tolerated the veneration of his person, he replied, "What can you do? People need an idol (*bozhka*)."[52] In the course of his well-known conversation with Stalin in 1937, Feuchtwanger confessed to finding some manifestations of the cult tasteless and excessive. Stalin agreed, claiming that he only answered a fraction of the hundreds of greetings he received and vetoed the publication of the majority, especially the most fervent. He insisted that he did not seek to justify the practice, but wanted to explain "the unrestrained, verging on saccharine enthusiasm for my person": in his view, workers and peasants were simply delighted to be freed from exploitation, and they attributed this to one individual: "of course that's wrong, what can one person do—they see in me a unifying concept, and light a fire of foolish raptures around me." Feuchtwanger then posed a very legitimate question: Why could he not put a stop to those manifestations that were causing embarrassment to some of Stalin's foreign friends? Stalin's response was that he had tried on several occasions, but that it was pointless, as people assumed he was just doing so out of a sense of false modesty. For example, he had been criticized for preventing celebrations of his fifty-fifth birthday. According to Stalin, the veneration of the leader was the result of cultural backwardness and would pass with time: "It's difficult to prevent people expressing their joy. It's a pity to take strict measures against workers and peasants." When Feuchtwanger went on to explain that what concerned him was not so much the feelings of workers and peasants, but the erection of busts and so on, Stalin proceeded to blame one of his favorite targets, bureaucrats. Claiming that officials were afraid that if they did not put up a bust of Stalin they would be criticized, he asserted that erecting a bust was a form of careerism, "a specific form of the 'self-defense' of bureaucrats: so that they are left alone, they put up a bust."[53]

While Stalin generally refrained from publicizing his comments on the subject of the cult, he made an exception for the largely sympathetic account of this conversation that appeared in Feuchtwanger's book, *Moscow, 1937*. The writer effectively paraphrased Stalin's interpretation of the cult and suggested that it was now in decline. The Russian edition of the book was published swiftly in a print-run of two hundred thousand copies—as Dmitrii Volkogonov points out: "It was probably the only book ever printed in the Soviet Union under Stalin which acknowledged the existence of the Stalin cult and provided some explanation for it."[54]

Stalin's carefully dosed-out words on this and other occasions were designed to cultivate the impression that he himself had no control over the escalating cult, that it was entirely the product of others' misguided efforts. In fact, behind the scenes, he was closely involved in the packaging of his public persona. Although not personally responsible for scrutinizing all the materials pertaining to his image (much of this work was delegated to his secretary, Poskrebyshev), he did express a particular interest in certain matters, including writings focused on his biography and the projection of his image in some core political rituals and celebrations. The remainder of the chapter will be devoted to detailed exploration of Stalin's words on these subjects.

The Biography of Stalin

The life story of the party leader came to serve as an integral part of Stalin's cult as well as those of other Communist leaders.[55] However, it is worth noting that this preoccupation with biography was not unique to communist political culture. Stimulated in part by the development of new technologies such as cinema, fascination with the biographical genre took off throughout the United States and Europe in the early twentieth century.[56] In the Soviet Union, the potential of biographical narrative was increasingly recognized by figures such as Maxim Gorky, who was well aware of the limits of historical materialism as a focus for mobilization efforts. In 1933 he founded what turned out to be a highly successful and long-lived series of biographies, *The Lives of Remarkable People.*[57] Also that year, Glavlit's B. M. Volin, the author of some brief biographical sketches of the Bolshevik leaders in the 1920s, acknowledged that the secondhand bookshops were full of illustrated collections of biographies from the pre-revolutionary period. Observing that these were very popular, especially with young people, he proposed producing similar volumes of revolutionary biographies (an excellent demonstration of how Bolsheviks quite consciously reworked pre-revolutionary culture to suit their own "neo-traditional" purposes).[58] As the 1930s progressed, biographical-hagiographical narrative rapidly came to dominate Soviet socialist-realist culture, and Soviet political culture more generally.[59]

Stalin's biography was, of course, the most crucial, but potentially the most problematic of all. Producing suitable narratives about his life was bound to be a torturous process, in part because of the demands of accommodating Marxist-Leninist ideological conventions concerning the role of the individual. There was a fine line between what was deemed to be useful publicity about Stalin's life and what was considered irrelevant and ideologically flawed. Where the line was to be drawn was not immediately obvious: it changed over time and was heavily dependent on the inclinations of Stalin himself, who exerted considerable influence over narratives relating to both his political biography and his personal life.

Stalin's Political Biography

Until the mid–1930s, Stalin created the deliberate impression that he wished to restrict the circulation of material about his life—it is certainly not the case that biographies about him were "appearing thick and fast" at this time.[60] Brandenberger has detailed the problems involved in the production of a Stalin biography in this period: Ivan Tovstukha's 1927 pamphlet was the only one available at the end of the 1920s, and although a new study was promised in 1929, it took another decade for a full Soviet-produced biography to appear.[61] Stalin himself appears to have intentionally thwarted some earlier efforts. In 1930 the influential journalist Mikhail Kol'tsov prepared a short biography, *The Life of Stalin*, for publication by *Krest'ianskaia gazeta.*[62] Kol'tsov apparently wanted Stalin to look at it, but no one dared to show it to him—Ordzhonikidze said, "he will beat you and thrash me." The proofs were sent to Glavlit, which forwarded them to

Stalin's secretariat. Stalin subsequently notified Kol'tsov by phone: "I've read the little book about Stalin—you praise me too much . . . it's unnecessary. Come and see me in the summer and I'll tell you what to include." A proposal to adapt the book for children (which would apparently have simply required replacing "Stalin" with "uncle Stalin") evidently did not materialize, and the manuscript appears to have languished in Stalin's personal archive.[63] Similar initiatives by Gorky and Emel'ian Iaroslavskii also failed. Iaroslavskii's attempt to produce a biography in 1935 was obstructed by Stalin, who responded curtly to his request for access to documentary materials: "I am against this venture with my biography. Maxim Gorky has similar intentions and asked me for help. But I have backed away from this. I do not think that the time has yet come for 'a biography of Stalin.' "[64]

Stalin also vetoed other projects aimed at publicizing his life story in the first half of the thirties. In July 1933 he expressed opposition to the Society of Old Bolsheviks' proposal for an exhibition focusing on his biography. On this occasion, he explicitly invoked the term "cult of personality," arguing that "such undertakings lead to the strengthening of the 'cult of personality,' which is harmful and incompatible with the spirit of our party." In the same year he forbade the Ukrainian party organization from publishing a brochure about his life to celebrate the fifteenth anniversary of the Komsomol. In 1935, when the journal *Obshchestvennoe pitanie* requested permission to publish a piece entitled "Stalin in the Sal'sk Steppes" to mark the seventeenth anniversary of the Red Army and fifteenth anniversary of the 1st Cavalry, Stalin opposed the project on the grounds that "my role is exaggerated, and there is little about other people."[65]

While initiatives focused exclusively on the person of Stalin were restricted at this stage, an increasing deluge of Stalin-centered writings dedicated to various aspects of party history did appear, notably Beria's infamous *On the History of the Bolshevik Organizations in the Transcaucasus* (1935).[66] Although Stalin himself did little to curtail this trend, he did periodically comment on and edit texts in a way that suggested he wished to be seen to be downplaying the significance of his own role vis-à-vis that of the party/CC and to be endorsing a correct Marxist-Leninist approach to historical writing.[67]

When the Institute of Marx-Engels-Lenin (IMEL) produced theses in connection with the thirtieth anniversary of the party in 1933, Stalin deleted a few of the most extravagant references to his own contributions. He amended another IMEL work dating from 1934, "Lenin—The Great Founder of Socialist Construction," which was packed with eulogies to Stalin and emphasis on his closeness to Lenin, removing his name from references to the "Lenin-Stalin party" and the "teachings of Lenin and Stalin."[68] A 1935 *History of the VKP(b)* that described him as the "wise leader of all the toilers" merited the comment: "An apotheosis of individuals? What happened to Marxism?" And when Stalin encountered mentions of both his own and Ordzhonikidze's contributions to the Revolution in Mamiia Orakhelashvili's 1936 biographical study of Ordzhonikidze, he wrote in the margins comments like: "And the CC? And the party?"[69]

Elements of this approach survived even when the cult was at its zenith in the late 1930s and the 1940s. Increasingly interested in theoretical matters, Stalin liked to reflect more explicitly and systematically on the need for what he termed "scientific history."[70] He was particularly concerned that the canonical party history of the Stalin era, the *History of the All-Union Communist Party (Bolsheviks): Short Course* (1938), should not exaggerate the importance of individuals.[71] This may appear counterintuitive, given that the book is often regarded as a quintessential example of how Stalin inflated his own cult—Khrushchev certainly portrayed it as such in his "Secret Speech."[72] Stalin of course bears ultimate responsibility for the *Short Course*'s ludicrously distorted and hagiographical rendition of his personal contribution to party history, and yet, paradoxical though it might seem, when discussing and editing the work, he still tried to sustain the impression of wishing to restrict the glorification of his person and to warn of the dangers of undue preoccupation with the role of individuals.

The *Short Course* was ultimately rather less focused on the role of the *vozhd'* and his colleagues than it would have been without Stalin's editing of Pospelov and Iaroslavskii's early drafts. The initial texts contained much factual material, including, at Iaroslavskii's suggestion, the detailed prerevolutionary biographies of Stalin and other Politburo members. Stalin insisted on removing these and shifting the emphasis to the theoretical framework. For example, he cut out an entire section entitled "Bolshevik Activity in the Years of Reaction." This considered Lenin's role in emigration and his own experiences of arrest and exile in the period 1908–13, and discussed the revolutionary biographies of other Bolsheviks, notably Sverdlov and Molotov. It commented explicitly on the personal experiences of Bolshevik leaders and their "will to struggle during terrible conditions," highlighting episodes such as Stalin's bravery while in Baku's Bailovsk prison, which was presented as a source of inspiration for his fellow prisoners.[73] Stalin evidently deemed this focus on individuals and their heroism to be superfluous and incompatible with the "scientific" approach of the book, replacing it with his own theoretical contribution entitled "On Dialectical and Historical Materialism."

Stalin's many other amendments included the elimination of a lengthy section dealing with his contributions to the Transcaucasian party organization in 1907–12 and its supposed significance for the party as a whole. He retained the reference to what was described as his "leadership" of the CC's new Russian bureau formed at the 1912 Prague Conference, but deleted an entire paragraph narrating how, after escaping from exile, "he traveled around the most important regions of Russia, built up the Bolshevik Party, organized *Pravda*, and led the Duma fraction . . .," etc. He also cut out several references to his role from the chapter on the October Revolution, including discussion of his contribution to the development of the constitution of the RSFSR. The "Brief Conclusions" to this chapter on the central episode of Bolshevik history are remarkable for the absence of any mention of Stalin—for example, the reference to his return from exile was removed from the sentence: "Decisive moments in the history of the party of this period [February–October 1917]: Lenin's return from emigration (and Stalin's from exile), Lenin's April theses, the April conference of the party and sixth party congress."[74]

Several of Stalin's colleagues duly complained about his revisions when asked for their comments. Both Iaroslavskii and Pospelov lamented the disappearance of references to the leader's contributions, particularly his activity in the Transcaucasus, while Mikoian also suggested that the latter should have received a fuller treatment. The revisions and the responses they elicited thus served to reinforce the image of Stalin as supremely modest: Iaroslavskii commented explicitly that the amendments were a sign of his "exceptionally great modesty, which decorates a Bolshevik."[75]

Stalin went to great lengths to justify the depersonalized approach of the *Short Course* in terms of the need to provide a properly "scientific" history for the new "Soviet intelligentsia" that was currently being promoted in the media at his instigation.[76] He explained to propagandists in September 1938 that a work which exaggerated the significance of individuals, as opposed to the laws of historical development, would be unsuitable for leading cadres. He observed that hitherto most history textbooks had been written according to a model of "educating people through characters (*na litsakh*), eulogizing these characters." In its initial conception, the *Short Course* had concentrated on individuals "who conducted themselves heroically, who escaped from exile so many times, who suffered so much for the cause, etc., etc." This was the wrong way to teach cadres, who should be educated instead on the basis of ideas and theory: "If there is that knowledge, then there will be cadres too, but if people don't have that knowledge—there won't be cadres, just an empty space. And what will individuals offer? I don't want to oppose individuals to ideas, although of course we have to speak about individuals, but only insofar as it's necessary. The essence is not in individuals, but in ideas, in the theoretical tendency."[77] He reiterated these points in a speech to the Politburo two weeks later: "History focused on individuals provides nothing for the education of our cadres, or very little, history should be focused on ideas. That's why there is little in the *Short Course* on individuals, that's why all the material is arranged according to the key points in the development of our party, in the ideas of Marxism-Leninism. This educates people more, it leads to less interest in particular individuals and *vozhdi*, it's more beneficial for the forging of the consciousness in order to become a real Marxist-Leninist."[78]

Stalin voiced similar concerns about the dangers of exaggerating and distorting the role of individuals in his intervention regarding an article by the historian M. Moskalev, "I. V. Stalin at the Head of Baku Bolsheviks and Workers in 1907–8," one of the numerous hagiographical writings that appeared around the time of the leader's lavish sixtieth birthday celebrations. Published in the journal *Istorik-Marksist* in January 1940, it was then summarized in *Pravda* by E. Gorodetskii on 4 February. On 10 February Stalin wrote a letter complaining about the article to the editors, authors, and members of the Politburo. In its concern with historiography and the use of primary sources, this letter was somewhat reminiscent of his more well-known letter to the editors of *Proletarskaia revoliutsiia*, although in contrast to the latter, this one was clearly marked "Not for publication."

Accusing the authors of factual inaccuracies and exaggerations, of violating "historical truth," Stalin firmly rejected claims that he had served as editor of the oil workers' newspaper *Gudok* and denied that Voroshilov's role in Baku had been so prominent: "Comrade Voroshilov was only in Baku for a few months, and then left Baku without leaving visible traces behind him" (this was, perhaps not coincidentally, a time when Voroshilov's reputation was under attack following the disasters of the Winter War with Finland).[79] Stalin also cast aspersions on the veracity of the memoirs used to support the article's propositions, suggesting that these might have been "dictated" by journalists (quite a well-founded assumption, as it happened!). Iaroslavskii, the editor of *Istorik-Marksist*, responded to Stalin's allegations on 27 April, furnishing a number of sources for the article's claims, including Stalin's official biography, Soviet encyclopedias, the Baku press, as well as the memoirs of the official editor of *Gudok*, A. Samartsev, and others. Iaroslavskii expressed regret that such evidently unreliable sources had been employed. Two days later, Stalin replied, disputing this evidence and reiterating his point that historians should approach so-called memoirs with greater skepticism. Maintaining that neither he nor Voroshilov needed to have false services ascribed to them, since they had enough real ones, he proceeded to express contempt for flattery and sycophancy: "Clearly this is necessary for the careerist-inclined authors of 'memoirs' and the authors of some suspicious articles 'about *vozhdi*' who want to promote themselves by way of excessive and sickening flattery of the leaders of party and government. Do we have the right to cultivate in our people these feelings of servility and groveling? Clearly not. Indeed it is our duty to exterminate these shameful and servile feelings in our people . . . Sycophancy is incompatible with scientific history."[80]

The potential of such hagiographical writing to inculcate servility was a theme to which he returned when commenting on his own biography after the war. Following various unsuccessful attempts to produce a Stalin biography, *Iosif Vissarionovich Stalin: A Short Biography*, prepared under the auspices of IMEL, finally appeared at the tail end of 1939, just in time for Stalin's sixtieth birthday celebrations.[81] Stalin was given a copy of the manuscript but alleged that he had "no time to look at it" (such pointed indifference was revealing in itself).[82] After the war, however, he did find time to consider an updated second edition, which was presented to him in 1946. He asked Pospelov to arrange a meeting to discuss it, and the latter's notes of the meeting, along with the recollections of one of its authors, V. Mochalov, provide some indication of how he approached the complicated question of his own biography.[83] With its fantastically distorted version of Soviet history, the *Short Biography*, like the *Short Course*, has often been considered a prime example of Stalin's thirst for self-aggrandizement, and indeed in many ways it was just that; however, once again, Stalin made a point of criticizing some of the work's cultic excesses and warning of the inherent dangers of personality cults.[84]

According to Mochalov, Stalin began the discussion of the biography by focusing on Lenin rather than himself, arguing that a good medium-sized biography of Lenin was necessary for the majority of people who studied Lenin not from his works, but from his biography. In Pospelov's version, Stalin remarked that the masses, the "simple people," could not begin the study of Marxism-Leninism on the basis of Lenin and Stalin's collected works—they needed biography. He suggested that a new Lenin biography should be prepared as "this is a proven way of helping the simple people begin their study of Marxism."[85] At the outset, then, he made it clear that he regarded biography not as an end in itself but as a means for popularizing Marxist-Leninist ideas.

He then went on to discuss the second edition of his own biography, complaining that it contained many mistakes and that the tone was poor and "SR-ish"—for example, he had been ascribed all manner of "teachings." Objecting to the excessive concentration on the individual, he observed that there was "a lot of praise in this biography, exaggeration of the role of the individual. What should a reader do after reading this biography? Go down on their knees and pray to me." He pointed out that this would not educate people in Marxism and stressed that they did not need idolaters. Stalin proceeded to comment on the erroneous "teachings" about war, communism, industrialization, collectivization, and so on that had been ascribed to him, as if Lenin had had nothing to say on these matters, concluding, "We have the teaching of Marx and Lenin . . . we don't need any additional teachings." He suggested that people were being turned into slaves ("*liudi rabov vospityvaiut*"), before anticipating with some prescience the repercussions of his own death: "and if I'm not here? . . . You're not inculcating love for the party . . . When I'm not around, then what?" Mochalov recorded that he continued to expatiate at length on this theme of educating people in love for party, love for ideas rather than worship of a single individual.

Turning to the book itself, Stalin was critical of the lavishly illustrated edition with which he had been presented, complaining that it made him nauseous. He praised the depiction of the Great Patriotic War included in the new edition, but objected to the exaggeration of his own role in some periods, such as the Baku period, where it appeared that the Bolsheviks had done nothing before his arrival. He argued that at other stages too, individuals such as Dzerzhinskii, Frunze, and Kuibyshev had made critical contributions, and he emphasized the importance of cadres in general. Stalin then insisted that he be portrayed as Lenin's pupil, as he had made quite clear in his conversation with Emil Ludwig: "I am Lenin's pupil. Lenin taught me, and not the other way round. No one can deny that I am Lenin's pupil. He laid down the road, and we go down this well-trodden road."[86]

Stalin's own editorial amendments to the manuscript followed similar lines. He removed some of the ubiquitous references to "under Stalin's leadership," "Stalin led," "*stalinskii*" (e.g., "Under Stalin's leadership the Caucasian union committee tirelessly propagandized the decisions of the third party congress . . .," "Stalin led the work of the [twelfth] congress," "the Stalinist policy of industrialization"). He deleted "all" from a phrase about how from the end of 1921 Stalin came to lead "all the work" connected with party leadership, replacing it with a rather more plausible "the main work." In a section on the home front during the war, he shifted some of the emphasis from his leadership to the role of the people, referring to the industry "created by the efforts of our people" as opposed to "under the leadership of comrade Stalin." In another sentence that read "all the peoples of the Soviet Union came to the defense of the motherland at the call of Stalin," he replaced "Stalin" with "the party."[87]

He frequently added the names of other (mostly deceased) leaders to the narrative of pre-revolutionary Bolshevik history. For example, he added to the sentence "Stalin—a member of the Transcaucasian committee of the RSDWP—leads its work" the words "along with com. Tskhakaia." He noted that the December 1904 strike in Baku was conducted under the leadership of Stalin "and Dzhaparidze," he added Sverdlov's name to his own and that of Molotov in the description of their revolutionary work in St. Petersburg, and he clarified that in 1917 Stalin "together with Molotov" led the work of the CC and the Petersburg party committee.[88]

Stalin also insisted on the correct portrayal of his relationship with Lenin, adding several phrases describing himself as the "outstanding pupil of Lenin" and Lenin as his "teacher" and "educator." He incorporated a section which claimed that he refused to allow himself to become conceited, citing as evidence his claim to Ludwig that he was "only Lenin's pupil." He made sure to add the words "after Lenin" to the start of one of the final sentences in the biography: "After Lenin no other leader in the world has yet had to lead such many millions of masses of workers and peasants as I. V. Stalin."[89]

Finally, Stalin slightly cut back on the ubiquitous references to his personal brilliance and greatness. He substituted the references to his "teachings" with other phrases such as "theses" or "theory." He sometimes deleted epithets such as "genius" and "brilliant"; for example, he removed the phrase "the work of genius" from a description of his "Foundations of Leninism" and deleted the words "with truly brilliant foresight" which preceded the sentence "com. Stalin uncovered the machinations of the igniters of war against the USSR." After his revisions, "great commander" became "com. Stalin," "Generalissimus Stalin" became "comrade Stalin," and the absurdly florid line "The beloved *vozhd'* and teacher of the toilers, the brilliant theoretician and leader of the Bolshevik Party, the experienced helmsman of the Soviet state and the greatest commander" became the comparatively modest "*vozhd'* and teacher of the toilers."[90]

Despite these editorial interventions by Stalin, the revised *Short Biography*, and other similarly hagiographical works, remained full-blown eulogies to the leader. At the same time, Stalin was careful to observe certain conventions in the treatment of his political biography. His contributions continued to be represented in a somewhat impersonal manner, as part of the broader trajectory of the party and Soviet state, and a residual notion of collective leadership survived. Particularly in the late 1940s, Stalin insisted that excessive concentration on his person would make it much harder for the party to sustain any legitimacy after his death. This desire to contain the focus on the leader within acceptable parameters was equally evident in Stalin's approach to the dissemination of material regarding his personal life.

Stalin's Personal Life: Childhood, Homes, Family

In his concern to keep the portrayal of the "personal" sphere of his childhood, family life, and domestic arrangements within certain limits, Stalin also adhered to well-established Bolshevik norms. Jeffrey Brooks has shown how personal life was marginalized in party discourse in the 1920s: "Bolsheviks promoted a world in which actual families and homes counted little . . ." He points out that this changed somewhat in the 1930s with the partial rehabilitation of the family and domestic sphere, not as a genuine private sphere, but as yet another arena for the promotion of the cult.[91] Although Stalin contributed toward this rehabilitation, permitting, for example, the (limited) publication of materials devoted to his mother and daughter, many taboos remained concerning the presentation of his personal life.

Stalin's *Short Biography* contains only a couple of laconic initial paragraphs devoted to his childhood:

> Joseph Stalin (Dzhugashvili) was born on December 21, 1879, in Gori, a town in the province of Tiflis. His father, Vissarion Dzhugashvili, a Georgian peasant from the village of Dido-Lilo in the same province, was a shoe-maker by trade, subsequently employed as a wage laborer at the Adelkhanov footwear factory in Tiflis. His mother, Ekaterina Dzhugashvili, was the daughter of a serf, named Geladze, from the village of Gamnareuli.
>
> In the autumn of 1888 Stalin was enrolled in the Gori Ecclesiastical School, and in 1894 he graduated from this school and entered the Tiflis Theological Seminary.[92]

This represented the official interpretation, which did not, however, preclude the publication of certain memoirs and literary depictions of the young Dzhugashvili. While Stalin preferred to avoid drawing attention to his early years, there were evidently political advantages to distributing some information, especially material aimed at young people for whom the leader was supposed to serve as an exemplar (it is interesting in this connection that Kol'tsov had tried to repackage his biographical study as a work aimed at children).[93] The editor of *Kolkhoznye rebiata* was probably being perfectly sincere when he informed Poskrebyshev in 1937 that he received many letters from children and teachers requesting popular biographical material about Stalin and complained that textbooks and brochures on party history did not provide enough.[94]

Information about Stalin's early years was disseminated primarily via a few select memoirs. The production of memoirs about Stalin developed into a major industry in the 1930s at the initiative of what Miklos Kun terms the "Beria brigade." As we have seen, Stalin was suspicious of such reminiscences, and only a small fraction was ever published.[95] The Georgian newspaper *Zaria vostoka* played a particularly active part in bringing this material to light; for example, in August 1936 it published a selection of reminiscences about Stalin's youth by M. Titvinidze, P. Kapanadze, G. Glurdzhidze, and D. Gogokhiia. A 1937 volume entitled *Tales of Old Workers about the Great Vozhd'*, based on memoirs originally published by *Zaria vostoka*, also contained accounts of his childhood. Many of these recollections were later republished, along with some unpublished material, in a special edition of *Molodaia gvardiia* devoted to Stalin's sixtieth birthday, while some were recycled in Iaroslavskii's 1939 biography of Stalin. Unlike the dry IMEL biography, Iaroslavskii's rather more animated *On Comrade Stalin* devoted an entire first chapter to Stalin's childhood and youth.[96]

There are numerous examples of Stalin's apparent sensitivity toward accounts of his childhood. In April 1939 *Komsomol'skaia pravda* requested permission to publish flattering memoirs by one of his oldest friends, G. Elisabedashvili, who had attended his school in Gori and seminary in Tiflis. The tone of these recollections was particularly hyperbolic, even by the standards of the cult in the late 1930s. Stalin was depicted as a young hero, adored by all: "Who won at 'Krivi' [a boxing game]? Soso! . . . Who could throw a ball the furthest? Soso! At the same time who read the most books? Soso! . . . Who sings better and more pleasantly than everyone? Soso!" Although these memoirs had been approved by the Tbilisi branch of IMEL, Stalin vetoed their publication, declaring that "apart from everything else, the author has shamelessly lied."[97] However, less effusive extracts from Elisabedashvili were published elsewhere. Evidently, Stalin's approach to the publication of memoir material centered on his early years was not always entirely consistent; for example, accounts that had been published in Georgian were occasionally deemed inappropriate for publication in Russian. In August 1936, *Komsomol'skaia pravda* requested permission to reprint the *Zaria vostoka* publication "The Young Years of the Great Vozhd'," but this request appears to have been refused.[98] In 1950 Stalin vetoed the publication of a Russian edition of P. Kapanadze's *Recollections of the Childhood and Youth of the Leader* on the basis that it contained "many fabricated and completely inaccurate elements." The memoirs had previously been published in Georgian and extracts in Russian had already appeared elsewhere.[99]

As well as objecting to the publication of certain memoirs, Stalin also expressed strong disapproval of various literary depictions of his early years that seem to have been produced without his prior authorization. The best-known example is his refusal to allow the publication of V. Smirnova's *Tales of Stalin's Childhood* by the Komsomol publishing house Detizdat in February 1938. Pointing out that the book was full of distortions and inaccuracies, Stalin referred explicitly to its potential to inculcate the "cult of personality, *vozhdi*, infallible heroes." He described this theory of masses and heroes as an "SR theory," which was unacceptable to Bolsheviks, and advised that the publishers burn the book.[100] In 1940 he objected similarly to E. Fedorov's *Kartalinskaia Tale*, which centered on the childhood and youth of Stalin. He complained to Zhdanov in September 1940 that "Com. Pospelov acted stupidly and unacceptably by commissioning a book about me from Fedorov without my agreement (and knowledge). Fedorov's book should be liquidated as rubbish and Pospelov given a good dressing down." Following this incident Goslitizdat notified Poskrebyshev about another book, K. Gamsakhurdiia's *Childhood of the Vozhd'*, edited by the Georgian party secretary and published in Tbilisi to mark Stalin's sixtieth birthday. Pospelov had suggested that it appear in Russian and proofs had already been prepared, but Stalin overruled this proposal.[101]

Stalin's desire to regulate the portrayal of his personal life extended to the treatment of places he had inhabited in various periods. He sometimes tried to discourage public interest in his former residences; for example a 1934 draft *Pravda* article on Stalin's exile in Turukhansk that included a picture of his house and its interior elicited Stalin's curt resolution

"Ru-bbish [*Che-pu-kha*]."[102] In 1935 *Molodaia gvardiia* published an account by G. El'-Registan of the writer's travels through the USSR. El'-Registan had written about several locations where Stalin had lived while in exile, however the journal was not permitted to publish these sections.[103]

Nor did Stalin always succumb to pressures from local authorities to memorialize his places of residence through the creation of museums (*dom-muzei*, or house museums, based on Lenin's homes had existed since the 1920s).[104] At the end of 1935, Western *oblast'* requested permission to restore the wing of the house in Smolensk where Stalin had stayed in 1919 in order to turn it into a museum to commemorate the civil war and the leader's part in this. Stalin asked that they not make a fuss about the fact he had lived there and certainly not undertake any "restoration" of the wing.[105] Even when such *dom-muzei* were eventually established (no doubt with Stalin's authorization) he insisted on imposing some restrictions on the way they were publicized in the press. When his birthplace in Gori was opened to the public in November 1937, TASS news agency asked to report on the opening of the museum and the flocks of visitors it had already attracted. Stalin refused to give his permission, evidently preferring not to draw attention to the matter. In January 1939 the agency asked to publish a telegram relaying the news that a hundred thousand people had visited the house in 1938, but once again Stalin's resolution was an emphatic "No!" In the same year he also denied TASS permission to publish telegrams about the Stalin *dom-muzei* in Leningrad and the restored house in Vologda where he had stayed while in exile.[106]

Another area of his personal life that Stalin generally preferred to keep out of the media spotlight was his family. His wife kept a deliberately low profile prior to her death in 1932, and while the promotion of family values in the mid–1930s was accompanied by occasional public glimpses of his mother and children, especially his daughter Svetlana, Stalin continued to take care over how they were portrayed, intervening when he considered boundaries had been overstepped.[107]

The leader's unusually well-publicized visit to his ageing mother in Tiflis in October 1935 was striking for its novelty. This was the first time Stalin had visited her in many years, and he was obviously not averse to the principle of according some publicity to the visit. When Poskrebyshev asked him to confirm a *Pravda* correspondent's report of the visit, which described his mother's rapture at seeing her son and discussed in some detail the contents of her room, Stalin replied simply that it was not his job to confirm or deny what was in the report.[108] However, the press obviously went beyond what he considered legitimate public interest. On 27 October *Pravda* reported an interview with his mother in which, among other things, she described how Stalin's father had taken him out of school to train him as a cobbler, despite all her protestations, and how she had later succeeded in returning him to education. Incensed by the press's intrusions, Stalin instructed Politburo members to stop "the vulgar rubbish" that was appearing in the central and local press, including alleged interviews with his mother and "all sorts of publicistic rubbish, even portraits."[109]

Stalin was not opposed to the very occasional portrayal of his children, particularly when these were included in child-oriented publications.[110] In 1935 the German journalist Maria Osten asked if she could include a photograph of Stalin and Svetlana in her *Hubert in Wonderland*, a book due to be published in Russian and other languages about the experiences of the German boy she and her partner Kol'tsov had adopted and brought to the USSR.[111] Stalin agreed to this request. He also permitted a picture of his children to be published in *Pionerskaia pravda*, telling Svetlana to "treasure it."[112] Although visual rather than verbal examples, these cases are nonetheless representative of the general trend that such glimpses of Stalin's personal life were the exception rather than the rule. He aimed to minimize excessive public interest in Stalin, the man, and there was no concerted attempt to humanize his image. Most accounts of his life were strikingly colorless and devoid of personal detail. This was, as others have aptly observed, a deliberately cultivated "cult of impersonality."[113]

Rituals and Ceremonies

Stalin took great interest in shaping the way his image was projected in the various forms of political ritual and ceremony that were an integral part of the post-revolutionary order.[114] As the cult intensified and his image became increasingly pervasive, Stalin often intervened to urge a calculated measure of restraint. Documentary evidence of his interventions is particularly plentiful for three areas: political meetings and ceremonial receptions; the slogans issued to mark May Day and the anniversary of the October Revolution; the practice of renaming places in honor of the *vozhdi*, which escalated dramatically in the 1930s.

Meetings and Receptions

Political gatherings on a variety of scales served as important "stages" for the performance of the cult, particularly when Stalin himself was in attendance.[115] Involving much pomp and ceremony, they provided an opportunity for speeches, resolutions, toasts, and interminable ovations honoring Stalin and other party leaders. Until the cult acquired mass dimensions in the mid–1930s, such occasions were usually confined to the party. In the case of formal party meetings, Stalin seemed particularly determined to adhere to Bolshevik conventions concerning the treatment of the leader and to avoid exaggerated displays of veneration.

Stalin expressed some irritation at the culture of congratulations and ovations that prevailed within the party even during the 1920s. At the fifteenth party congress in 1927 he attacked the complacency of some Bolsheviks who liked to swim with the current, failed to look ahead, craved a constant "celebratory and triumphal" (*prazdnichnoe i torzhestvennoe*) atmosphere and celebratory meetings, wished "for there to be constant applause, and for each of us to take turns as honorary members of all kinds of praesidia."[116] He depicted these practices as detrimental to the proper conduct of party work, a shield behind which incompetent officials could protect themselves. Similarly, at a CC meeting devoted to the coal industry in 1931, he criticized party leaders who engaged in what he described as "theater" rather than real business: "When you write 3-yard resolutions in which you praise Soviet power, the CC, the *vozhdia, vozhdei, vozhdiam*, decline and conjugate the names of *vozhdi*—it's theater, declarations, empty, unnecessary 'for the general line,' 'for the *vozhdi*,' 'for the CC' and the devil knows what else. It's nonsense, it's playing games."[117]

On several occasions during the 1930s Stalin publicly condemned the prolonged ovations accorded to him at party gatherings. He voiced irritation particularly when these occurred at meetings of leading cadres, whom he suspected of clapping loudly rather than taking their responsibilities seriously. At a time of particular political tension in October 1932, he rebuked applauding delegates attending a meeting of sovkhoz directors: "why are you applauding—you should be ashamed," before proceeding to accuse them of ignoring the plan for meat procurement: "if a plan is drawn up, it's not there to be applauded, but to be fulfilled."[118] Likewise, when Zhdanov introduced him to defense industry workers in June 1934 to the habitual "stormy applause, which turned into an ovation," Stalin responded, "it always happens like this with us; when they want to turn a serious matter into a joke, they start to applaud." He warned them against complacency: "You are very kindly disposed and welcome your *vozhdi*—however damned they may be—with applause. With us, rays of joy and kindness etc. never leave our faces. But we have capitalist encirclement, so we're surrounded by enemies, enemies who are civilized and more cultured than us . . ."[119] Addressing the November 1934 CC plenum, he reminded delegates: "comrades here in the CC it's not customary to applaud. It's not a mass meeting [*miting*] or a conference."[120] He urged similar restraint at the discussion of the *Short Course* with party propagandists in 1938: "Comrades—this isn't a mass meeting here. Why are you wasting so much time applauding? I didn't expect that qualified people would applaud. It's not right . . . We don't need praise here, but help, help in the form of corrections, in the form of comments, in the form of instructions arising from your experience as propagandists. That's what's needed, not praise and applause."[121]

Stalin seems to have been anxious to demonstrate his respect for Bolshevik protocol in these matters. According to Dmitrii Shepilov, he distinguished between practices that were acceptable at ordinary celebrations or meetings and those that were suitable for plena of the CC and Politburo. Shepilov describes how some CC members started to applaud when Stalin appeared on the stage at the plenary meeting of the CC in October 1952. Stalin "at once gestured at them in displeasure, muttering something like, 'Never do that here.' " Shepilov suggests that this represented continued observance of the legacy of Lenin, who, he claims, opposed personality cults.[122]

Whereas intense adulation of Stalin was deemed inappropriate for the party's business meetings, it was tolerated at the much more overtly ceremonial congresses, *soveshchaniia* (conferences) and Kremlin receptions (*priemy*) presided over by party leaders and attended by groups ranging from shock

workers and Stakhanovites to Red Army commanders and Comintern
officials.[123] A vital part of the cult, creating the impression of direct communication between Stalin and Soviet citizens, these events were widely
reported in the press and illustrated with photographs of the leader among
"his" peoples, often members of minority nationalities. They were particularly frequent in the period from November 1935 (following Stalin's return
from vacation) to the middle of 1936.[124] In April 1936 Stalin felt obliged
to apologize to Gorky for not having written to him sooner, explaining
that he had been terribly busy: "they've been wearing me out with endless
soveshchaniia and *priemy* of delegations."[125] The occasions evidently proved
to be *too* popular, for in January 1936 the Politburo was compelled to send
out a letter forbidding the spontaneous influx of delegations descending
on Moscow and demanding celebratory *soveshchaniia* and receptions with
the *vozhdi*. Such "*stikhiinost'*" (spontaneity) did not accord with the leadership's aspirations for central control, and it was announced that delegations arriving without permission would be sent home, including those
recently arrived from the Udmurt and Kirghiz republics.[126] Stalin clearly
became disenchanted with the meetings, for in November 1936, when the
Turkmen leadership asked if it might send a delegation to report to him
about the overfulfillment of cotton production, the Politburo, at Stalin's
instigation, warned local party organizations not to dispatch delegations
to Moscow as they had done the previous year since there was no opportunity to receive them.[127] Kremlin receptions did continue in the late 1930s,
but tended to have a less obviously populist character.[128]

   The tone of these ceremonial events was naturally more extravagant than
that of the party's business meetings. Despite, or perhaps because of this,
Stalin still felt the need periodically to use these opportunities to convey
to delegates his vision of the relationship between the *vozhdi* and other
social forces, and to warn against unduly exaggerating the significance of
the former. Some, but not all, of the words he uttered on these occasions
were published in *Pravda*. At the first All-Union Congress of Kolkhoz
Shock Workers in February 1933 he reminded his audience that the time
had long gone when *vozhdi* were considered the sole creators of history,
for the history of states and nations was now decided primarily by millions
of workers.[129] He reiterated this message at a Kremlin reception for Red
Army participants in the 1934 May Day parade: "I don't deny that *vozhdi*

have significance, they organize and lead the masses, but *vozhdi* without the masses are nothing. People like Hannibal, Napoleon were ruined as soon as they lost the masses. The masses decide the success of any matter and the fate of history. Everything depends on whom the masses follow. Among you there are sitting brave, young people. We may not know the names of most of you, but you are the strength and power of our country." Voroshilov's response to these words was to accentuate, on the contrary, the role of *vozhdi* and of Stalin in particular: "Masses without real *vozhdi* are powerless to decide matters. We are happy that we have such a *vozhd'*— the great, beloved, our teacher, comrade and friend com. Stalin."[130]

Addressing graduates of Red Army academies at a Kremlin reception in May 1935, Stalin objected to the notion that all Soviet achievements should be attributed to the *vozhdi:* "we talk too much about the contributions of leaders, the contributions of *vozhdi* . . . It's not just a matter of *vozhdi'*." He then announced the important new slogan "cadres decide everything."[131] He conveyed a similar message to leaders and Stakhanovites of the metal and coal industries in October 1937, noting that it was customary to make toasts to leaders: "That, of course, is not bad. But apart from the big leaders there are also the middling and small leaders." He went on to utter his famous words about how important it was for leaders to have the trust of the people, proclaiming that "leaders come and go, but the people remain. Only the people are immortal."[132]

Stalin expanded on the role of leaders in history, and his own role in particular, at a small Kremlin reception held in Voroshilov's apartment following the parade to celebrate the twentieth anniversary of the Revolution in 1937.[133] A much more private and exclusive affair than the receptions discussed hitherto, it was attended by Politburo members and other officials, including the Comintern head, Georgi Dimitrov. In such a relaxed and intimate setting, Stalin probably felt able to expatiate on this subject at greater length than usual. The dinner incorporated typically elaborate rituals—the toastmaster, Mikoian, apparently made thirty toasts! Voroshilov then gave the floor to Stalin, who spoke about the strength and unity of the Soviet state, before toasting Lenin, "our forefather." Dimitrov responded, recalling the greatness of Lenin, and observing how fortunate it was that he had been followed by Stalin, whom he proceeded to toast. Stalin then argued that Dimitrov was incorrect from a Marxist perspective, and, echoing his words of the previous week, declared that "individuals always appear if the cause that gives rise to them is not rotten. Individuals come and go, the people remain forever, and if the cause is not rotten, then the individual will appear."

He went on to interpret the struggle with the various opposition groups in the party in this light. In his view, the opposition had failed because it did not take account of the will of the "average [*seredniatskaia*] masses," the "backbone" of the party. Unlike most official histories dating from this time, Stalin downplayed his own significance in the period after Lenin's death, when, in his words, the prominent figures in the party had been people like Trotsky, Bukharin, Tomskii, Rykov, Zinoviev, and Kamenev. He himself was merely in charge of organizational work in the CC, "what was I compared with Il'ich? A poor specimen [*zamukhryshka*]." Molotov, Kalinin, Kaganovich, Voroshilov were all unknowns. So how did it transpire that all these unknowns were able to prevail over the more prominent members of the party? According to Stalin, it was because "the party itself wanted it." Acknowledging that he was a poor orator compared with the leaders of the opposition, he argued that the latter had not taken into account the feelings of the party masses who valued actions above speeches.

No doubt with the recent purges of the Red Army in mind, he explained that if an army and state had good officers, but poor generals, the officers would overthrow the generals:

> The people will put forward those who will lead them to victory, individuals in history come and go, the people remain and are never mistaken. If there hadn't been that backbone in the party, that basic of basics, those figures could have won, it's not the personality [*lichnost'*] that matters. It's very difficult to say who raised [*vospital*] me. Did you raise me, or I you? You say that I am an outstanding person, it's not true. A righteous fear of failing the trust the masses and people have placed in you in the struggle with those figures—that's what was decisive, the fear of failure, and we emerged as leaders. Comrades Molotov, Voroshilov, Kalinin, Kaganovich, Mikoian, Chubar', and others worked intensively.

Stalin concluded this speech with a toast to the average man (*seredniak*), the officer corps.

As was by now the custom following Stalin's displays of self-effacement, Voroshilov and Dimitrov responded by praising his contribution. Dimitrov said that it was now clear to him that without the backbone nothing would have succeeded, but this backbone would not have formed in such quantity and quality, or in such short a time, if Stalin had not encouraged it. Stalin then explained further that in 1927 720,000 party members had voted for the CC—"us *zamukhryshki*," while 4,000 to 6,000 voted for Trotsky and 20,000 abstained. He argued that the party's officers could only be created if they were led properly, and that in Russia they developed from 1900 thanks to favorable conditions in the country; the "brilliant Lenin" led them in concrete economic and political circumstances. Communist Parties in other countries were weak because they lacked the officers. Stalin concluded by reiterating his message about the need for leaders to fear failure if they were to retain popular trust. In an intriguing commentary on Kirov's murder, he added, "We needed Kirov's sacrifice to understand that. Kirov with his own blood opened the eyes of us idiots (excuse the blunt expression)."

In this important speech at what was a crucial juncture in Soviet history, Stalin thus outlined his own path to power in characteristically impersonal terms. Arguing that "it's not the personality that matters," he was quick to downplay his personal talents, acknowledging that he did not possess charismatic qualities such as oratorical brilliance. The only attributes to which he laid claim were the capacity for hard work and an understanding of and commitment to the desires and needs of that crucial force, the "average masses."

While this reception was a small, private affair, other gatherings with Stalin in attendance were accorded considerable publicity. Stalin took great care over how they were reported in the press, editing draft articles for *Pravda* to ensure that certain principles were observed. *Pravda* editor I. Bogovoi was apparently well aware of the leader's preferences. He noted that when Stalin received a huge ovation at a reception to mark Lenin's death held at the Bol'shoi Theater in January 1935, Stalin sat down, indicating that the applause should cease, but it only increased, compelling him to stand up again. Bogovoi suggested cutting back on the description of the ovation in the *Pravda* report, claiming that Stalin "doesn't like it. He did not even permit a welcome for him at the session."[134] In his own editing of the draft reports Stalin would sometimes (although not always) eliminate or tone down the references to the ovations that accompanied these occasions. He also made attempts to dilute some of the most effusive cult language and to redirect attention towards other leaders and participants.

When the original title of a draft article for *Pravda* in November 1933 referred to a delegation of kolkhozniks from Odessa *oblast'* being received by Stalin alone, Stalin himself added the names of Kalinin, Molotov, and Kaganovich.[135] He also corrected the text of a report of a conference of leading agricultural workers in December 1935, deleting the words: "For a long time the cries of welcome do not die down: 'Long live our *vozhd'* and teacher com. Stalin!' 'Hurray!' 'Long live com. Molotov!' 'Long live com. Voroshilov!' '*Vozhd'* of the people—com. Stalin—Hurray!' "[136] The tone of the final article was somewhat more restrained as a result. Likewise he removed some of the references to Stalin from the *Pravda* report of a *soveshchanie* of leading workers of MTS and agricultural organs that took place in January 1936, and appended Voroshilov's name to the end of the text that had hitherto included "hurrays" addressed only to Molotov and Stalin.[137]

Stalin edited the report on the Kremlin reception for participants of the 1937 May Day parade, eliminating the phrase "great was the joy of the people who had the happiness of seeing their own Stalin and his government," and toning down the sentence "Comrade Voroshilov sounds inspirational when he speaks of the greatest man of our times who is loved without limits by our Red Army and entire Soviet people—great and dear Stalin," replacing it with the more modest: "Then comrade Voroshilov speaks about Stalin who is loved by the Red Army and entire Soviet people." He added references in Voroshilov's speech to Lenin's role as party leader, but did not alter the words about his own role as Lenin's successor (although he did strike out Voroshilov's description of Stalin as a "man of genius"). He also deleted an extravagant-sounding sentence: "The participants of the 1 May parade expressed the thoughts and feelings of the entire Red Army, wholeheartedly dedicated to and loving without limits their friend and teacher, *vozhd'* of the peoples, Stalin." The report mentioned the concert laid on at the reception, and Stalin insisted on including some of the names of individual performers.[138]

He amended the report of the October 1937 Kremlin reception of leaders and Stakhanovites of the metal and coal industries in a similar fashion, deleting some cries of "Long live beloved com. Stalin" and the phrase "leader of the peoples," while adding applause and ovations to the speeches of other Politburo members. At this reception Kaganovich, who clearly enjoyed inventing elaborate toasts to Stalin, made an impressively lengthy and florid toast, invoking the images of "furnace worker" and "steel founder" to describe Stalin, who had been responsible for destroying "the harmful admixtures and dross from the metal of the accursed Trotskyite-Bukharinite wreckers and spies, the hirelings of Japanese and German fascism, and has smelted steel of a higher and unprecedented category—the wonderful united cadres of the builders of socialism, Stakhanovites, and shock workers . . . The great steel founder of our socialist construction leads our socialist furnace without accidents and slowdowns . . ." The toast, which continued in that vein, was eliminated entirely by Stalin.[139] Interestingly, however, he did not seem to object to the publication of a similarly lengthy and elaborate toast made by Kaganovich at the reception of railway workers in July 1935 that was based on the metaphor of Stalin as the "first engine driver of the Soviet Union."[140]

Vladimir Nevezhin suggests that Stalin may have deleted the October 1937 toast because he disliked the imagery—as will become clear in the following chapter, manual labor was out of favor with Stalin by this stage—or because he felt more secure in his position and no longer required such adulation from Kaganovich.[141] Certainly Kaganovich's words conflicted with the anti-cult messages that were being propagated in 1937 at occasions such as the February-March plenum. They would also have seemed particularly jarring when juxtaposed with the words Stalin had uttered at this reception: "leaders come and go, but the people remain." Clearly it would be possible to speculate endlessly about Stalin's motives for making particular modifications to the reports of these events. What is certain, though, is that he played an active role in the management of his image in the press, consistently intervening to keep—and be seen to be keeping—the focus on his person within acceptable proportions.

Slogans

The annual celebrations to celebrate May Day (1 May) and commemorate the anniversary of the October Revolution (7 November) were the major highlights of the Soviet political calendar, and the series of slogans (*lozungi*, or, from 1943, *prizyvy*) devised by the CC to mark the festivities thus constituted a further important element of Soviet political ritual.[142] In their quantitative analysis of May Day slogans, Yakobson and Laswell suggest that "the history of the Soviet Union could easily be written in terms of changing slogans."[143] This may overstate the case; however, it is true that the slogans served as a kind of ideological weathervane, and, as fundamental political texts, were the object of Stalin's close scrutiny.

The Bolsheviks had always attached great significance to correctly formulated slogans. Lenin recognized that a phrase such as "All power to the Soviets!" could possess great mobilizing power in the right circumstances.[144] Stalin too devoted much attention to the question of slogans and their wording. In his 1923 article "On the Question of the Strategy and Tactics of the Russian Communists," he defined a slogan as "a concise and clear formulation of the immediate or distant goals of a struggle given by a ruling group," asserting that in wartime military slogans could prove as decisive as artillery: "Successfully formulated decisions that reflect the goals of a war or a particular battle, and are popular among the troops, sometimes have a decisive significance at the front as a means of inspiring an army to action, support its morale, and so on. Corresponding orders [*prikazy*], slogans, or appeals to the troops have as much importance for the whole course of the war as first-class heavy artillery or rapid tanks." Slogans, he continued, carried even more weight in the political arena as a means of handling millions of people with differing needs and wants. In his view, the function of slogans varied according to their context: depending on the nature of its audience, and the immediacy of its goals, the same slogan could be designed for propaganda, agitation, or action, or it could become a directive (a direct appeal). It was important not to confuse these tasks.[145]

The formulation of the key May Day and October Revolution slogans was always a major operation for the party leadership. From the late 1920s, the slogans were drafted by the CC's Agitprop department, then considered and amended by the Orgburo, before being presented to the Politburo, which assumed responsibility for the ultimate revisions. While some other Politburo members did make changes and suggestions at this stage (particularly prior to the mid–1930s), usually only Stalin undertook any substantial revisions. The drafts were even sent to him during his vacations: Kaganovich wrote to him on 23 October 1934, "I didn't want to burden you, but in view of their importance I'm sending you the draft slogans and ask that you send your opinion by telegraph."[146]

The slogans themselves followed a reasonably predictable and formulaic structure in the Stalin years. They usually began with international appeals, which were followed by domestic appeals, including addresses to specific groups such as workers, peasants, and women, and they concluded with general slogans on the subject of the party and its leadership. As will become evident in the next chapter, Stalin amended draft slogans on a broad range of issues; however here we will concentrate on the revisions directly associated with his own image. Stalin's interventions followed the customary pattern, that is, with some notable exceptions, he rarely sought to inflate the cult; on the contrary he aimed to create an impression of wishing to curb the excesses of others.

Prior to the late 1930s, Stalin's name was usually absent from the published slogans, except in the form of quotations attributed to him. However, from the end of the 1920s, the important concluding slogans began to focus more consistently on the leadership of the party and CC rather than on the workers, as had often been the norm. Stalin himself added a final party-centered slogan to the draft for May Day 1929: "Raise higher the banner of the VKP, the organizer of October! Workers and toilers, unite around the VKP, the leader of socialist construction."[147] The emphasis on Lenin also increased markedly around this time: quotations from his speeches and writings featured more frequently, and in 1930 there appeared a slogan addressed to the Young Pioneers, which would recur in various incarnations on subsequent anniversaries: "Children of the revolution, Young Pioneers! Be prepared to carry on and complete the cause of Il'ich!"[148] Slogans for November 1930 and 1931 described the party as "organizer and *vozhd'* of the victorious socialist revolution," and as "Leninist" after one of Stalin's additions ("Under the leadership of the Leninist party and its Central Committee, forward to new victories!")[149] The terminology remained similar in the concluding slogans of 1932–33, although for some inexplicable reason Stalin chose to eliminate the description of the party as "*vozhd'* " from the drafts for May 1932.[150]

The practice of including Stalin quotations only commenced in 1932. Before then, attempts to cite his words were overruled by Stalin himself;

for example, he deleted from the draft for November 1931 a slogan that mentioned the "six conditions of com. Stalin" (a reference to his speech of 23 June 1931). Although he eliminated a further reference to his "six conditions" from the draft for May 1932, over the course of this year other quotations attributed to him did begin to creep in, often at the instigation of his close colleagues.[151] The slogans for May 1932 incorporated— apparently without any objections from Stalin—his statement about the defense of the Soviet Union: "We don't want one inch [*piad'*] of others' land. But our land, we won't give away a single inch [*vershok*] of our land to anyone." This practice was encouraged by other Politburo members, such as Postyshev, who proposed that the slogan also be added to the November 1932 series.[152] At Voroshilov's initiative, Stalin's words about the need for Bolsheviks to master technology (taken from his speech of 4 February 1931) were included in an additional slogan addressed to the Red Army for November 1932.[153] As the cult entered a more intense phase in 1933, quotations from Stalin's speeches and writings began to proliferate. Stalin himself did make some effort to set limits on this practice, deleting a couple from the May 1933 slogans and insisting that Kaganovich remove two of his utterances and a further reference to his "six conditions" from the drafts for November 1933.[154] On both these occasions, however, other Stalin quotations remained in place.

It is striking that Kaganovich also tried to incorporate Stalin's name in another way in 1933, coupling it with that of Lenin in the November slogan addressed to the Pioneers, which became: "Young Pioneers—children of October! Strengthen proletarian discipline in the school. Master the basics of science. Be prepared to continue and complete the great cause of Lenin-Stalin, the cause of world October!"[155] This innovation was retained in the published version. It is unclear whether Stalin endorsed it, as a draft amended by him is not available. He certainly did not raise the issue in his abovementioned letter to Kaganovich, although this may simply have been because he had not seen the revisions at that point. The slogan was clearly out of line with the prevailing conventions, which only allowed for Stalin's name to appear in the context of quotations and did not yet include the Lenin-Stalin linkage. This phrase did not recur in published slogans for several years, which suggests it may have been yet another example of Kaganovich's personal zeal for cult-building in the early 1930s.

From 1934, as the focus of party rhetoric shifted decisively in favor of outstanding individuals from the past and present, the concluding slogans also began to highlight individuals more explicitly.[156] Stetskii's draft of the May 1934 slogans ended: "Under the banner of the Bolshevik Party and its Leninist CC—forward to new victories! Long live the great, invincible banner of Marx, Engels, Lenin, Stalin!" However, Stalin objected to this formulation, decoupling his own name from the holy trinity of Marx, Engels, Lenin.[157] This became the standard ritual for the next few years, with Stalin usually deleting his own name from the quartet and from the phrase "the cause of Lenin-Stalin" (*delo Lenina-Stalina*). For example, the draft for November 1934 culminated on an extravagant note: "With the banner of Marx-Engels-Lenin-Stalin we were victorious in the battles for the October Revolution. With the banner of Marx-Engels-Lenin-Stalin we were victorious in the battles for socialism. With the same we will be victorious in the proletarian revolution throughout the whole world. Long live the great and invincible banner of Marx-Engels-Lenin-Stalin!" Stalin eliminated most of this, leaving only the final phrase, which he changed to "Long live the great and invincible banner of Marx-Engels-Lenin!" He also deleted his name from the formula "the cause of Lenin-Stalin," which had been included in the slogan addressed to Pioneers.[158] He modified the May 1935 slogans in a similar fashion, very deliberately removing his name from the phrases "party of Lenin-Stalin," "theory of Marx and Engels, Lenin and Stalin," "banner of Marx-Engels-Lenin-Stalin," and "cause of Lenin-Stalin." However, he left in words about "Leninist-Stalinist irreconcilability" toward what he termed the "enemies of Leninism" (his more pointed substitute for "deviation"), as well as generally sharpening the focus on Lenin and Leninism, adding "Long live Leninism" to the final slogan.[159] The slogans followed a similar pattern from then until November 1937: quotations attributed to Stalin remained, but Stalin continued to delete his name from phrases such as "Marx-Engels-Lenin-Stalin."

The twentieth anniversary of the Revolution constituted something of a watershed in the portrayal of the Lenin-Stalin relationship, as well as in the official interpretation of Soviet history more generally.[160] From then on, it became acceptable to couple Stalin's name with Lenin's in slogans. Stalin did not modify the words in the November 1937 draft: "Proletarians throughout the world! Oppressed peoples of the colonies! Higher the banner of Lenin-Stalin, the banner of victorious socialist revolution," nor did he touch a further reference to "the cause of Lenin-Stalin." However, he did adhere to the practice of decoupling his name from Marx-Engels-Lenin in the final slogan.[161] The published May 1938 slogans included for the first time (apart from the anomalous case of 1933) "the cause of Lenin-Stalin" in the slogan addressed to Pioneers, while in November 1938 yet another significant shift occurred: Stalin did not attempt to amend the crucial concluding slogan "Long live the great unbeatable banner of Marx-Engels-Lenin-Stalin! Long live Leninism!"[162] The new formula "Marx-Engels-Lenin-Stalin" was retained until the war.

Whereas in the immediate pre-war years Stalin seemed content with the new prominence of his name in Soviet domestic slogans, including the direct connection with Marx, Engels, and Lenin, he continued to express reservations about the way he was depicted in slogans designed for international consumption. Dimitrov records Stalin's displeasure with a section of the draft Comintern proclamation for May Day 1939 that read "Long live our Stalin! Stalin means peace! Stalin means communism! Stalin is our victory!" He accused its chief editor, Comintern secretary Dmitrii Manuilskii, whom he suspected of having had Trotskyite leanings and of being generally unreliable, of "toadying."[163] Stalin insisted that his name be removed from "under the banner of Marx-Engels-Lenin-Stalin" in the Comintern draft, although it had been included in the CC's slogans for May 1939 (with his authorization).[164] He explained: "It is not a question of *prestige*, but a question of *principle*. Slogans are our own 'national business,' and in this case we slipped up; there was no call to write them like that! But this is *an international appeal:* here we have to put things more precisely!"[165] He was clearly acutely sensitive to the potential nuances of the Stalin image, adopting different strategies depending on whether slogans were oriented toward a domestic or an international audience.

As has been amply demonstrated, Stalin generally preferred to restrict the use of his image in slogans or allow others to take the initiative when it came to including his name. However, there were some notable exceptions to this pattern. With war on the horizon, Stalin himself encouraged the personification of the party and its ideology. In May 1940 he chose to replace the words "cause of communism" with "cause of Lenin-Stalin" in the proposed Pioneer slogan, as well as completely eliminate the reference to socialism: "Children are our future. Let us raise Soviet children as fiery patriots of the socialist motherland, ready to continue the struggle for the cause of communism" thus became "Children are our future. Let us raise Soviet children as patriots of our motherland, ready to continue the struggle for the cause of Lenin-Stalin."[166] The emphasis on the party, socialism, and communism continued to decline markedly during the Great Patriotic War as the focus moved to the Red Army, the motherland, and victory over the enemy. In November 1941 the drafts contained only a couple of references to the party, including the final slogan "Long live the All-Union Communist Party of Bolsheviks—the organizer of the struggle for victory over the German-fascist robbers!" At this critical juncture in the war, there appears to have been some temporary uncertainty as to how much prominence the *vozhd'* should be accorded, for his name was virtually absent from the drafts, apart from a few quotations attributed to him. Stalin decided to rectify this, adding to the final slogan the words "party of Lenin-Stalin," the term he had also employed in his famous speech of 3 July 1941.[167] Subsequent wartime slogans included habitual references to the "party of Lenin-Stalin" and "under the banner of Lenin, under the leadership of Stalin."[168]

The end of the war ushered in another period of rhetorical instability that lasted until 1947. In 1945 a new slogan was added to the draft for the anniversary of the October Revolution, which was innovative in its exclusive focus on the person of Stalin rather than his relationship with the party and/or Lenin: "Long live the *vozhd'* of the Soviet people—the great Stalin!"[169] However, Stalin removed this slogan from the May 1946 series, while retaining the usual slogan "Under the banner of Lenin, under the leadership of Stalin." He left "Long live the *vozhd'* of the Soviet people—the great Stalin!" in slogans for November 1946 and May 1947, but in November 1947 appeared to change his mind yet again, deleting it, as well as substituting "government" for "Stalin" in the slogan "Glory to the kolkhozniks, MTS and sovkhoz workers, agricultural specialists who honorably fulfill the obligations they have made to comrade Stalin."[170] After this unstable period, the slogans of the late 1940s and early 1950s began to exhibit a more uniform pattern. Stalin's name continued to appear in the phrases "party of Lenin-Stalin" and "under the banner of

Lenin, under the leadership of Stalin" in the two important concluding slogans. All the slogans addressed to children contained the words "the cause of Lenin-Stalin,"[171] apart from the intriguing and anomalous case of the October 1952 slogans—the last series to be issued before Stalin's death—which exhorted children to prepare to be "true Leninists, loyal sons of our great motherland" rather than the usual "active fighters for the cause of Lenin—Stalin."[172] In contrast to earlier years, when Stalin had exercised careful, if not always consistent, control over the process of formulating slogans, in his final years in power he appears not to have been actively involved in undertaking any significant revisions to his image in these texts.

Naming Places

The final cult practice to be considered in detail is the naming of places in honor of Stalin (and, for the purposes of comparison, other *vozhdi*). This included both renaming, as in the case of Tsaritsyn to Stalingrad discussed above, and the addition of the phrase "named after Stalin" (*imeni Stalina*) to existing names. Although this was a well-established practice, it only began to acquire truly epidemic proportions from the mid–1930s. While Khrushchev attributed this escalation to competition among Politburo members to "claim" the most factories, towns, and so on, Malte Rolf shifts the perspective to the interests of the local authorities who, he argues, vied to acquire the symbolic capital associated with the names of Stalin and other *vozhdi*: "The center of centers, Moscow, definitely profited from this dynamic and would have found ways to stop it, if it had wanted to put an end to it. The center had to do very little on its own to keep the process going. The process worked smoothly as an autonomous and decentralized cycle of inflation."[173] Although Rolf is quite right that "the center" allowed the epidemic to spread, it is also the case that Stalin and some other Politburo members did make a number of attempts to regulate and restrict some of its most egregious manifestations. Stalin's well-known resistance to Ezhov's attempt to rename Moscow "Stalinodar" is entirely consistent with his concerns about other less-familiar initiatives.[174]

The process of naming places in honor of Bolshevik leaders that began after the Revolution gained momentum following the sudden deaths of Kirov and Kuibyshev. The Politburo was responsible for sanctioning the deluge of requests from the localities, and these became regular items on its agenda in these years. After Kirov's assassination, Leningrad led the way in early December 1934, proposing a raft of measures to immortalize their local chief, including the renaming of key locations in his honor. The party organizations of Moscow and Ukraine soon followed, and the practice of requesting name changes to commemorate Kirov spread rapidly throughout the USSR without letting up for the next couple of years.[175] Kuibyshev's demise in January 1935 acted as an additional catalyst, and before long the toponymical changes were occurring on such a scale that confusion sometimes ensued: for example, both Samara and Kainsk were renamed Kuibyshev in early 1935, which inevitably led to postal difficulties (it was later suggested that Kainsk become Kuibyshevsk).[176]

While the names of deceased leaders, such as Kirov and Kuibyshev, were bestowed frequently and uncontroversially in the mid–1930s, name changes involving living *vozhdi* also escalated dramatically at this time.[177] Stalin was the obvious and most popular choice, but his close associates were recognized too: Kaganovich was particularly in vogue at this stage, while leading Politburo members such as Mikoian, Ordzhonikide, Voroshilov, Molotov, Kalinin, and Kosior also figured prominently. Others of lesser stature who attracted interest included the likes of Piatakov, Demchenko, Khrushchev, Khataevich, Mirzoian, Kosarev, and Beria.

Although the requests for toponymical changes were normally approved automatically and without comment, Politburo materials do betray the existence of a measure of concern and tension regarding the scale and nature of the practice. For example, Stalin was clearly anxious to ensure that decisions about name changes be framed in accordance with Bolshevik conventions. In November 1935 the Politburo considered a request to rename Lugansk "Voroshilovgrad," a name it had apparently borne informally for some time. The proposal was phrased in terms of the commemoration of a decade of Voroshilov's tenure as Commissar of Defense. Stalin disapproved of this wording on the grounds that it was not Soviet practice to mark the fact that someone had been commissar or secretary for ten years. He proposed a less personalized formulation, suggesting that the name change mark the forthcoming anniversary of the October Revolution instead.[178] In this way, the renaming was firmly identified with Voroshilov as a symbol of the Revolution rather than with his personal status.

There was also some concern that name changes should not be accorded too much publicity. Sometimes a resolution would be labeled "not for publication," or "for publication in the local press," such as the decision to bestow Stalin's name on two sovkhozy in Kazakhstan in October 1935, which was marked "not for the central press." This reluctance to publicize the resolutions was of course particularly evident when the process involved figures who had fallen out of favor: when Ambrolaurskii district, renamed Enukidze district in August 1933, had its original name restored in September 1935 following Enukidze's disgrace, the Politburo stipulated that this should only be mentioned in the local press.[179]

Most significantly, perhaps, Stalin and other Politburo members were increasingly inclined to veto proposals for name changes in their own honor. There were recent precedents for this: in February 1935, Stalin responded to alleged "rumors" that workers at the new Moscow metro wished to name the metro after him with a suggestion that they nominate Kaganovich instead: "In view of the categorical disagreement of com. Stalin with such a suggestion, and in view of the fact that com. Stalin equally categorically insists that the metro be named after L. Kaganovich, who is the immediate and direct leader of the successful organization and mobilizational work of the construction of the metro, the CC VKP(b) asks the collective of the metro not to pay attention to com. L. Kaganovich's protests and take a decision to name the metro after com. L. Kaganovich."[180]

Other Politburo members also adopted this practice. Mikoian seems to have been one of the most consistently vocal objectors: when asked to approve the name change of Veleso-Lopanskii district to Mikoian district at the end of September 1935, he wrote, "Why is this necessary? I am against."[181] The following month, after Kuibyshev Building Institute requested permission to take his name, Mikoian again expressed his opposition, and asked for the item to be removed from the agenda, remarking, "In general lots of these suggestions have started arriving recently, which is bad."[182] (Mikoian's objections notwithstanding, the changes went ahead.) While Mikoian appears to have been exceptional in the frequency and consistency of his objections in 1935, by the following year other *vozhdi* were beginning to voice similar reservations. When it was proposed in March that Mizinskii district in Gor'kovskii krai be renamed Voroshilovskii district, Voroshilov wrote, "I don't see any need for this." In April Molotov noted alongside a proposal that Vostochno-Sibirskii krai rename Zabaikal'skii railway in his honor, "Against. I ask to discuss this at the Politburo"; Stalin overruled himself resolving, "Molotov is wrong. I suggest that the decision is formalized." Even Kaganovich opposed a proposal to name the Katavskii plant after himself in March. On 7 April the Politburo considered several requests for name changes including two involving Kaganovich, who wrote, "I vote against the first paragraph [which referred to him] and ask the Politburo not to accept it." In May he also tried to veto a couple of proposals to rename locations on the railways in his honor. Around the same time Ordzhonikidze wrote on proposals to name a factory in Perm and the town Enakievo (formerly Rykovo) after him: "there's no need for this."[183]

Stalin also expressed growing unease at the scale of the phenomenon. In March 1936 he resorted to his previous strategy of suggesting alternatives to the use of his own name, proposing that Khar'kov Electromechanical Plant bear the name of another leader, such as Kalinin, Molotov, Voroshilov, Kosior, or Postyshev. Other Politburo members disagreed on the grounds that the plant had held Stalin's name informally for eight years following a decision by the local authorities and that it was simply seeking to formalize this.[184] The general concern about the sheer number of name changes reached a climax in May 1936. On 5 February Ivan Akulov had sent the Politburo requests received by the Central Executive Committee for several renamings: a factory in Vitebsk after Stalin, a Simferopol sovkhoz after Kalinin, a sanatorium of the Central Asian railway after Kaganovich, and a factory in Makeevsk after Postyshev. Stalin responded: "As regards the naming after Stalin, I'm totally against. As for the others, I do not object." His lukewarm words "I do not object" served to convey his general lack of enthusiasm, and Molotov resolved that the question of reducing the torrent of name changes be discussed at the Politburo. On 20 May 1936, Stalin raised the item "On renaming towns, etc.," as a result of which the Politburo agreed to ban the renaming of towns, small towns, district centers, and railway stations from 1 June 1936.[185]

Despite this signal from the center, requests to rename towns and other locations continued to pour in. In particular, the accusations leveled against "rightists" in the autumn of 1936 prompted a deluge of proposals for name changes, such as the removal of Tomskii, Rykov, and Bukharin's names from sugar refineries in the Odessa, Voronezh, and Chernigov regions, and their replacement with those of E. I. Veger, Mikoian, and Kosior.[186] Stalin continued to rebuff some of the suggestions: in September 1936 he vetoed a personal appeal by the secretary of the Cheliabinsk obkom, Ryndin, for Cheliabinsk to become "Kaganovichgrad," despite Ryndin's insistence that the name Cheliabinsk was associated with backwardness.[187] Politburo members also continued to voice objections to name changes in their own honor. In the second half of 1936 Ordzhonikidze was a popular choice as he celebrated his fiftieth birthday in October, but he spoke out against some of the proposals, such as the renaming of a Narkomzdrav RSFSR research institute to which he "categorically" objected.[188] Mikoian also continued to reject various suggestions.[189]

The continuing failure to stem the tide of requests, along with the complications and instability arising from the Great Terror, may have prompted a further decree of 26 October 1936 "On the renaming of *krais*, regions, towns, districts, factories, institutes, sovkhozy, kolkhozy, etc.," which informed party committees that "in light of the fact that recently there has been a bacchanalia of suggestions for renaming *krais*, regions, towns . . . the CC VKP(b) suggests ceasing further attempts at renaming."[190] In the aftermath of this decree numerous requests for name changes were refused, such as the proposal from Donetsk obkom that one of the region's mines be named after Ezhov: this item was removed from the agenda of the CC Secretariat in connection with the decree of 26 October.[191]

From then on, the name changes became notably less frequent. Some did still proceed, often those involving places that had borne the names of enemies of the people, or those aimed at honoring the new hero of the moment, Ezhov. For example, on 22 November 1936, the Politburo sanctioned the Ukrainian CC's request for the Slavutsk Border Guard to take Ezhov's name, while on 23 October 1937 Stalin expressed his enthusiasm for a proposal to name a Krasnodar college after Ezhov instead of the disgraced Sheboldaev, writing an emphatic "Correct!" on the voting paper.[192] Stalin continued periodically to intervene to regulate the changes. In March 1937 he rejected a proposal to name Rykov district and village in Sakhalin region after the recently deceased Ordzhonikidze, suggesting that they should bear Kirov's name instead.[193] The immediate pre-war period witnessed many name changes involving Molotov, particularly in the wake of his appointment as Commissar of Foreign Affairs in 1939. This process reached a climax in connection with his birthday celebrations in March 1940 when he was awarded the Order of Lenin and honored with several name changes. Stalin's editing of the decree on the renaming of Perm and the Perm region after Molotov sheds interesting light on how he wanted the practice to be viewed in this period. The original decree was expressed in terms of the need to "satisfy the request of workers of community organizations of Perm and the region to rename them Molotov and Molotov region in connection with the fiftieth birthday of the head of Sovnarkom, Molotov." Stalin substituted the original phrase "to satisfy the request of" with "we will meet the wishes of [*idem na vstrechu pozhela-niiam*]," implying that this was a reluctant concession. He also completely removed the reference to Molotov's fiftieth birthday, no doubt uneasy about the excessive personalization of the process.[194]

As with so many other manifestations of the cult, Stalin strove to convey an impression of some discomfort at the escalating use of his name (and those of his colleagues). Further evidence of this is his deletion from the proofs of the second edition of his biography the sentence: "Therefore many industrial giants in which the country takes pride bear Stalin's name."[195] While it is indisputable that many places did, with his sanction, bear his name (the trend, if anything, only increased after the war), he sometimes preferred not to draw too much attention to this fact or be perceived to be wholeheartedly endorsing the practice.

Some of modern history's most extravagant leader cults flourished in the Soviet Union in the first half of the twentieth century. However, the existence of these cults was always the source of some tension for the Bolsheviks. The notion that a leader should be aggrandized in such extreme fashion sat awkwardly with the party's stated commitment to Marxism and seemed uncomfortably redolent of the SRs' proclivity to exaggerate the significance of heroic personalities.

Although Lenin did not make a particularly concerted effort to rein in the incipient cult tendencies focused on his self, he adopted a modest persona and voiced principled objections to the glorification of the individual. His words set an important precedent for his successors to follow. Before the emergence of his own full-blown cult, Stalin also denigrated various cult practices, without doing very much to terminate them. Once his cult was in full swing in the 1930s, he was under even more pressure to cultivate a modest self-image and to choose his words carefully to mini- mize any impression that he was encouraging the blatant adulation. Stalin embarked on a quite delicate balancing act. On the one hand, he tacitly endorsed the cult, allowing it to escalate to quite epic proportions, largely thanks to initiatives undertaken by others and without any need for specific encouragement or much positive guidance from him. At the same time, he let it be known that he was criticizing and restraining it in line with Bolshevik norms.

Stalin himself was only one of many people involved in the packaging of his image for public consumption, but his interventions played a decisive role. We now have a much clearer picture of the significance he attached to these matters. He exercised quite careful supervision over issues he considered important, prescribing detailed changes designed to ensure that the cult remained within certain boundaries. He was particularly concerned to monitor writings relating to his political biography and personal life and to scrutinize the projection of his image in major political rituals and ceremonies. Although it is true that Stalin did relatively little to halt the ever-increasing emphasis on his leadership, at certain stages he did make some effort to limit the diffusion of his image. Moreover, at his insistence, the cult remained a largely impersonal phenomenon, minimally focused on the personality and personal life of the *vozhd'*. The cult of the leader continued to be linked to a broader cult of the party, and Stalin strove to retain a residual notion of collective leadership, insisting that the contributions of other Bolshevik figures were not entirely overlooked. Stalin's utterances thus played an important role in the shaping of the cult. Ultimately, his balancing act proved quite successful, containing some of the ideological and political tensions of the cult, as well as enabling the system to outlive him, in the short term at least.[196]

5

THE WORKING CLASS

Like the great leader, the heroic industrial worker served as a central symbol of the Soviet order. "Class" was of course essential to the Bolsheviks' worldview, and the "working class" or "proletariat"[1] of Bolshevik imagination was revered as an inherently virtuous and collectivist "messiah," destined to preside over the inevitable downfall of capitalism. The "proletarian" Revolution of October 1917 was presented as a vindication of Marxist claims, providing incontrovertible proof of the historical significance of the working class. In the first years after the Revolution, the heroic figure of the manual worker dominated Soviet iconography, while affirmative-action policies were designed to encourage the real as well as symbolic progress of this newly privileged "ruling class" under the "dictatorship of the proletariat."[2]

Yet, although the exalted status of the imagined proletariat was never in doubt, there remained some ambivalence about actual flesh-and-blood workers that pre-dated 1917 and persisted long after the Revolution.[3] Lenin's well-known hesitations concerning the political maturity of the working class as a whole encouraged him to depend on an elite vanguard of "advanced" proletarians who would guide the "backward" toward the promised land of socialism. Once in power, he expressed increasing frustration at the relative backwardness of the Russian worker, describing him unflatteringly as a "bad worker compared with people in advanced countries" and advocating the use of strict discipline within the factories. Other prominent leaders, including Trotsky, shared some of Lenin's misgivings.[4]

This sense of Russian/Soviet workers' backwardness became a leitmotif in Bolshevik discourse, sitting uncomfortably alongside the idealized image of the conscious proletarian. At the same time, tension mounted over the question of just how much significance should be attached to an individual's working-class origins and/or service at the bench (*stazh*). Although theoretically wedded to the principle of proletarian hegemony, many leading Bolsheviks simultaneously opposed the "fetishization" of working-class identity and advocated a less socially restrictive approach to matters such as party membership and selection for higher education.[5] All of this simply compounded the ambiguities surrounding the status of workers in the "workers' state."

How did Stalin discuss the sensitive matter of the Soviet working class? Memoirs such as those of Kaganovich indicate that among close colleagues at least, he was sometimes inclined to adopt a dismissive tone: when asked by Felix Chuev for his opinion of Khrushchev, Kaganovich replied that the latter was able and had been promoted by him. "You see, Stalin said to me: 'You have a weakness for the working class.' I had a weakness for promoting workers because at that time there were few able ones. He was an able worker, without doubt."[6] To what extent was this comment typical of Stalin's stance? His published speeches and writings certainly suggest that whereas before the 1930s he was inclined to paint an optimistic picture of a cohesive, heroic proletariat, his approach changed with the onset of industrialization. From then on he started to represent workers in a more variegated light, moved steadily away from the notion of proletarian hegemony, and concentrated on raising the status of other social groups, particularly the intelligentsia. However, the relative paucity of comment on these matters in his published *Works* has limited our understanding of this important subject.

Recent archive-based studies have begun to cast more light on the various different ways in which Stalin chose to portray the working class. David Priestland, for example, has situated Stalin's ideas about workers in the context of broader currents in Bolshevik thought that he labels "revivalist" and "technicist." According to Priestland, Stalin's stance oscillated according to whether he was operating predominantly in technicist or revivalist mode.[7] With the benefit of a more comprehensive range of archival sources, we are now in a position to explore the evolution of Stalin's approach more systematically. Exactly what kinds of messages about Soviet workers did he seek to convey in different periods, and why? How did he choose to frame the discussion of sensitive issues such as poor labor discipline and low productivity? How did he handle the contentious issue of class origins? What precisely did Stalin contribute to the presentation of the "status revolution" that resulted in the workers' "fall from grace" and the new ascendancy of the intelligentsia?[8] The unpublished materials provide more complete answers to these questions.

The Heroic Ruling Class? Workers and NEP

Bolshevik ambivalence toward the working class appeared particularly pronounced during the partial return to capitalism represented by NEP. The existence of private enterprise and trade, unemployment, a conciliatory attitude toward sections of the intelligentsia, and pro-peasant policies all seemed to threaten the hegemonic status of the worker, as the many leftist critics of NEP were quick to point out. Yet the *principle* of proletarian hegemony remained intact along with the commitment to a socialist future. During NEP, the working class became the repository of many Bolshevik hopes and fears about Soviet power and its future, since its perceived strength or weakness was regarded as central to the prospects for constructing socialism. Images of the working class veered between the optimistic and pessimistic, the confident and despairing, while the contemporary vogue for eugenicist thinking encouraged regular assessments of the "health" of the proletariat in terms of biological metaphors.[9]

The early 1920s were marked by considerable pessimism about a working class that appeared to have been devastated over the course of the civil war. By 1921, the industrial proletariat had shrunk to less than half its size in 1917. The perception that "the proletarian coach that had brought Cinderella to the revolution had turned into a pumpkin" was reinforced when workers inconveniently persisted in striking and protesting against Bolshevik policies, most seriously at the time of the Kronstadt uprising. It is hardly surprising, then, that "unprecedentedly critical and jaundiced remarks" about workers began to be voiced at the start of the 1920s.[10] There was much agonizing over the so-called declassing of the proletariat, as some Bolsheviks tried to explain away workers' supposedly "unproletarian" behavior (i.e., their lack of enthusiasm for the new order). At the eleventh party congress in 1922, Lenin distinguished between what he termed the "true proletariat" and "any old" workers:

> Very often when you say "workers," people think you mean the factory proletariat. It doesn't mean that at all. Since the war people who are not at all proletarian have come to the factories, and have come to hide away from the war, and surely it's not the case that the social and economic circumstances are currently such that a real proletariat comes to the factories? It's not true. It's correct according to Marx, but Marx did not write about Russia, but about capitalism as a whole from the fifteenth century. Over the course of six hundred years it's correct, but for contemporary Russia it's not true. Most often those coming to the factories are not the proletariat but any old people [*vsiacheskii sluchainyi element*].[11]

Aleksandr Shliapnikov, of the dissident Workers' Opposition, did respond to this by suggesting that Lenin and other Bolsheviks were discrediting the proletarian base in order to explain their ebbing support, but his was a marginal voice.[12] Meanwhile, Zinoviev issued a strong warning against the "idealization" of factory workers, employing biological metaphors to argue that once heavy industry had recovered there would be a gradual process of gathering, consolidation, and strengthening of the class, but that currently "what we have now is not the most vital, the most healthy, the oldest part, but that stagnant part of the proletariat that remained at the factories," the "petit bourgeois" part that arrived at the factories during the war.[13]

As the economy started to revive from 1923, a more optimistic vision developed centering on claims that the working class had been "gathered" and was regaining its former vitality.[14] The year 1924 saw the launch of the "Lenin levy" to recruit more workers from the bench to the party, as well as campaigns to purge and proletarianize higher education.[15] However, concerns remained that with the influx of peasants into industry, the new arrivals were "diluting" the strength of established workers. This issue played an important part in the factional disputes of the mid–1920s. Whereas those on the left adopted more militant pro-worker rhetoric, their opponents tended to be cautious about the strength of the proletariat. For example, at the fourteenth party congress in 1925, Tomskii expressed concerns that the new arrivals from the countryside were like "guests" in the factories, with their self-seeking ("*rvacheskii*") ethos. He and others on the right advocated a prolonged period of education (*vospitanie*) of the former peasants.[16] Those further to the left, such as Zinoviev and Krupskaia, accused the Right in turn of "pessimism," of "fear of the working class" and of the "unboiled (*neperevarennyi*) element." They favored recruiting more workers into the party, underlining the importance of cadre workers and their desire to "boil" the new workers.[17]

Although Stalin maintained a fundamentally optimistic tone throughout NEP, he did recognize the problem of dilution. Like others, he tended to attribute labor problems of the 1920s to the "new strata of workers," the "semi-peasants," the "arrivals from the countryside."[18] He also suggested that socioeconomic differences among workers might affect their political allegiances. In 1926, he analyzed what he called the heterogeneity (*razno-rodnost'*) of the working class, distinguishing between three categories of workers: the main mass of "pure-blooded" (*chistokrovnykh*) proletarians, the "permanent contingent," who had decisively broken with the capitalists and were their most reliable support base; recent recruits from non-proletarian backgrounds who were unstable and potentially susceptible to anarchist and "ultra-leftist" influences; and a workers' aristocracy, the top level (*verkhushka*) of the working class, with its desire for compromise with the bourgeoisie and susceptibility to reformists and opportunists.[19] Stalin's tripartite classification undoubtedly influenced analyses of working-class political attitudes and behavior during NEP.[20]

While he acknowledged the existence of differentiation, Stalin was nevertheless increasingly inclined to construct an image of the Soviet working class as cohesive and mature. On several occasions in the mid–1920s he claimed that the class was no longer atomized and declassed, but was now a "full-blooded proletariat" with growing political consciousness as well as increasing material and cultural requirements that the party had an obligation to fulfill. He regularly adopted an anti-bureaucratic line, berating officials for ignoring the needs of this "ruling class." In February 1927, for example, he blamed insensitive bureaucrats for strikes and distur-bances in the textile industry, arguing that the protests reflected workers' rising political awareness.[21]

Stalin's optimistic pro-worker stance intensified in tandem with the "cultural revolution as class war" that aimed to mobilize disgruntled workers against "class enemies" and forge a new "proletarian intelligentsia."[22] He continued to invoke paternalistic and anti-bureaucratic language, demanding that workers' needs be met. He focused ever more sharply on the notion of workers as members of a "ruling class," while also introducing a new motif—the idea of proletarians as human beings and *heroes* rather than as an anonymous "productive force." This vision of heroic workers may have owed something to the romanticism of Gorky, whose influence was steadily growing at this time. What Priestland calls the "revivalism" of Stalin in 1927–28 contrasted with the more "technicist" approach of many on the right who preferred to concentrate on raising the technical skills of workers rather than unleashing their latent heroism.[23]

The discovery of "wrecking" by "bourgeois specialists" at the Shakhty mines in spring 1928 acted as an immediate catalyst for Stalin's fresh approach. During the discussion of the Shakhty affair at the April 1928 CC plenum, Stalin expressed indignation that heroic miners had been misled by managers who had ignored Soviet legislation specifying a six-hour day for underground work: "They have stifled [*oglushili*] workers, telling them that the party expects a seven-hour day underground from them,—and workers work for they are prepared to work more if the party orders them. Who needs this deception and why is it being carried out? Why is there this mockery of workers who have every right to be called heroes and not simply workers?" Stalin went on to warn of the risk of squandering the "moral capital" they had accumulated among this class.[24] Reporting on the plenum to the Moscow party organization, he reiterated this message, describing the miners as "not simply workers, but heroes."[25]

Stalin was adamant that members of the "ruling class" should be respected and treated as human beings. In December 1928, during a Politburo discussion about the work of Donugol', the trust responsible for the Shakhty mines, he insisted that managers should treat their workers better.[26] He compared the USSR unfavorably with the United States in this respect, citing an American engineer, Cooper, who could not understand why a Soviet worker turned up for work at 6:00 am when his boss only appeared at 12:00 pm: "we'd have ruined America if that had been the case." Emphasizing that workers would not work if they lacked good bosses, Stalin argued that managers had to be able to talk to their workers, not just focus on making a profit. He continued: "these are people, not things. And which people? From the ruling class. These are not just phrases. If some bosses or *spetsy* (specialists) do not relate to the workers as people of the ruling class, that is, people whom it's necessary to convince, whose needs must be fulfilled, if the worker waves his hand, twenty times asked for improvements in technology in Lisichansk, and they did nothing, what kind of attitude to the worker is that, if not to a thing."[27] In conversation with worker-peasant correspondents at the end of 1928, he echoed this line, challenging the common image of the workers as "labor power." Acknowledging the existence of strikes, he argued that it was wrong to consider workers simply as "labor power": "The working class is not only labor power, they're living people, they want to live . . ." As in February 1927, he asserted that strikes could be averted if workers' needs were considered: "If a manager thinks that his working class is labor power and not the ruling class and that he needs to bang out a profit, then such a manager cannot and should not be at the factory."[28]

This workerist language with its emphasis on the potential of self-sacrificial labor heroism played an essential part in the debates about the pace of industrialization that dominated 1928. As Stalin had previously observed, belief that the building of socialism was possible in the USSR required confidence that "the Soviet proletariat could through its own strength overcome the Soviet bourgeoisie."[29] He and others who favored a strategy of rapid industrialization articulated this faith in the heroic powers of workers, dismissing the concerns of skeptics. For example, at the CC plenum in November, Pavel Postyshev claimed that "the broad masses of proletarians, real proletarians, the main cadres of the proletariat" were prepared to defend industrialization.[30] Molotov admitted to the July plenum that it would not be easy for workers: they might have to eat black rather than white bread, but they would understand this sacrifice and the need to increase productivity, because the working class was the ruling class, not an exploiter, and with "his own callused hand he's hauling the proletarian state along."[31] At the November plenum, Molotov echoed Stalin's "heroic" language, arguing that the working class, as the leading class, would have to shoulder the burden of socialist construction, which would be impossible "without the exceptional heroism of workers, the exceptional self-sacrifice, determination, and discipline of the proletarian ranks."[32]

Hiroaki Kuromiya suggests that Molotov's statements at the July plenum were characterized by the "pretence of optimism."[33] "Pretence" or not, this optimistic image of self-sacrificing Soviet worker-heroes with their callused hands served important political goals and was articulated with considerable conviction by Stalin and his associates. Their words contrasted sharply with those of the critics of rapid industrialization, who expressed greater skepticism about the powers of the proletariat, often adopting metalworking images, such as "tempering" and "boiling," to describe the difficult process by which proletarians were "forged." At the July plenum Krupskaia asserted that the working class had become more peasantized since 1925. Although, in her view, this was leading to growing working-class influence over the peasants, it also meant that the "hardened cadres" (*zakalennye kadry*) of the working class were being weakened and were "dissolving" into the peasant contingent.[34] Tomskii agreed with Krupskaia that they did have "good, crystallized [*vykristallizovavshiesia*] cadres of proletariat," but these had been severely diluted by newly arrived young workers who "did not make the Revolution, did not struggle for the Revolution, weren't at the fronts, are not used to viewing factories as the fruits of their own victory, whose roots are still in the countryside and whom we have not yet boiled (*perevarili*) and whom it's still very difficult to boil."[35]

The contrasting images of the working class constructed by both the Right and the Left played a significant role in the industrialization debates. Both sides articulated a shared understanding that class mattered, and that rapid industrialization could not be accomplished without a strong, healthy, class-conscious proletariat. Ultimately Stalin and his allies' optimistic vision of a heroic, self-sacrificing, unified proletariat, and their faith in the "callused hand" of the manual worker, proved more politically attractive than the pessimism of the Right. But how far did this image withstand the test of the first five-year plan?

"Advanced" and "Backward" Workers

The introduction of the frenzied first five-year plan was accompanied by unprecedented changes in the size and composition of the working class. The number of industrial workers almost doubled between 1928 and 1932, largely thanks to recruits from the countryside.[36] This, along with the multiple teething problems of the "planned" economy, led to intense preoccupation with workers' behavior and attitudes. Widespread public criticism of the Soviet worker marked the start of the first *piatiletka*, and although on a larger scale than that of the early 1920s, it echoed some of Lenin's concerns, with a number of Bolsheviks warning against "idealizing the working class" as a homogeneous entity.[37]

Stalin himself was now much less inclined to describe the working class as a homogeneous, heroic proletariat. His response to the manifestly unheroic behavior of some industrial workers was to divide the class into two distinct categories: on the one hand were the workers he labeled as "honest," "advanced," "shockworker," or "Stakhanovite," whereas on the other were those he classified as "dishonest," "backward," "non-shock-worker," or "non-Stakhanovite." Some signs of this emerging binary model were already in evidence in October 1928, when Stalin added an extra, tougher-sounding appeal to the slogans issued to mark the eleventh anniversary of the 1917 Revolution: "Down with absenteeism and laxity at factories and plants, mines and railways! Long live labor discipline and honest proletarian labor that strengthen the power of our workers' state."[38] If this slogan merely hinted at the new approach, Stalin's confidential letter to Molotov of 28 September 1930 was more forthright. Complaining about the poor state of labor discipline, he differentiated clearly between two groups: those "who labor honestly in accordance with socialist competition" and "others (the majority) [who] are irresponsible and transient."[39] Initially Stalin was inclined to identify the former category as "proletarian," along the lines of his new slogan ("honest proletarian labor"), while equating the latter with inherently "self-seeking" ex-peasants. However, this class-based interpretation was gradually superseded by the binary classification of workers according to their skills and performance rather than simply their social origins or *stazh*.

In his writings and speeches, Stalin defined "backward" and "advanced" workers in quite particular ways. Although many of his utterances on the sensitive subject of "backward" workers were not published at the time, they were still influential, shaping the language used by the party leadership and the press. At first, Stalin tended to attribute persistent labor problems, such as turnover, to recent arrivals from the countryside. During Politburo discussions about Donugol' at the end of 1928, he referred to a report from Shakhty about workers who took sick leave twenty-five days a month and were considered "heroes" at their workplace. Arguing that it was the responsibility of the unions to prevent this kind of attitude, he implied that the shirkers were new recruits, since enterprises contained "old cadres who are closely tied to the factory and love it, and new cadres who have arrived, in the majority, who regard the factory or the mine as a milk cow to be milked maximally, then left—'the devil take their technological improvements, their mechanization, and so on,' 'live while you can,' and so on." He then raised the question of influence, adopting the Rightist argument about peasant influence over the worker: "Who remakes whom is still a question: Do cadre workers remake new ones, or do new workers with a self-seeking psychology infect the cadre workers? I think the latter often happens." Stalin suggested that the unions often sided with the majority, that is, the recent arrivals, and warned that if nothing changed, industry would suffer. Workers had to understand that the factory was socialist property and that their prosperity depended on its success.[40]

This narrative attributing labor problems to those with rural origins and attachments continued into the early 1930s, when turnover was becoming a particularly critical problem, exceeding 150 percent in 1930.[41] Many explanations have been offered for the scale of turnover, notably the unsatisfactory state of labor planning and the workers' quite natural inclination to move around in search of better wages and living standards.[42] However, Stalin regularly pointed the finger at ex-peasants, presenting the crisis almost exclusively as a direct consequence of new workers returning to their villages to help out with the harvest or take up lighter work. He maintained that life in the countryside had improved thanks to collectivization, and that it was the rise, rather than fall, in the general standard of living that was creating high turnover. Of course there was some truth in the argument that large numbers of new workers, particularly in the construction and mining industries, did view their jobs as temporary, in line with the traditional seasonal patterns of the *otkhod*, and that some also returned to the countryside during the first wave of collectivization to check up on their property and families.[43] However, there were clearly many other reasons for turnover that Stalin simply chose to ignore.

Stalin was determined that his vision should dominate political discourse. In September 1930, when the newspapers were full of stories about the latest economic crisis, falling productivity, and so on, he wrote to Molotov, asking him to stop the press focusing on "breakdowns," "failures," and "disruptions," in what he described as a "hysterical Trotskyist-Right-deviationist tone" that was "*not justified* by the facts" and was "*unbecoming to the Bolsheviks.*" The papers did not explain why workers were migrating to the countryside, he claimed. It could not be related to poor food supply, since this year was no different from the previous year. In his view, the problem lay in the self-seeking attitudes of former peasants: workers were leaving for the kolkhozy to help with the harvest to ensure that they would receive their full share. This was the message the press should concentrate on rather than panic-mongering.[44]

Likewise, at the 4 November 1930 meeting of the Politburo and Presidium of the Central Control Commission, which discussed the case of S. Syrtsov, V. Lominadze, and their associates, accused inter alia of attributing high turnover to falls in real wages, inadequate supplies of food, and so on, Stalin alleged that, on the contrary, real wages were actually rising along with the standard of living. Nor was turnover caused by deteriorating supplies, since the "semi-peasant elements" (*polukrest'ianskie elementy*), as he described these workers in the unedited version of his speech, had always left for the countryside during the summer months; turnover was only higher now thanks to better rural conditions: "The workers themselves say that the wife writes from the countryside: why are you sitting in the mines, come back, the harvest is good, the kolkhozniks are giving out the shares, they say you won't get a share because you're not working." Stalin anticipated that labor recruitment would become a growing problem in the future as conditions in the countryside continued to improve, for it was only logical that miners would prefer rural employment to dangerous work down mines. The solution was simply to mechanize the countryside.[45] He reiterated these points in May 1931 during a CC conference devoted to the Donbas coal industry, which was particularly afflicted by problems of turnover. He rejected as "prejudice" the common view that the recent serious exodus of workers from the region was due to the deteriorating availability of food, water, and housing, since in fact the situation was no worse, and in some respects better, than that of the previous year. The real reason for the exodus was that life in the kolkhoz had improved, for in the past hunger had driven peasants to the factories and mines. Once again, Stalin's answer to the problem was to focus on technological innovation.[46]

A couple of months later, at a Politburo session attended by cooperative workers, he restated the same general theory, although with a slightly different emphasis, as he was by then prepared to acknowledge that food supplies in the towns were inadequate and to attribute the flight to the countryside to this factor as well as to the improvements in rural areas. He suggested explicitly that workers were departing for the countryside in search of better food: "What's the worker's mood now? 'I'll go to the kolkhoz for a couple of months, feed myself up, then come back.'" On this occasion, his solution was to improve the systems of urban food supply and distribution.[47]

Although such stereotypes about self-seeking, undisciplined peasant-workers did not entirely disappear from Soviet discourse in the 1930s, Stalin himself increasingly dispensed with this class approach, preferring to associate poor labor discipline with those identified simply as "backward," regardless of their social origins or *stazh*. Matt Payne observes that in this process "very real workers were defined out of the working class as 'backward elements' and 'class aliens.' As chauvinists and opponents of shock work were purged, socioeconomic criteria such as length of service in industry or urban origin became irrelevant to the regime's conception of its 'ruling class.'"[48]

Stalin's new approach was particularly evident when the subject of backward workers resurfaced in connection with the emergence of the Stakhanovite movement in 1935. As we shall see, discussions about the issue of backwardness had abated somewhat after the early 1930s, but Stakhanovism brought it back into focus, as controversies arose over just how far output norms should be raised to reflect the capabilities of the more advanced workers. Some interesting debate occurred at the December 1935 CC plenum, where Robert Eikhe mentioned the problem of those "backward groups" about whom Lenin had said that "they expect to receive more from the state and to give it less." He insisted they should be "unmasked."[49] Postyshev refuted any notion that backward workers were a meaningful force, arguing that the Soviet worker had changed. He did not deny that some "petit bourgeois" characteristics remained, but disagreed that the majority of workers tried "to give the state less, to take more from it." Although there were some like this, they were now under the influence of advanced and Stakhanovite workers—a fact that should be taken into account when reviewing norms.[50] Stanislav Kosior preferred to concentrate on what he called the "average masses," observing more realistically that the revision of norms had led to "very many negative moods and great doubts among workers." There were only "a handful or a few dozen Stakhanovites." Hundreds of thousands of workers remained "the average masses [*seredniatskaia massa*], among whom these attitudes toward productive labor have not yet been broken. We must not forget that these people still live with well-known survivals [*perezhitki*]."[51]

Stalin offered his own contribution to this discussion at the First All-Union Conference of Stakhanovites in November. He drew a distinction between advanced workers and the rest, arguing that norms should be adjusted to reflect the differences between workers. The old norms had been drawn up two or three years earlier when they did not have "good qualified workers with a grounding [*podkovannye*]," when "we were backward."[52] Current norms relied on the idea of backwardness, made a fetish of it, but, at the same time, new norms could not be set too impossibly high. Without attempting to estimate the size of each contingent, Stalin identified three categories of workers whose varying capacities had to be taken into account when setting norms: "There are the advanced workers, at the front—they need to be given the road, let them march ahead! There are the backward ones—they must be pulled up. There are the average ones [*seredniaki*], who link the advanced with the backward." This tripartite model differed from the more common contemporary binary division of workers into advanced and backward, and, unsurprisingly, the published version of the speech was more conventional, mentioning only the advanced workers and those that lagged behind.[53] The model was also markedly different from the tripartite scheme Stalin had proposed in the mid–1920s (see above). Unlike the latter, this made no mention of socioeconomic differences: workers were now classified merely as "advanced" and "backward" (or, much more rarely, as "average").

From 1930, Stalin increasingly sought to dampen down public discussions about the awkward subject of backward workers and to reorient attention toward the achievements of the advanced.[54] Gorky had warned him in November 1929 that the harsh anti-worker tone of the Soviet press was creating a bad impression abroad, and that Western workers "cannot learn anything about Soviet revolutionary-cultural progress, industrialization's success, our workers' enthusiasm . . . It is therefore necessary to arrange for a more objective coverage of current events. Negative reports must be balanced by positive reporting . . . The press should keep reminding itself and its readers that socialism is being built in the USSR not by sloppy individual hooligans and raving morons, but by a genuinely new and mighty force—the working class."[55] In his response to Gorky of January 1930, Stalin vigorously defended the need for self-criticism, but agreed with the recommendation that critical press comment should be balanced by more positive coverage.[56] A few days later, he went on to discuss the reporting of "socialist competition" with newspaper editors, urging them to pay greater attention to outstanding individuals as well as highlighting problems in the workplace.[57] Similarly, at the May 1931 CC conference on the coal industry, he called for the names and achievements of the Donbas region's "self-sacrificing, true revolutionaries, shock workers" to be given greater prominence in the meeting's resolution. Mentioning these "advanced people, the best people of the Donbas" was "a way of supporting them, a means to get the backward [*otstaiushchie*] to copy them."[58] A public campaign designed to spread this message, "The Country Needs to Know Its Heroes," was launched that year.[59]

Stalin began to voice objections to references to Soviet workers' backwardness and lack of "culture." In December 1930 he struck a patriotic note, chiding the poet Dem'ian Bednyi for slandering the Russian working class—"the avant-garde of Soviet workers"—and for attributing Oblomov-like characteristics to workers in his recent newspaper feuilletons.[60] He was particularly concerned to refute foreign stereotypes about the apathy of the Russian/Soviet worker: during his conversations with the German Emil Ludwig in 1931 and the American Colonel Raymond Robins in 1933 he criticized clichés about Soviet workers' alleged laziness, their inability to work with machines, and so on. Acknowledging to Robins that they still had too few "cultured" workers, he explained that this was a temporary problem and that Soviet workers were learning how to use machines astonishingly quickly, not because they possessed any special abilities, but because of the socialist nature of the economy. He strongly objected to what he termed the "biological" (racist) underpinnings of stereotypes about workers of different nations and races.[61] By 1934, sensitivity toward the public image of the Soviet worker had reached such a height that (ironically) Gorky himself was censored in part because he had alluded to the backwardness of Soviet factories. According to Kaganovich, he had written an article for *Pravda* that stated: "the ancient, tormented, still wild countryside is going to the factories, plants, and cities." When Stalin was informed of this, he instructed *Pravda*'s editor, Mekhlis, not to publish the article in its current form.[62]

Stalin himself helped to define the dominant image of the "advanced" Soviet worker by reworking some of the language he had previously associated with the entire working class. At the sixteenth party congress in June 1930 he announced that as a result of socialist competition, labor was no longer a burden, but "a matter of honor, a matter of glory, a matter of valor and heroism." The Soviet worker aspired to be a "hero of labor," a "hero of shock work."[63] Stalin now wanted selected workers to be described as heroes rather than the proletariat as a whole. He harnessed the language of heroism in a similar fashion in the famous "New Conditions, New Tasks" speech of 23 June 1931, proclaiming that "the great majority of workers have accepted these demands of Soviet power [for discipline, competition] with great enthusiasm and fulfill them heroically." This appraisal contrasted markedly with his complaint to Molotov the previous year that only a minority of workers labored "honestly in accordance with socialist competition" while the "majority" were "irresponsible and transient."[64] By 1931, in public at least, the honest, heroic minority had become the majority.

Advanced Soviet worker-heroes were to be identified by their particular material and cultural requirements. Although Stalin's paternalist rhetoric about the party's obligation to satisfy workers' needs, defend workers' interests, and so on did not evaporate in the 1930s, it was increasingly associated with the more advanced workers rather than workers as a class. In his letter to Molotov of 28 September 1930, Stalin expressed outrage that workers were receiving the same rewards regardless of performance, decreeing that henceforth each enterprise should identify a group of shock workers who would receive preferential allocations of food, clothes, housing, benefits, and so on.[65] The "New Conditions, New Tasks" speech, as well as advocating wage differentials based on qualifications, also called for the satisfaction of the material and cultural requirements of workers and outlined a kind of social contract according to which workers who were "heroically" fulfilling the state's demands for discipline and shock work had the right to expect that their own needs were fulfilled in return.[66]

In Stalin's vision, the growing needs of workers, and advanced workers in particular, were closely related to the development of their "cultured-ness" (*kul'turnost'*) and taste.[67] When the Politburo met with cooperative workers in July 1931, Stalin demanded better provisions for workers, arguing that it was a sign of their *kul'turnost'* that they had these increasing require-ments. On this occasion he also invoked traditional class terminology more reminiscent of the late 1920s, such as "workers' interests" and "workers' state," claiming that cooperative workers had lost their sensitivity to "workers' interests" and describing how workers had been "robbed" of their rightful rations at the Stalingrad tractor factory. He questioned how this could occur in a "workers' state" and voiced indignation at such squandering of the party's "moral capital."[68] Workerist rhetoric also featured at the November 1934 CC plenum, where Stalin accused the Urals party secretary, I. Kabakov, of ignoring the question of workers' everyday life. He alleged that there was "very little care about the workers in the Urals," that everyday life in the region was "medieval." However, he also made a point of singling out advanced workers in particular, noting that cities such as Moscow, Leningrad, Kharkov, Kiev, and Baku contained many qualified workers, "people with taste, who want to live, who know how to live, who earn proper money."[69]

The culmination of all these tendencies was the Stakhanovite movement, which quite explicitly identified and rewarded the most advanced, cultured worker-heroes. Stalin made it clear in his speech to the First All-Union Conference of Stakhanovites that class origins and *stazh* counted for little anymore, identifying Stakhanovites as "new people," often young, as well as highlighting the key role played by figures such as "yesterday's kolkhoznik" Aleksandr Busygin (although the reference to "yesterday's kolkhoznik" was removed from the published version of the speech). He deliberately accentuated the intellectual, rather than physical, prowess of Stakhanovite workers, referring repeatedly to their superior "cultural and technical knowledge."[70] In Stalin's eyes, Stakhanovism was important because it heralded the birth of the process of overcoming the distinction between mental and manual labor. Manual labor itself was increasingly identified with "backwardness," a tendency that would only accelerate in the second half of the 1930s.

Proletarian Identity and the Great Terror

While the image of the "backward worker" in all its different guises provided a convenient scapegoat for persistent economic problems, Stalin increasingly chose to blame what he defined as politically subversive activities on more dangerous "enemies" emanating from within the working class—not only the predictable targets, ex-kulaks and class aliens who had "wormed their way" into the factories and the party, but even those with long-standing proletarian credentials. In an echo of Lenin's words in 1922, he regularly pointed out that the working class contained "all sorts" and that worker credentials alone were not a sufficient guarantee of political loyalty.

Throughout the 1920s, the party had been concerned about how to recruit more workers, especially workers "from the bench." With the massive expansion of the working class from the end of the decade, this task became in some respects easier. At the start of 1930, 65.3 percent of party members were classified as being of working-class origin, and nearly half (46.3 percent) as currently workers by occupation.[71] However, in February 1930 Stalin cautioned against blanket assumptions about workers' suitability for party membership. When questioned by Sverdlov Communist University students about the party's attitude to mass applications for membership from entire factory shops, he welcomed the fact that large numbers of workers wanted to join, but warned that not all could do so. He insisted that the party maintain an individual approach rather than accept mass applications, noting rather ominously that within the factories were "all sorts of people, including wreckers."[72]

Whereas this comment appeared in *Pravda*, the majority of Stalin's statements casting doubt on workers' loyalty were not published. For example, he presented a similar picture of a politically heterogeneous working class in a private letter of 22 April 1930 to a certain comrade N. I. Kin. Kin had written to Stalin following the latter's "Dizzy with

Success" article, criticizing his policies and accusing him of being cut off from the real situation in the country. Kin concluded by proudly describing his proletarian roots: from 1911 to 1929 he had worked as a faceter (*fasetchik*) at a mirror factory, where his father still worked. Stalin picked up on this in his curt response: "I would like to give you one bit of advice: do not boast about the fact that you are a worker at a mirror factory. There are all sorts of people among workers, good and bad—I know old workers with a long production *stazh* who still drag behind in the tail of Mensheviks and still cannot free themselves from the longing for the old bosses—the capitalists. Yes, com. Kin, there are all sorts of workers in the world."[73]

Such language became more common as strikes and disturbances continued in the early 1930s, reaching their apogee with the events of April 1932 in Ivanovo-Vosnesensk.[74] The harsh labor laws of 1932 directed against "pseudo-workers" were accompanied by increasingly stern words warning against the idealization of workers. Kaganovich advised the Ninth All-Union Congress of Unions at the end of April that they "should not flatter the workers, this is not one of our Bolshevik traditions," before addressing the problem of how to deal with what he, at least, defined merely as "backward" workers.[75] At the November 1932 joint session of the Politburo and Presidium of the Central Control Commission, which considered the case of the Smirnov-Eismont-Tolmachev "opposition," Stalin adopted a tougher stance, arguing against the "fetishization" of some ranks of the working class and citing precedents in favor of the use of force against workers where necessary. Although he affirmed that "the working class is the basis and source of existence of our party," he recalled that in the past some sections of this class had "with weapons in their hands" opposed Soviet power; for example, during the civil war. The use of coercion against workers had been justified then because the party still enjoyed the support of the *majority* of the working class. Stalin then went on to assert that even within their own socialist factories there were cases of "sabotage" and "anti-Soviet machinations": "Should we beat these saboteurs and anti-Soviet 'activists'? Of course we should. And as is well known, we do," he declared. He argued (less controversially) that the same was even more true of the kolkhozniks.[76] In front of a larger audience at the CC plenum in January 1933, Stalin's words were rather more circumspect: rather than associating genuine proletarians with "wrecking," he claimed instead that "former people" had "wormed their way into factories," and even the party, by donning "the mask of a worker."[77]

In unpublished communications, Stalin voiced growing suspicion of leading Communists with proletarian origins. By 1933, he was already employing the term "hereditary proletarian" in an ironic and derogatory way. The previous year he had complained that the first secretaries of Ukraine, the Urals, and part of Nizhnii Novgorod *oblast'* were too preoccupied with industry and were neglecting agriculture; in April 1933 he repeated this accusation in a telegram to the heads of the Urals obkom and oblispolkom: "Kabakov and Oshvintsev think that as hereditary proletarians they are not obliged to get involved in agriculture. This narrow parochial [*tsekhovaia*] view has led to a situation where the great agricultural opportunities of the Urals remain unused."[78]

This dismissive tone only intensified as the momentum of the Great Terror started to pick up and Stalin sought to convey the controversial message that proletarian origins should not confer immunity on potentially dangerous enemies. While he tended not to associate himself directly with this message, he made sure that it was communicated via other channels. The "closed letter" issued by the CC after Kirov's assassination warned that Bolsheviks with worker origins, such as R. Malinovskii, could turn out to be provocateurs, while at a conference of regional party secretaries in 1935 Ezhov complained that insufficient vigilance toward workers was obstructing the hunt for Trotskyists. Arguing that activists were ignorant of Marxism-Leninism, he accused them of wrongly "venerating" the worker: "For them, you know, workers represent an inaccessible category. Look here, this veneration for the worker is completely un-Bolshevik and un-Marxist. This veneration for the party member—if he is a member of the party, if he has a party card—this means that he is inviolable in his person, and so on. We must put a stop to all this, comrades."[79] The transcript of the August 1936 Moscow show trial—which Stalin presumably helped to shape—contains a line recited by one of the accused: "Let everybody remember that not only a general, not only a prince or a nobleman can become a counterrevolutionary; workers or those who spring from the working class, like myself, can also become counterrevolutionaries."[80]

At the same time it was explained that those with bourgeois origins should not *automatically* be viewed as suspect. Stalin himself uttered the words "a son does not answer for his father" at a meeting of combine operators in December 1935 (it is interesting that in contrast to other published statements by Stalin, his comment was not widely discussed at the time). Zhdanov informed a meeting of local party officials in August 1935 that there should be "no schematism in relation to former people," that their attitudes and behavior, rather than their social origin, would dictate how they were to be treated.[81]

This message about social origins had to be reiterated time and time again, such was the attachment to what Stalin called "biological" interpretations. At the height of the Great Terror in August 1937, during a CC/Sovnarkom conference of cotton industry workers attended by Stalin, Molotov attacked a simplistic biographical approach to rooting out enemies. He identified two individuals, Korotkov and Kisel'nikov, originally from the working class, who turned out to be "such rotten, bourgeois rubbish, alien to the working class, like many other saboteurs and spies." Molotov pointed out that because it was customary to think that wreckers emanated from hostile bourgeois backgrounds, people tried to identify them primarily by considering "their biographies, their origins, their kin, relationships, etc." He warned that experience showed that wreckers could emerge from within the working class. They currently faced quite a number of these cases, and it was necessary to deal with each one on an individual basis rather than citing factors such as origins, services, or long party *stazh*.[82]

Although Stalin himself generally avoided making allegations against those with worker origins in very public settings, he drew similar conclusions about the "biological" approach in more intimate circles. In his speech at the Military Council of the Commissariat of Defense on 2 June 1937 following the arrest of Tukhachevskii, Iakir, and other military "conspirators," he dismissed arguments attributing Tukhachevksii's treachery to his noble origins. If the nobility as a class was hostile to working people, it did not follow that certain members of the nobility could not serve the working class. He cited the obvious examples of Lenin and his noble origins; Engels, the son of a factory owner, who ran his own factory that helped to support Marx; and Chernyshevskii, the son of a priest. Conversely, those originating from worker backgrounds could end up as enemies. He pointed out that Serebriakov was a worker, "and you know what a scoundrel he turned out to be," while Livshits, a "semi-literate worker," also turned out to be a spy: "When one talks about hostile forces, one means a class, an estate, a stratum (*prosloika*), but not every individual from a given class can be a wrecker. Some members of the nobility [and] the bourgeoisie worked for the benefit of the working class, and worked well. For example, many revolutionaries emerged from the stratum of advocates. Marx was the son of an advocate, not the son of a farm laborer (*batrak*) or worker. There are always people from these strata who can serve the working class not worse but better than pure-blooded proletarians." Stalin announced that the general rule that "he's not the son of a *batrak*" was an old rule, not applicable to individuals. It was not a Marxist, sociological approach but "a biological approach." He then proceeded to argue that it was equally wrong to condemn someone on the basis that they might have voted for Trotsky once. The most sensible approach was to judge people by their deeds over the course of several years.[83]

Similarly, in a speech to air force commanders the following year, Stalin recounted how Mekhlis had criticized the deputy head of the air force, Ia. Smushkevich, writing a completely "unnecessary note" in which he recalled whose son he was, where he had been, and generally engaged in excavating the past. Stalin reminded his audience: "Someone can be the son of a non-proletarian family, and work honestly, and, on the contrary, he can be the son of proletarian parents, and a scoundrel. He can be the son of non-proletarian parents, but a good person. There are those." He urged them to be aware of the fluidity of class identities, recalling once again Serebriakov, who was considered to be the son of a worker, but whose father, they had recently discovered, was a provocateur. Smirnov, also of worker origin, was "a scoundrel." Stalin then introduced a comparatively rare personal note, citing his own biography as an example:

> For example, I am not the son of workers, my father was not born a worker, he had a workshop, he was a deputy foreman [*podmaster*], an exploiter. We did not live badly. I was ten when he was ruined and joined the proletariat. I would not say that he joined the proletariat with enthusiasm. He swore all the time about how unlucky he was to have joined the proletariat. The fact that he was unlucky, that he was ruined, has been of use to me. I assure you, it's funny. I remember when I was ten I was unhappy that my

father was ruined, not knowing there would be plusses for me forty years later. But those plusses are completely undeserved.

Stalin then returned to the subject of Smushkevich, who, he claimed, was being unfairly victimized: "It's all rubbish. I see how he works. He can work."[84]

Stalin's words notwithstanding, social origins and the biological approach continued to play some role in the identification of enemies as it always had done. Although the rhetoric of 1937–38 targeted "enemies of the people" rather than the usual "class enemies," old habits died hard.[85] This was partly because the anti-bureaucratic thrust of the purges had overtones of "class struggle" (and was certainly interpreted at the grassroots in this light). The mass operations directed against those with "alien" social origins, particularly ex-kulaks, also seemed to contradict Stalin's message about class.[86] The leadership's apparent ambivalence about the whole question and the lack of publicity accorded to Stalin's pronouncements only served to obfuscate matters.[87]

After the Great Terror had subsided, Stalin continued to condemn the principle that working-class credentials should confer any superiority or special immunity. He was particularly incensed by those who used their class origins as an excuse for complacency, for failing to "work on themselves" or improve their skills. In September 1940, the writer A. Avdeenko, who had hitherto enjoyed great favor, was berated at a CC meeting for his controversial screenplay *The Law of Life*.[88] As well as criticizing his work, Stalin also attacked Avdeenko's character, accusing him of lacking "culture," being semi-literate, not knowing Russian, and not "working on himself." He had apparently been admitted to the party on the basis of a recommendation by the disgraced Urals obkom chief, Kabakov (the "hereditary proletarian" mentioned above, who was a victim of the purges):

> What does he rely on? The fact that he is of working-class origin . . . The working class as a whole is a revolutionary, advanced class, but in the working class there are certain people. And your friend Kabakov was also from the workers, but he wanted to sell Russia, a good fifth of Russia, to the Japanese, Poles, Germans. Surely you know this? Tomskii, too, was a former worker, but see they supported Trotsky. That's former workers for you. You think that

every worker is worth his weight in gold? You are wrong, and if you take all Citrine's imperialists and the rest-that's former workers. Among advanced workers there is one stratum that uses its workers' origins and chooses everything accordingly in order to arrange its own affairs and then in a more advantageous way to itself to betray the interests of the working class. That is the law of life. Nine-tenths of the working class are gold, one-tenth, or one-twentieth, or even one in a thousand are bastards who have betrayed the interests of the working class. They are everywhere, in all countries, and here too in the likes of Tomskii, Kabakov, Zhukov, Evdokimov, and others; these aren't accidental people. This is the law of life.[89]

One of the many striking features of this diatribe was its statistical vagueness—according to Stalin, the traitors could number as few as one in a thousand, or as many as one in ten. In a sense, of course, the numbers were immaterial: what mattered was that every "worker" was potentially suspect.

This motif of "working on oneself" recurred a couple of months later in a speech at a 7 November reception reported in Georgi Dimitrov's diary. Stalin chose this opportunity to criticize the country's lack of military preparedness, complaining that he alone had to assume responsibility for these matters. According to Dimitrov, Stalin addressed himself particularly to Kaganovich and Beria. He denounced the complacency of those who rested on their laurels, who refused to study despite the opportunity to do so, singling out particularly those with lower-class origins: "People think that since they are from worker and peasant stock, since they have calluses on their hands, then there is nothing they cannot do, and there is no sense in learning anything new or working to improve themselves. And meanwhile—they are real dolts." Honesty and bravery were no longer sufficient: "you have to know something, you need skills . . ."[90]

Stalin uttered similar words regarding the need for skills and professionalism rather than workers' calluses in May 1940 during a Politburo discussion on the subject of how to reward directors. He insisted that competence rather than class should now be the decisive criterion when making senior appointments. "At the head of our enterprises and organizations there should be engineers, people who know the business. Now we cannot rely on calluses. We cannot retain power on worker origins." Stalin also spoke disparagingly about the experience of involving the working class in management, referring to the proposed new Commissariat for State Control as an advance on earlier failed experiments such as the Workers' and Peasants' Inspectorate (Rabkrin), which he described as "taking the entire working class through the school of state administration."[91] As was the case with the identification of enemies, however, the biological approach to making appointments evidently continued. In February 1941 Malenkov was forced to remind delegates to the eighteenth party conference: "We must put an end to the biological approach in the selection of cadres and judge cadres on performance, evaluating them on their work, and not just going on what is in their personal dossiers. Up to the present, despite the party's instructions, when an official is appointed in many party and economic organs, people spend more time establishing his genealogy, finding out who his grandfather and grandmother were, than studying his personal managerial and political qualities [and] his abilities."[92]

Over the course of the 1930s, Stalin expressed increasing skepticism about the use of worker origins and service as criteria for evaluating individuals. He rejected displays of what he called "weakness for the working class," insisting that individuals should be judged on their merits rather than their calluses.[93] Not surprisingly, cardinal Bolshevik tenets concerning the hegemony of the proletariat were also subjected to fundamental revision during these years.

"Proletarian Hegemony" Challenged

As Stalin expressed growing disenchantment with the myth of the proletariat and embraced a less divisive vision of Soviet society, the privileges and status workers had enjoyed as the "ruling class" were gradually dismantled. Economic, social, and political discrimination in favor of workers was abandoned, and, as Fitzpatrick has observed, the achievement of "proletarian hegemony" was followed by a distinct shift away from "proletarian" language in favor of more politically neutral terms such as "worker" and "working class."[94] By the 1940s, even these neutral terms were falling out of favor. Stalin's interventions in relation to key political texts played a major part in the definition and justification of the new approach.

Although change had been underway since 1931, in terms of socioeconomic privileges, a major turning point came in the form of the decision of the November 1934 CC plenum to end the policy of bread rationing, which had favored workers by providing them with relatively cheap bread. Commenting on the plenum's resolution, Stalin described this policy as a "gift from the state to the working class," a "class policy of gift in relation to the working class at the expense of the peasantry." He also implied that rationing was spoiling the working class, since it encouraged speculation, leading even "decent" and "honest" workers to compete with the state by selling bread.[95] This pejorative evaluation of a "class policy" heralded the demise of a whole raft of socioeconomic policies designed to benefit workers and their families, such as quotas for higher educational institutions and technical schools for those of worker origin, which were lifted at the end of 1935.[96]

The theory of working-class political hegemony also came under fire from a variety of angles. Stalin signaled the start of a new direction when he edited the 1936 draft Komsomol statutes. These had described the youth organization as "a mass, in its essence proletarian, organization, uniting in its ranks the broad strata of advanced, class-conscious, politically literate youth." He eliminated the "proletarian" and "class" terminology from the drafts, defining the Komsomol instead as "a mass non-party organization, uniting in its ranks the broad strata of advanced, politically literate toiling youth of the town and countryside."[97] However, it was the new constitution of 1936 that offered the clearest public exposition of Stalin's more inclusive vision. In his widely broadcast speech on the draft, he explained why the old idea of "proletarian hegemony" was untenable. There were no longer any exploiting classes in the socialist USSR; what remained were the non-antagonistic "classes" of workers and peasants, plus the intelligentsia "stratum," which had itself experienced profound changes.[98] Turning his attention to the Soviet working class, Stalin observed that it was often called the proletariat from habit, but this was no longer appropriate since the term "proletariat" denoted an exploited class, whereas the Soviet working class was a completely "new class" that owned the means of production along with the rest of the Soviet people.[99] Although Stalin did not dispense entirely with the principle of the superiority of the working class, describing it at one point as "the advanced class in society," the speech did nevertheless represent a decisive shift.[100] The end of class antagonism and clear-cut hierarchies was embedded in the constitution itself, which labeled the USSR "a socialist state of workers and peasants" where power belonged to the "toilers of town and country" represented in soviets, and where all citizens were assured of equal rights.

As in the case of the leader cult, Stalin took considerable trouble to ensure that the key May Day and 7 November slogans aligned with his evolving vision. During NEP, Stalin had insisted that the principle of worker hegemony be retained in slogans despite the pro-peasant orientation of this period. For example, one of the draft slogans for the tenth anniversary of the Revolution had read: "The USSR is the only country in the world where workers and peasants run the state. In the next decade there should not be a single worker, a single peasant, or a single laboring woman who is not participating actively in the work of the Soviets." Stalin deleted this slogan, writing in the margin "The peasants do not *run* the state on a par with the workers."[101] The slogans issued during the industrialization drive at the end of the decade were characterized by a much more aggressively proletarian idiom. Stalin made many modifications to the draft slogans for May Day 1929 to reinforce the impression of workers' hegemony in the new proletarian revolution, adding multiple references to the working class and proletariat (his additions appear in bold):

> The competition of factories and plants, mines and workshops, is a powerful weapon for the socialist education of the masses and the involvement of millions of **workers** in the running of the economy.
>
> Long live socialist rationalization, the basis of the material and cultural development of the working class **in the land of the dictatorship of the proletariat!**
>
> Let us create cadres of Red specialists **from working-class people.**
>
> Strengthen the link between science, technology, and production **under the leadership of the working class.**[102]

Likewise, he changed the first slogan for the 1929 Revolution anniversary from "Long live the twelfth anniversary of October" to "Long live the twelfth anniversary of the dictatorship of the proletariat."[103]

While this "proletarian" accent remained in force in 1930, from 1931 the approach became less consistent. Stalin was increasingly inclined to replace terms such as "proletarian" and "proletariat" with the more neutral "workers" or "workers and peasants." For example, in 1931 he substituted "workers" for "proletarians" in draft May Day appeals addressed to "proletarians, kolkhozniki, *bedniaks*, and *seredniak-edinolichniks*" and "proletarians of factories and plants."[104] However, he did not completely abandon the term. References to "iron proletarian discipline," "proletarian youth," and "the best proletarians" remained in other May Day slogans for that year.

From then on, the word "proletarian" was used much more sparingly, except in the case of slogans referring to the struggle of the international proletariat. When the term continued to appear in the drafts, Stalin often changed it; for example in 1934 he altered "proletarian greetings" to "Bolshevik greetings" in one of the 7 November slogans addressed to the builders of the Moscow metro.[105] But his approach remained variable in the mid–1930s. Whereas the Revolution was described as a "proletarian revolution" in the 1935 November slogans and as "the great proletarian socialist revolution" in the 1937 May Day slogans, Stalin amended the drafts for November 1934 and 1936, labeling it simply "socialist." However in the latter case, the modified slogan—"Long live the nineteenth anniversary of the great socialist revolution in the USSR"—appeared directly below the *Pravda* headline, which read: "CC slogans for the nineteenth anniversary of the great proletarian revolution in the USSR"! Clearly some of Stalin's revisions had a somewhat arbitrary, haphazard quality.[106] Until 1936, the formulations "the dictatorship of proletariat" and "proletarian state" were generally preserved, although Stalin replaced "proletarian state" with "Soviet state" in a slogan for May 1932 and with "worker-peasant state" in one for November 1934.[107] Following the adoption of the new constitution, such "proletarian" terminology completely vanished. The slogans for May and November 1937 included the words "let us strengthen the dictatorship of the working class of the USSR—state leadership by the working class of all our society!"[108] By 1938, even this exclusive "working-class" language had fallen out of favor, and the slogan was removed by Stalin from drafts of both the May and November slogans.[109]

By the late 1930s, then, the working class was no longer accorded any special symbolic status. In 1939–40 it was presented as on a par with the peasants and the newly prominent intelligentsia with three slogans that proclaimed "long live our victorious working class," "long live our victorious kolkhoz peasantry," and "long live our socialist intelligentsia" (Stalin even deleted "victorious" from "working class" and "kolkhozniks" in the drafts for November 1940).[110] The slogans stayed in this form in May 1941. During the war, Stalin went so far as to eliminate the term "working class" entirely. For example, the draft slogans for May 1944, presented to him by Malenkov and Shcherbakov, contained appeals addressed to various groups, including workers, peasants, the intelligentsia, women and youth, as well as military personnel. The one that appealed to "workers and women workers, engineers, and technical personnel" to support the war effort with their self-sacrificial labor concluded with the words "Long live the working class of the Soviet Union."[111] Stalin actually deleted this—the only slogan he removed in its entirety—while retaining the analogous slogans about agricultural workers and the intelligentsia. The omission of a slogan referring specifically to the working class clearly surprised Voroshilov, who asked Poskrebyshev to convey his view that "it would be correct to give one additional slogan: 'Long live the workers and women workers of the Soviet Union.'"[112] Voroshilov's suggestion was ignored, however, and Stalin's deliberate neglect of the working class continued in the slogans for November 1944, which included numerous appeals addressed to particular groups, but none specifically focused on the working class as a whole.[113] After the war, the term "working class" did not feature in any of the May Day or October Revolution anniversary slogans.

Legitimizing the Intelligentsia

As "calluses" and "class" fell out of favor, attention shifted to the most able Soviet citizens, who were celebrated not for their social origins or length of service, but for their skills, education, and attainments. The new pantheon of heroes included not only those workers singled out for being "advanced" but also, by the end of the 1930s, members of a rather amorphous category, the "Soviet intelligentsia," which was said to comprise 13–14 percent of the population in 1939.[114] The term "intelligentsia" has had different meanings at various stages in Russian and Soviet history, from independently minded critics of autocracy to educated professionals. Stalin's loose definition came to encompass all those who were engaged in mental (non-manual) labor, including engineering and technical workers (ITR) and white-collar workers (*sluzhashchie*).[115] He challenged the long-standing Bolshevik (and popular) ambivalence about these "intellectual laborers," describing them as an integral part of the "Soviet working class" or "Soviet people."

Lacking a clearly defined position in the class structure, the category "intelligentsia" had always occupied an ambiguous place in Marxist thought. Although the intelligentsia was generally understood to be part of the capitalist system of oppression, it was also considered capable of detaching itself from this system and aiding the struggle to bring the proletariat to consciousness. By the early twentieth century, Russian Social Democrats drew a distinction between backward-looking "bourgeois *intelligenty*" and the revolutionary intelligentsia that identified with the interests of the proletariat.[116] Lenin, while berating the liberal *intelligenty*, endorsed the elitist notion of a party made up of a "workers' intelligentsia" that would lead the masses to salvation. Others, notably Aleksandr Bogdanov, were uneasy at the domination of the workers' movement by intellectuals at the expense of workers' own self-organization and activity. After 1917, similar criticisms of the Bolshevik Party were voiced by dissident groups such as the Workers' Opposition, who resented what they saw as the deproletarianization of the party and its domination by those who may once have been workers, but now had no connections with the factory. This so-called *makhaevshchina* (after Jan Machajski, a Polish syndicalist associated with anti-intellectualism) was condemned by mainstream party leaders.[117] The post-revolutionary attitude to the "bourgeois" *intelligenty* was also complicated. Lenin was prepared to countenance those members of the bourgeois intelligentsia ("specialists") whose skills he considered necessary for the building of socialism.[118] However, many other Communists, especially among the rank and file, were instinctively hostile to any cooperation, assuming that specialists' interests were necessarily opposed to those of the working class. The "intelligentsia" as a category was thus shackled with a whole host of negative associations that Stalin had to deal with as the 1930s unfolded.

From his early years as a revolutionary *intelligent*, Stalin, like some other Bolsheviks, identified closely with the party's intelligentsia and placed a high premium on knowledge and education.[119] At the same time, he was reputedly opposed to the "old" intelligentsia during the revolutionary period. Scholars have highlighted his well-known antipathy to the use of what he termed "so-called military specialists from the bourgeoisie" in the civil war, which led to clashes with both Trotsky and Lenin. Kendall Bailes hints at a connection between his civil war stance and the hounding of specialists associated with the Shakhty affair and its aftermath.[120]

Certainly, Stalin was *retrospectively* concerned to create the impression that he had recognized the importance of the intelligentsia during the Revolution, although he always insisted on the importance of distinguishing carefully between different categories of *intelligenty*. In conversation with H. G. Wells in 1934, he acknowledged the crucial role played by the intelligentsia in the revolutionary struggle, describing the party as a necessary "auxiliary force" (*vspomogatel'naia sila*), which included the best sections of the intelligentsia. Anxious not to underestimate its significance, he said, "it's just a matter of which intelligentsia we're talking about, because there are various kinds of *intelligenty*."[121] Recalling the civil war from the perspective of 1940, he contrasted his attitude with that of Trotsky; whereas the latter had enthusiastically embraced "old officers, specialists, who often turned traitor," he himself chose "people loyal to the Revolution, people connected with the masses, by and large non-commissioned officers from the lower ranks . . ." However, he also claimed to have been "clearly aware of the enormous value of honest specialists" and was concerned to correct Lenin's misapprehension that he did not "give a damn for specialists."[122]

Contemporary evidence indicates that during the 1920s Stalin did indeed express a cautious welcome for the limited use of the non-Communist intelligentsia, particularly in parts of the USSR where indigenous *intelligenty* were perceived to be in short supply.[123] In 1925, for example, he argued in favor of employing the non-party intelligentsia of Kirghizia in soviet and cultural work, suggesting that this would promote their "sovietization." But at the same time he objected categorically to their involvement in any kind of ideological or political activity, stating, "We didn't take power so that the political and ideological education of youth would be handed over to bourgeois non-party *intelligenty*."[124] His stated preference, like that of many Bolsheviks, was for the fabrication of a new and

untainted *Soviet* intelligentsia that would share the party's goals and partici-
pate in political life; as Bukharin put it in 1924: "We will turn out intellectuals, we will manufacture them, just as in a factory."[125] This nascent
intelligentsia was to be organically related to the proletariat, "linked . . .
by ties of blood," according to one Bolshevik, Platon Kerzhentsev.[126] Such
kinship imagery would become increasingly common in the later 1930s as
Stalin sought to legitimize the Soviet intelligentsia to a still rather skeptical
public.[127]

In 1925 Stalin was already encouraging the "Soviet Red intelligentsia"
to join the party, drawing a distinction between it and its bourgeois coun-
terpart. At an Orgburo session that debated the categories to be used for
party admission, Stalin pressed for three categories: first, workers—primarily
industrial workers, then other workers and farm laborers (*batraki*); second,
peasants and craftsmen (*kustari*), with craftsmen taking precedence; and
finally, *sluzhashchie* and intelligentsia, with the "Red intelligentsia" in first
place. He proposed singling out "our Soviet Red intelligentsia" because
"as it is we have tormented it too much. He was a worker, but over the
course of these years he managed to study a bit, has a bit of knowledge
and skill, has worked a lot. It's wrong to place such a Soviet Red intelligent
in the same category as the 'un-Soviet intelligentsia.'" Stalin proceeded to
highlight the importance of creating "our own commanding officers, our
engineers, technical personnel, and so on, otherwise we won't be able to
govern."[128]

The campaign to legitimize the Soviet intelligentsia stepped up following
the decision of the fourteenth party congress to embark on industrialization. In his April 1926 speech to the Leningrad party organization, Stalin
made it clear that the party must concentrate on "forging" its own leading
cadres for the industrialization "front," just as it had created its own
commanders in the civil war. These cadres were to be drawn from the ranks
of workers and Soviet intelligentsia, "that same Soviet intelligentsia that
linked its fate with the fate of the working class and that is building along
with us the socialist foundations of our economy."[129] An increasingly militant "class war" tone was already audible at the fifteenth party congress,
where Stalin emphasized what he perceived to be growing differentiation
within the intelligentsia. He declared that whereas the "new bourgeoisie"
was dissatisfied with Soviet power, hundreds and thousands of the "laboring

intelligentsia" were coming over to its side, especially the technical intelligentsia, which was closely involved in production and could see its
benefits, as well as the rural intelligentsia. Now the party's task was to
isolate the bourgeois intelligentsia and encourage the "*smychka*" of the
"laboring intelligentsia" with the working class.[130] The exposé of politically
unreliable "bourgeois specialists" in Shakhty in March 1928 represented
the logical culmination of this strategy. The Shakhty affair added fresh
momentum to the parallel drive for a "cultural revolution" aimed at creating
an entirely new Soviet intelligentsia through the massive expansion of
education and worker promotion (*vydvizhenie*).[131]

To forestall any backlash against the new "laboring intelligentsia" in the
wake of Shakhty, Bolshevik leaders hastened to criticize residual anti-
intellectualism within the party. At the April 1928 CC plenum, the "showcase proletarian" Tomskii ridiculed Communists who disdained workers
who had received an education: "With us it's like this: you're not educated,
you're a worker from the bench, you are one of us, we like and respect
you. When you are removed, go to rabfak [workers' faculty], graduate
from a VUZ [higher education], you're another person, you've become
alien, you're no longer one of us, you're an *intelligent* . . ." He pointed
out that if he, Uglanov, or Voroshilov had benefited from a higher education, they would be in a somewhat stronger position, "but with us to be
an *intelligent* is considered shameful." He insisted that the technical intelligentsia that had emerged from the ranks of workers should be evaluated
in a different way.[132] Stalin echoed these words a few weeks later in his
speech to the eighth Komsomol congress. He reaffirmed that the working
class required its own intelligentsia, arguing that the "bravery" typical of
the civil war era was no longer enough. Juxtaposing *kul'turnost'* with
backwardness, he deplored the "barbaric" attitude often displayed toward
those who had acquired *kul'turnost'* and left the factory bench: "If you
are illiterate or don't write properly and boast about your backwardness,
you are a worker 'from the bench,' you have honor and respect. If you
have escaped from *nekul'turnost'* (lack of culturedness), become literate,
mastered science, you are alien, 'you've broken away' from the masses,
have ceased to be a worker."[133] Clearly Stalin's words did not succeed in
eradicating the engrained antipathy toward the new intelligentsia, and
doubtless the officially sponsored harassment of the "old" intelligentsia

during the cultural revolution only inflamed the prejudices of those convinced that anyone with an education might not share the interests of the workers.

By early 1931, once the militant phase of the cultural revolution had already passed, the official attitude toward the old intelligentsia was becoming more conciliatory, paving the way for its eventual rehabilitation and incorporation into a broader concept of a Soviet intelligentsia that embraced both "old" and "new" regardless of class origins. Ordzhonikidze has often been identified with this tendency, but Stalin himself was clearly not opposed to the conciliatory line. Whereas his speech to the Conference of Workers in Socialist Industry in February 1931 had included hostile references to specialists and sabotage, provocative phrases such as "old, worn-out specialists" were expunged or toned down for the published version.[134] By May, he was advocating greater toleration of old specialists and technical personnel: at the CC meeting concerning the Donbas coal industry, he wondered aloud why the question of the "so-called *spetsy* (specialists)" had not been raised in the meeting's resolution. He asked rhetorically whether they were all "scoundrels" or if some were decent, and, since the latter was indeed the case, suggested this be mentioned in the resolution as a way of showing them some moral support. Stalin asserted that although there were some specialists and technical personnel who deserved to be put on trial, most were in fact loyal. He proceeded to describe the intelligentsia as "the most vacillating element of all the strata": for three or four years they had hoped for Western intervention and the collapse of Soviet power, believing that the kolkhoz system was doomed, but once it became apparent that these beliefs were unfounded, a large section of them, probably the majority, were starting to lean toward Soviet power. It was therefore high time to draw them in and encourage them to work.[135] These conciliatory words were followed by the more well-known "New Conditions, New Tasks" speech of 23 June 1931, in which Stalin expressed his support for the old intelligentsia and spoke out against specialist-baiting (*spetseedstvo*).[136]

This signaled the start of a more positive interpretation of the intelligentsia as a whole. Nevertheless it is clear that the term "intelligentsia" continued to provoke controversy. Tomskii alluded to some of the semantic confusion at the January 1933 CC plenum, noting that although their "own proletarian intelligentsia" had almost been created, there was still a need for the old intelligentsia: "it's no longer that intelligentsia, even the word 'intelligentsia' isn't quite suitable, for when we talk about the intelligentsia, we, old Marxists, somehow go around in a circle of former understandings about the intelligentsia as a kind of 'interclass stratum' [*mezhklassovoi prosloike*]." (In the corrected version of the stenographic report these final words were changed to "understandings and arguments about the intelligentsia as part of the bourgeoisie or as a kind of interclass stratum.") Tomskii's slight discomfort with some of the connotations of the term prompted a retort from Skrypnik, who argued that old Marxists had never thought about the intelligentsia in this way. Tomskii then distinguished the new Soviet intelligentsia from its predecessor, describing it as an integral part of the working class, as "proletarian": "It's a completely different intelligentsia, which poses the very concept of 'the intelligentsia' in a new way, for this layer [*sloi*; "this new proletarian intelligentsia" was added to the corrected stenogram] is a group within the working class, an inseparable part of the working class, and the question of the creation and strengthening of the power of the working class, the question of who whom [*kto kogo*], is being decided irrevocably in the main."[137]

At this stage the question of how the intelligentsia should be regarded was still far from being resolved. The reevaluation and rehabilitation of the category was a protracted process, and one that owed much to Stalin's choice of words in slogans and other key political texts. Although the term "intelligentsia" did not feature in the important May Day and Revolution anniversary slogans until the end of 1938, Stalin used a variety of other terms to publicize those engaged in non-manual labor. In 1933 he personally added an extra sentence to a draft May Day slogan focused on science and technology: "long live workers of science, technical personnel, and engineers who lead work at shock tempos,"[138] while in 1934 he added the phrase "engineers and technical personnel" to several May Day slogans that had been addressed purely to "workers" in various branches of industry (his formulation "workers, engineers, and technical personnel" was retained in subsequent years). At a time when patriotic discourse was becoming ever more prominent, Stalin carefully amended the words of one of these slogans to identify scientific and technical workers with patriotic rather than party allegiance: "Long live workers of science and technology, moving hand in hand with the working class ~~and party~~ in the great matter of the construction of socialism and strengthening of the defense of the ~~USSR~~ **our motherland**" (his addition is in bold and his deletions are struck through).[139] This appeal also featured in the November 1934 slogans, while in May 1935, in recognition of the prominence of the arts, it became an appeal to "workers of science and technology, art and literature," who were now described as "walking hand in hand with the working class [Stalin added 'and peasantry'] and strengthening the technical and cultural might of the Socialist Motherland!"[140]

While Stalin's famous "cadres decide everything" slogan of May 1935 added some momentum to the campaign,[141] the decisive turning point came with the introduction of the new Soviet constitution that defined the "people's intelligentsia" as a unified "stratum" that recruited from other classes. In his speech on the subject of the constitution at the end of 1936, Stalin used the umbrella term "intelligentsia" to stand for an otherwise rather disparate group consisting of "the intelligentsia, ITR, workers on the cultural front, *sluzhashchie* in general." He maintained that this was no longer the "old backward [*zaskoruzlaia*] intelligentsia, which tried to stand above classes but the majority of whom in fact served the landowners and capitalists." Instead, this Soviet intelligentsia was a new phenomenon with its roots in the workers and peasants; 80–90 percent of its members were from the working class, peasantry, and other laboring groups. Its function had also changed to one of serving the people, and it therefore enjoyed equal rights with others.[142] Stalin clarified that the first article of the constitution, which described the USSR as a "socialist state of workers and peasants," could not include the intelligentsia because it always had been, and remained, a stratum (*prosloika*) that recruited from other classes.[143]

Stalin elaborated on these ideas a few weeks later during his conversation with the writer Lion Feuchtwanger, who was interested in this definition of the intelligentsia as what he called an "interclass" (*mezhklassovoi*) stratum.[144] Feuchtwanger suggested that an intelligentsia that was not linked to a single class had fewer prejudices and greater freedom of judgment, but because of that fewer rights. Stalin then claimed that he had simply outlined the normal Marxist conception of the intelligentsia and had not added anything new. A class was merely a social group of people with a definite, constant position in the production process. Whereas workers, capitalists, landowners, and peasants all occupied definite positions in the production process, the intelligentsia served other classes as a "service [*obsluzhivaiushchii*] element, not a social class." He argued that when the intelligentsia tried to pursue independent goals and to ignore the interests of society, as in 1870s Russia, it was doomed to utopianism. The more the intelligentsia recognized and served the interests of the ruling classes, the greater its social significance. Stalin agreed that under capitalism the intelligentsia had fewer rights because *intelligenty* generally lacked capital, but that in the USSR everyone who worked had equal rights, including the intelligentsia.[145]

Stalin's words heralded the start of a more concerted campaign by the leadership to sell the intelligentsia to continuing skeptics. This involved accentuating the organic links between the intelligentsia and the workers/ people, as well as emphasizing the functional necessity of well-educated citizens in a modern, progressive state. For example, in April 1937 Molotov used familiar biological metaphors, describing the new technical intelligentsia as from "the same flesh and blood as the industrial working class."[146] As we have seen, Stalin increasingly spoke about the need for the country to be run by educated people. At the rather secretive October 1937 CC plenum he argued that if the plenum's delegates were a real intelligentsia, they would avoid "cheap demagogy" and support the election of members of the intelligentsia to the new Supreme Soviet: "Some people think that if enough combine harvesters, tractor drivers, women tractor drivers, flax pullers, and so on are proposed as candidates for the Supreme Soviet everything will be fine, but we also need experienced politicians of a regional and central stature in the Supreme Soviet." He highlighted the importance of achieving a balance between politically inexperienced worker and peasant deputies and experienced politicians. The party intelligentsia, regional and republican leaders, professors, and military commanders should not be forgotten, and to rely on tractor drivers would be "the cheap demagogy of a seeming intelligentsia. And surely you are not in that position of being a seeming intelligentsia? No, you are not in that position. The balance between politically experienced and inexperienced deputies must be observed not along the lines of demagogy but along the lines of Bolshevik leadership."[147]

This campaign to promote the intelligentsia in 1937–38 was considerably complicated by the unfolding Great Terror. Many of its most prominent victims could be classified as *intelligenty*, and it had the effect of unleashing a wave of populist, anti-official, anti-intelligentsia sentiment.[148] As the Terror subsided, Stalin's attention was increasingly focused not only on the matter of the intelligentsia's theoretical grounding, but also on the question of how to elevate its status in the eyes of the public. In this connection, the publication of the *History of the All-Union Communist Party (Bolsheviks): Short Course* in September 1938 proved to be a particularly important development.[149]

Stalin clearly attached great significance to the dissemination of the *Short Course*, since over the course of two weeks in late September–early October he delivered no less than three major speeches on the subject of propaganda in connection with the text. In his first speech to a meeting of propagandists from Moscow and Leningrad,[150] he emphasized that the book was designed primarily not for ordinary factory workers or *sluzhashchie*, but for those he described variously and somewhat confusingly as "the intelligentsia," "cadres," "leading cadres," "*sluzhashchie*," "administrative apparatus," "commanding staff," "people who work with their intellect." He also singled out students—"tomorrow's commanders." He mentioned a figure of eight million cadres in all areas of the economy and administration.

Stalin claimed that it was this group that, overburdened with practical political work, suffered from theoretical "backwardness" and required a grounding in theory, "bolshevization." Hitherto these non-manual workers had been neglected, in part because of the legacy of *makhaevshchina*, the "theory" that the intelligentsia should be driven from the party, that so-called callused hands were required. He argued that, on the contrary, calluses were now no longer obligatory at factories since "our factory is something like a laboratory, something like a chemist's, where it's clean and there are no calluses. Is this bad or good? I think it's good, very good. Calluses are a matter of the past." Eventually, Stalin suggested, all workers and peasants would join the ranks of the intelligentsia. Echoing his words of 1928, he criticized attitudes to yesterday's worker, who was respected when he worked at the bench, but as soon as he managed to get an education and move up: "'intelligentsia,' they spit at him."

Stalin went on to emphasize the critical importance of the intelligentsia in the USSR, explaining that the Soviet state could not possibly manage without this stratum. He tried to create a sense of urgency, referring to the perennial issue of Soviet backwardness and the danger of falling behind bourgeois states: "Either we create our own genuine intelligentsia and respect it, either we follow the course of respecting the intelligentsia that has emerged, either we care for and respect students—our future commanders in all areas of administration—either we do this or we will perish." These words contained what may have been a deliberate echo of his famous speech of 4 February 1931 in which he argued that the USSR must catch up with advanced countries in ten years: "Either we do that or we will be crushed."[151]

Stalin drew a clear distinction between workers and the intelligentsia, suggesting that the latter would approach the *Short Course* very differently from the former, "who works an eight-hour day, has a family, is busy and cannot devote much time to this." The worker would require simple explanations, and propagandists would have to avoid frightening him with theoretical complications, whereas non-manual workers might use the book as a springboard for their own further study of Marxist-Leninist classics. Stalin also insisted that despite his stress on the intelligentsia, workers and peasants should not be ignored by propagandists.[152]

He reiterated some of these points and expanded on others in a further speech at a meeting of propagandists on 1 October and at a Politburo session devoted to propaganda on 11 October. At the latter, he aimed for slightly greater precision in his classification of non-manual workers. He explained that the book would be particularly useful for *cadres*, that is, "the low, middle, and high commanding officers of the entire state apparatus." He observed that the term "cadre" had traditionally been applied to party cadres, whereas other state employees had been described as "*sluzhashchie*," a word that he admitted had pejorative connotations.[153] But the state could not exist without these *sluzhashchie*, and without what he termed "the intelligentsia" and "people who live by their intellect."

Returning to the issue of *makhaevshchina* and perceptions of the intelligentsia, Stalin observed a general reluctance in people to identify themselves as members of the intelligentsia. He generated some amusement by citing Khrushchev as an example: "Comrade Khrushchev thinks that to this day he remains a worker, when in fact he's an *intelligent*."[154] Makhaev was, he went on, "a fool, a complete idiot, because he did not understand that it's not only necessary to value one's intelligentsia, but also to make the whole working class, the peasantry, into an intelligentsia." Stalin described those who disdained workers who had left the bench "as worse than enemies . . . pitiful, unhappy people, Makhaevites, with nothing in common with Marxism" because they risked destroying the state and socialism. Complaining that old attitudes to the "bourgeois intelligentsia" were sometimes mechanically applied to the new "worker-peasant intelligentsia," he defended the Soviet intelligentsia, defining it as "on the one hand it's us, old Bolsheviks, and on the other, nine-tenths young people from the workers, peasants, and petty laboring intelligentsia." He added that it was these who also constituted the great bulk of *sluzhashchie*.

Stalin confirmed that although the *Short Course* was aimed primarily at the intelligentsia, this did not mean that it was not suitable for workers or peasants. However, it was propaganda efforts among the intelligentsia that required most urgent attention. In a deliberate reference to the Great Terror, he pointed out that neglect of this matter had had serious political consequences, namely, that some cadres had been drawn to the ideas of figures such as Bukharin and Trotsky. Stalin distinguished between the people (*narod*) who followed the party and cadres-*sluzhashchie*, some of whom, experience had shown, did not: "*Sluzhashchie* are not workers from the bench or kolkhozniks who will stand behind us with all their heart because they see the results of our policies in practice. A *sluzhashchii* is someone who thinks with his head, works with his intellect . . . who will not blindly follow us."[155]

Stalin's concern to promote the intelligentsia and *sluzhashchie* in this period was noted by *Pravda* journalist Lazar Brontman, who recorded in his diary that the *vozhd'* was in constant contact with the newspaper when it was publishing the *Short Course* in September 1938. One night he apparently telephoned the editors to explain that the *Short Course* was not a "textbook" but a "doctrine/teaching" (*uchenie*) designed primarily for the intelligentsia. He then urged *Pravda* to include more material about the lives of *sluzhashchie*, repeating the word "*sluzhashchie*" three times. Brontman observed that they immediately had to start working out plans and themes: "It's a new matter."[156]

This unequivocal rehabilitation of the intelligentsia, and especially the subcategory of *sluzhashchie*, was reflected in the 7 November slogans, which were published a few weeks after these meetings and included one slogan directed specifically at *sluzhashchie* and another calling on unions to care for workers and *sluzhashchie*. The first slogan incorporating the term "intelligentsia" also appeared at this time. Stalin slightly amended the original version from: "The Soviet intelligentsia is a new intelligentsia, the likes of which the history of humanity has never known. More attention to the political education and Bolshevik tempering [*zakalka*] of the Soviet intelligentsia-cadres of our state apparatus!" to "Long live our Soviet people's [*narodnaia*] intelligentsia! More attention to the political education and Bolshevik tempering of the Soviet intelligentsia!" The accent was thus placed firmly on the connections between the intelligentsia and the "people," and on the intelligentsia as a coherent group rather than the looser-sounding entity "intelligentsia/cadres."[157] The new tone was even more striking in 1939: whereas in previous years the slogans had often included the sentence "Long live the union of workers and peasants—the basis of Soviet power!," for May 1939 this became "Long live the united front of workers, peasants, and intelligentsia!" after Stalin's intervention. He changed this yet again for 7 November, using the language of kinship to accentuate the organic connections more explicitly: "Long live the fraternal cooperation of workers, peasants, and intelligentsia of our country!"[158]

Stalin laid out his vision in forceful terms at the eighteenth party congress in 1939, where he described the "new, people's, socialist intelligentsia" that was "flesh from flesh and blood from blood of our people" as one of the most important results of the "cultural revolution."[159] He also criticized the continuing confusion within the party about the status of the Soviet intelligentsia and the ongoing suspicion of and hostility toward the educated. He explained that the new intelligentsia was radically different from the old bourgeois intelligentsia that, with a few brave exceptions, had served the landowners and capitalists. Remnants of the old had now "dissolved" into the new Soviet intelligentsia, the majority of whom were prepared to serve the people faithfully and truthfully. He warned that those who still believed that former workers and peasants with an education were second-class people were essentially propagating backwardness and ignorance.[160]

Although his vision of the Soviet intelligentsia was overwhelmingly positive, it is worth pointing out that Stalin was not devoid of contradictions and never completely lost the habit of using the word "*intelligent*" in a derogatory sense. In a letter to Molotov he once characterized Bukharin as "a typical representative of the spineless effete *intelligent* in politics . . ." As we saw in the previous chapter, he described Shatunovskii's expressions of personal devotion to him as an "empty and unnecessary intelligentsia trinket." As late as 1941, he derided the "frightened little *intelligenty* [*intel-ligentiki*]" who overestimated the strength of the fascist enemy.[161] However, what is more striking than these occasional lapses is the consistency with which he sought to invest the term "intelligentsia" with positive meaning over the course of the 1930s. His very public pronouncements at the nineteenth party congress completed this long process, paving the way for the further consolidation of the Soviet intelligentsia in the 1940s.[162]

The 1940 Legislation, "Labor Power," and the Younger Generation

Stalin's vigorous promotion of the intelligentsia in the immediate pre-war period coincided with a renewed spell of pessimism about the working class that reached a climax in 1940. By this stage, the perennial Soviet problems of low productivity and labor shortages had been exacerbated by the effects of the Great Terror and the rapid expansion of the armed forces at the end of the 1930s.[163] Tough labor legislation enacted in December 1938 failed to resolve the problems and was followed in 1940 by the controversial edict of 26 June that introduced an eight-hour work day and criminalized unauthorized job-quitting, absenteeism, and, most notoriously, lateness for work of twenty minutes or more.[164] The need for such drastic measures naturally reflected badly on Soviet workers, and the publicity surrounding the edict depicted what were described as a minority of workers in remarkably unflattering terms.

According to the Commissar of Armaments, Boris Vannikov, Stalin agreed only reluctantly to the introduction of the 1940 edict, as he was more inclined to believe that effective leadership was needed to tackle the problem. Khlevniuk implies that this reluctance may have been insincere.[165] Stalin certainly refrained from making public statements about the edict, presumably in an attempt to distance himself from what was a highly unpopular measure. However, in front of more limited audiences he defended the legislation, justifying it in part on the basis of poor productivity and the delinquent behavior of some Soviet workers, but also invoking anti-management and anti-union rhetoric familiar from earlier periods.

At a meeting on 19 June attended by the Deputy Chair of Sovnarkom, V. A. Malyshev, Stalin spoke quite candidly about Soviet workers' low productivity. As was his habit when seeking to justify a particularly controversial policy, he compared the Soviet Union unfavorably with other countries, claiming that whereas workers in capitalist states labored for ten to twelve hours, their Soviet counterparts only worked for seven hours, and badly at that. He argued that the introduction of the seven-hour day in 1927 had been a mistake; they "understood the economy poorly then." Now the time had come to ask workers to make sacrifices and work an extra hour without any additional pay. After this negative assessment of Soviet workers' productivity, he proceeded to address the ongoing problem of labor turnover. Following quite heated discussions, he proposed prohibiting the voluntary movement of workers (and *sluzhashchie*) from enterprise to enterprise, describing those who moved around as the "10–15 percent of loafers, self-seekers, and drifters who mix up all our cards." It is worth noting that these figures were considerably higher than those mentioned in the All-Union Central Council of Trade Unions' (VTsSPS) address to workers, ITR, and *sluzhashchie* published on 26 June, which specified that only 3–4 percent were responsible for turnover, absenteeism, and discipline problems, and that the majority had nothing to fear. Just as he had done at the end of the 1920s, Stalin attributed some of the blame for workers' misdemeanors to the "corrupting" influence of the unions, which he described as "not a school of communism, but a school of self-seekers."[166] At a further meeting, he accused the VTsSPS secretary, Nikolai Shvernik, of a "reformist policy": "Surely the unions are corrupting the workers if union representatives come in and turn off the lights in the shop when workers want to do overtime?!"; "Unions encourage self-seeking moods among the workers."[167]

As various scholars have pointed out, the actual implementation of the 26 June edict proved to be highly problematic. These difficulties were considered by the CC plenum of July 1940, which Stalin addressed.[168] On this occasion he chose to depict workers in a rather more favorable light, speaking out against excessive reliance on repressive measures and criticizing factory directors who were incapable of properly regulating the labor force. In particular, he opposed a proposal to punish workers who fulfilled the same norms in eight hours as they had done in seven.[169] Arguing that the majority of workers were "honest," he claimed that the problems stemmed from a minority of "hooligans" and from poor management: "In this case it's a question of a handful or dozens of hooligans. The great majority of workers, who work honestly, won't allow such a thing. If there were real directors, then I'm sure that nine-tenths of the decree would be unnecessary, but since the directors of our enterprises are not real bosses, can't manage properly, tolerate these hooligans, these hooligans don't respect them, don't respect labor in general, and because of this, we have to compensate for directors' leadership failings with repression, and nevertheless there must be limits to this repression."[170]

Stalin's repeated use of the word "hooligan" here is noteworthy. "Hooliganism" was the term used to designate a range of offenses, some minor, some more serious, including public drunkenness and disorder, and a general disregard for social norms. It had been customary to attribute hooligan behaviors to the working class, for example in the second half of the 1920s hooliganism had been associated with poor discipline among workers.[171] On this occasion, Stalin also chose to link lax labor discipline with hooliganism, presumably aware that the 26 June edict had inadvertently encouraged some workers who were desperate to be fired to engage in disorderly conduct and petty theft.[172] The use of the term also implied that the main culprits were young, since traditionally it tended to be the more youthful, male workers who were accused of the offence.[173] Certainly the VTsSPS address had stated quite clearly that "young workers" were responsible for turnover and discipline problems.[174] Large numbers of younger workers had in fact been recruited in response to the labor shortages arising from military mobilization, and whereas in the past Stalin had blamed ex-peasants or generally "backward" workers for labor problems, he was now more inclined to incriminate *youth* in particular.[175] Concerns about the younger generation figured prominently in Stalin's immediate pre-war discourse (it was a central theme of the *Law of Life* episode discussed above), contributing to a growing sense that young people, on

whom the country would have to depend during war, might not be sufficiently well integrated.[176] Many of the fears that had previously been
expressed about ex-peasants in the factories, for example, were now simply
projected onto young workers, whose allegedly unreliable behavior was
contrasted with that of the supposedly more "honest" cadre workers.

In his speech to the plenum, Stalin once again drew unfavorable comparisons between the Soviet Union and capitalist states, claiming that "if foreign
economic experts had a look today, they'd be horrified." If a Soviet worker
wanted to be fired, he engaged in hooligan behavior or petty theft, which
never happened under capitalism because of the constant fear of unemployment. In the USSR, the land of full employment, some workers came to
the factory for two or three months in order to work for three or four days
and then take the rest of the week off. If prohibited from leaving, they
then engaged in criminal activity and undermined discipline. Stalin drew
a distinction between cadre workers, who considered it an honor to work
in socialist industry and stayed in the factories, and younger workers, who
treated coming to work as a day out: "The conditions are such that he can
be a hooligan as much as he likes and nothing will happen to him. He does
not value work, he can live in the kolkhoz, there's a demand for labor
everywhere." Stalin used the vocabulary of "spoiling" more reminiscent
of the late 1920s, arguing that Soviet workers had not been "spoiled," but
that the existence of full employment simply allowed them to quit whenever
it suited them.[177]

While asserting that the workforce had not yet been spoiled, he nevertheless highlighted worrying trends, particularly the heavy reliance on
convict labor. Expressing regret that in distant parts of the north, one-third
of the labor force were criminals, he claimed: "In some far-flung places
gulag labor can be used, but in the machine-building industry, in towns,
where on one side there's a criminal working, and on the other a non-
criminal, I don't know about that, I'd say that's very irrational and not
really proper."[178] This dependence on convict labor was a response to the
long-standing Soviet conundrum: How to secure a regular supply of labor
to meet the demands of an expanding economy? This question had preoccupied Stalin since the early 1930s; however, by the end of the decade the
problem had become particularly acute.[179] According to his interpretation,
the supply of labor from the countryside had dried up since living standards

in the kolkhoz were now relatively high, while another source, the petite bourgeoisie, no longer existed. He warned that unless the workforce expanded, industry would be forced to contract. Rejecting the "scourge of unemployment" used by the bourgeoisie—"We consider, *as representatives of the working class* [our emphasis], that if such a scourge existed we should not use it"—he argued that other methods should be found. Repressive measures were necessary, but repression alone could not solve the underlying problem.[180]

Stalin's solution was radical: to create a new generation of workers who would be dependent on and loyal to the state. This was the thinking behind the proposed Labor Reserve scheme, designed to mobilize teenagers for an initial period of factory training followed by four years of compulsory factory work. Stalin envisaged recruiting youngsters from the large pool of Soviet orphans, as well as from families with multiple children "who are happy to be free of one or two sons or daughters." They would learn a trade for a year to eighteen months in a factory school "to give them the taste for city life, the requisite taste for working in industry." It would be necessary to recruit five to six million, starting with one or two million initially. Stalin described these recruits as "young people who depend on us and respect us."[181]

While the Labor Reserve scheme would suffice for the moment, Stalin proceeded to outline another longer-term plan for replenishing the working class. Earlier, at the May 1939 CC plenum, he had suggested that some of those he defined as "parasites"—the 30 percent of peasants who apparently earned less than fifty "labor-days" annually—should be "shaken out" of the kolkhoz and drawn into industry to help satisfy the insatiable demand for labor.[182] He reiterated this proposal to the July 1940 plenum, announcing that in future they would need to try to extract these "parasites" from the kolkhozy and force them to work. Currently anyone performing the minimum amount of work for the kolkhoz could spend the rest of the time "spitting at the ceiling" and would not starve because he had a plot, animals, and no housing expenses: "Why the devil would he go underground, to the mines?" According to Stalin, there were large numbers of these idle hands (*lishnye ruki*) in the countryside who would become increasingly redundant with mechanization. The main problem was how to drive them out of the kolkhoz. Until it was possible to achieve a "substantial natural influx" from the countryside to the cities, it would be necessary to rely on a Labor Reserve scheme rather than resorting to gulag labor. Stalin concluded that the use of Labor Reserves and *lishnye ruki* from the countryside was preferable to employing repressive measures, reiterating that repression on its own would solve nothing.[183]

Stalin returned to the question of the Labor Reserve scheme at the Politburo in September shortly before the system was introduced the following month. He justified the scheme on the grounds that it would allow them to control the composition of the working class, introduce continuity, and plan the use of labor power. Current factory schools (FZU) were unable to do this because of their voluntary status. He admitted that since the June edict was clearly insufficient, the only solution was to mobilize: "We cannot be indifferent to who's joining the working class. If this goes on in a spontaneous way, the composition of the working class may spoil, and correspondingly, the regime as a dictatorship of the working class may spoil. But at present, they grab anyone who turns up for a job. The formation of the working class cannot be left to spontaneity. The composition of the working class is changing, but how it's changing, no one is interested."[184]

If this represents a faithful record of Stalin's words (and Malyshev seems generally reliable), then the choice of terminology is interesting. Stalin's concern about the "composition of the working class," and how this might affect the regime as a "dictatorship of the working class" (as well as similar references in his plenum speech to the party as representative of the working class), differed markedly from much of the language of this period. By 1940, terms such as "dictatorship of the working class" had, with some exceptions, fallen out of favor. Clearly Stalin was not always consistent in his choice of words, and no doubt it was politically expedient to resurrect elements of this workerist language at a time when the party was adopting such controversial policies toward what had been considered its natural support base. In general, however, Stalin's vision of the working class in 1940 contrasted sharply with that of the 1920s. Whereas in 1928 he had insisted that "the working class is not only labor power, it's living people, they want to live . . .," by 1940 he was more inclined to talk about workers precisely in terms of "labor power" (*rabsila*), to portray them as an awkward problem for the state rather than a heroic ruling class.[185]

We now have a more complete picture of the various ways in which Stalin chose to interpret the important and controversial subject of the Soviet working class. The previously unpublished sources permit a fuller understanding of just how multifaceted his vision was. Stalin's ambivalence toward the proletariat/working class was part of a long-standing Bolshevik tradition: optimism concerning workers' theoretical role in the socialist transformation had always coexisted with doubts about their actual capabilities and allegiances. The experiences of rapid industrialization served merely to amplify concerns about the "backwardness" of the working class (as well as Soviet backwardness more generally).

Anxious to promote a vision of the USSR as a modern, cohesive state, Stalin gradually reworked the Bolshevik language of class. He continued to use terms such as "working class" throughout the 1930s, while simultaneously deemphasizing the importance of class in various ways. He challenged the very notion of the hegemony of the proletariat and he questioned the validity of the "biological" approach to evaluating individuals. He tried to divert attention from workers as a heroic class toward the select contingent of "advanced" worker-heroes, who were increasingly singled out for special treatment on the basis of their intellectual and cultural development rather than their callused hands. By the end of the 1930s, Stalin was speaking in quite disparaging terms—to certain audiences at least—about manual labor with all its connotations of backwardness. Thanks to a concerted campaign spearheaded by him, the newly prominent Soviet intelligentsia came to share the limelight occupied by workers and peasants. During the war, the term "working class" did not even feature in the important May Day and 7 November slogans.

This tendency only intensified after the war, along with Stalin's concerns about the international reputation of the Soviet Union. In 1946, he criticized the depiction of Soviet workers in *The Great Life*, Leonid Lukov's controversial film about the post-war reconstruction of the Donbas. Complaining that one worker "is impossible to wake unless he smells vodka and hears the sound of glasses," he questioned why the filmmakers "who live among golden people, among heroes" could not portray them correctly. Stalin observed that the film had the flavor of the olden days "when a manual worker was appointed instead of an engineer, like, you are one of us, a worker, you will lead us, we don't need an engineer. They push aside the engineer, appoint a simple worker, he will be in charge." Claiming that workers used to think like this in the early years of Soviet power, he stressed that much had changed since then, particularly as a result of mechanization, and insisted that if the film were to be corrected "all the spirit of *partizanshchina* [partisanism], that we don't need educated people, we don't need engineers" would have to be eradicated.[186]

Stalin's words were clear enough, and during his final years the status of the intelligentsia remained high relative to that of the "simple worker." The premium placed on education and culture grew ever more pronounced, with the leader himself conspicuously venturing into the terrain of scholarly debate.[187] Of course, the manual worker never completely disappeared from view: the hammer and sickle remained as emblems of Soviet power, although they no longer corresponded closely with Stalin's vision of modern Soviet society. A more unambiguously positive image of the ordinary manual worker was revived only under Khrushchev, that "able worker" whom Kaganovich had promoted because of what Stalin called his "weakness for the working class." As Amir Weiner observes, during Khrushchev's ascendancy "an intense media campaign celebrated the honor and worth of manual labor, praising citizens who were not afraid of soiling their hands rather than 'sitting in their offices and filing papers.'"[188] It seemed that callused hands were back in fashion once again.

6

SOVIET CULTURE

The relationship between the Bolshevik Party and the arts was never an easy one. According to Plekhanov, "Social consciousness is determined by social existence. For a man who maintains such a view it follows that art, and so-called belles-lettres, expresses the strivings and the mood of a given society, or, if we have to do with a society divided into classes, of a given social class."[1] While all Bolsheviks subscribed to this conventional Marxist wisdom, they differed in their understanding of what it might actually mean for cultural policy after the Revolution. How far should culture directly reflect the interests and aspirations of the newly ascendant proletariat? What was the role of the party, as vanguard of this class, in artistic affairs?

Lenin did not provide any tidy solutions. In his 1905 article "Party Organization and Party Literature" he made some ambiguous statements about the need for "*partiinost'*" (party spirit) in literature and the formation of a literature closely allied to the proletariat.[2] After 1917, he often argued that artists must build on the achievements of "bourgeois" culture, and he remained skeptical of the semi-autonomous Proletkul't movement, which aimed to stimulate a distinctive proletarian culture and class consciousness. When Lenin subordinated Proletkul't to Narkompros (Commissariat of Enlightenment) in 1920, he made it clear that the arts were merely one branch of public education and, as such, should serve the political needs of, and be supervised by, the state.[3] However, Lenin was never particularly concrete about these matters, and throughout the 1920s heated debates continued about the relationship between class, party, and culture.

Stalin's *Works* contain relatively few references to the arts and until the opening up of the Soviet archives it was often assumed that he had little to say on this subject.[4] Recent studies have shown this to be very far from the case.[5] While Stalin generally preferred not to publish his utterances, in part, no doubt, because he wished to minimize the impression of undue interference in the cultural process, behind the scenes he commented regularly on artistic affairs, and his words often circulated quite widely, leaving a strong imprint on Soviet discourse. Although it is now clear that the concept of "totalitarian culture" is inadequate on many levels and that "Stalinist" cultural policies and practices were not simply imposed from on high but were the result of a more complex process of interaction among the party-state, artists, and public, it is nonetheless important that we do not lose sight of the crucial role played by Stalin and his particular vision of Soviet culture.[6]

This vision was never static or one dimensional. Stalin always insisted that, as a powerful political weapon, culture must serve the dominant class/Soviet state. He increasingly favored subordinating artists to party control, and from 1932 he expected them to work within the confines of socialist realism. And yet, this authoritarian, dogmatic stance was always counterbalanced by a rather more tolerant, flexible rhetoric: as Evgenii Gromov points out, Stalin was sometimes inclined to present himself in the guise of a well-informed cultural "moderate" and to vilify those who advocated a more simplistic, sectarian approach.[7] He liked to create the impression that he regarded the arts as more than just a form of party propaganda, emphasizing that culture constituted a distinct sphere with its own intrinsic aesthetic requirements. This chapter will explore his multifaceted vision as it evolved from the 1920s, focusing particularly on the more verbal arts of literature, theater, and cinema, for which he felt most responsible in his role as "guardian of the texts."[8]

Debating "Proletarian Culture"

During the 1920s discussions about culture became increasingly fraught and intertwined with political debates about NEP and the very future of the Soviet Union. The young militants centered on VAPP (All-Russian Association of Proletarian Writers), the "On Guard," and

"October" groupings regarded art first and foremost as a political instrument for the party, arguing that it was the latter's responsibility to endorse only an expressly partisan, proletarian-oriented culture in order to hasten the advent of socialism and prevent bourgeois "infection" of the working class.[9] However, moderates such as the editor of *Krasnaia nov'*, A. Voronskii, insisted that it should tolerate and even welcome a more pluralistic culture capable of accommodating the work of the non-Communist "fellow travelers" (*poputchiki*), as Trotsky labeled them, who were broadly sympathetic to the Bolsheviks' cause and possessed the talents and experience required to produce art that would broaden the workers' perspective and further their "cognition of life." In contrast to their opponents, the moderates believed that "all art is class art; but . . . it is not *only* that."[10]

Leading Bolsheviks, who had largely abstained from direct intervention in cultural matters during the turmoil of the civil war, participated enthusiastically in the polemics of the early 1920s. In the conciliatory spirit of NEP, most favored a more flexible and inclusive "soft line" and opposed the radical sectarianism of the proletarian militants.[11] Both the party's main spokesmen on artistic affairs, Trotsky and Bukharin, rejected a reductive class-based approach, particularly the crude and misleading application to the arts of the labels "bourgeois" and "proletarian." Whereas Trotsky questioned whether a specifically "proletarian" culture could develop in what he anticipated would be a relatively brief transition period before the advent of a classless society, Bukharin was consistently more sympathetic to the idea of proletarian culture, but remained adamant that it could only evolve if open to non-proletarian influences. Both concurred that although the *poputchiki* might not share all the party's values, they could still play a useful role, and, with sufficient nurture, might ultimately be won over to the cause.[12]

For example, in *Literature and Revolution*, Trotsky maintained that the artistic realm was relatively autonomous and should not be approached in exactly the same manner as politics and the economy: "art must make its own way and by its own means. The Marxian methods are not the same as the artistic." While accepting the principle of party involvement in the arts, he rejected the notion of rigid control, proposing that the party should help and protect art, but not "command" it.[13] Trotsky accused the proletarian wing of espousing an excessively narrow approach: writing to one of their leading advocates, L. Averbakh, in 1924, he criticized their vision of art as a self-contained entity, a "microcosm" rather than "part of a macrocosm." According to Trotsky, Averbakh and his supporters were only interested in literature and ignored other forms of political influence. Although the works of writers such as Gorky, for example, contained much politically dubious material, they were far from being the only influence on workers, and served to broaden the worker's "field of vision" (*pole zreniia*) rather than completely altering his "angle of vision" (*ugol zreniia*). Trotsky insisted that it was important to differentiate between categories of writers: while "White" (anti-Soviet) writers were incapable of enlarging the workers' field of vision, the *poputchiki* could do so because they were often able to reveal what others failed to see. He conceded that it would be ideal if all literature was communist, but currently this was not feasible. Workers derived from literature what they did not get from other spheres, and a *poputchik* who broadened a worker's field of vision was more valuable than a Communist who was incapable of adding anything new.[14]

Trotsky defended the pluralist position at the May 1924 meeting of the CC's press department that was held to try to address the growing clamor from militants for party intervention. Following presentations by representatives from both sides, I. Vardin and Voronskii, Trotsky spoke out emphatically against the very possibility of proletarian culture. Bukharin justified the policy of party neutrality in a somewhat more conciliatory manner, arguing that proletarian literature could only thrive in an atmosphere of "free anarchic competition."[15] Pressure mounted for a clearer statement of the party line, however, and this resulted in the important CC resolution on literature of 1925.

This resolution, whose principal contributors included Bukharin, was a classic compromise typical of NEP, steering a middle course between the two extremes—advocating "free competition" between different artistic tendencies and backing the fellow travelers on the one hand, but pledging to encourage the development and eventual hegemony of proletarian culture on the other.[16] The resolution has been variously interpreted, with some maintaining that the proletarians gained ground and others regarding it as a victory for Voronskii's line.[17] However, in light of what followed, it could be argued that a less immediately obvious beneficiary was the principle of a unified, party-directed "Soviet" culture, since the underlying message of the resolution was that the party was responsible for the overall direction of cultural policy, the ultimate aim of which should be the creation of a "Soviet literature" (a term mentioned in the final sentence) accessible to "millions." As we shall see, this is a position with which Stalin would have sympathized.[18]

What, then, was Stalin's stance in this period? Unlike Trotsky and Bukharin, Stalin tended to distance himself from the public discussions of the mid–1920s, preferring to cultivate an impression of lack of expertise.[19] For example, at the height of the debates in February 1925, he gave a deliberately non-committal response to Lunacharsky's request for his opinion on whether honors should be bestowed on the Bol'shoi's N. Golovanov, N. Obukhova, and K. Derzhinskaia in connection with the centenary of this most traditional of theaters: "I'm not strong in artistic matters, as you yourself know, and I do not dare say anything decisive in this area."[20] This cultivated self-deprecation was a recurring motif in his correspondence. Although reticent in public, in more private settings he did express certain views, which are in some ways quite consistent with his subsequent interventions. From early on, he portrayed himself as an advocate of an inclusive "Soviet" rather than a "proletarian" culture, arguing that it would be more productive to attempt to win over a broad spectrum of artists instead of alienating them with "communist arrogance." However, he simultaneously offered considerable moral support to the proletarians and their ambitions for a culture aimed at political mobilization. In this respect, his stance was in harmony with the conciliatory spirit of the 1925 resolution.

The kernel of some of Stalin's subsequent views on the need to use organizational measures to unify and control a broad range of "Soviet" writers can be detected as early as 1922, a time of considerable Bolshevik anxiety about the pernicious influence of writers in the semi-free market of NEP.[21] In June Trotsky warned the head of Gosizdat's editorial board: "Literature is now acquiring the greatest significance. Almost every day little books of poems and literary criticism are appearing. Ninety-nine percent of these publications are filled with anti-proletarian moods and essentially anti-Soviet tendencies." In his opinion, censorship was not the only solution; rather a proactive approach to the publication of more politically suitable works should be undertaken.[22] Trotsky went on to

present the Politburo with various concrete proposals about the assimila-
tion of young writers and artists who were sympathetic to the Bolsheviks
but potentially susceptible to the influence of the bourgeoisie. These
included the creation of a register of artists centered on Glavlit, professional
encouragement and material support for sympathizers, and the establishment of a non-party literary journal.[23]

Stalin also expressed an interest in this question, although, not surprisingly, his vision was rather different from that of his rival. His own suggestions to the Politburo were framed explicitly in terms of the need to support
what he called "Soviet culture" and "Soviet-minded" writers. He maintained that the "creation of Soviet culture (in the narrow sense of the
word), about which much was written and spoken at one point by some
'proletarian ideologues' (Bogdanov, etc.)," was only just beginning, and
that this culture would emerge in the course of a struggle of young writers
drawn to their cause with various counterrevolutionary tendencies. Stalin
expressed a desire to unite "Soviet-minded" writers in a single "core" and
support them in this struggle. Arguing that the involvement of an official
censorship body (Glavlit) would only alienate artists, he proposed instead
uniting them in an independent *organization* such as a "society for the
development of Russian culture," ideally headed by a non-party, "Soviet-
minded" writer such as Vsevolod Ivanov.[24] Stalin's suggestions were based
on a paper that the deputy head of Agitprop, Ia. Iakovlev, had produced
at his request. Iakovlev identified six categories of potential sympathizers:
(1) older writers who had come over to their side in the early stage of the
Revolution such as Briusov and Gorky; (2) proletarian writers, Proletkul't;
(3) Futurists such as Mayakovsky; (4) Imaginists (Esenin, etc.); (5) the
Serapion Brothers (Vs. Ivanov, Shaginian, etc.) and political waverers such
as Pil'niak and Zoshchenko; (6) writers attracted to them via *Smena vekh*,
including Alexei Tolstoi and Erenburg. Iakovlev proposed that they be
encouraged to join a *non-party* "organizational center," and emphasized
that the "communist minority" must desist from "communist arrogance"
in their approach to such writers. He suggested that this center could be
based on the existing All-Russian Union of Writers, or on an entirely new
body such as a "society for the development of Russian culture," or on a
combination of both.[25] This co-optation of existing institutions was typical
of Bolshevik strategy at the time, while the emphasis on *Russian* culture

was deliberately designed to appeal to the influential *Smena vekh* current within the intelligentsia.[26]

A Politburo decree of 6 July, "On Young Poets and Artists," incorporated some of both Trotsky's and Stalin's proposals. A register was to be created and a subsidized non-party publishing house set up under Gosizdat to encourage the publication of works of a "general Soviet" orientation. Iakovlev was put in charge of a commission to discuss the notion of an organization of young poets headed by a reliable non-party figure. This commission ultimately concluded that a newly established publishing house, *Krug*, might form the basis for the creation of such a society.[27] Evidently Stalin's proposal for a "Russian/Soviet" umbrella organization was considered problematic from the outset, given the diversity of the artists concerned and their potential resistance to any form of organization, whether party or non-party. As Schull observes, even the attempt to unify them via *Krug* resulted in failure: "instead of uniting people, it succeeded in alienating nearly everyone."[28]

Stalin nevertheless continued to espouse similar ideas about the absorption and unification of writers of various persuasions. In 1928 he endorsed Gorky's proposal that the Federation of Organizations of Soviet Writers (FOSP), the loose coalition of writers' groups that had eventually emerged in 1927 in the wake of the 1925 resolution, be permitted to publish its own weekly newspaper. According to Stalin, this initiative was designed to win over young writers, and he made it clear that although technically the newspaper would be a non-party publication, in practice it would be in the hands of the party. The result of the proposal was the establishment of the influential *Literaturnaia gazeta*.[29] Stalin's support for a major FOSP initiative exemplifies his consistent preference for the "gathering" of writers under an ostensibly non-party "Soviet" umbrella, a preference that would be finally realized in 1932.

While endorsing the inclusive strategy of the 1920s, Stalin appears to have simultaneously expressed considerable sympathy for the proletarian wing and its aspirations for an overtly agitational art.[30] His close relationship with the proletarian "poet laureate" Dem'ian Bednyi in the 1920s has been amply documented in their personal correspondence.[31] Stalin also had private communications with the leadership of VAPP at the height of the debates about culture. He supported their call for a conference of proletarian writers, albeit with some irony, writing to Vardin and G. Lelevich in January 1925, "You frightened me to death with the 'bitter class struggle' between you and Voronskii, in view of which I went and voted out of fear for your suggestion regarding a conference. Don't frighten me any further, I'm frightened enough as it is."[32] He went on to meet with the VAPP leadership three times in early 1925 to discuss the question of proletarian literature.[33] However, this apparent sympathy for their cause did not extend to support for their exclusive, sectarian approach, and throughout NEP Stalin continued to endorse the work of talented fellow travelers such as Mikhail Bulgakov.[34] His more tolerant stance did not completely evaporate even with the launch of a full-scale "cultural revolution" and the drive for "proletarian hegemony" at the end of the decade.

The "proletarian" cultural crusade gained momentum at the end of the 1920s, when it seemed to dovetail neatly with the party's campaign for cultural revolution. Whereas in 1924 the CC had refused a request to hold a congress of proletarian writers, in November 1927 it sanctioned an All-Union of Congress of Proletarian Writers, which took place in April–May 1928. At this meeting, RAPP (Russian Association of Proletarian Writers, the heir to VAPP[35]) was commended by Lunacharsky for its willingness to serve the immediate political needs of the party, and the organization expanded rapidly thereafter.[36] In December 1928 an important CC resolution, "On the provision of literature to the mass reader," ordered the publication of literature designed for mass consumption, proclaiming that mass literature of all types (including belles-lettres) should serve more than ever as "an instrument for the mobilization of the masses" behind the party's current political and economic tasks. Publishers were instructed to rely particularly on *Communist* authors and to recruit new authors from the proletarian and peasant masses.[37]

This signaled the start of a more narrowly utilitarian approach to the arts that was, ostensibly at least, favorable to RAPP. The organization now appeared to enjoy privileged status: according to *Pravda*, it represented the "party line on literary issues."[38] Although this new policy must have been sanctioned by Stalin, his words betray an ambivalence regarding RAPP and its claims to hegemony. Fitzpatrick suggests that he probably considered the proletarian writers politically useful without ever fully endorsing their approach.[39] RAPP's fixation with party-minded literature, its concern with dialectical materialism rather than the study of literary technique, and its combative attitude to other artists seemed out of step with his own pronouncements on the arts, which continued to be rather more moderate and conciliatory. In certain respects at least, Stalin's words in this period did not differ markedly from the spirit of the 1925 resolution, which had not in fact been formally revoked.[40] He continued to speak up in favor of a range of artists and a variety of approaches, if, in his view, these could make a useful contribution toward *Soviet* objectives, particularly the urgent task of mass mobilization. He objected to RAPP's attempts to monopolize literary affairs, upholding what he called the party's (and his) "duty" to supervise the arts.

In early 1929 Stalin began to exercise this duty more regularly, acting as arbiter in the increasingly acrimonious conflicts between rival literary camps and between competing institutions, often, it should be noted, at the instigation of artists and officials themselves.[41] He expressed a particular interest in theater, which he described as the art form best suited to the task of mass mobilization.[42] In the late 1920s, much of the debate centered on the legitimacy of the plays of Bulgakov, whose fellow-traveling credentials and association with *Smena vekh* made him an obvious target for the militants. Bulgakov's controversial works, including *Days of the Turbins*, which portrayed the Whites sympathetically, and the satirical *Zoia's Apartment*, had been playing in MKhAT to large audiences since 1926 thanks to earlier interventions by Stalin and the Politburo.[43] The works were subject to unrelenting criticism from Communist critics and repeated attempts to ban them. With the onset of the cultural revolution, this criticism of Bulgakov and all that he symbolized became increasingly vehement. Finally, in December 1928, a group of self-proclaimed proletarians, the "Proletarian Theater" group (led by the playwright V. Bill'-Belotserkovskii), were emboldened to appeal to Stalin for support. The group sent him a letter, warning of a "Right danger" in art mirroring that in politics. One symptom of this was the recent decision, supported by Narkompros, to allow MKhAT to stage Bulgakov's *Flight*,[44] which they accused of idealizing White emigrants. The group complained that Bulgakov was receiving special treatment, mentioning rumors about Stalin's alleged sympathy with this "Right 'liberal' course." They requested that Stalin respond with the kind of "clearly orienting" answer that they had come to expect from him.[45]

Stalin obliged them on 1 February, following a Politburo decision to ban *Flight*.[46] He began by denying the existence of a direct correlation between art and party politics, emphasizing that there could not be a "Left" and "Right" in literature mirroring the split in the party. Theater and literature constituted a much broader, non-party sphere and works of art should only be categorized using class terminology, or concepts such as "Soviet"/"anti-Soviet," "revolutionary"/"anti-revolutionary," and so on. Bulgakov's *Flight* was neither "Right" nor "Left," but anti-Soviet (in its current form) in its attempt to elicit sympathy for the White Guard. Stalin did not reject the work entirely, simply observing that it required some correction. His defense of Bulgakov was presented in pragmatic terms: his plays were performed in the absence of superior alternatives by "their own" (*svoikh*) authors, and a play such as *Days of the Turbins* did more good than harm, since it demonstrated the strength of Bolshevism, even if this was not Bulgakov's intention. Stalin argued that only through "competition" with non-proletarian literature would a strong proletarian literature eventually emerge. He concluded by urging them to ignore rumormongering about his alleged "liberalism."[47]

In some respects, the language of this letter resembled that of Trotsky and Bukharin in the mid–1920s. Although Stalin's priority was the mobilization of the masses behind state objectives rather than "broadening the workers' perspective," like Trotsky, he denied that art was directly reducible to politics and that political categories could be mechanistically applied to artists and their works. Like Trotsky, he also argued pragmatically that the work of fellow travelers should be tolerated in the absence of high-quality communist alternatives, while his remarks about the need for healthy competition between proletarian and fellow-traveling literature contained more than an echo of Bukharin. Not surprisingly, the moderate Lunacharsky was eager for this letter to be published immediately, but Stalin was evidently less enthusiastic, appearing anxious to distinguish between his own "personal" communications and "official" party pronouncements.[48] In June 1929 he did send Gorky a copy of the letter, along with his subsequent correspondence with RAPP (see below), but was adamant that this represented "*personal* correspondence" (Stalin's emphasis).[49] As we shall see, the letter to Bill'-Belotserkovskii was only published in Stalin's *Works* twenty years later at a time of similar debate about *partiinost'* and culture.

Stalin's intervention notwithstanding, the campaign against *Days of the Turbins* did not die down. Just ahead of Stalin's meeting with Ukrainian writers on 12 February, the former Proletkul'tist and current deputy head of Agitprop, Platon Kerzhentsev, launched a public attack on MKhAT and Narkompros for staging a play so damaging to the interests of Ukraine.[50] The meeting itself focused on several issues, including nationalities policies and the development of Ukrainian culture; however, it was *Days of the Turbins* that attracted the most controversy. Delegates were anxious for the play to be banned, objecting to its portrayal of Ukrainians and elements of what they perceived to be *Smenovekhovstvo*.

In his speech to the meeting, which he clearly preferred not to publicize too widely, Stalin reiterated and developed many of the points he had made in his letter to Bill'-Belotserkovskii.[51] He argued that art should be judged by different criteria from party politics, and questioned the very concept of *partiinost'*: "But surely literature is not *partiinaia?*" Literature was broader than the party, and labels such as "Left" and "Right" did not apply to it. Instead distinctions such as Soviet/anti-Soviet, proletarian/anti-proletarian, revolutionary/non-revolutionary should be used.

He also denied that writers must be Communists or that they should write about Communists. Although Ukrainian culture should be "national in form, socialist in content," it did not follow that every writer should become a Marxist or a socialist. In his view, so-called "fellow travelers" such as Vs. Ivanov and B. Lavrenev had been more useful with their works *Armoured Train* and *Break* than ten, twenty, or even a hundred Communist "writers" who did not know how to write. Workers liked Ivanov and Lavrenev and were not worried about Right-Left distinctions. Lavrenev had captured aspects of proletarian life, while Ivanov's work possessed great "educational significance." Likewise, Stalin continued, they could not expect Bulgakov to be a Communist. When one delegate suggested withdrawing *Days of the Turbins* and replacing it with Kirshon's play *Baku Commissars*, Stalin retorted that they could not just write about Communists, since the reality was that out of a population of 140 million, only about half a million were party members. He explained that it was very easy to ban plays, but the needs and preferences of the public also had to be considered.

At the same time, Stalin conceded that Bulgakov himself was "alien" (*chuzhoi*), "not Soviet," "not one of us" (*ne nash*). His plays failed to show that their protagonists, for all their noble and honest qualities, were exploiters, but *Days of the Turbins* was nevertheless "useful" overall, since it demonstrated the strength of Bolshevism. Stalin distinguished between the outlook of the author and the work itself, observing that a play could be useful even though the author may not have intended this. He also emphasized that an individual's interpretation of the play depended partly on his or her perspective: a White Guardist would not like it, workers would see the strength of Bolshevism, while the more discerning would perceive the elements of *Smenovekhovstvo* and distortion of Ukraine as well as the play's positive features. Stalin expressed a similar pragmatism toward the classics, which could be both harmful and useful. He argued that there were few absolutely good works, identifying only four—*Voice of the Deep* (Bill'-Belotserkovskii), *The Rails Are Humming* (Kirshon), *Break* (Lavrenev), and *Armored Train* (Ivanov).[52]

In the end, despite Stalin's tolerant-sounding words, *Days of the Turbins* was eventually withdrawn in March 1929, partly, no doubt, to assuage its critics. However, it was revived in the rather different political climate of January 1932,[53] and Stalin continued to personally encourage a despondent Bulgakov after 1929, most notoriously with his widely discussed phone call of 1930.[54] Stalin's semi-public defense of Bulgakov was designed to demonstrate that he stood above the warring factions with the power to arbitrate and intervene to protect writers—not only Bulgakov himself, but also those of an altogether different political complexion.

One of these he protected in this way was Bill'-Belotserkovskii himself. The latter had quit RAPP to establish the "Proletarian Theater" group following public censure by the RAPP leadership (he had been described by Averbakh as a "déclassé lumpen" and "class enemy" for welcoming the departure to the West of the director Meyerhold and the MKhAT actor-director Mikhail Chekhov in the summer of 1928). When the leadership of RAPP continued their offensive against him, which included posting negative reviews of his play *Voice of the Deep*, the "Proletarian Theater" group decided to write to Stalin and Agitprop head A. Krinitskii. Meanwhile, in a separate letter, V. Osinskii also alerted Stalin to the campaign of discreditation.[55] In his response to Osinskii of January 1929, Stalin expressed support for Bill'-Belotserkovskii and *Voice of the Deep*, describing him as one of "the most able (of our) dramaturgists," and promising to do everything possible to protect him.[56] He subsequently defended Bill'-Belotserkovskii during a conversation with Averbakh, while on 28 February he justified his stance in a lengthy letter of response to "writer-Communists" of RAPP.

This letter argued that although Bill'-Belotserkovskii had not been entirely correct in his judgments, especially regarding Meyerhold, RAPP's criticism of him was excessive, and its description of him as a "class enemy" absurd: "*That's* not the way to gather (*sobirat'*) people from the Soviet camp. *That's* the way to disperse them and confuse them for the benefit of the 'class enemy.'" Using an extended military metaphor, Stalin criticized RAPP for its failure to be a good commander and deploy all its troops correctly. "The commander who is unable to take account of the particularities of all his varied units and use them *in different ways* in the interests of a *single, united* front—what kind of a commander is he . . . ?" While boasting about their careful approach to fellow travelers, RAPP's leaders were simultaneously seeking to destroy the likes of Bill'-Belotserkovskii. Stalin criticized the fellow-traveling Pil'niak, who was only capable of depicting "the back end of the Revolution," and questioned why RAPP was emphasizing its careful approach to him and not to Bill'-Belotserkovskii. He concluded by denying that his earlier letter to Bill'-Belotserkovskii and the "Proletarian Theater" group signified a change in his attitude to RAPP, insisting that his own relations with the organization remained close and friendly. He noted that he would continue to communicate with a range of writers: "This is necessary. This is useful. This is, finally, my duty."[57]

Gorky, to whom Stalin had sent a copy of this letter, as well as his earlier correspondence with the "Proletarian Theater" group, was, like Lunacharsky, eager that Stalin publicize his conciliatory words. At the end of November 1929, he appealed to Stalin's didactic urges, suggesting that he might expand and develop the ideas expressed in his "very good" letter to members of RAPP in the form of an article for the journal *Literaturnaia ucheba* on the theme of "the party's view of belles-lettres, its cultural-revolutionary significance." Undeterred by Stalin's silence, he reiterated his request in January, insisting that an article "will be useful for beginning writers. Very." Once again, however, Stalin resisted, pleading lack of time, and deliberately belittling his abilities: "Apart from that, what kind of critic am I, devil take me!"[58]

Although reluctant to commit to a public statement, throughout the period of RAPP's dominance Stalin continued to cultivate his image as protector and "gatherer" of writers from across the spectrum, and to counter RAPP's monopolistic tendencies. In 1930 he offered strong support to Aleksandr Bezymenskii, a prominent member of the newly formed extreme left Litfront faction, which was challenging the current RAPP leadership and its categorical devotion to realism and preoccupation with individual psychology (the "living man") in literature. Litfront claimed that this "psychologism" was overshadowing coverage of topical social issues and advocated greater diversity of approach, including elements of romanticism.[59] When Bezymenskii's play *The Shot* was attacked by RAPP for its schematism and lack of psychological depth, the author appealed directly to Stalin, who responded with a defense of the work.[60]

Stalin began his letter by presenting himself in a characteristically self-deprecatory light: "I am not an expert in literature and, of course, not a critic," however, since Bezymenskii had insisted, he would express his views. He declared that the writer's *The Shot* and *Day of Our Life* contained "nothing petit bourgeois or anti-party," describing them as "models of revolutionary proletarian art for our time" (the phrase "for our time" was carefully chosen). As in the Bulgakov case, he depicted himself in the role of a just arbiter, carefully weighing up the strengths and weaknesses of the contested works. In his view, they were not flawless and contained some "Komsomol avant-gardism," but they also served to draw attention to the issue of bureaucratism, and in this respect their benefits outweighed their minor faults.[61] Having earned Stalin's seal of approval, Bezymenskii subsequently enjoyed the privilege of speaking out publicly against the leadership of RAPP at the sixteenth party congress in June 1930.[62]

Likewise, in 1931 the fellow-traveling writer Marietta Shaginian received a letter from Stalin promising to help expedite the publication of her mammoth production novel, *Hydrocentral,* and to defend her from unwarranted criticism (he alleged not to have time to write a foreword for the book, however).[63] He also approved Konstantin Stanislavsky's request that MKhAT be granted permission to stage Nikolai Erdman's controversial play *The Suicide,* even though he claimed to be personally unenthusiastic about the work. His letter to Stanislavsky ended on yet another note of self-deprecation: "The supers (*superami*) will be comrades who know about artistic matters. I am a dilettante in these matters."[64]

Stalin's reputation among the literary intelligentsia was certainly enhanced by these carefully worded personal letters, as well as by other gestures such as his facilitation of Zamiatin and Pil'niak's travel to the West in 1931, his support for the son of the nineteenth-century satirist Saltykov-Shchedrin, and, of course, his ostentatious courting of Gorky, the ultimate "symbol of reconciliation" who returned permanently to the USSR in 1933 following a series of earlier sojourns.[65] A secret police report from March 1932 detailing Leningrad writers' reactions to the government's assistance to Saltykov included several glowing remarks about Stalin (who received a copy of the document). One comment by the critic V. Medvedev indicates that although Stalin intervened in a deliberately informal, personal, and low-profile manner, knowledge of his support quickly, and no doubt intentionally, reached a wide audience: "Stories like this Saltykov one betray facts, however strange it might seem at first glance, of a second essential point about Stalin, who is above all a most decisive and severe politician: his essence as a great liberal and patron in the best sense of that word. Every day we hear either about a conversation between Stalin and some writers, or about some assistance rendered at his initiative to one of the masses of writers. In Stalin, literature and writers have a great friend."[66]

Creating "Soviet Culture"

Stalin's consistent defense of a diverse range of writers from attacks by the overly aggressive leadership of RAPP paved the way for the introduction of a series of initiatives with momentous consequences: the abolition of RAPP, the creation of a Union of *Soviet* Writers, and the launch of "socialist realism."

The landmark decree dissolving RAPP, "On the *perestroika* of literary-artistic organizations," represented only one of several new ideological currents that were emerging in 1932. New economic policies allowed a greater role for the market and for consumption—the so-called neo-NEP. The seventeenth party conference announced that the foundations of a socialist economy had been built, and that a "classless socialist society" was imminent. This move away from class-war militancy toward an apparently more conciliatory stance was also manifest in the cultural *perestroika* of the period.[67]

Stalin was closely involved in this *perestroika* as a member of the Politburo commission set up in March 1932 to consider the future of RAPP, and as editor of the draft decree.[68] The latter justified the liquidation of RAPP on the grounds that the party had endorsed proletarian cultural organizations in order to combat the unhealthy tendencies of NEP; however, with the emergence of new writers and artists from worker and peasant backgrounds, RAPP was now impeding the development of *Soviet* literature and obstructing those who did not share their platform but were prepared to support Soviet power. A new Union, containing a Communist fraction, was to unite all writers who "supported the platform of Soviet power" (Stalin's substitute for "stand for the policies of Soviet power"). Analogous measures were to be undertaken in other fields of art.[69]

The decree alarmed the RAPPists and was welcomed by fellow travelers in equal measure. For many of the latter, it appeared to herald the start of a "thaw," "an act of reconciliation with non-party writers": Valerii Kirpotin, head of Kul'tprop's literature section, recalled how Meyerhold expressed his delight at the news by hanging a framed copy of the decree on the wall of his living room![70] However, the new measures certainly did not put an end to the conflicts and uncertainties plaguing the literary establishment—if anything it simply exacerbated them. Stalin himself attempted to introduce some clarity at his two well-known meetings with writers held at Gorky's residence in October 1932, a few days before the important first plenum of the Orgkomitet of the Writers' Union. These informal meetings and their location were an unusual departure, but not entirely without precedent: Kirov had apparently held a similar meeting with Leningrad writers in 1931 in the flat of the fellow traveler Mikhail Slonimskii.[71] The location sent out an important signal that Stalin wanted to reach out to writers beyond the party, and whereas the first meeting was restricted to Communists, non-party writers attended the second. Although no official stenograms were made, some of those present produced their own records of the meetings that were later handed over to the CC. Despite several suggestions from writers that these should be published, they were—characteristically—consigned to the archives. Knowledge of Stalin's words at the meetings spread widely, however.[72]

At the first session on 20 October, Stalin laid out his utilitarian vision for the arts. He stated explicitly that writers should be working toward the goals set by the party. This had not been possible because of the constant squabbles and infighting for which RAPP had, in large measure, been responsible. RAPP had been "in essence the central, leading group," and although useful at one stage, it should have been disbanded by 1931. Stalin explained that RAPP's monopolistic tendencies had become counterproductive, since it was unable to manage and unite even Communist writers, let alone non-party writers—the newly emerging literary forces and those members of the intelligentsia who had come over to the side of Soviet power. Even after the April 1932 decree it had been slow to change. Communist writers were now expected to abandon the ongoing sectarianism and work toward the party's goals. Stalin then turned to aesthetic questions before concluding with another critique of RAPP's conflictual approach and a defense of the much-maligned Bill'-Belotserkovskii, who "gave us several necessary plays."[73]

A selection of non-party writers, including L. Leonov, Vs. Ivanov, and L. Seifullina, were summoned to the second meeting with Stalin on 26 October, when he addressed the critical question of the relationship between non-party and Communist writers. Explaining that the previous meeting had followed the party tradition of members gathering to "purge [*chistim*] one another" before reaching a consensus, Stalin emphasized that it was the role of non-party people to check up on the work of party members (and vice versa). He confirmed that the decision to liquidate RAPP had been taken because the organization was incapable of working with those outside the party: "It is easy to alienate a sympathizer . . . and much harder to win him over." The new Union would have a Communist fraction at the center to guide the others. There would be conflict within the fraction—"there's only unanimity at the graveyard"—but ultimately it would need to be united if it was to exercise effective leadership. The Union would support all "Soviet" writers (those accepting Soviet power), including the large numbers of non-party writers who "know life and can portray it. They also do serious work."[74]

On the surface, Stalin's words seemed reasonably clear: this new, theoretically independent Writers' Union was designed to attract a wide spectrum of writers to the Soviet cause. Less obviously spelled out was the idea that it would come to serve as a powerful conduit for subordinating writers to direct control by the party apparatus. However, the question of the party's dominance over writers, particularly the ever-assertive proletarian contingent, was a recurring motif in Stalin's private correspondence in the early 1930s. One well-known example was his letter to the proletarian poet Bednyi, much of which was later published in his *Works*. When Bednyi's poems "Get Down off the Stove!" and "Without Mercy" were criticized by the CC Secretariat at the end of 1930 for being too scathing about Russia and implying that laziness and "sitting on the stove" were virtually national characteristics, the poet complained to his erstwhile patron, Stalin. In his response, the latter condemned Bednyi's attitude toward a decision of the CC, suggesting that instead of regarding it as a "yoke," he should think hard about it and rectify his mistakes. He wrote: "Perhaps a CC decision is not obligatory for you? Maybe your poems are above all criticism? Don't you think that you have become infected with some unpleasant disease called 'conceit'?"[75]

Likewise, in September 1933 Stalin insisted that a former prominent member of RAPP, A. Afinogenov, should be reminded of his subordinate status. In a letter to Kaganovich, he raised the question of Afinogenov's play *Lie*, which was due to be performed in Moscow. Stalin had read an earlier draft and had suggested, inter alia, that the writer depict the Bolshevik characters in a more positive light. Clearly he remained unconvinced that the new version would turn out any better, for he advised Kaganovich to consider the revised version and ban it if necessary, warning that "Afinogenov and co. should not think that they can ignore the party."[76] He deployed similar words in relation to former RAPP leaders during the run-up to the Writers' Congress in August 1934. Kaganovich had informed Stalin that a campaign against the leadership of the Union's Orgkomitet was being waged by Kirshon, Afinogenov, and B. Iasenskii, and suggested that the former RAPPists were trying to assert themselves using Gorky's influence. Stalin responded emphatically: "It must be explained to all Communist writers that the boss [*khoziain*] in literature, as in all other areas, is only the CC and that they are obliged to subordinate themselves unconditionally to the latter." He asked Kaganovich to explain to Kirshon and the rest that they would not tolerate even a partial restoration of RAPP.[77]

For a decade, Stalin had advocated the incorporation of *Soviet* writers, regardless of party affiliation, into a theoretically non-party organization. The abolition of RAPP and establishment of the Writers' Union in 1932 seemed to represent a logical conclusion to this process. Although some of his more private communications conveyed the message that the real "boss in literature" was now the Central Committee of the party, Stalin presented RAPP's demise as a step toward greater freedom and opportunity for writers of various persuasions. Likewise, the newly proclaimed artistic "method" of socialist realism was depicted as a way of encouraging, rather than suppressing, diversity of approach.[78]

Stalin was directly involved in the initial formulation of the concept of "socialist realism" in 1932. Following objections by some of RAPP's former leaders to the harsh criticism of their organization, a Politburo commission that included Stalin, Kaganovich, Postyshev, Stetskii, and I. Gronskii was set up in May to consider their concerns.[79] Gronskii, editor of *Izvestiia* and head of the Orgkomitet of the Writers' Union, relates how Stalin met him in advance of a meeting with the objectors in order to discuss "creative questions" (the "organizational questions" having already been resolved).[80] When Stalin asked for his opinion of RAPP's "dialectical-materialist" approach, Gronskii argued that it was wrong to apply this mechanically to the arts. He himself described Soviet literature as the heir to the traditions of Russian nineteenth-century critical realism viewed from the perspective of the working class and socialist revolution. He proposed the terms "proletarian socialist realism," or "communist realism." While Stalin apparently liked these formulations, he suggested that it was no longer necessary to underline the "proletarian" character of Soviet art, given the aspirations for unity, and, since communism was too distant a goal, he recommended instead the more inclusive term "socialist realism." Gronskii's memoirs should be treated with some caution; however, his explanation for why this meeting was not minuted—"Stalin did not like putting things down on paper"—does ring true.[81]

How did Stalin himself define socialist realism and its tasks? At his second meeting with writers on 26 October he uttered his famous words about writers as "engineers of human souls," and spoke rather vaguely about the need for "truthfulness": the most important thing was for artists to "portray life truthfully. And if he shows our life truthfully, then he cannot help but notice and show what is leading it to socialism. That will be socialist art, that will be socialist realism."[82] He was a little more expansive at his meeting with Communist writers, where he repeatedly emphasized that the function of the arts in the Soviet state was to contribute toward the building of socialism by what he called the "refashioning of the human psyche." The chief duty of writers was to mobilize the millions, and plays were the most effective form of mobilization: "Writers should give us the necessary plays." Other forms were necessary too (he provided examples of two useful books dealing with the current preoccupation, collectivization, Panferov's *Ingots* and Sholokhov's *Virgin Soil Upturned*), but plays were particularly valuable. He pointed out that not enough books were being produced because of paper shortages, and that after an eight-hour day not every worker had the energy to read a book: "But we are concerned that a good work of art, which helps the construction of socialism, helps the refashioning of the human psyche toward socialism, should be available to millions of workers." Books could not yet serve those millions, whereas plays could. Stalin emphasized popular demand for drama, reporting that tickets for good plays, such as Afinogenov's *Fear*, were sold out, and singling out Bill'-Belotserkovskii's "necessary plays" for special mention.[83]

However, Stalin also explained that these injunctions concerning the need for writers to mobilize the masses did not mean that "all the variety of forms and shades of literary creation" would be destroyed: "On the contrary. Only with socialism, only here can and must the most varied forms of art grow and expand, all the fullness and multifacetedness of forms, all the variety of shades of every type of creation, including, of course the multifacetedness of forms and shades of literary creation." At the same time, he warned that this did not imply a license to write anything—diversity did have its limits. He mentioned writers, such as Pil'niak, who wrongly understood the new approach to mean that now everything was permitted. These writers were slow to understand what was happening, to come over to the side of the working class, but they needed support rather than impatience.[84]

Stalin insisted that writers should not be forced into the straitjacket of the dialectical method, arguing that great writers such as Tolstoy, Cervantes, and Shakespeare still managed to portray their respective epochs successfully without any knowledge of dialectics. Such knowledge might help a writer to interpret reality correctly, but it took a long time to acquire, and non-party writers should not be criticized for lacking it. He pointed out that he himself had taken some time to master dialectics and accused RAPP's leaders of adopting a vulgarized approach to this question, stressing that it was important for writers to study not only Marx, Engels, and Lenin, but also the literary classics. He cited Lenin on the importance of learning from the classics, and suggested that writers could even learn from some "counterrevolutionary" authors.

Stalin then turned to the contested question of romanticism, which he defined as "the idealization, the embellishment of reality." He argued in favor of Shakespeare's romanticism rather than that of Schiller, since the latter's work was "infused with noble-bourgeois idealism." Gorky's early work contained much romanticism, "the romanticism of a new class, rising up for a struggle for power." The idealization of a new man and a new order was the romanticism they needed, "the romanticism that will move us forward." Stalin denied that romanticism should be counterposed to revolutionary realism. Revolutionary socialist realism would be the main tendency in Soviet literature; however, this should not exclude use of the romantic method. It was just a question of knowing "when, why, and how to apply one or other method."[85]

The question of whether Stalin ever endorsed two distinct approaches, realism and romanticism, was the subject of much subsequent debate. According to Gronskii, Stalin never spoke of two equally valid methods, socialist realism and revolutionary romanticism; he interpreted the speech at Gorky's house to mean that Stalin viewed romanticism as just one facet of the main method of socialist realism.[86] Stetskii implied that Stalin's concept of "realism" necessarily entailed an element of idealization, recounting how when Stalin met with RAPP leaders in May 1932, he explained that there was no need for writers to study dialectics: "'Anti-Dühring' must not be directly transformed into novels or poems." Instead a writer should focus on reality and "write the truth." But this "truth" had to be perceived correctly: "if you bring a man to a building site in the initial period of construction, he will see nothing but the turned-up soil, the building materials, crushed stones and rubbish. The sensible man will see ahead to the building rising up in this chaos. That will be the truth."[87]

Whatever Stalin's original intention, his words were evidently interpreted by many contemporaries as a signal that henceforth a variety of styles and approaches would flourish. Several speeches at the lively plenums of the Orgkomitet certainly implied this, including that of Lunacharsky at the second plenum in February 1933.[88] So too did many of those at the Writers' Congress in August 1934. Described by Erenburg in his memoirs as a "great and marvellous festival," the Writers' Congress occurred at a time of relative political détente and seemed in some ways to herald a new era of artistic freedom and creativity, in stark contrast to the situation in Nazi Germany.[89] As he was on vacation, Stalin did not attend the congress, which probably suited him well, as he was thus able to distance himself from the event while simultaneously exercising remote control over its proceedings, vetting keynote speeches and receiving regular updates from Kaganovich and others.[90]

In his speech to the congress, Stalin's spokesman, Zhdanov, emphasized the need for tendentious literature, for the "truthful" portrayal of reality "in its revolutionary development" and for "the ideological remolding and education of the toiling people in the spirit of socialism." At the same time he appeared to suggest that socialist realism would encourage diversity of approach, declaring that artists: "have many different types of weapons. Soviet literature has every opportunity of employing these types of weapon (genres, styles, forms and methods of literary creation) in their diversity and fullness, selecting all the best that has been created in this sphere by all previous epochs."[91] Zhdanov also focused on the importance of literary quality and technique, and the need to learn from the classics, echoing the discussions that had dominated both the third Orgkomitet plenum and the literary press earlier in the year. A consensus seemed to have emerged that crude agitational works were no longer necessary or desirable, and that as well as serving a political purpose, art must, after all, be art.[92]

This was certainly a theme of Bukharin's controversial speech to the congress. Bukharin criticized the outdated agitational poetry of Bednyi, Bezymenskii, and even Mayakovsky, while praising the artistic qualities and originality of Pasternak's more complex oeuvre. His speech was remarkable for its stress on freedom and diversity ("Unity does not mean that we must all sing the same song at the same time," "People approach a problem from different angles . . . 'Prohibitive' measures are therefore absurd"), while his subsequent apologetic letter to the congress Presidium echoed the language of the 1925 resolution, arguing that literature was different from politics and that there should be "broad freedom of competition" in poetry.[93] Bukharin had sent a copy of his speech to Stalin before the congress, and whatever his reservations, the latter certainly did not prohibit it, although he did subsequently complain to Zhdanov that Bukharin "had messed things up, introducing hysterical elements into the discussion (D. Bednyi rebuked him well and venomously)."[94]

Literary figures at the congress lined up to welcome the new era of freedom and diversity. A few examples will suffice: in his keynote speech, Gorky insisted that the task of the Writers' Union was to promote a variety of tendencies—not to limit individual creativity, but to provide the greatest opportunities for its further development.[95] The critic I. Bespalov declared: "We must mobilize a variety of forms, genres, means of artistic influence," and "The literature of socialist realism cannot but be a varied, passionate literature."[96] Erenburg criticized simplified, bureaucratic understandings of the "social command,"[97] while the scriptwriter N. Zarkhi summarized what many evidently understood to be the official position: "We should demand from our artists great talent . . . but not engage in the regimentation of how they do it." He continued, "We should tell our artists, 'everything is permitted.' Everything that serves the defense of the motherland, its strengthening, the victory of Communist, Bolshevik ideas, everything that leads to the development of Soviet culture and the flourishing of the creative individuality of people, growing not in spite of the collective, but because of it."[98]

While the congress has often been regarded as a kind of smokescreen, an elaborate piece of theater staged primarily in order to present a positive image of the USSR to impressionable Western guests, others have argued that the optimism expressed in many speeches should be interpreted in its own terms, as the product of a critical juncture in Soviet cultural life when as yet nothing was preordained and the prospects for pluralism within the context of socialist realism seemed reasonably bright.[99]

Even after the end of what has come to be seen as the mini cultural "thaw" of 1932–34, Stalin himself continued to talk about diversity and artistic freedom and to question simplistic notions of "social command."

He also took care to maintain his image as defender of writers with his deliberately well-publicized interventions in high-profile cases such as the arrests of Mandel'shtam and members of Akhmatova's family.[100] The Writers' Union and its bureaucracy now replaced RAPP as a prime target of his admonitions. In 1935 he sent out a clear message that the Union should refrain from an overly prescriptive approach, asking its secretary, V. Stavskii, to pay attention to the writer L. Sobolev, whom he described as "a great talent, to judge by his work *Major Overhaul*." Sobolev was capricious and unstable but so were most great writers, and he should not be forced to write another *Major Overhaul*, or about collective farms or Magnitogorsk. "You can't force him to write about such things." Stalin was adamant that he should be allowed to write about what he wanted, when he wanted. Like his earlier interventions, this plea for tolerance apparently became widely known in literary circles: the editor of *Literaturnaia gazeta*, O. Voitinskaia, mentioned "comrade Stalin's letter to Sobolev" in the context of her report to Zhdanov on the troubling situation in the Writers' Union in 1938. She recounted how she had cited the letter to a disgruntled Ukrainian poet, P. Tychina, as an illustration of the Union's failure to draw the correct conclusions. Tychina had responded tellingly: "If such a great man as Stalin has the time to deal with us, it means we are necessary."[101]

Stalin also chose to emphasize his support for freedom and diversity in the seemingly inauspicious setting of the notorious CC meeting held in 1940 to criticize Aleksandr Avdeenko's screenplay for the film *The Law of Life*. The main purpose of this meeting was to reprimand the writer for his portrayal of immoral conduct within the Komsomol, and Stalin was duly critical of Avdeenko's failings. He took this opportunity to reaffirm the political significance of art, asserting that what he called the "true" (*pravdivyi*) and "objective" approach did not imply that literature should be passionless, "a camera," for the artist must always sympathize with some of his heroes and not others. He declared that "truthfulness and objectivity are the truthfulness and objectivity that serve a certain class," citing Plekhanov: "literature cannot but be tendentious."[102] Yet Stalin also made some more moderate-sounding remarks on this occasion. Having rebuked the Writers' Union for taking insufficient care of average writers, the so-called ballast, Stalin announced: "You have to give freedom to art [*nado dat' voliu iskusstvu*]. You have to let people express themselves. You have to convince people who are wrong, if they are reformable." Following Stalin's praise for Wanda Wasilewska's "honest" and "truthful" depictions of ordinary people and everyday life, the poet Nikolai Aseev called into question the influence of Stalin's taste on Soviet literature, expressing concern that henceforth everyone would be instructed to write like her, just as Bednyi had once been canonized. While Aseev acknowledged it was important to take into account Stalin's preferences for a certain work or picture, "that doesn't mean that it must be copied, that the work or picture should be copied three hundred thousand times." Stalin concurred with this view. Later Sobolev also warned against the canonization of a single approach, citing Stalin's own words in support of this: "Sometimes they announce a main road, some kind of method, some kind of approach, and suddenly it's decided that everyone should do it that way. That's wrong. Comrade Stalin said that there should be discussion. Comrade Stalin said that there are various tendencies, let's bring these tendencies together, find out what they want to do and we will discuss it." Once again, Stalin agreed, confirming: "There is one artistic line [*ustanovka*], but it can be reflected in different ways, various methods, approaches, and ways of writing, why not argue about this? There will never be any standard in these questions."[103]

More predictably, perhaps, Stalin was anxious to communicate this vision of Soviet cultural freedom to international audiences, and his lengthy dialogue with the German writer and Soviet sympathizer Lion Feuchtwanger in January 1937 provided an ideal opportunity.[104] Having explained to Feuchtwanger that artists always serve class interests—as members of the intelligentsia, they themselves do not constitute a "class" but act as the servants of other classes, a "*sluzhebnyi element*" (a service element)—he distinguished between progressive and reactionary writers and a third group, who, "under the flag of falsely understood objectivism," tried to unsuccessfully sit between both stools. At the same time, as in the case of Bulgakov, he objected to simplistic attempts to identify a writer's own political outlook with his works: Gogol's conservatism, for example, did not preclude him from producing *Dead Souls*, which, "with its artistic truth," had had an enormous influence on the revolutionary-inclined intelligentsia. In response to Feuchtwanger's question about the possibility of criticism within Soviet literature, Stalin went on to insist that "if you eliminate attempts at propaganda against Soviet power, the propaganda of fascism and chauvinism, then writers here enjoy the broadest freedom, broader than anywhere else."[105]

Stalin's vision of Soviet culture was always characterized by a duality—on the one hand he strove to promote the notion of artists as political servants under party control, while on the other he stressed the importance of artistic freedom and diversity (albeit within limits), and demanded that art should be of the highest quality. Although, as Alexei Yurchak reminds us, this duality was a perennial source of tension for the party-state, the contradictory elements were particularly difficult to reconcile in the Stalin era.[106] These contradictions reached a crescendo during the culturally barren post-war period.

The war years have traditionally been regarded, with some justification, as an interlude of relative cultural relaxation.[107] This period of détente did not end abruptly in May 1945, however. Indeed, throughout 1945 and into 1946, many members of the intelligentsia, anticipating a new era of freedom, became increasingly assertive in their dealings with their masters. Journal editors were at the forefront of campaigns to reduce excessive bureaucratic interference in the arts. For example, A. Tarasenkov, deputy editor of *Znamia*, complained to Malenkov about the dictatorial secretary of the Writers' Union, D. Polikarpov, describing him as worse than the former leader of RAPP, Averbakh. Polikarpov was removed in April 1946, partly because of this complaint.[108] Panferov, the editor of *Oktiabr'* and one of Stalin's longtime favorites, issued a remarkably candid appeal for change, initially in the form of a letter to Malenkov of November 1945, in which he proposed that writers be given greater independence and that the interference of countless editors (i.e., censors) be minimized. He recommended that his journal focus primarily on works about the present and that writers should be able to portray difficulties and problems, arguing that it was wrong to gloss over controversial issues such as the initial setbacks during the war, since the Soviet people did not need a "literature of consolation." It is striking that Panferov invoked Stalin's words to legitimize his plea for a more careful approach to writers: "Comrade Stalin has often said to us in conversations: 'Literature is a delicate affair.' 'Do not administer the writer.' 'Take care of the writer.' 'Remember that the writer sometimes sees more than us politicians.' 'Do not rush and do not push Marxism onto a writer: it makes no difference, for by studying reality, the writer will arrive at Marxism, for Marxism is a wall.'"[109]

Panferov elaborated on these themes in a forthright article published in *Oktiabr'* in 1946, in which he castigated editors and critics who did not understand art. The article cited several hitherto unpublished statements by Stalin, including those quoted in the letter to Malenkov, which suggests that it must have been authorized by Stalin's secretariat, as was customary with all publications incorporating Stalin's unpublished words.[110] However, Agitprop insisted the article could only be printed if accompanied by a critical rejoinder in *Pravda*.[111] The uncompromising tone of the *Pravda* response was characteristic of the mounting campaign for a tougher line that culminated in the infamous clampdown identified with Zhdanov, the "Zhdanovshchina."

Zhdanov was, as ever, merely Stalin's spokesman. In his own speeches at the infamous Orgburo meetings of 9 August 1946, Stalin himself readily adopted a firm stance in an attempt to restore the party's dominance over the unruly intelligentsia. At the session devoted to Leningrad's literary journals, he rebuked writers and editors who "think that politics is a matter for the government, the CC. Politics is not our business, they say. If someone's written well, artistically, beautifully, it should be published, despite the fact that it contains rotten parts that disorient our youth, poison it." Culture was a political matter and journal editors and writers had an obligation to consider "only the interests of the state, the interests of educating the younger generation correctly." He drew similar conclusions in his speech criticizing the films *Admiral Nakhimov* (dir. V. Pudovkin), *Ivan Groznyi* (dir. S. Eisenstein), and *A Great Life* (dir. L. Lukov), in which he also highlighted the political importance of Soviet cinema for the USSR's reputation abroad.[112] This renewed emphasis on culture as a political weapon both domestically as well as internationally made the post-war epoch one of the most stultifying for the creative intelligentsia.

However, Stalin's vision was never one-dimensional, and he continued to speak out intermittently against an overly dogmatic and regimented approach to the arts. Some of the themes of Stalin's pre-war "tolerant" utterances resurfaced; for example, he reiterated his objections to oversimplified understandings of "social command." In his memoirs, Konstantin

Simonov recounts how in May 1947, at a meeting held to discuss various matters, including the new campaign for "Soviet patriotism," Stalin questioned the value of sending writers on official trips (*komandirovki*) against their will, citing the example of Lev Tolstoy, who managed without such expeditions. When Fadeev then observed that Tolstoy wrote about the estate where he lived, Stalin responded, "when a serious writer works seriously, he himself will go if it's necessary."[113] Dmitrii Shepilov, then in charge of the CC's Agitprop department, also recalls that Stalin "often scoffed at statements that a certain writer was 'in search of themes' or had gone on a 'creative trip' to find a subject for a novel or 'collect material' for a story," and that he once pointed out that a seemingly "banal" plot about a married woman who falls in love with another man who does not understand her and then commits suicide formed the basis of Tolstoy's *Anna Karenina*.[114]

Simonov claims that Stalin also continued to criticize monopolistic "*partiinyi*" positions and to advocate greater pluralism in his final years. The period from 1949 witnessed a limited reaction against Zhdanovshchina, which had triggered what Swayze terms a "scissors crisis" of declining artistic quality and increasing political demands.[115] Stalin's interventions seem to have been designed to help resolve this cultural "scissors crisis" and to alleviate growing tensions in the literary community, one example of which was dissatisfaction with the RAPP-like dominance of the Writers' Union by characters such as A. Sofronov.[116] Stalin's 1929 letter to Bill'-Belotserkovskii was finally made public for the first time in the eleventh volume of his *Works* in 1949.[117] He also spoke up in favor of greater diversity and higher artistic quality, reprimanding those perceived to be suppressing it in terms reminiscent of those he had used two decades earlier.

Stalin was closely involved in decisions concerning the award of Stalin Prizes for the arts.[118] At the 1950 prize meeting attended by Simonov, he questioned recent criticism of the play *Voice of America*, whose author Boris Lavrenev had apparently been accused of exhibiting a "non-party" approach. By recalling Lavrenev's play *Break*, which he had praised in 1929 as an example of a "useful" work by a fellow traveler, Stalin drew implicit parallels between the two situations. Referring to Lenin's 1905 work "Party Organization and Party Literature," he explained that it was incorrect to invoke the slogan "Down with non-party writers," as Lenin had only used this when the party was in opposition, whereas once in power, the party was responsible for the whole of society, including Communists and non-Communists alike. He resurrected the ghost of the RAPP leader, Averbakh, "who had been necessary at first, but became a curse for literature."

Stalin then proceeded to dissect a controversial article by a literary critic, Aleksandr Belik, recently published in the journal *Oktiabr'*.[119] Belik attributed some of the problems of Soviet literature to writers' and critics' inadequate knowledge of Marxism-Leninism and dialectical materialism. He argued that many works were not sufficiently socialist realist and stressed that socialist realism required *partiinost'*, the "party depiction of reality," citing Lenin's 1905 article to this effect. The critic attacked the notion that socialist realism could accommodate competing tendencies, criticizing in particular a recently published work by Tarasenkov, who had argued that "Soviet prose writers follow different paths; they choose different literary styles to embody their creative concepts." The younger generation chose to follow the style of Tolstoy, Chekhov, Turgenev, or Gogol, claiming that socialist realism as developed by Gorky offered the greatest opportunities for the development of "the most varied creative individualities with which our literature is so rich." Tarasenkov chided some literary critics for forgetting about this need for variety. Belik in turn criticized Tarasenkov's "free-for-all" conception of socialist realism. Of course, he argued, there should be individuality, but socialist realism still had its own rules that must be obeyed: "Socialist realism is not a counter [*zheton*] that is given out to every Soviet writer just because he is Soviet."

Stalin denounced this attitude of "Down with non-party writers," labeling Belik a "RAPPist of our times" who was resurrecting "neo-RAPP theory." He accused him of wanting all heroes to be positive, for everyone to be an ideal (this was, of course, a simplification and distortion of RAPP's ideas), and pointed out that neither Gogol nor Tolstoy depicted totally positive heroes.[120] The *Pravda* article that appeared shortly afterward echoed Stalin's words, reprimanding Belik for his high-handed "administrative" tone, his distortion of Lenin's 1905 article, and his attempt to counterpose party and non-party writers. Belik was described as a "neo-RAPPist" who was trying to revive RAPP theories and mechanically transfer party concepts to literature. The article deliberately recalled the polemics of the late 1920s, referring explicitly to Stalin's recently published letter to Bill'-Belotserkovskii. It condemned the development of sectarianism, typical of the journal *Oktiabr'*, and the promotion of a nihilistic approach to the classics.[121]

Gromov argues that Stalin's stance in this period was motivated by a desire to improve relations with writers in the wake of the unpopular anti-cosmopolitanism campaign, just as his previous attacks on RAPP had won him popularity.[122] However, it should also be viewed in the general context of Stalin's post-war interventions in scholarly debates, analyzed most recently by Pollock. In his contributions to the discussions about linguistics in 1950, for example, Stalin expressed a desire to stimulate a "battle of opinions" and discourage "Arakcheev regimes," claiming that "Marxism is the enemy of all kinds of dogmatism." This opposition to intellectual monopolies evidently extended to literature too, and there were obvious parallels between Stalin's appeal for greater focus on objective laws in science and his comments about a more measured approach to the question of *partiinost'* in literature.[123]

Judging Socialist Realism

Belik's critique of Tarasenkov illustrates how, even into the late 1940s, there remained much uncertainty about precisely what was required of Soviet socialist realist art. What did those hallowed phrases embodied in the Statutes of the Writers' Union actually mean: "a truthful, historically concrete depiction of reality in its revolutionary development," "the ideological refashioning and education of the workers in the spirit of socialism"?[124] The lack of definitive guidelines explaining how the rather opaque pronouncements from on high, including Stalin's own, should be translated into practice left open the possibility of multiple interpretations. As Panferov observed in his aforementioned 1945 letter to Malenkov, "Comrade Stalin defined the contemporary direction of literature as 'socialist realism.' It's strange, but for some reason our critics are silent about this, even though the concept of 'socialist realism' is still unclear to many, many people."[125] In practice, what was acceptable and desirable was decided on a case-by-case basis and was frequently subject to the whims of party officials.[126] Stalin's judgments about particular works of art played an important role, of course, and the remainder of this chapter will be devoted to closer examination of some of these.

Stalin acted as a judge of socialist realist works of art in a literal sense through his participation in the award of Stalin Prizes. He also devoted considerable time to assessing them in other less formalized ways, often making judgments in cases where there was some conflict or uncertainty about the merits of a literary work or film, or where an issue of particular political importance was at stake. As well as his written evaluations, we draw on accounts of his oral contributions to the Stalin Prize meetings held after the war and the notes of remarks he made to the head of GUKF, Boris Shumiatskii, during the private film screenings that he and other Politburo members attended in the mid–1930s.[127] Although not necessarily a completely accurate record of Stalin's words on these occasions, this evidence does provide a reasonable indication of the kinds of criteria he invoked when evaluating films and works of literature. Given the broad scope of both his written and oral comments, our aim is to identify those criteria that recurred regularly over the course of the two decades after the proclamation of socialist realism in 1932.

Stalin's judgments were generally framed in utilitarian terms: How useful was the book/poem/film/play in question? How great was its "didactic" or "mobilizational" significance? What Stalin considered necessary and useful in a work of art varied according to the precise context, but three criteria were invoked with some regularity: topical subject matter, mass appeal, and "truthfulness." Although explicitly political priorities were central to all Stalin's assessments, he certainly did not ignore aesthetic considerations; indeed he often liked to flag up the artistic qualities of a given work. Shepilov claims that he could be quite demanding when adjudicating the Stalin Prizes for literature: "Stalin's views on art were exceedingly varied. Sometimes he set exceedingly high artistic standards and ridiculed attempts to push through a prize for some work simply because of its politically topical subject matter." He recalls that when discussion at the Stalin Prize meeting in 1949 turned to the contemporary significance of A. Korneichuk's play *Makar Dubrava*, and in particular its portrayal of a "genuine Soviet miner," Stalin interjected: "The question is not whether Makar Dubrava is a miner, whether he is of proletarian origin. We're talking about the play's artistic merits—does it create an artistic image of a Soviet miner? That's the decisive factor." However, Shepilov admits that political considerations frequently overrode other criteria: "'This is a revolutionary work,' he would say. 'This is a useful theme. This story is on a currently vital theme.' And the work got a Stalin Prize despite its artistic weakness."[128] Simonov also claims that although Stalin valued purely aesthetic criteria, when it came to awarding Stalin Prizes, the political utility of a work of art generally outweighed its artistic significance. For example, during the 1948 prize adjudication he praised V. Smirnov's novel *Sons*, which centered on the Russian countryside at the start of the twentieth century. Having observed that the book was well written, he then asked, "Do we need this book now?"[129]

This question—do we need the book *now?* [our emphasis]—was central to many of Stalin's judgments. He regularly assessed works of art in terms of whether or not they addressed immediate political objectives. Particular importance was attached to this criterion when the sensitive matter of the Soviet Union's international relations was involved; in such cases he was often interested in the *timing* of the publication or performance of works on strategically important themes and would accelerate or retard their appearance in light of changing political imperatives.

In March 1932 *Pravda* editor Mekhlis asked Stalin if it was an appropriate moment to publish a poem by Bezymenskii, "Song of Warning," which was considered strategically sensitive because of its allusions to the Far East and Japanese military maneuvers close to the Soviet border. Stalin's resolution was: "It's a fine piece. But it should not be published now."[130] In 1935 he adopted a similar line toward a poem by Bednyi that poked fun at the French for prevaricating over the question of a pact with the Soviet Union. When Mekhlis requested permission to publish the poem in *Pravda* in April, Stalin resolved: "*For the time being* it's not worth including it in view of the fact that new talks with the French have begun."[131] By contrast, Kirshon's play *The Court*, centered on the struggles of the German communist movement, was deemed appropriate for immediate performance: the author sent it to Stalin on 9 October 1932, asking for instructions, and the latter responded within a week, recommending that it come out quickly (the play was staged in three major theaters in 1933).[132]

A similarly strategic approach characterized Stalin's approach to the award of Stalin Prizes to works with foreign-policy implications. Simonov explains that in 1946 a first prize was awarded to a novel about the Russo-Japanese War, A. Stepanov's *Port Arthur*, even though it had been published much earlier, in 1940–41. It received the prize following the defeat of Japan and the return of Port Arthur, which Russia had lost in 1905. The book was judged to be useful at that particular moment, since it underlined how Russian forces had fought bravely but had lost because of the nature of tsarist autocracy. The contrast with the victorious Soviet system was self-evident.[133]

In 1952, the Stalin Prize committee was censured for having overlooked several important works the previous year, particularly V. Latsis's *Toward New Shores*, O. Mal'tsev's *Yugoslav Tragedy*, and D. Eremin's *Storm over Rome*, all of which had some immediate bearing on Soviet relations with other states and had attracted Stalin's attention.[134] *Toward New Shores*, a novel about collectivization in the Latvian Republic written by the chairman of Latvia's Council of Ministers, had been widely criticized, partly as a result of infighting within the Latvian political elite.[135] In February 1952 *Pravda* published an article defending the book. Although the author of the piece was ostensibly a "group of readers," its real author was in fact Stalin, who presumably wished to avoid any impression that he was intervening personally in the affair. His review targeted a *Literaturnaia gazeta* article by M. Zorin, who had reported negative comments made about the work at a discussion of the Artistic Council of Latvia's Gosizdat. Stalin attributed these negative views to Zorin himself (whom he claimed had adopted the ruse in order to absolve himself from responsibility). Accusing Zorin of incorrectly identifying the main protagonist and plot of the work, he offered his own politicized evaluation: the real hero was the Latvian people who had broken with their bourgeois ways and were building new socialist ways, while the main plot was the transformation of Latvian peasants into kolkhozniks. He described criticisms of the work as "leftist" (*levatskie*).[136] According to Simonov, Stalin did not consider the book to be strong from an artistic point of view, but judged the subject matter to be politically necessary "for the Baltic republics as well as for abroad." *Toward New Shores* was duly awarded a first-class prize for 1952.[137] Simonov also recalls how Stalin unexpectedly decided to bestow a third-class prize on Eremin for his (in Simonov's view) mediocre novel *Storm over Rome*. Justifying his decision, Stalin complained that other writers all wrote about the same subjects, that there was no variety; Eremin, on the other hand, had tried to describe something unfamiliar, the political situation in Italy, and "the book will play a useful role."[138] Presumably he regarded it as useful in a climate in which the Soviet Union was beginning to emerge from a period of isolation and seeking to extend its contacts with the West.

A further criterion frequently invoked by Stalin was, not surprisingly, the mass appeal of a work of art. To succeed in its task of mobilizing and educating, Soviet culture had to be attractive and intelligible to the masses/the people. This theme was especially prominent in the mid–1930s, as Stalin sought to consolidate the shift away from the generally unpopular culture characteristic of the first five-year plan era.[139] He expressed his preoccupation with the question of mass appeal particularly forcefully in the course of his discussions about Soviet cinema with Shumiatskii, emphasizing to the latter just how highly he valued what he considered to be entertaining, clear, and simple films.

As the quintessential modern mass art form, cinema was the object of Stalin's constant scrutiny and support from the early 1930s.[140] According to Shumiatskii, Stalin himself encouraged the production of fast-paced, lighthearted comedies on the grounds that these would appeal to the masses more than overtly political, serious films such as E. Piscator's *Revolt of the Fishermen* (Stalin described the latter as "tedious," "gloomy," "deliberately cold," and "unnecessary, cheerless").[141] Until 1933–34, Soviet filmmakers had tended to steer clear of comedies, either because they considered them to be a frivolous distraction from serious, politically engaged films, or because they were afraid to poke fun at aspects of Soviet reality. As Shumiatskii pointed out to Stalin, creative workers avoided satirical treatments of contemporary phenomena, while critics cultivated a "puritanical" attitude to comedy.[142] Stalin insisted that the public should have more choice. One evening he asked Shumiatskii to show a comedy film: "You come back after work to rest a bit. Therefore you want your nerves to relax. Surely you should give the viewer the right to such a choice and not only give him films of a single dramatic genre, with the very rare exception of *Jolly Fellows*?" When Shumiatskii replied that the viewer did indeed have the right to choice, but that they had only recently embarked on comedies and the atmosphere was still not supportive enough, Stalin retorted: "Make it supportive. It's an important matter." On another occasion he remarked: "Cinema workers must take great care to ensure that films are varied, that along with serious ones there are funny ones, like at the theater, so that the viewer . . . can choose what best to see today."[143]

Stalin personally intervened to support the much-maligned *Jolly Fellows*, Grigorii Aleksandrov's lighthearted musical comedy about a shepherd who becomes the conductor of a jazz orchestra. Throughout its production, the film was subject to a barrage of criticism for its allegedly apolitical, Hollywood-like qualities, and it is possible that the completed film would have been jettisoned had it not been for Stalin's interventions. He was apparently delighted with the film when he first saw it in July 1934. Commenting that Soviet filmmakers tried to be original with their gloomy "rehabilitations" and "reforgings," he declared that although he was not opposed to these themes on principle, they too should be treated in a joyful and funny manner. He remarked that he had come away from *Jolly Fellows* feeling as if he had had a day off—the first time he had felt this after watching a Soviet film. He was particularly complimentary about Liubov' Orlova's and Leonid Utesov's acting and the film's jazz music. He thought that "the masses" would like the song "March of the Jolly Fellows," and that gramophone recordings should be produced to popularize it.[144] Success at the Venice Film Festival in the summer of 1934 did not protect *Jolly Fellows* from incessant attacks, particularly from writers, but Stalin continued to defend it.[145] When Kaganovich reported that some writers were criticizing the "hooligan" aspects of the film, Stalin argued that it was really jolly, even if the theme was not profound. He judged that it would be popular and "the people will be happy."[146]

Stalin also demonstrated his concern with the mass appeal of Soviet films by rating them according to how clear and comprehensible to the public he perceived they were likely to be. For example, he commended *Chapaev* (dirs. Vasilievs) for being a model of simplicity and accessibility, whereas he objected to *Paths of Enemies* (dirs. O. Preobrazhenskaia and K. Pravov) because it contained "unintelligible" sections, and claimed that many viewers would not understand *Pepo* (dir. A. Bek-Nazarov).[147] He often suggested ways of clarifying the messages of films, for example, through the use of explanatory inscriptions for complicated historical films such as *The Youth of Maksim* (dirs. G. Kozintsev and L. Trauberg) and *The Last*

Masquerade (dir. M. Chiaureli).[148] He insisted that Fridrikh Ermler alter the ending of his *Peasants* to make it less ambiguous for "the people," explaining to the director that it might appear that the kulak character had simply escaped, whereas "the people want clarity in relation to him, demand punishment for the subversive work, the terrorist activity. But you chased after symbolism."[149]

While Stalin was generally critical of "symbolism" on the grounds that it created ambiguity and confused the public, it is worth noting that he was prepared on occasion to demonstrate some flexibility. This was certainly the case with Aleksandr Dovzhenko's *Aerograd*. Stalin was favorably disposed toward Dovzhenko and his work, unlike some critics, and had facilitated the filming of *Aerograd* when this had been obstructed by the military.[150] According to Shumiatskii, when the film was screened in November 1935, Stalin commented adversely on Dovzhenko's fondness for symbols, observing, "He cannot do it more simply," while acknowledging nevertheless that the film was interesting and patriotic. After Shumiatskii argued that it could have been simplified, Stalin proceeded to defend Dovzhenko on the basis that an artist is entitled to his own style and, crucially, that the film would be *popular* with viewers: "Yes, but what he did is in his style, both in his style and his understanding of things. It's unlikely that he could have done it differently. And since what he has shot comes across as interesting and uplifting, then, as they say, 'long live' [he used the Ukrainian terms], all the more so because it's all being done for the first time and the viewer will welcome it and think highly of it because it deals with Soviet patriotism."[151] In this case, the utility of the film for the purposes of mass mobilization outweighed its other faults.

Such a flexible approach contrasted strongly with the more stringent line of the 1936 anti-formalism campaign, the initial target of which was music. In late December 1935, Stalin expressed strong approval for Lev Arnshtam's film *Girlfriends*, highlighting its "mobilizational significance." However he criticized the "lyricism" of Dmitrii Shostakovich's accompanying music for being out of step with the overall tone of the film and "impeding reception."[152] In January Shostakovich was once again in the firing line for his opera *Lady Macbeth of Mtsensk District*. Although it had attracted much critical acclaim since its first performance in 1934, times had changed, and it was now accused of being "leftist" and unintelligible

in the notorious *Pravda* article "A Muddle [*sumbur*] instead of Music."
The nature and extent of Stalin's influence on this article remains uncertain,
although it does contain much typically Stalinist lexicon.[153] According to
Shumiatskii, Stalin described the article as a "program" for music, urging
composers to write music that was clear and intelligible to the masses "and
not rebuses and riddles, in which the sense of the work is destroyed." He
praised what he described as the "realistic music" of Soviet films, and
commended the use of melody, highlighting *Jolly Fellows*, in which "all the
songs are good, simple, melodic."[154] Thereafter simplicity and accessibility
became mandatory for all the arts.

A final, very important criterion Stalin considered when assessing a work
of art was whether or not it depicted its subject matter correctly, or "truthfully," as he often put it. What constituted a "truthful" representation in
Stalin's eyes was never entirely obvious, however. Of course, it went without
saying that a partisan, pro-Soviet stance was essential, but beyond that
much remained unclear. As far as depictions of the contemporary Soviet
Union were concerned, a "truthful" approach seemed to require positive
heroes, idealization, and a capacity to imagine the radiant socialist future
(the building rather than the building site).[155] And yet, on various occasions, Stalin appeared to object to the total "varnishing" (*lakirovka*) of
Soviet reality, the absence of conflicts and problems, and unrealistic black-
and-white depictions of Soviet citizens. In his 1940 Orgburo speech, for
example, he praised Chekhov's depiction of "gray people" rather than
unambiguously heroic characters, arguing that black-and-white images of
heroes and villains were untruthful. He declared "we need truthfulness,
depicting the enemy fully [*polnotsenno*] not only with negative qualities,
but also positive qualities." A "truthful" representation was one that
recognized that few people were entirely good or bad.[156] Socialist *realism*
did sometimes require a dose of verisimilitude.

It is well known that Stalin did not refrain from criticizing works of art
that portrayed life in the USSR in an unacceptably negative light. For
example, he often objected to images of Soviet cultural and economic
backwardness, such as the manual harvesting depicted in Igor Savchenko's
film *Accordion* and the slow tempo of rural life in Ermler's *Peasants*, both
of which reflected poorly on the post-collectivization countryside.[157]
Likewise, his 1940 Orgburo speech contained criticisms of Avdeenko for

his portrayal of Soviet people "in a black light, in the light of backwardness, cultural malaise" and his focus on naturalistic "tavern love" (*traktir-
nuiu liubov'*).[158] After the war Stalin was particularly concerned by works
of art that he claimed might damage the prestige of the victorious Soviet
Union. As we have seen, during the August 1946 Orgburo sessions he
targeted Leonid Lukov's film about post-war reconstruction in the Donbas,
A Great Life, on the grounds that it depicted the USSR as culturally and
economically backward, with its emphasis on workers' drinking habits,
poor-quality housing, and the lack of mechanization in industry.[159]
Zoshchenko's satire, *Adventures of a Monkey*, was also singled out on this
occasion for its preoccupation with the seamier side of Soviet reality: when
the writer Vsevolod Vishnevskii highlighted Zoshchenko's obsession with
"invalids," "bars," and "scandals," Stalin interjected sharply, "and the
bathhouse."[160]

   At other times, however, Stalin was rather more subtle in his approach,
implying that "truthful" art must address some of the real problems
and conflicts of Soviet life and, equally important, show how these were
being resolved. In this respect he could at times appear more flexible
than certain officials, critics, and overzealous colleagues who preferred to
avoid any allusions to the "negative" features and "backwardness" of the
USSR.

   Stalin valued comedy films in part because they served as potent weapons
for exposing and ridiculing symptoms of Soviet "backwardness," such
as the flaws of officialdom. Commenting on two silent comedies about
contemporary Soviet life and its problems, *The Stadium Flag* (dir.
B. Kazachkov) and *Last Prince of the Republic* (dir. E. Ioganson), Stalin
observed that making fun of backwardness was always "useful."[161] On
another occasion, he criticized the excision of potentially sensitive episodes
from the comedy *Alena's Love* (dir. B. Iurtsev) on the grounds that the
cuts made the film less convincing. One character, a director, had been
replaced by a deputy director, as it was deemed inappropriate that the
former should be the object of comedy. Details of the extremely run-down
barracks were excluded even though these were necessary to show how in
the second half of the film the barracks had been cleaned up. According
to Stalin, it had been a mistake to cut these sections, as the film would
have been more amusing if they had been retained. As he put it, it was

important to expose the obstacles to be overcome, "otherwise everything in the film appears too smooth, or rather not even smooth, but well ordered, that is, lacking emotion."[162]

Works of art were particularly prone to excite controversy if they hinted at any backwardness and shortcomings within the armed forces. Stalin sometimes intervened in their defense. For example when Voroshilov accused a film about the relationship between a tank commander and a young student, *Hectic Days* (dirs. A. Zarkhi, I. Kheifits), of portraying "idiots" untypical of the Red Army and petit bourgeois (*meshchanskie*) relationships, Stalin argued that as well as flaws, it had many strengths. He also invoked the criterion of mass appeal, observing that the film would be popular among soldiers because of its lively tone and positive characters.[163] Later Voroshilov expressed reservations about Iulii Raizman's film *Fliers*, in which two different characters—Rogachev, the disciplined, older head of a flying school, and Beliaev, the younger, more impulsive trainee pilot—compete for the affections of the female pilot Bystrova. Voroshilov objected to the film's portrayal of what he considered to be behavior untypical of the armed forces, such as the failure to punish Beliaev and Bystrova for their "hooligan" acts. He disliked the way the senior pilot, Rogachev, had been sent to the personnel department along with junior pilots and posted to Sakhalin with no allowance for his rank or services. Stalin disagreed, maintaining that the ideological and artistic merits of the film outweighed its flaws. He concluded that the bad behavior had been sufficiently punished and that Rogachev's fate was a necessary expression of "artistic license." He insisted that the film had successfully captured the inner world of their "new people."[164]

In 1942, at a critical juncture in the war, Stalin endorsed Korneichuk's heavily promoted play *The Front*, which addressed the conflict between a modern, professional approach to warfare and the older "heroic" tradition associated with the civil-war generation. *The Front* painted the older generation of military leaders and their contribution to the Great Patriotic War in an unflattering light, and following its publication in *Pravda* on 28 August, Marshall Timoshenko sent Stalin a telegram expressing his concern that it "will harm us for a long time" and recommending that it be banned and its author reprimanded. Stalin responded that on the contrary it would have great "educational significance" for the army and its leadership since it drew attention to failings that needed to be recognized and eliminated.[165]

After the war, in his adjudication of works nominated for Stalin Prizes, Stalin continued to voice support for some relatively complex portrayals of Soviet society. According to Simonov, "Zhdanovshchina" was not intended by Stalin to be a call for the "varnishing" (*lakirovka*) of reality, for simplistic depictions of life, although this was how many interpreted it. In fact, Simonov notes, Stalin favored quite controversial works in this period, including Vera Panova's *Traveling Companions* and *Kruzhilikha*, Viktor Nekrasov's *In the Trenches of Stalingrad*, and Emmanuil Kazakevich's *The Star*, all of which were awarded Stalin Prizes for 1946 and 1947.[166]

At the height of the anti-Western campaign in 1948, Stalin questioned a proposal to award Erenburg's *The Storm* a second-class rather than a first-class Stalin Prize on the grounds that it portrayed the French more successfully than the Russians. He praised the author for depicting average (*srednye*) people, for focusing on how over the course of the war "petty" people with flaws had found themselves and were transformed. He was also prepared to accept Erenburg's controversial portrayal of a relationship between a Soviet citizen and a Frenchwoman: "But I like this Frenchwoman, she's a nice girl. And besides, such things do happen in real life."[167]

As this episode suggests, Stalin seemed willing to condone depictions of complicated personal relationships in this period. The theme of personal life became much more prominent in the literature of the 1940s and early 1950s, but, as ever, the boundaries of what was acceptable were never explicit.[168] Works such as Panova's *Kruzhilikha* and Antonina Koptiaeva's *Ivan Ivanovich* that tested the boundaries were often denounced by reviewers for their negative portrayals of relationships. *Kruzhilikha* addressed the conflict between work and family life in a particularly stark fashion: Listopad, the successful factory manager devoted to his work, neglects his wife, who eventually dies in childbirth. Critics admonished Panova for being too "objective" and "detached," for depicting characters such as Listopad as an ambiguous mix of good and bad qualities.[169] However, Stalin defended the "truthful" approach of the book: "Look, everyone's criticizing Panova for the fact that in the novel there's no unity between the personal and the social, criticize her for that conflict. But surely in life things are not decided so easily, so easily combined? It happens that they are not combined . . . Her people are shown truthfully."[170] He made a similar point about Koptiaeva's hugely popular and sensational (for its time) *Ivan Ivanovich*, which had drawn criticism for its portrayal of marital relations—the story focuses on how the busy Ivan Ivanovich neglects his wife, who then turns to another man. Stalin maintained that love triangles existed in the USSR and that it was important for literature to address these.[171]

By 1952, the whole question of how contemporary Soviet life was to be represented had come to a head. At the Stalin Prize committee meeting, chaired for the first time by Malenkov, Stalin criticized Olga Ziv's novel *Hot Hour* for its failure to depict the everyday life (*byt*) of workers and complained generally about the tendency of Soviet novels to focus on "competition" rather than *byt*, with the notable exception of Vsevolod Kochetov's tale of a dynasty of workers, *The Zhurbin Family*.[172] He contested the award of a prize to a typically "conflictless" work, Ianka Bryl's *Light beyond the Marshes:* "But why is it good? Because all the peasants are good? All the kolkhozes are advanced? No one argues with anyone? Everyone is in full agreement? There's no class struggle? In general everything is fine, therefore the story is fine. Yes? But artistically—is it a good book?" He was only prepared to consider it for a prize once its artistic merits had been established.[173] Stalin went on to question why Soviet dramaturgists thought they were not allowed to write about negative phenomena and why critics demanded idealized portrayals of life, citing the example of Semen Babaevskii, who had been rebuked for depicting "backward" people: "Immediately they turned on him saying that could not be, demanding that everything should be ideal with us, saying that we should not show the bad side of life [*nekazovuiu storonu*], when in fact we should show the bad side. They talk as though we don't have any bastards . . ." Stalin argued that on the contrary there were still many "false people, bad people" and that not to portray them was "to sin against the truth." He insisted that they needed Gogols and Saltykov-Shchedrins, rejecting the theory of the secretary of the Writers' Union, Sofronov, that writers were unable to write decent plays because of the lack of conflict in Soviet life. Conflicts existed and should be addressed.[174] A raft of leading articles in *Pravda* and the literary press echoed his words, and the matter was considered of sufficient importance to be dealt with at the nineteenth party congress, where Malenkov reiterated the call for an end to "varnishing" and *bezkonfliktnost'* (conflictlessness) in Soviet culture.[175]

While Stalin's judgments concerning Soviet works of art were quite wide-ranging, he did consistently invoke certain criteria when justifying his evaluations. Purely aesthetic considerations were never disregarded, but political priorities remained his overriding concern: how far did a given novel or film address topical subject matter, would it appeal to the masses, and to what extent was it "truthful" in its approach? This was how works of socialist realism were to be judged.

Stalin's comments about individual works of art and about Soviet culture in general were rarely made public at the time or were published anonymously. The large corpus of unpublished or recently published speeches, correspondence, resolutions, and remarks therefore sheds new light on his vision of the arts. Even in an unpublished form, his words helped to circumscribe the boundaries for public discussion about the phenomenon that was "Soviet culture." These boundaries were always rather fluid, however, in part because Stalin's approach was itself multifaceted.

Stalin consistently depicted art as a political weapon and artists as servants who must be harnessed tightly to the goals of the Soviet state. While the expectations for "socialist realism" were never clearly defined, Stalin evidently wanted Soviet culture to conform to certain political priorities: to be topical, "truthful," and aimed at the masses. Nevertheless he tempered this dirigiste line with other more tolerant pronouncements that suggested that the arts were not reducible to party propaganda tout court. He expressed a desire for an aesthetically high-quality, enjoyable, and diverse culture, and for artists to be given a degree of autonomy to create this. He chastised institutions and officials who were perceived to be suppressing artistic creativity. His more benevolent words, as well as his tendency to associate figures such as Zhdanov with the most hard-line public rhetoric, go some way to explaining why, paradoxical though this may seem, he could come across to some at least as a "great liberal and patron."

The heterogeneity of his words allowed a certain scope for maneuvering by both Stalin and other officials, who were able to vary their approach according to the exigencies of a given situation, and also by artists themselves, who could invoke his words to further their own interests and aspirations. However, this heterogeneity also generated significant tensions that, by the early 1950s, were becoming increasingly glaring and increasingly hard to reconcile. The cultural "thaw" that followed Stalin's death was timely and not without some antecedents in Stalin's own discourse.

CONCLUSION

Over two decades ago, Arch Getty wrote of Iosif Stalin, "He continues to fascinate us: books about him sell year after year and specialists endeavour to understand him and his deeds. Yet we know practically nothing about him."[1] Despite his immense importance for twentieth-century history, Stalin often comes across as a rather faceless and intangible figure in the numerous biographies written about him in the West during the Cold War. His biographers frequently seem disappointed with their subject, describing him as enigmatic, "a hard man to know."[2] In part this is a reflection of the limitations of the source materials with which they had to work. The well-known problems of archival access were compounded by the fact that, as we have seen, Stalin carefully managed the presentation of his own biography.

Now that substantial quantities of archival material and memoirs have become available, more rounded portraits of Stalin are beginning to emerge.[3] The release of Stalin's "personal archive" was a particularly exciting development, and our study has made extensive use of this as well as other related materials. While these sources do not offer "revelations," they have allowed us to get to know Stalin as a man and a political actor rather better than before. What comes across particularly vividly is the sheer amount of time he devoted to reading, writing, and editing. Stalin's world was a world of words. He consumed vast quantities of written information in the form of reports, correspondence, scholarly works; he was constantly writing speeches and letters or editing resolutions.

These materials have allowed us to come closer to comprehending how Stalin approached some of the matters that preoccupied him most, ranging from domestic and foreign threats to the relationship between the state and the arts. What is striking is that, in many cases, there was no great gulf between his published utterances and those that were confined to the archives. For that reason, some have argued that Stalin was no cynic, that he truly believed what he said and wrote.[4] The question of "belief" is always a complex one: we will never be in a position to ascertain whether the vision he communicated to various audiences aligned with the way he *really* saw the world. Moreover, we have only worked with a selection of the relevant sources, albeit a very significant selection: we cannot know for certain how much other material was either lost or deliberately destroyed, and if it was destroyed, according to what principle. Equally important to bear in mind is that the content of Stalin's innumerable conversations over the phone or in person was almost never recorded and must remain a matter for speculation. Nevertheless, on the basis of the evidence we do have, it is possible to draw conclusions about certain aspects of Stalin's vision.

The first aspect we considered was the manner in which Stalin interpreted (and misinterpreted) information about matters ranging from the domestic and foreign threats he faced to the consequences of overambitious plans. We examined how the information system functioned and what systematic biases came to be built into intelligence and other information reports before Stalin properly took power. It was entirely logical for Bolshevik leaders to remain concerned with internal and external threats to the Revolution after the civil war had ended, but they developed a grossly exaggerated sense of the danger posed by "capitalist encirclement" abroad and by actual and potential subversives at home. This has nothing to do with "paranoia" in the sense of a clinical condition. The threat in the civil war was very real, and the Bolsheviks' perception that a successful communist revolution posed a mortal threat to capitalism predisposed them to think that there would inevitably be some kind of confrontation from which only one would emerge victorious. The persistent drone of establishment anti-communism kept Bolshevik nerves on edge. For all the self-inflicted damage done by these exaggerated fears—not least the mass repression of 1936–38—the world war that ensued only served to convince Stalin and senior officialdom that they had been right all along.

The chapter on Bolshevik leadership took the story of information and its interpretation in a slightly different direction. As Priestland has observed, there was a persistent tension between what he calls the "technicist" and "revivalist" strands of Bolshevism: Bolsheviks tended to think both that their plans were "scientific" and that the plans were unleashing an almost boundless potential.[5] We highlighted the tension in Stalin's vision between the technicist's attention to nurturing leadership and administrative skills, and the revivalist's feeling that the right person in the right place could solve all problems. The key point is that toward the end of the first five-year plan Stalin closed off any discussion about the realism of plan targets. When he did so, he eliminated the single most important source of information any leader has: the ideas, doubts, and concerns of those who implement policy. To be sure, Stalin knew the outlines of what was going on from agencies checking the fulfillment of decisions and other sources, but he gave the impression of never adequately grasping that bureaucratic resistance, foot-dragging, and other forms of recalcitrance and corruption were products of the system he had created. He appeared not to realize that *he* had given birth to the "double-dealer" (*dvurushnik*) whom he so feared and loathed.

The second part of the volume concentrated on Stalin's efforts to establish hegemonic interpretations of subjects that had always served as a source of tension for the Bolshevik Party: the place of leader cults within a Marxist polity, the status of the Soviet "working class," and the relationship between the party-state and the arts. Although by no means the only person involved in this process, as "master" of the word, Stalin played a critical role. He allotted considerable time to the process of correctly formulating speeches, newspaper articles, letters, slogans, and other core texts in an attempt to ensure that audiences ranging from close colleagues to the broader Soviet public saw the world through a very particular set of lenses.

As Stalin developed this vision, he had to perform a delicate balancing act, taking into account the exigencies of state-building as well as the party's commitment to Marxism-Leninism. The Marxist-Leninist framework strongly shaped his interpretations, but was flexible enough to accommodate a degree of adaptation and change of emphasis. Concerned to refute perceptions of the USSR as unstable, fragmented, and backward, Stalin strove to promote a vision of a cohesive, modern, and progressive

Soviet political community. In his vision, this community was united around the leader as an emblem of the party-state rather than as an individual in his own right. There was little place for a romantic view of manual labor, with all its connotations of backwardness, or for the outdated and divisive principle of working-class hegemony; instead advanced workers and the new Soviet intelligentsia marched together at the head of one Soviet people. Finally, artists were united in their aspiration to serve the party-state by producing a high-quality, politically useful *Soviet* culture that catered to the population as a whole. Stalin's vision contained many tensions and contradictions, but the authoritative nature of his words went some way to containing these. How others responded to his vision is a question that this study has been able to address only in passing; one thing is clear however—the words of the infallible leader were difficult to ignore.

How important are Stalin and his vision for explaining "Stalinism"? The question of Stalin's personal influence is one that historians have wrestled with long and hard. Some have argued that the system was bound to turn out as it did: Stalinism was the logical outcome of Marxism-Leninism, an ideology that was doomed from the outset not merely for its utopianism, but also because it was an alien graft that fatally weakened the regime's legitimacy and compelled it to rule by force.[6] Others have looked to contextual factors to explain Stalin-era developments, from Russia's political culture and relative socioeconomic backwardness to pan-European tendencies associated with the rise of the modern interventionist state.[7] But for many scholars, Stalinism still cannot be explained without reference to the agency of Stalin himself.

We now know considerably more about the nature and extent of Stalin's power. He certainly did not lack for ambition to control and shape the political, economic, social, and cultural landscape of the USSR. His interventions were usually decisive. He was the final arbiter of any dispute on which he chose to express a view. In many ways, he did shape the era that bears his name. And yet these findings have not discredited the arguments of those who sought to observe the limits of Stalin's power. For all his immense power, he was not always able to obtain the outcomes he sought. The archival evidence shows his frustration and anger with a party-state apparatus that from his perspective all too frequently failed to conform to his will. It also demonstrates the paradox that, although the state was strong, Stalin and others in his inner circle, and well beyond it, perceived that it was facing mortal threats.

Gauging the relative significance of structure and agency is always a difficult task, all the more so in the case of an individual who has been branded a "dictator." What we have tried to show is that the way Stalin saw the world was substantially limited by the structures in which he found himself. His interpretation, and misinterpretation, of information demonstrates this all too clearly. And yet he was not a total captive of these structures. He was capable of molding them in various ways, of creating a vision that bore his own personal stamp. Analysis of Stalin's distinctive vision is essential if we are to make sense of the extraordinary phenomenon that was Stalinism.

NOTES

Introduction

1. O. V. Khlevniuk, R. W. Davies, L. P. Kosheleva, E. A. Rees, and L. A. Rogovaia, eds., *Stalin i Kaganovich: Perepiska, 1931–1936 gg.* (Moscow, 2001), 19; Leonid Maksimenkov, *Sumbur vmesto muzyki* (Moscow, 1997), 3.

2. Pierre Bourdieu, *In Other Words: Essays towards a Reflexive Sociology* (Stanford, Calif., 1990), 134–37.

3. Here we paraphrase the point made by Ludwig Wittgenstein in his *Philosophical Investigations* (Oxford, 1958), 146.

4. John Lewis Gaddis, *We Know Now: Rethinking Cold War History* (Oxford, 1997), 14.

5. We chose not to attempt to cover some themes that , although important, have received extensive treatment elsewhere. Collectivization, for example, has been thoroughly documented in V. Danilov, V. Vinogradov, L. Viola, L. Dvoinikh, N. Ivnitskii, S. Krasil'nikov, R. Manning, O. Naumov, E. Tiurina, and Khan Chzhong Suk (Hahn Jeong-Sook), eds., *Tragediia sovetskoi derevni: Dokumenty i materialy v 5 tomakh, 1927–1939* (Moscow, 1999–2006).

6. Alter Litvin and John Keep, eds., *Stalinism: Russian and Western Views at the Turn of the Millennium* (New York, 2005), 4–7; Jan Plamper, *The Stalin Cult: A Study in the Alchemy of Power* (New Haven, 2012), 125–27. We are grateful to Arch Getty for clarifying some of these matters. Stalin's personal archive is in the process of being digitized by Yale University Press.

7. J. Arch Getty and Oleg V. Naumov, eds., *The Road to Terror: Stalin and the Self-Destruction of the Bolsheviks* (New Haven, 1999), 24–27, 455; Erik Van Ree, *The Political Thought of Joseph Stalin* (London, 2002), 16; Ethan Pollock, *Stalin and the Soviet Science Wars* (Princeton, N.J., 2006), 3.

8. John Adams, "Argument in Defense of the Soldiers in the Boston Massacre Trials," December 1770; L. Kinvin Wroth and Hiller B. Zobel, eds., *Legal Papers of John Adams*, vol. 3 (Cambridge, Mass., 1965), 260–70.

9. RGASPI 558/11/96, 100, 105, 108, 112, 115–17.

10. Silvio Pons's *Stalin and the Inevitable War* (London, 2002) was one of the more recent contributions to the "debate." Among those who consider that ideology dominated Stalin's thinking are Martin Malia, *The Soviet Tragedy: A History of Socialism in Russia, 1917–1991* (New York, 1994), and Stephane Courtois et al., *The Black Book of Communism: Crimes, Terror, Repression* (Cambridge, Mass., 1999). See especially the introduction by Courtois, 1–31.

11. David Priestland, *Stalinism and the Politics of Mobilization: Ideas, Power and Terror in Inter-war Russia* (Oxford, 2007).

12. Andrea Graziosi, "The New Soviet Archival Sources: Hypotheses for a Critical Assessment," *Cahiers du monde russe* 1–2 (1999), 34.

13. Ibid., 36–39.

14. Stalin first used the phrase in a speech of April 1928. I. Stalin, *Sochineniia*, vols. 1–13 (Moscow, 1946–51) and vols. 1–3/vols. 14–16 (Stanford, Calif., 1967), vol. 11, 58.

15. Peredovaia, "Iskusstvo partiinogo rukovodstva," *Bol'shevik* 5 (1930), 10. See also Peredovaia, "Na dva fronta," *Bol'shevik* 6 (1930); Peredovaia, "Industrializatsiia SSSR k XVI s"ezdu VKP(b)," *Bol'shevik* 9 (1930).

16. Joseph Berliner, *Factory and Manager in the USSR* (Cambridge, Mass., 1957).

17. Most recently, Van Ree, *Political Thought of Joseph Stalin*.

18. N. Kozlova, "The Diary as Initiation and Rebirth: Reading Everyday Documents of the Early Soviet Era," in Christina Kiaer and Eric Naiman, eds., *Everyday Life in Early Soviet Russia* (Bloomington, Ind., 2006), 296.

19. Jochen Hellbeck, *Revolution on My Mind* (Cambridge, Mass., 2006), 19; Michael Gorham, *Speaking in Soviet Tongues* (DeKalb, Ill., 2003), 9–12.

20. R. V. Daniels *The Conscience of the Revolution* (Cambridge, Mass., 1960), 306–7.

21. Ibid.; Igal Halfin, *From Darkness to Light: Class, Consciousness and Salvation in Revolutionary Russia* (Pittsburgh, 2000), 37.

22. Eric Naiman, "Introduction," in Evgenii Dobrenko and Eric Naiman, eds., *The Landscape of Stalinism* (Washington, D.C., 2003), xii.

23. Eric Naiman, "Discourse Made Flesh: Healing and Terror in the Construction of Soviet Subjectivity," in Igal Halfin, ed., *Language and Revolution* (London, 2002), 299.

24. Katerina Clark and Evgenii Dobrenko, eds., *Soviet Culture and Power* (New Haven, 2007), xii–xiv; Katerina Clark, "The Cult of Literature and Nikolai Ostrovskii's 'How the Steel Was Tempered,' " in Klaus Heller and Jan Plamper, eds., *Personality Cults in Stalinism* (Göttingen, 2004), 415–16. See also Gorham, *Speaking in Soviet Tongues*, 121–23.

25. Alexei Yurchak, *Everything Was Forever, Until It Was No More* (Princeton, N.J., 2006), 10–14, 39–44.

26. N. Bukharin, "Ekonomika sovetskoi strany," *Izvestiia* 12 May 1934.

27. A. V. Kvashonkin, L. P. Kosheleva, L. A. Rogovaia, and O. V. Khlevniuk, eds., *Sovetskoe rukovodstvo: Perepiska, 1928–1941 gg.* (Moscow, 1999), 277–79, 282–95.

28. On "speaking Bolshevik," see Stephen Kotkin, *Magnetic Mountain: Stalinism as a Civilization* (Berkeley, 1995).

29. A. Artizov and O. Naumov, eds., *Vlast' i khudozhestvennaia intelligentsiia* (Moscow, 1999), 745 n.17; RGASPI 558/11/88/21–23.

30. In March 1935 Stalin assumed official responsibility for supervising the CC's Department of Culture and Propaganda. A. V. Kvashonkin, A. V. Lishvin, and O. V. Khlevniuk, eds., *Stalinskoe politbiuro v 30-e gody* (Moscow, 1995), 143.

31. Dmitrii Shepilov, *The Kremlin's Scholar* (New Haven, 2007), 229.

32. Ibid., 26–27; D. Volkogonov, *Triumf i tragediia* (Moscow, 1989), vol.1, part 1, 221; vol. 2, part 2, 153.

33. Volkogonov, *Triumf*, 184.

34. Shepilov, *Kremlin's Scholar*, 23.

35. Lion Feuchtwanger, *Moscow, 1937* (London, 1937), 125.

36. Norman Naimark, "Cold War Studies and New Archival Materials on Stalin," *Russian Review* 1 (2002), 11; Maksimenkov, *Sumbur*, 3.

37. D. L. Brandenberger and A. M. Dubrovsky, " 'The People Need a Tsar': The Emergence of National Bolshevism as Stalinist Ideology, 1931–1941," *Europe-Asia Studies* 5 (1998), 873–92; Priestland, *Stalinism*, 244–49; David Hoffmann, *Stalinist Values* (Ithaca, N.Y., 2003), ch. 5.

Chapter 1.   "Bolshevik" Leadership

1. See, for example, J. Arch Getty, *Practicing Stalinism: Bolsheviks, Boyars, and the Persistence of Tradition* (New Haven, 2013); E. A. Rees, "Stalin: Architect of Terror," in James Harris, ed., *Anatomy of Terror: Political Violence under Stalin* (Oxford, 2013); Oleg Khlevniuk, *Master of the House: Stalin and His Inner Circle* (New Haven, 2009); James Harris, "Was Stalin a Weak Dictator?" *Journal of Modern History* 75 (2003), 375–86.

2. R. W. Davies, "Making Economic Policy," in Paul Gregory, ed., *Behind the Facade of Stalin's Command Economy: Evidence from the Soviet State and Party Archives* (Stanford, Calif., 2001), 69. See also R. W. Davies, *The Industrialisation of Soviet Russia*, vol. 4: *Crisis and Progress in the Soviet Economy, 1931–1933* (Basingstoke, England, 1996).

3. Paul Gregory, "The Dictator's Orders," in Gregory, *Behind the Facade*, 22. See also Paul Gregory, *The Political Economy of Stalinism: Evidence from the Soviet Secret Archives* (Cambridge, England, 2004).

4. R. W. Davies, "The Soviet Economy and the Launching of the Great Terror," in Melanie Ilic, ed., *Stalin's Terror Revisited* (Basingstoke, England, 2006), 11–37.

5. In this, I am in agreement with Gregory, "Dictator's Orders," 33.

6. The best single source for these behaviors remains Joseph Berliner, *Factory and Manager in the USSR* (Cambridge, Mass., 1957), chs. 6–10. See also Eugenia Belova, "Economic Crime and Punishment," in Gregory, *Behind the Facade*, 131–58; James R. Harris, "The Purging of Local Cliques in the Urals Region," in Sheila Fitzpatrick, ed., *Stalinism: New Directions* (London, 1999), 262–85.

7. Andrei Markevich provides the best treatment of the imperfections of the system: "How Much Control Is Enough? Monitoring and Enforcement under Stalin," *CEFIR/ NES Working Paper Series*, Working Paper No. 10, December 2007. See also Belova, "Economic Crime and Punishment," 156–57; J. Arch Getty, "Pragmatists and Puritans: The Rise and Fall of the Party Control Commission," *Carl Beck Papers*, University of Pittsburgh, 1997.

8. Isaac Deutscher, *Stalin: A Political Biography* (Harmondsworth, England, 1986), 234; E. A. Rees, *State Control in Soviet Russia: The Rise and Fall of the Workers' and Peasants' Inspectorate, 1920–1934* (New York, 1987).

9. V. I. Lenin, "How We Should Reorganize the Workers and Peasants Inspectorate," in *Polnoe sobranie sochinenii*, vol. 45 (Moscow, 1963), 389–406.

10. I. Stalin, *Sochineniia*, vols. 1–13 (Moscow, 1946–51) and vols. 1–3/vols. 14–16 (Stanford, Calif., 1967), vol. 5, 62–112.

11. This particular battle between Stalin and Trotsky was fought in meetings of the CC and in correspondence between meetings. RGASPI 558/11/816.

12. Stalin, *Sochineniia*, vol. 5, 197–222.

13. Stalin's address to the Fourth Conference of Leading Officials of the Republics and Provinces (12 June 1923). RGASPI 17/165/4/47, 127. See also his 28 December 1923 article in *Pravda*: Stalin, *Sochineniia*, vol. 5, 363–65.

14. RGASPI 17/165/4/127.

15. *KPSS v rezoliutsiiakh i resheniiakh s"ezdov, konferentsii i plenumov TsK* (Moscow, 1984), vol. 3, 74, 99; James Harris, "Stalin as General Secretary: The Appointments Process and the Nature of Stalin's Power," in Sarah Davies and James Harris, eds., *Stalin: A New History* (Cambridge, England, 2005).

16. Stalin, *Sochineniia*, vol. 5, 362–70.

17. Ibid., vol. 7, 42–47.

18. Ibid., vol. 6, 53–58.

19. Ibid., vol. 6, 186.

20. Ibid., vol. 6, 53.

21. Ibid., vol. 6, 277–78.

22. Ibid., vol. 6, 269–70.

23. Ibid., vol. 7, 171–72.

24. Indeed, so great was the shortage of cadres, exclusion from the party generally did not mean exclusion from "responsible" (*otvetstvennye*, or "leading") posts. RGASPI 17/68/35.

25. Stalin, *Sochineniia*, vol. 7, 349–50.

26. A standard which, according to a resolutions of the fifteenth party conference (October–November 1926), "the Soviet Union would catch up to and exceed in a minimal historical period." *XV konferentsiia vsesoiuznoi komunisticheskoi partii(b): Stenograficheskii otchet* (Moscow, 1927), 773–92. See also the CC resolution on the rationalization (24 March 1927), in *KPSS v rezoliutsiiakh*, vol. 4, 161–67; I. Kraval', "Sotsialisticheskaia ratsionalizatsiia proizvodstva i upravlenie," *Bol'shevik* 9 (1927), 43–45.

27. RGASPI 17/85/212/4–7 (23 March 1927).

28. See, for example, the letter from Said Gabiev (Dagestan) to Stalin on regional family groups protecting the region from challenges and demands of the center. RGASPI 558/11/725/81–83.

29. Stalin, *Sochineniia*, vol. 9, 157–58.

30. L. Kosheleva, V. Lel'chuk, V. Naumov, O. Naumov, L. Rogovaia, and O. Khlevniuk, eds., *Pis'ma I. V. Stalina V. M. Molotovu, 1925–1936 gg.: Sbornik dokumentov* (Moscow, 1995), 91.

31. He was not especially clear on how that distinction was to be made. See Stalin's speech to the Leningrad Gubkom (12 April 1926), RGASPI 558/11/1107/108, 149–51; Stalin, *Sochineniia*, vol. 8, 132–39.

32. See, for example, Stalin's address to the Orgburo (3 May 1927), RGASPI 558/11/1110/150–63; RGASPI 17/69/269/49, 80–81 (November 1927 reports to the Orgburo on the development of inner-party democracy).

33. K. Bauman, "Osnovnye momenty raboty partiinykh organizatsii," *Bol'shevik* (1927), 56–67.

34. Lynne Viola, V. P. Danilov, N. A. Ivnitskii, and Denis Kozlov, eds., *The War against the Peasantry, 1927–1930: The Tragedy of the Soviet Countryside* (New Haven, 2005), 17.

35. Stalin, *Sochineniia*, vol. 10, 329–33.

36. V. Danilov, V. Vinogradov, L. Viola, L. Dvoinikh, N. Ivnitskii, S. Krasil'nikov, R. Manning, O. Naumov, E. Tiurina, and Khan Chzhong Suk (Hahn Jeong-Sook), eds., *Tragediia sovetskoi derevni: Dokumenty i materialy v 5 tomakh, 1927–1939* (Moscow, 1999–2006), vol. 1, 108–14.

37. Ibid., 136–37.

38. Stalin's address to the Siberian Regional Party Committee (20 January 1928), RGASPI 558/11/118/63, 78.

39. See notes 2 and 3 above.

40. Stalin, *Sochineniia*, vol. 11, 19.

41. See, for example, the letter of A. Z. Gol'tsman (Urals region) to Sergo Ordzhonikidze on the impact of Molotov's visit. A. V. Kvashonkin, A. Ia. Livshin, and O. V. Khlevniuk, eds., *Sovetskoe rukovodstvo: Perepiska, 1928–1941* (Moscow, 1999), 18–19. The April 1928 CC plenum subsequently criticized some organizations for "excesses" (*peregiby*) in the purges.

42. Stalin, *Sochineniia*, vol. 11, 27–31; N. Speranskii, "K voprosu ob uluchshenii partapparata," *Bol'shevik* 6 (1928); M. Vasil'ev, "O promkadrakh," *Bol'shevik* 8 (1928); Peredovaia, "Komandnye kadry i kul'turnaia revoliutsiia," *Bol'shevik* 9 (1928).

43. See Daniel R. Brower, "The Smolensk Scandal and the End of NEP," *Slavic Review* 4 (1986), 689–706. Other less well-publicized scandals of the time included the Artemovsk scandal and the Sochii scandal. RGASPI 17/69/494/4, 10.

44. The Presidium of the Central Control Commission and Collegium of the People's Commissariat of the Workers' and Peasants' Inspectorate (Rabkrin) passed its

resolution on the Smolensk organization on 9 May 1928. RGASPI 613/1/78/45. The scandal hit the national press nine days later. See *Pravda*, 18 May 1928; V. Feigin, "Smolenskii signal," *Bol'shevik* 10 (1928).

45. Stalin, "Rech' na VIII S"ezde VLKSM" (16 May 1928), in *Sochineniia*, vol. 11, 66–77.

46. Peredovaia, "O lozunge samokritiki," *Bol'shevik* 10 (1928); "Obrashchenie TsK VKP(b) ko vsem chlenam partii, ko vsem rabochim o razvertyvanii samokritiki" (2 June 1928), in *KPSS v rezoliutsiiakh*, vol. 4, 338–42.

47. Kvashonkin et al., *Sovetskoe rukovodstvo*, 38–39.

48. Catherine Merridale, *Moscow Politics and the Rise of Stalin: The Communist Party in the Capital, 1925–1932* (Basingstoke, England, 1990); James Hughes, *Stalin, Siberia and the Crisis of the New Economic Policy* (Cambridge, England, 1991), ch. 6.

49. James Harris, *The Great Urals: Regionalism and the Evolution of the Soviet System* (Ithaca, N.Y., 1999), ch. 3.

50. Kvashonkin et al., *Sovetskoe rukovodstvo*, 33–35.

51. Stalin, *Sochineniia*, vol. 11, 234–35.

52. Ibid., 318; Peredovaia, "O predstoiashchei chistke Partii," *Bol'shevik* 4 (1929).

53. Stalin, *Sochineniia*, vol. 11, 246–47.

54. Ibid., 187.

55. Stalin, "Pis'mo A. I. Mikoianu," in I. Stalin, *Sochineniia*, ed. Richard Kosolapov, vol. 17 (Tver'na, 2004), 281–82.

56. RGASPI 613/1/77/38, 46.

57. RGASPI 558/11/1112/301–2, 309–10.

58. RGASPI 558/11/36/95, 103; 558/11/153/21, 22, 28, 29, 34–35, 55, 57–8.

59. See, for example, Stalin, *Sochineniia*, vol. 11, 1–107, especially 10–11, 17.

60. L. Shatskin, "Doloi partinuiu obyvatel'shchinu," *Komsomol'skaia pravda*, 18 June 1929; Ia. Sten, "Vyshe kommunisticheskoe znamia Marksizma-Leninizma," *Komsomol'skaia pravda*, 21 July 1929. For Stalin's letter to Molotov, see Lars Lih, Oleg V. Naumov, and Oleg V. Khlevniuk, eds., *Stalin's Letters to Molotov, 1925–1936* (New Haven, 1995), 162–63.

61. Lih, Naumov, and Khlevniuk, *Stalin's Letters to Molotov*, 169. In this case the translation is mine, from the original Russian.

62. Stalin, *Sochineniia*, vol. 12, 118–35.

63. Harris, *Great Urals*, especially ch. 3.

64. Stalin, *Sochineniia*, vol. 12, 144. Stalin rarely made a speech in this period without attacking the Right. His marginal notes on a report on the evolution of the Five-Year Plan are revealing of his attitude to Gosplan. See RGASPI 558/11/133/3, 8, 23.

65. Stalin, *Sochineniia*, vol. 12, 174–75. See also Stalin's speech to the Orgburo on the reorganization of the apparat (30 December 1929), RGASPI 558/11/1113/175–84.

66. Stalin, *Sochineniia*, vol. 12, 191–99.

67. Peredovaia, "Iskusstvo partiinogo rukovodstva," *Bol'shevik* 5 (1930), 10. See also Peredovaia, "Na dva fronta," *Bol'shevik* 6 (1930); Peredovaia, "Industrializatsiia SSSR

k XVI s"ezdu VKP(b)," *Bol'shevik* 9 (1930); E. Iaroslavskii, "Bor'ba protiv opportu-nizma v period mezhdu XV i XVI s"ezdami VKP(b)," *Bol'shevik* 9 (1930), 11–18.

68. Stalin, *Sochineniia*, vol. 12, 304, 308, 311–13, 327. See also the resolutions of the congress in *KPSS v rezoliutsiiakh*, vol. 5 129–33, 140–42.

69. Stalin, *Sochineniia*, vol. 12, 357–61; "S"ezd razvernutogo sotsialisticheskogo nastupleniia," *Bol'shevik* 13 (1930), 4–5.

70. Kosheleva et al., *Pis'ma Stalina Molotovu*, 193–95, 218–19. Stalin ordered Molotov to put an end to "hysterical reporting" in the press. "Stop them going on about catastrophes, breakdowns, and endless failures. It's not justified by the facts, and it's not becoming of Bolsheviks." Ibid., 219.

71. Danilov et al., *Tragediia sovetskoi derevni*, vol. 2, 599–600.

72. Ibid., 627.

73. Ibid., 628–29.

74. *KPSS v rezoliutsiiakh*, vol. 5, 201.

75. Ibid., 201–2 (quotation), 198–207; *Pravda*, 3 September 1930.

76. Kosheleva et al., *Pis'ma Stalina Molotovu*, 222–23.

77. Lominadze had been demoted to this post having been associated with the earlier Shatskin-Sten incident. For more detail on these events, see R. W. Davies, "The Syrtsov-Lominadze Affair," *Soviet Studies* 1 (1981), 29-50.

78. Kosheleva et al., *Pis'ma Stalina Molotovu*, 231; A. V. Kvashonkin, A. V. Lishvin, and O. V. Khlevniuk, eds., *Stalinskoe politbiuro v 30-e gody* (Moscow, 1995), 96–97, 100–101.

79. See, for example, S. Shpilev, "Dvurushnichestvo i Pravo-'Levyi' Blok," *Partiinoe stroitel'stvo* 21 (1930); Peredovaia, *Partiinoe stroitel'stvo* 22 (1930).

80. Stalin, *Sochineniia*, vol. 13, 29–42.

81. Ibid., vol. 13, especially 80; RGASPI 17/165/27/2–3 (Molotov), 14 (Kuibyshev); Oleg Khlevniuk, *In Stalin's Shadow: The Career of "Sergo" Ordzhonikidze* (Armonk, N.Y., 1995), 47. See also O. V. Khlevniuk, R. W. Davies, L. P. Kosheleva, E. A. Rees, and L. A. Rogovaia, eds., *Stalin i Kaganovich: Perepiska, 1931–1936 gg.* (Moscow, 2001), 66, 68, 72, 711.

82. Kaganovich, Stalin's second in command at the time, had recommended "deci-sively rejecting" their pleas, but Stalin overruled him.

83. Danilov et al., *Tragediia sovetskoi derevni*, vol. 3, 199–200.

84. For Stalin's correspondence with regional officials in this period, see RGAE 7486/37/147; RGASPI 558/11/40, 41.

85. As in this letter from Kaganovich to Stalin on recent communications with the Ukrainian Politburo. Khlevniuk at al., *Stalin i Kaganovich*, 164, 169. Even then, Kaganovich thought they would have to give Ukraine some grain, but Stalin subse-quently told him not to.

86. Ibid., 205–10.

87. Ibid., 298–99.

88. RGASPI 558/11/1116/141–42. The same sort of analysis can be found in Stalin, *Sochineniia*, vol. 13, 229–31; *KPSS v rezoliutsiiakh*, vol. 6, 26–29.

89. Danilov et al., *Tragediia sovetskoi derevni*, vol. 3, 525, 575, 625–30; RGASPI 55/11/787/25–26.

90. R. W. Davies, "The Management of Soviet Industry, 1928–1941," in William G. Rosenberg and Lewis H. Siegelbaum, eds., *Social Dimensions of Soviet Industrialization* (Bloomington, Ind., 1993), 105–23.

91. Indeed, both in public and in private Stalin described party policy as almost self-evidently correct. See, for example, his speech to the seventeenth party congress: *Sochineniia*, vol. 13, 367.

92. From an address to a conference of the rural Komsomol (2 February 1933), RGASPI 558/11/1117.

93. Stalin, *Sochineniia*, vol. 13, 213.

94. Ibid., 229–31.

95. The new institution was called the "political department" of the recently created Machine Tractor Stations. See *KPSS v rezoliutsiiakh*, vol. 6, 26–29.

96. Ibid., 46–47.

97. "Nekotorye itogi," *Partiinoe stroitel'stvo* 10 (1933).

98. Stalin, *Sochineniia*, vol. 13, 365–66, 370.

99. Kosheleva et al., *Pis'ma Stalina Molotovu*, 247–48; Khlevniuk et al., *Stalin i Kaganovich*, 318–34; Kvashonkin et al., *Stalinskoe politbiuro*, 133; Kvashonkin et al., *Sovetskoe rukovodstvo*, 261–62.

100. RGASPI 56/1/143/73, 83–103; 56/1/144/2, 4, 5; 558/11/152/53, 68, 74–76.

101. RGASPI 558/11/49/94.

102. Khlevniuk et al., *Stalin i Kaganovich*, 480.

103. RGASPI 558/11/64/88–89ob.

104. Khlevniuk et al., *Stalin i Kaganovich*, 511.

105. See, for example, Peredovaia, "Ovladet' bol'shevistskim stilem organizatsionno-prakticheskogo rukovodstva," *Partiinoe stroitel'stvo* 9 (1934), 1–8; A. Shcherbakov, "Neudovletvoritel'noe rukovodstvo i ego rezul'taty," *Partiinoe stroitel'stvo* 9 (1934), 2–7; E. Iaroslavskii, "Pervye itogi chistki partiinoi organizatsii," *Bol'shevik* 15 (1935), 9–23; M. Rubenshtein, "Ne zaznavat'sia, ne uspokaivat'sia!" *Bol'shevik* 16 (1934), 18–35; Peredovaia, "17 let oktiabria i organizatsionnaia rabota partii," *Partiinoe stroitel'stvo* 21 (1934); E. Sh., "Bor'ba s narusheniiami partiinoi i gosudarstvennoi distsiplinoi," *Partiinoe stroitel'stvo* 23 (1934), 11–15.

106. These tensions have been discussed at length elsewhere, so will not be discussed here in any detail. See, for example, Gabor Rittersporn, *Stalinist Simplifications and Soviet Complications: Social Tensions and Political Conflicts in the USSR, 1933–1953* (Chur, Switzerland, 1991); J. Arch Getty, *Origins of the Great Purges: The Soviet Communist Party Reconsidered, 1933–1938* (Cambridge, England, 1985); Harris, *Great Urals*, chs. 5, 6.

107. See, for example, Kvashonkin et al., *Sovetskoe rukovodstvo*, 245, 248, 258; Khlevniuk et al., *Stalin i Kaganovich*, 317, 329, 361–62, 364–67, 389, 505. Regional party officials occasionally requested an audience with Stalin in order to discuss conflicts in their organizations. See, for example, RGASPI 558/11/64/109, 112; 558/11/150/120.

108. See, for example, Stalin, *Sochineniia*, vol. 1/14, 56–64.

109. See Lewis Siegelbaum, *Stakhanovism and the Politics of Productivity in the USSR, 1935–1941* (Cambridge, England, 1988); Francesco Benvenuti, "Stakhanovism and Stalinism, 1934–1938," *CREES Discussion Papers No. 30*, SIPS, University of Birmingham, 1989; Robert Thurston, "The Stakhanovite Movement: Background to the Great Terror in the Factories, 1935–1938," in J. Arch Getty and Roberta Manning, eds., *Stalinist Terror* (Cambridge, England, 1993).

110. See chapter 2 of this volume.

111. A. Shcherbakov, "Glavnoe—povyshenie bol'shevistskoi bditel'nosti," *Partiinoe stroitel'stvo* 1 (1936), 18. However, some organizations got into trouble for going too far.

112. J. Arch Getty and Oleg V. Naumov, eds., *The Road to Terror: Stalin and the Self-Destruction of the Bolsheviks* (New Haven, 1999), 250–55.

113. See, for example, Getty and Naumov, *Road to Terror*, ch. 11; J. Arch Getty, "The Fall of the Clans: The Rise and Fall of Vainov of Iaroslavl," in Harris, *Anatomy of Terror;* Barry McLoughlin and Kevin McDermott, eds., *Stalin's Terror: High Politics and Mass Repression in the Soviet Union* (Basingstoke, England, 2003); Harris, "Purging of Local Cliques."

114. Yoram Gorlizki and Oleg Khlevniuk, *Cold Peace: Stalin and the Soviet Ruling Circle, 1945–1953* (Oxford, 2004).

Chapter 2.   Spymania

1. Using "Terror" or "Great Terror" as a label for the political violence of 1936–38 is a matter of controversy. At the height of the Cold War, scholars like Merle Fainsod, Carl Friedrich, and Zbigniew Brzezinski portrayed Soviet political violence as an "instrument of rule." They suggested that the regime deliberately terrorized the population—instilled a generalized fear—in order to overcome resistance to revolutionary change. We now know this not to be the case, so to some historians "Terror" seems no longer to be an appropriate term. The authors of this volume use it in the sense that it is applied to a specific phase of the French Revolution, a phase of mass executions, widespread denunciations amid a generalized fear of domestic and foreign enemies. The parallels have their limits, but they are strong enough that we prefer it to the less familiar and perhaps less appropriate alternatives, such as Yezhovshchina, Great Purges, and Mass Repression. For more on the parallels between the French and Soviet "Terrors," see Arno J. Mayer, *The Furies: Violence and Terror in the French and Russian Revolutions* (Princeton, N.J., 2000).

2. On popular opinion in the thirties, see Sarah Davies, *Popular Opinion in Stalin's Russia: Terror, Propaganda and Dissent, 1934–1941* (Cambridge, England, 1997); Sheila Fitzpatrick, *Everyday Stalinism: Ordinary Life in Extraordinary Times—Soviet Russia in the 1930s* (Oxford, 1999); Lesley A. Rimmel, "Another Kind of Fear: The Kirov Murder and the End of Bread Rationing in Leningrad," *Slavic Review* 56 (1997), 481–99; A. K. Sokolov, ed., *Golos naroda: Pis'ma i otkliki riadovykh sovetskikh grazhdan o sobytiiakh, 1918–1932 gg.* (Moscow, 1997); Lewis Siegelbaum and Andrei Sokolov,

eds., *Stalinism as a Way of Life* (New Haven, 2000); Andrei Sokolov, ed., *Obshchestvo i vlast', 1930-e gody: Povestvovanie v dokumentakh* (Moscow, 1998); and A. Ia. Livshin and I. B. Orlov, eds., *Pis'ma vo vlast', 1917–1927: Zaiavleniia, zhaloby, donosy, pis'ma v gosudarstvennye struktury i bol'shevistskim vozhdiam* (Moscow, 1998). On the situation of workers, see Donald Filtzer, *Soviet Workers and Stalinist Industrialisation* (London, 1986); David Hoffmann, *Peasant Metropolis: Social Identities in Moscow, 1929–1941* (Ithaca, N.Y., 1994); E. A. Osokina, *Ierarkhiia potrebleniia* (Moscow, 1993); E. A. Osokina, *Za fasadom 'stalininskogo izobiliia'* (Moscow, 1997).

3. N. Werth and G. Moullec, eds., *Rapports secrets sovietiques* (Paris, 1994), 209–16; Jeffrey Rossman, "Weaver of Rebellion and Poet of Resistance: Kapiton Klepikov (1880–1933) and Shop-Floor Opposition to Bolshevik Rule," *Jahrbücher für Geschichte Osteuropas* 44 (1996), 374–407; Rossman, "The Teikovo Cotton Workers' Strike of April 1932: Class, Gender and Identity Politics in Stalin's Russia," *Russian Review* 56 (1997), 44–69.

4. *Oni ne molchali* (Moscow, 1991), 422, 427–28; Iu. Aksiutin et al., *Vlast' i oppozitsiia: Rossiiskii politicheskii protsess XX stoletiia* (Moscow, 1995), ch. 5; A. V. Gusev, "Levokommunisticheskaia oppozitsiia v SSSR v kontse 20-x godov," *Otechestvennaia istoriia* 6 (1996), 85, 93. Gusev quotes Stalin speculating in his collected works that there were twenty thousand members of the party who sympathized with Trotsky.

5. Oleg Khlevniuk, "The Objectives of the Great Terror, 1937–1938," in Julian Cooper, Maureen Perrie, and E. A. Rees, eds., *Soviet History, 1917–1953: Essays in Honour of R. W. Davies* (London, 1995), 158–76.

6. These are too numerous to mention, but articles published under Stalin's editorial supervision include "O nekotorykh kovarnykh priemakh verbovochnoi raboty inostrannykh razvedok," *Pravda*, 17 May 1937; "Podryvnaia rabota Iaponskoi razvedki," *Pravda*, 5 August 1937; "Shpionskii internatsional," *Pravda*, 21 August 1937; RGASPI 558/11/203/62–88, 93–100.

7. The archives of the main agencies that conducted this work from France, Britain, Japan, Poland, and elsewhere remain closed, so sources for the study of espionage activities against the USSR are few and indirect.

8. Soviet leaders understood that they were exaggerated. See, for example, Feliks Chuev, *Molotov: Poluderzhavnyi vlastelin* (Moscow, 1999), 466, 473–75. Stalin himself manipulated evidence when it served his political purposes. See William Chase, "Stalin as Producer," in Sarah Davies and James Harris, eds., *Stalin: A New History* (Cambridge, England, 2005); Wladislaw Hedeler, "Ezhov's Scenario for the Great Terror and the Falsified Record of the Third Moscow Show Trial," in Barry McLoughlin and Kevin McDermott, eds., *Stalin's Terror: High Politics and Mass Repression in the Soviet Union* (Basingstoke, England, 2002), 34–55.

9. Ernest R. May, *Knowing One's Enemies: Intelligence Assessment before the Two World Wars* (Princeton, N.J., 1984); Walter Laqueur, *Terrorism* (London, 1977), 13–17; Michael Miller, *Shanghai on the Metro: Spies, Intrigue, and the French between the Wars* (Berkeley, 1994), 215, 306.

10. Miller, *Shanghai*, 99.

11.   See, among others, Paul Haggie, *Britannia at Bay: The Defense of the British Empire against Japan, 1931–1941* (Oxford, 1981); R. Dallek, *Franklin Roosevelt and American Foreign Policy, 1932–1945* (Oxford, 1975); Jonathan Haslam, *The Soviet Union and the Threat from the East, 1933–1941* (London, 1992).

12.   This fear was whipped up by journalists, filmmakers, and novelists, among others. Films portraying the threat of infiltration and invasion included *The Airship Destroyer* (1909), *The Invaders* (1909), *O.H.M.S.* (1913), and *The German Spy Peril* (1914). Among the writers of novels depicting the threat to Britain from abroad, the most famous, perhaps, was William Tufnell Le Queux, whose works, *The Invasion of 1910* (1906) and *Spies of the Kaiser* (1909), were serialized by the British publishing magnate Lord Northcliffe.

13.   See, for example, John Price Jones, *The German Secret Service in America* (Boston, 1918); French Strother, *Fighting Germany's Spies* (Garden City, N.Y., 1918); Joseph Caillaux, *Devant l'histoire: Mes prisons* (Paris, 1920); Sidney Theodore Felstead, *German Spies at Bay* (London, 1920); Walter Nicolai, *Geheime Machte: Internationale Spionage und ihre Bekämpfung im Weltkrieg und Heute* (Leipzig, 1923); Cesare Petorelli Lalatte Finzi, *I. T. O. (Informazioni truppe operanti): Note di un capo del servizio informazioni d'armata, 1915–1918* (Milan, 1934); Marthe Richer, *I Spied for France* (London, 1935); Franz Von Rintelen, *Dark Invader: Wartime Reminiscences of a German Naval Officer* (London, 1933); Ernst Carl, *One against England: The Death of Lord Kitchener and the Plot against the British Fleet* (London, 1935); Alexander Bauermeister, *Spies Break Through: Memoirs of a German Secret Service Officer* (London, 1934); Amleto Vespa, *Secret Agent of Japan* (London, 1938). The above are examples of what were claimed to be nonfiction. There were as many, if not more, novels of spying and sabotage, though the boundary between fiction and nonfiction was anything but clear.

14.   RGASPI 558/11/1180/38–40 (from an unpublished collection of Stalin's writings on military themes).

15.   See, for example, Sir R. H. Bruce Lockhart, *Memoirs of a British Agent* (London, 1932). The Cheka exposed much of this activity in its first great intelligence operations, "Trest" and "Sindikat-1." See Christopher Andrew and Oleg Gordievsky, *KGB: The Inside Story of Its Operations from Lenin to Gorbachev* (London, 1990).

16.   Andrew Cook, *On His Majesty's Secret Service: Sidney Reilly Codename ST1* (London, 2002); John W. Long, "Plot and Counterplot in Revolutionary Russia: Chronicling the Bruce Lockhart Conspiracy, 1918," *Intelligence and National Security* 1 (1995), 122–43; A. L. Litvin, ed., *Savinkov na Lubianke: Dokumenty* (Moscow, 1990). Other revolutionary parties were also trying to assassinate Soviet leaders. Supporters of the Socialist Revolutionaries were among the most active, assassinating the head of the Petrograd Cheka and two weeks later shooting Lenin, though not fatally.

17.   For Dzerzhinskii's reports to the Politburo, see, for example, RGASPI 76/3/364/4–8, 12–13, 21–22, 25. See also James Morris, "The Polish Terror: Spy Mania and Ethnic Cleansing in the Great Terror," *Europe-Asia Studies* 5 (2004), 743; Terry Martin, "The Origins of Soviet Ethnic Cleansing," *Journal of Modern History* 4 (1998), 860.

18. R. W. Davies, Oleg V. Khlevniuk, E. A. Rees, Liudmila P. Kosheleva, and Larisa A. Rogovaya, eds., *The Stalin-Kaganovich Correspondence, 1931–36* (New Haven, 2003), 180.

19. Though the Soviet ambassador complained that there was no sign of any decrease in acts of sabotage. RGASPI 55/11/790/123.

20. William Chase, *Enemies within the Gates? The Comintern and Stalinist Repression, 1934–1939* (New Haven, 2001), 51, 122–25. By 1936, Stalin doubted the loyalty of political émigrés generally.

21. RGASPI 558/11/185/76 (intercepted correspondence). It is not possible to convert such a figure into rubles, but the average monthly wage of a Japanese skilled worker in 1935 was around 90 yen per month. Andrew Gordon, *The Evolution of Labour Relations in Japan* (Cambridge, Mass., 1985), 193. Thanks to Steven Tolliday for this reference.

22. For example, see the correspondence of the American ambassador to Japan, Joseph Grew, intercepted by the Foreign Department of the OGPU. RGASPI 558/11/185/128.

23. RGVA 4/19/13/2–8, 25.

24. There were several other ongoing investigations at the time, including that of an espionage ring in Kamchatka that had been infiltrated and whose members were rounded up in 1933. RGVA 9/39/5/76–116.

25. RGVA 4/19/13/2–15; 558/11/187/60–61.

26. RGVA 9/39/5/76–116.

27. RGASPI 55/11/186/118; RGVA 9/39/5/211–20.

28. RGASPI 558/11/185/77–79.

29. "Record of a Conversation of 31 January 1939 between Himmler and General Oshima, Japanese Ambassador at Berlin," in *Trial of the Major German War Criminals before an International Military Tribunal, Nuremberg*, vol. 1. (Washington, D.C., 1947), document no. 2195-PS, 852.

30. See the Dzerzhinskii fond, RGASPI 76/3.

31. These pervade the special folders of the protocols of Politburo decisions. RGASPI 17/162.

32. On the legacy of the civil war, see Sheila Fitzpatrick, "The Civil War as a Formative Experience," in Abbott Gleason, Peter Kenez, and Richard Stites, eds., *Bolshevik Culture: Experiment and Order in the Russian Revolution* (Bloomington, Ind., 1985), 57–76.

33. Limits on the Cheka were discussed by the CC at the beginning of February 1918 and instituted by a decision of the Council of People's Commissars fewer than ten days later, but the limits were suspended almost immediately with the beginning of the German offensive. *Istoriia sovetskikh organov gosudarstvennoi besopasnosti* (Moscow, 1977).

34. For Lenin's opinion of the need for the Cheka to change its tactics, see his *Polnoe sobranie sochinenii*, vol. 40 (Moscow, 1969), 115.

35. V. N. Khaustov, V. P. Naumov, and N. S. Plotnikova, eds., *Lubianka: Stalin i VChK-GPU-OGPU-NKVD, ianvar' 1922–dekabr' 1936* (Moscow, 2003), 11–15.

36. For example, in September 1922 the GPU pressed for the right to execute criminals without the approval of the Commissariat of Justice "in exceptional circumstances, and for the right to investigate all crimes and not just cases of counterrevolutionary activity." Ibid., 64–66.

37. Ibid., 77–78, 103.

38. The Politburo resolved in May 1922 that there should be no shortfall in the provision of wages and supplies to GPU workers, but the GPU, like other party and Soviet institutions, faced regular budget cuts through the first half of the 1920s despite Stalin's advocacy. Ibid., 27–29, 37–39, 95–96, 791–92. On Kamenev and the OGPU budget, see Donald Rayfield, *Stalin and His Hangmen* (London, 2005), 96.

39. RGASPI 76/3/362; A. V. Kvashonkin, ed., *Bol'shevistskoe rukovodstvo: Perepiska, 1912–1927* (Moscow, 1996), 277.

40. Richard B. Spence, "Russia's *Operatsiia Trest:* A Reappraisal," *Global Intelligence Monthly* 1 (1999), 19–24.

41. Like Boris Savinkov and the "Narodnyi soiuz zashchity rodiny i svobody." O. B. Mozokhin, "Iz istorii bor'by organov VChK-OGPU s terrorizmom," *Voenno-istoricheskii zhurnal* 5 (2002), 5; *Istoriia sovetskikh organov*, 159–60.

42. On several occasions. *Istoriia sovetskikh organov*, 151; RGASPI 17/162/2/157, 160; and Khaustov et al., *Lubianka: Stalin*, 108.

43. *Istoriia sovetskikh organov*, 129–30.

44. See, for example, *Kniga ucheta lits sostoiavshikh na osobom uchete byvshikh belykh ofitserov v organakh GPU Ukrainy*, 4 vols. (Kharkov, 2011–12).

45. Politburo resolutions on these reports can be found in RGASPI 17/162. The materials of the Politburo commission that discussed sentences for the accused (Komissiia po politdelam) remain in the Presidential Archive. Some reports were deemed suitable for publication in the national press. See, for example, the case of Kinderman, Volscht, and Ditmarin. *Pravda*, 23 June 1925; Khaustov et al., *Lubianka: Stalin*, 105–6.

46. Some of the reports that Dzerzhinskii received and passed on to Stalin between late 1924 and the first half of 1926 can be found in RGASPI 76/3/331/1–3; 76/3/364/4–8, 12–13, 21–25, 58.

47. This paid for, among other things 2,600 new border guards, 925 horses, 25,000 rifles, 30 one and a half ton lorries, and 102 motorcycles with sidecars.

48. RGASPI 76/3/362/11. At that stage the OGPU was freed from the oversight of the Commissariat of Justice on appeal to the Politburo. See, for example, RGASPI 17/162/3/56 (April 1926).

49. *Istoriia sovetskikh organov*, 189.

50. Ibid., 191.

51. On the same day, he ordered Voroshilov to report on the danger of war and defense plans drawn up by the Commissariat of Defense. RGASPI 17/162/4/3, 4.

52. These committees extended the existing system, created in 1922, to prevent the infiltration of Party committees by SRs, Mensheviks, and other "anti-Soviet elements." V. I. Lenin, "Khoroshii kommunist v to zhe vremia est' i khoroshii chekist," *Istochnik* 1 (1996), 115–19.

53. *Istoriia sovetskikh organov*, 214.

54. Ibid., 191. RGASPI 17/162/4/70, 89, 94–96. Some of these documents are also published in Khaustov et al., *Lubianka: Stalin*, 125–28.

55. *Istoriia sovetskikh organov*, 194. It was not long before the Commissariat of Justice was trying to claw these new rights back. See Krylenko's note to the Politburo, 1 July 1927, in Khaustov et al., *Lubianka: Stalin*, 137–38.

56. Khaustov et al., *Lubianka: Stalin*, 144. He made a similar statement to Henri Barbusse in September 1927. " 'U nas malo rasstrelivaiut': Beseda I. V. Stalina s A. Barbiusom," *Istochnik* 1 (1999), 101–5.

57. RGASPI 76/3/362/10–11.

58. Khaustov et al., *Lubianka: Stalin*, 143–45.

59. Hiroaki Kuromiya, "The Shakhty Affair," *South East European Monitor* 2 (1997), 41–64.

60. V. A. Kovalev, a Russian minister of justice, presents a fascinating assessment of the evidence and the conduct of the trial in *Dva stalinskikh narkoma* (Moscow, 1995), 48–59.

61. It is not clear what methods the OGPU employed for obtaining confessions, but one accused person at the Promparty trial testified that he had been interrogated for eighteen straight hours, by which time he was ready to sign whatever his interrogators showed him. Ibid., 90.

62. The OGPU report on the affair, as edited by Stalin, can be found in RGASPI 558/11/132/1–20. Stalin did not alter the substance of this report, which was widely distributed among party members, enterprise directors, trades unions, and OGPU officials in mid-March.

63. See, for example, the case of the British spy ring, October 1927. Khaustov et al., *Lubianka: Stalin*, 143, 798–99; *Pravda*, 18 October 1927.

64. Khaustov et al., *Lubianka: Stalin*, 155–63; A. V. Kvashonkin, L. P. Kosheleva, L. A. Rogovaia, and O. V. Khlevniuk, eds., *Sovetskoe rukovodstvo: Perepiska, 1928–1941 gg.* (Moscow, 1999), 28, 91–94.

65. Hiroaki Kuromiya, *Stalin: Profiles in Power* (London, 2005).

66. *Dva stalinskikh narkoma*, 58.

67. RGASPI 17/162/8/1, 3, 5, 13, 136, 138, 157; Khaustov et al., *Lubianka: Stalin*, 166–74, 177–89.

68. Khaustov et al., *Lubianka: Stalin*, 256–57. For further detail on Stalin's thinking, see his September letter to Molotov in Lars Lih, Oleg V. Naumov, and Oleg V. Khlevniuk, eds., *Stalin's Letters to Molotov, 1925–1936* (New Haven, 1995), 195–96.

69. Khaustov et al., *Lubianka: Stalin*, 256–57.

70. *Istoriia sovetskikh organov*, 226–27.

71. Ibid., 227, 243–34; Mozokhin, "Iz istorii bor'by," 14–19. In November 1931, Stalin was informed that he had narrowly escaped assassination while walking from the Kremlin to Staraia Square. Khaustov et al., *Lubianka: Stalin*, 286.

72. See, for example, the 26 November 1932 OGPU report to Stalin. Khaustov et al., *Lubianka: Stalin*, 341–42.

73. Mozokhin, "Iz istorii bor'by," 19; *Istorii sovetskikh organov*, 246;

74. Khaustov et al., *Lubianka: Stalin*, 262, 805.

75. " 'Diktatura iazykocheshyshchikh nad rabotaiushchimi': Poslednaia sluzhebnaia zapiska G. V. Chicherina," *Istochnik* 6 (1995), 108–10.

76. *Istoriia sovetskikh organov*, 234–35; Khaustov et al., *Lubianka: Stalin*, 277–79.

77. Khaustov et al., *Lubianka: Stalin*, 262, 275–77, 805–6.

78. Mozokhin, "Iz istorii bor'by," 19–20; Robert Thurston, *Life and Terror in Stalin's Russia, 1934–1941* (New Haven, 1996), 10.

79. Khaustov et al., *Lubianka: Stalin*, 427, 445–50, 811; Thurston, *Life and Terror*, 5.

80. Khaustov et al., *Lubianka: Stalin*, 429–35.

81. RGASPI 17/162/14/123–24.

82. O. V. Khlevniuk, R. W. Davies, L. P. Kosheleva, E. A. Rees, and L. A. Rogovaia, eds., *Stalin i Kaganovich: Perepiska, 1931–1936 gg.* (Moscow, 2001), 429; Khaustov et al., *Lubianka: Stalin*, 549, 818–19.

83. See the telegram of Ia. S. Agranov (First Deputy People's Commissar of Internal Affairs) to Stalin in August 1934. RGASPI 558/11/50/46.

84. This is from Nikolai Ezhov's concluding speech to the February–March 1937 CC plenum. We know that this was indeed the direction the investigation took, but according to others, after being told of the Kirov murder, Stalin immediately asked if the assassin was carrying any foreign documents. Robert Tucker, *Stalin in Power: The Revolution from Above, 1928–1941* (New York, 1990), 293. See also "O dele tak nazyvaemogo 'Moskovskogo tsentra,' " *Izvestiia TsK KPSS* 7 (1989), 69.

85. Michal Reiman, *The Birth of Stalinism: The USSR on the Eve of the "Second Revolution"* (Bloomington, Ind., 1987), appendixes.

86. Ibid., 126–27.

87. I. Stalin, *Sochineniia*, vol. 11 (Moscow, 1950), 313–17; *Pravda*, 24 January 1929; Tucker, *Stalin in Power*, 126.

88. Copies of these TASS bulletins are in Anastas Mikoian's personal archive. RGASPI 84/1/135/3–51.

89. Reiman, *Birth of Stalinism*, 127.

90. Rayfield, *Stalin and His Hangmen*, 230. Stalin and the OGPU consistently interpreted "remove" as "kill."

91. RGASPI 558/11/1114/49–54. "They played at staging a coup," Stalin wrote to Molotov on 23 October. This conclusion was based on denunciations by B. G. Reznikov, secretary of a party cell at the Institute of Red Professors. Lih, Naumov, and Khlevniuk, *Stalin's Letters to Molotov*, 223, 263.

92. RGASPI 558/11/1114/49.

93. RGASPI 558/11/1114/56.

94. Smirnov was the deputy chairman of the RSFSR Council of People's Commissars and a secretary of the CC. Eismont was RSFSR People's Commissar for Trade and Tolmachev was the head of Glavdortrans RSFSR (the Main Roads and Transport Administration).

95. I. V. Kurilova, N. N. Mikhailov, and V. P. Naumov, eds., *Reabilitatsiia: Politicheskie protsessy 30–50-kh godov* (Moscow, 1991), 442.

96. J. Arch Getty and Oleg V. Naumov, eds., *The Road to Terror: Stalin and the Self-Destruction of the Bolsheviks* (New Haven, 1999), 50–52.

97. See Andrew and Gordievsky, *KGB*, 119–21; J. Arch Getty, *Origins of the Great Purges: The Soviet Communist Party Reconsidered, 1933–1938* (Cambridge, England, 1985), 121.

98. Broue thinks that Stalin was not aware of the existence of the coalition until 1935. Pierre Broue, "Party Opposition to Stalin and the First Moscow Trial," in John W. Strong, ed., *Essays on Revolutionary Culture and Stalinism* (Columbus, Ohio, 1990), 106.

99. Amy Knight, *Who Killed Kirov?* (New York, 1999), 178; Robert Conquest, *The Great Terror* (London, 1968), 41. In September, Iagoda had criticized the Leningrad NKVD for being complacent in the struggle against counterrevolution. Khaustov et al., *Lubianka: Stalin*, 569–71.

100. The idea of foreign involvement did not completely die away. A January 1935 letter to local NKVD organs on the failures of the Leningrad branch in the Kirov murder demanded vigilance against the threat posed by foreign terrorist organizations planning to assassinate Soviet party and state leaders. Khaustov et al., *Lubianka: Stalin*, 592–93.

101. Ibid., 578–79.

102. This interpretation of the investigation of the Kirov murder is heavily indebted to the work of Iurii Zhukov in parts of the Ezhov archive that remain secret. See Iu. N. Zhukov, "Sledstvie i sudebnye protsessy po delu ob ubiistve Kirova," *Voprosy istorii* 2 (2000), 33–51.

103. Zinoviev and Kamenev were arrested after only two. "O dele 'Leningradskoi kontrrevolutsionnoi zinov'evskoi gruppy Safarova, Zalutskogo i drugikh,' " *Izvestiia TsK KPSS* 1 (1990), 39.

104. Ibid., 42–43.

105. Khaustov et al., *Lubianka: Stalin*, 599–612, 617–19, 626–50. Kamenev denied any involvement.

106. See Getty, *Origins of the Great Purges*, 90–91.

107. Paul Hagenloh, " 'Socially Harmful Elements' and the Great Terror," in Sheila Fitzpatrick, ed., *Stalinism: New Directions* (New York, 2000); David Shearer, "Crime and Social Disorder in Stalin's Russia: A Reassessment of the Great Retreat and the Origins of Mass Repression," *Cahiers du monde russe* 1–2 (1998), 119–49.

108. See Iagoda's 11 March 1935 letter to regional NKVD organs: "O perestroika operativnoi raboty i raboty s kadrami," in A. I. Kokurin and N. V. Petrov, eds., *Lubianka: Organy VChK-OGPU-NKVD-NKGB-MGB-MVD-KGB* (Moscow, 2003), 548–52.

109. This was largely a response to the criticisms of regional party and NKVD organizations. Getty and Naumov, *Road to Terror*, 187–88.

110. Khaustov et al., *Lubianka: Stalin*, 738–41.

111. *Istoriia sovetskikh organov*, 266–69, 276–77; Khaustov et al., *Lubianka: Stalin*, 468–69, 489, 495, 506–8, 565–66, 741–42, 751.

112. Which was once again on the defensive, accused by the NKVD of posing an obstacle to their work against anti-Soviet elements. Khaustov et al., *Lubianka: Stalin*, 744–47.

113. *The Case of the Trotskyite-Zinovievite Terrorist Center* (Moscow, 1936), 88–92 (V. P. Ol'berg), 75, 103 (N. Lur'e).

114. "O tak nazyvaemom 'antisovetskom ob"edinennom Trotskistsko-Zinov'evskom tsentre,' " *Izvestiia TsK KPSS* 8 (1989), 83.

115. On 21 August, at the trial of the "Trotskyist-Zinovievite center," Vyshinskii told the court that in view of the fact that some of the accused had "referred to Tomskii, Bukharin, Rykov, Uglanov, Radek, Piatakov, Serebriakov and Sokol'nikov as being to a greater or lesser degree involved in the criminal counter-revolutionary activities for which the accused in the present case are being tried," he had given orders for a new investigation. *Case of the Trotskyite-Zinovievite Terrorist Center*, 115.

116. Chase, *Enemies within the Gates?* 163–74.

117. B. A. Starkov, *Dela i liudi Stalinskogo vremeni* (St. Petersburg, 1995), 18. Starkov has had access to many archives that otherwise remain closed to researchers, but he does not identify his source in this case.

118. Davies et al., *Stalin-Kaganovich Correspondence*, 359–60.

119. RGASPI 17/3/981/58; Getty and Naumov, *Road to Terror*, 273.

120. RGASPI 558/11/1120/15.

121. Kokurin and Petrov, *Lubianka: Organy*, 569–82.

122. RGASPI 558/11/1120/49.

123. RGASPI 558/11/1088/82.

124. See Robert Tucker, "Stalin, Bukharin, and History as Conspiracy," in Robert Tucker and Stephen Cohen, *The Great Purge Trial* (New York, 1965); Hedeler, "Ezhov's Scenario," 34–55. See also Chase, "Stalin as Producer," for an excellent analysis of the trial transcripts.

Chapter 3.   Capitalist Encirclement

1. Leon Trotsky, *Moia zhizn': Opyt avtobiografii* (Berlin, 1930) vol. 2, 64.

2. Jonathan Haslam, *Soviet Foreign Policy, 1930–1933: The Impact of the Depression* (London, 1983), 18–19; Haslam, "Litvinov, Stalin and the Road Not Taken," in G. Gorodetsky, *Soviet Foreign Policy, 1917–1991: A Retrospective* (London, 1994), 57. Derek Watson wrote an excellent review of the literature on this issue in his discussion paper for the CREES SIPS seminar series at the University of Birmingham. Derek Watson, "Stalin, Molotov and Decision-Making in Soviet Foreign Policy, 1930–1946," 1–3.

3. Up to 1938. I have taken the figures from Watson, "Stalin Molotov and Decision-Making," 7.

4. As he did with Litvinov in 1935. O. V. Khlevniuk, R. W. Davies, L. P. Kosheleva, E. A. Rees, and L. A. Rogovaia, eds., *Stalin i Kaganovich: Perepiska, 1931–1936 gg.* (Moscow, 2001), 564.

5. This is not to say that intelligence gatherers did so cynically, not believing that such threats existed. There were many believers and much evidence to support their beliefs, but the relationship of the gatherers and the consumers of intelligence gave little space to skeptics who might otherwise have identified the limits of threats.

6. Michael Jabara Carley has written extensively on anti-communist sentiment in the interwar period. See his articles "Episodes from the Early Cold War: Franco-Soviet Relations, 1917–1927," *Europe-Asia Studies* 7 (2000), 1275–1305; "Down a Blind Alley: Anglo-French Soviet Relations: 1920–1939," *Canadian Journal of History* 2 (1994), 47–172; "Behind Stalin's Moustache: Pragmatism in Early Soviet Foreign Policy, 1917–41," *Diplomacy and Statecraft* 3 (2001), 59–174.

7. R. V. Daniels, *The Conscience of the Revolution* (Cambridge, Mass., 1960); A. Ulam, *Expansion and Coexistence: Soviet Foreign Policy, 1917–1973* (New York, 1974); and, more recently, Leonid Nezhinskii, "Byla li voennaia ugroza v kontse 20-kh–nachale 30-kh godov?" *Istoriia SSSR* 6 (1990).

8. Silvio Pons, *Stalin and the Inevitable War, 1936–1941* (London, 2002); Vladimir Pozniakov, "The Enemy at the Gates: Soviet Military Intelligence in the Interwar Period and Its Forecasts of Future War, 1921–1941," in Silvio Pons and Andrea Romano, eds., *Russia in the Age of Wars* (Milan, 2000), 215–33.

9. See, for example, RGASPI 558/11/29/116-116ob for a coded telegram from the Central Asian bureau to Stalin on British support for the Basmachi. RGVA 25895/846/2 has intelligence from the Central Asian Military District on British support for the Emir of Bukhara.

10. RGASPI 558/11/1180/53 from an unpublished collection of Stalin's writings on military issues. See also *Pravda*, 25, 26 May 1920.

11. See, for example, Stalin's commentary in *Pravda*, 18 December 1921. This was reprinted in I. Stalin, *Sochineniia*, vols. 1–13 (Moscow, 1946–51) and vols. 1–3/vols. 14–16 (Stanford, 1967), vol. 5, 118–20.

12. Stalin, *Sochineniia*, vol. 5, 120. See also Maxim Litvinov's correspondence with members of the Politburo about the imminent threat of war with Poland and Romania in the early part of 1922. RGASPI 359/1/3.

13. The existing cooperation between Germany and Soviet Russia made the Polish very nervous, given that neither state had an interest in its continued independence. A revolution would leave Poland surrounded and doomed to a communist takeover.

14. *Politbiuro TsK RKP(b)-VKP(b) i Komintern, 1919–1941 gg.: Dokumenty* (Moscow, 2004), 185–202.

15. See V. I. Lenin, *Polnoe sobranie sochinenii*, vol. 43 (Moscow, 1963), 4.

16. Alfred Senn, *Assassination in Switzerland: The Murder of Vatslav Vorovsky* (Madison, Wis., 1981). I thank William Chase for bringing this book to my attention.

17. RGASPI 558/11/789/2-4. The letter from CC secretary Ian Rudzutak on behalf of the Politburo to regional bureaus of the party warning of the imminent invasion was published in Val'ter Krivitskii, *Ia byl agentom Stalina* (Moscow, 1998), 215.

18. See, for example, his 10 October 1923 article in *Die rote Fahne*, quoted in F. I. Firsov, "Stalin i Komintern," *Voprosy istorii* 8 (1989), 2–6.

19. RGASPI 74/2/38/8; RGASPI 558/11/708/15; *Politbiuro i Komintern*, 198.

20. See his comments from September in *Politbiuro i Komintern*, 169–71.

21. Stalin, *Sochineniia*, vol. 6, 236–40, 276. In the latter letter to the poet Dem'ian Bednyi, Stalin seems to base his judgment about the growing hatred of the bourgeois order on a few meetings with French, German, and English workers attending the fifth Comintern congress.

22. Stalin, *Sochineniia*, vol. 6, 236–40, 280–301; vol. 7, 11–14, 52–58, 90–101, 156–211.

23. Stalin included this detail in his November 1924 article in *Bol'shevik*, "K mezhdunarodnomu polozheniiu." Stalin, *Sochineniia*, vol. 6, 286. A few months later (5 February 1925), Dzerzhinskii informed Stalin that the counterintelligence operation "Iaroslavets" was revealing an unexpectedly large number of groups and individuals from Britain, France, and America willing to finance anti-Soviet terrorist activity. RGASPI 76/3/356/2–8.

24. A. Plekhanov, *VChK-OGPU v gody novoi ekonomicheskoi politiki, 1921–1928 gg.* (Moscow, 2006), 282; V. N. Khaustov, V. P. Naumov, and N. S. Plotnikova, eds., *Lubianka: Stalin i VChK-GPU-OGPU-NKVD, ianvar' 1922–dekabr' 1936. Dokumenty* (Moscow, 2003), henceforth *Lubianka: Stalin*, 795.

25. N. S. Simonov, "The 'War Scare' of 1927 and the Birth of the Defence-Industry Complex," in John Barber and Mark Harrison, eds., *The Soviet Defence-Industry Complex from Stalin to Khrushchev* (Basingstoke, England, 2000), 35.

26. *Lubianka: Stalin*, 101–2.

27. For example, see Ian Berzin's report to Mikhail Frunze on the state of the Polish armed forces. RGVA 37977/3/98/241.

28. L. Kosheleva, V. Lel'chuk, V. Naumov, O. Naumov, L. Rogovaia, and O. Khlevniuk, eds., *Pis'ma I. V. Stalina V. M. Molotovu, 1925–1936 gg.: Sbornik dokumentov* (Moscow, 1995), 30–31.

29. Plekhanov, *VChK-OGPU*, 295.

30. RGASPI 76/3/364/23–31.

31. Stalin, *Sochineniia*, vol. 7, 263–88.

32. RGASPI 76/3/362/3.

33. On 14 April 1926, Iagoda wrote to Stalin about "materials in our possession which confirm beyond doubt that on the instructions of the English, the Polish and other general staffs of countries on our western borders have begun broad subversive work against the USSR and have increased their espionage network on our territory . . . Measures are being taken." *Lubianka: Stalin*, 117.

34. Stalin largely limited the Soviet response to expressions of moral support for the striking workers. Efforts to fund the striking British miners in the summer of 1926 had provoked a fierce response from the British government and press. See Alfred Meyer, "The War Scare of 1927," *Soviet Union/Union Soviétique* 1 (1978), 4; Kosheleva et al., *Pis'ma Stalina Molotovu*, 56–59.

35. Kosheleva et al., *Pis'ma Stalina Molotovu*, 61–63.

36. RGASPI 76/3/364/57. He had been warning about the anti-Soviet links between England and Poland since the spring of 1925. RGASPI 76/3/364/4–8, 12–14.

37. RGASPI 76/3/364/70.

38. RGASPI 76/3/364/58.

39. *Polibiuro i Komintern*, 406; Stalin, *Sochineniia*, vol. 8, 359.

40. See, for example, Stalin, *Sochineniia*, vol. 7, 296–97.

41. RGASPI 17/162/4/30.

42. Stalin, *Sochineniia*, vol. 9, 170; *Pravda*, 3 March 1927.

43. Plekhanov, *VChK-OGPU*, 62, 285, citing FSB sources.

44. *Lubianka: Stalin*, 133–34.

45. *Pravda*, 9, 10 June 1927; *Lubianka: Stalin*, 134, 795.

46. *Politbiuro i Komintern*, 468–69. Within a week it was clear that the Committee would be no help because the General Council of British Trades Unions had distanced itself from the Communists. Stalin was none too pleased, and ordered that the press observe that they were "helping their masters prepare a war." Kosheleva et al., *Pis'ma Stalina Molotovu*, 104.

47. The Profintern, or "Trades Union International," coordinated the activities of Communists within trades unions much as the Comintern coordinated the activities of the Communist parties.

48. *Politbiuro i Komintern*, 477–8. Like the earlier effort with the British Trade Union Committee, the lack of any positive response served only to further convince Stalin that European Social Democrats were at heart enemies of the USSR.

49. Ibid., 474–75.

50. *Lubianka: Stalin*, 135.

51. Ibid., 134–35, 795.

52. Stalin, *Sochineniia*, vol. 9, 311–12.

53. Ibid., vol. 10, 271–90.

54. Plekhanov, *VChK-OGPU*, 285–6.

55. *Lubianka: Stalin*, 148–61. See also Stalin's comments at the April plenum of the CC and the Central Control Commission. *Sochineniia*, vol. 11, 53.

56. RGASPI 17/163/727/43.

57. See, for example, F. Notovich, "Pakt Kelloga, imperialisty i SSSR," *Bolshevik* 17–18 (1928), 9–26.

58. RGASPI 558/11/136/8; *Politbiuro i Komintern*, 515–16, 525.

59. RGASPI 558/11/800; 17/163/729/65, 116. Stalin first publicly defended the idea in a speech to the July 1928 CC plenum. *Sochineniia*, vol. 11, 152.

60. *Politbiuro i Komintern* (15 September 1927), 488–89; (29 February 1929), 579–80.

61. Stalin, *Sochineniia*, vol. 11, 27–64, 116–17, 157–96, 197–204.

62. Ibid., 245–90. The quotation is from 247–48.

63. RGVA 33988/2/682/36–40.

64. *VChK-OGPU*, 286–7.

65. *Dokumenty Vneshnei Politiki SSSR* (*DVP SSSR*) (Moscow, 1967), vol. 12, 66–70. Stalin was not inclined to think that the signatories would hold themselves to these pacts, but he knew that they would deepen the challenge for the signatories of gaining public support for the idea of war against the USSR.

66. *Pravda*, 10 March 1929.

67. A. V. Kvashonkin, L. P. Kosheleva, L. A. Rogovaia, and O. V. Khlevniuk, eds., *Sovetskoe rukovodstvo: Perepiska, 1928–1941 gg.* (Moscow, 1999), 68.

68. *Perepiska Stalina Molotovu*, 139, 144–45, 154–55; *DVP SSSR*, vol. 12, 429–30.

69. *Politbiuro i Komintern*, 606–7; *Perepiska Stalina Molotovu*, 167.

70. Mostly the foreign department of OGPU in this instance.

71. For the response of the Politburo to events on the KVZhD in July and August, see *Politbiuro i Komintern*, 607, 608, 610–12.

72. "General'naia repetitsiia budushchei voiny," *Bol'shevik* 15 (1929), 37.

73. Stalin, *Sochineniia*, vol. 12, 247–56.

74. Anti-communist demonstrations had followed news of the suffering of ethnic Finns during collectivization. The significance of the "peasant" march twelve thousand strong on Helsinki and the adoption of anti-communist legislation called the Protection of the Republic Act was exaggerated in Moscow. *Politbiuro i Komintern*, 234–41.

75. Ibid., 604–5.

76. V. Mitskevich-Kapsukas, "Ekonomicheskii krizis, Pol'sha i limitrofy," *Bol'shevik* 13 (1930), 105–24.

77. Kosheleva et al., *Pis'ma Stalina Molotovu*, 209 (1 September 1930).

78. *Lubianka: Stalin*, 256–57. Stalin was unconcerned or unaware that Ramzin had agreed to provide the testimony demanded of him in exchange for guarantees of reinstatement in the Academy of Sciences. Stalin instructed Menzhinskii to make the plans for an attack on the USSR the central issue of the trial and to interrogate the other accused "very severely" in order to make clearer the outlines of the plans for invasion. Donald Rayfield, *Stalin and His Hangmen* (London, 2005), 160–61.

79. *Lubianka: Stalin*, 257; RGASPI 17/162/9/53–54.

80. Kosheleva et al., *Pis'ma Stalina Molotovu*, 209–10 (1 September 1931); RGASPI 17/162/9/31.

81. O. N. Ken, *Mobilizatsionnoe planirovanie i politicheskie resheniia, konets 1920-seredina 1930-kh* (St. Petersburg, 2002), 209; Lennart Samuelson, *Plans for Stalin's War Machine: Tukhachevskii and Military-Economic Planning, 1925–1941* (London, 1999), 119.

82. Simonov, " 'War Scare' of 1927," 35–36.

83. Stalin received Tukhachevskii's note "On the Reconstruction of the Red Army" on 11 January 1930. RGASPI 558/11/446/13–18. This was supplemented a month later by a further note with General Shaposhnikov's judgments. RGASPI 558/11/446/19–32. For more detail on these proposals, see Samuelson, *Plans for Stalin's War Machine*, 92–109; Stalin's response to Tukhachevskii's proposals can be

found among his correspondence with Voroshilov. RGASPI 74/2/38/58. It was also was published in " 'Moia otsenka byla slyshkom rezkoi.' I.V. Stalin i rekonstruktsiia RKKA. 1930–1932 gg.," *Istoricheskii arkhiv* 5–6 (1998), 147–52.

84. In mid-December, the Politburo wrote a formal letter of protest to the French government presenting the findings of the Soviet Supreme Court on the involvement of French nationals in the Industrial Party affair. RGASPI 17/162/9/96.

85. Kosheleva et al., *Pis'ma Stalina Molotovu*, 258–59.

86. Stalin, *Sochineniia*, vol. 13, 38–39.

87. For Molotov's draft of the speech, see RGASPI 82/2/238/1–50. His notes for the speech are in 82/2/241/125–77.

88. Jonathan Haslam has argued that this was the case, in *Soviet Foreign Policy*, 69.

89. Khlevniuk et al., *Stalin i Kaganovich*, 71, 75, 76, 113, 114; RGASPI 17/162/11/1.

90. RGASPI 558/11/76/76–76ob; *Politbiuro i Komintern*, 645–46; Kvashonkin et al., *Sovetskoe rukovodstvo*. 116–17.

91. Kvashonkin et al., *Sovetskoe rukovodstvo*, 161–62.

92. RGASPI 558/11/185/1–9.

93. Kvashonkin et al., *Sovetskoe rukovodstvo*, 167–68 (13 January 1932).

94. R. W. Davies, "Soviet Military Expenditure and the Armaments Industry, 1929–1933: A Reconsideration," *Europe-Asia Studies* 4 (1993), 594. The figures are from table 3, "Military orders financed from the state budget appropriations to NarKomVoenMor (million rubles at current prices)."

95. Kvashonkin et al., *Sovetskoe rukovodstvo*, 171–72 (7 May 1932); " 'Moia otsenka byla slyshkom rezkoi,' " 147–52.

96. See Stalin's correspondence with Voroshilov on the fulfillment of military orders in the summer of 1932. Kvashonkin et al., *Sovetskoe rukovodstvo*, 236–38, 240–41 (9, 21 June).

97. *Lubianka: Stalin*, 298–308, 807.

98. RGASPI 558/11/185/65–70.

99. *DVP SSSR*, vol. 15, 214–17.

100. RGASPI 558/11/206/39–41.

101. RGASPI 558/11/43/116; Kvashonkin et al., *Sovetskoe rukovodstvo*, 135, 141, 220–21.

102. Kvashonkin et al., *Sovetskoe rukovodstvo*, 173–74; Khlevniuk et al., *Stalin i Kaganovich*, 136, 143, 156–57.

103. Haslam, *Soviet Foreign Policy*, 98.

104. Ken, *Mobilizatsionnoe planirovanie*, 286–89 n. 11.

105. Khlevniuk et al., *Stalin i Kaganovich*, 274.

106. Shortly after the Bliukher incident, Stalin found out that the Far Eastern OGPU had been sending its agents on sabotage missions to Manchuria without permission of the Politburo. When one of these was exposed, Stalin demanded that categorical denials of involvement be issued to the Japanese and that "draconian" measures be taken against the members of the Far Eastern OGPU who had approved the missions. "To whom is

that sort of thing useful, except to the enemies of Soviet power?" he wrote to Kaganovich. Ibid., 208.

107. Ibid., 120–22.

108. Ibid., 139–40.

109. He also accepted interviews with foreign journalists if he thought he could positively influence public opinion. See, for example, his interview with Emil Ludwig, 13 December 1931, in Stalin, *Sochineniia*, vol. 13, 104–23; with Ralph Barnes, 3 May 1932, in Stalin, *Sochineniia*, vol. 13, 258.

110. *Politbiuro i Komintern*, 694.

111. Davies, "Soviet Military Expenditure," 580–81.

112. Kvashonkin et al., *Sovetskoe rukovodstvo*, 162.

113. For Stalin's assessment of the progress of negotiations in June 1932, see Kvashonkin et al., *Sovetskoe rukovodstvo*, 182.

114. At one stage they took the risky step of fabricating a story for the press about meetings with American officials, but the plan backfired when the article generated a denial. Khlevniuk et al., *Stalin i Kaganovich*, 199–200, 222. See also *DVP SSSR*, vol. 15, 392–93; Kvashonkin et al., *Sovetskoe rukovodstvo*, 215–16.

115. Khlevniuk et al., *Stalin i Kaganovich*, 192–93.

116. M. Lechik, "Vo frantsuzsko-pol'sko-rossiiskom treugol'nike. 1922–1934," in E. Durachinskii and A. N. Sakharov, eds., *Sovetsko-pol'skie otnosheniia v politicheskikh usloviiakh 30-kh godov XX stoletiia* (Moscow, 2001), 120–23.

117. Haslam, *Soviet Foreign Policy*, 98.

118. Stalin, *Sochineniia*, vol. 13, 162–68, 182–85.

119. This was the gist of a (less public) speech Voroshilov made a couple of weeks later. RGASPI 74/2/19/90.

120. *Izvestiia*, 25 January 1933; *Pravda*, 27 January 1933.

121. Kosheleva et al., *Pis'ma Stalina Molotovu*, 245.

122. *Komintern protiv fashizma* (Moscow, 1999), 291–97.

123. For advice given to Stalin on the matter, see RGASPI 558/11/790/23–25, 42, 45–50, 52–56, 59–63.

124. Jonathan Haslam, *The Soviet Union and the Threat from the East* (London, 1992), 8.

125. Ibid., 45.

126. See, for example, RGVA 9/39/5c/2–21, 76–82, 109–16.

127. RGASPI 558/11/185/97–102.

128. Karakhan to Enukidze, in Kvashonkin, Livshin, and Khlevniuk, *Sovetskoe ruko-vodstvo*, 235–36 (4 June 1933). On the progress of those negotiations, see ibid., 288, 296, 297, 303, 309; *DVP SSSR*, vol. 16, 837–38.

129. Kvashonkin, Livshin, and Khlevniuk, *Sovetskoe rukovodstvo*, 342, 361, 363, 375. For decisions on the publication of brochures, books, and further articles, see also 383–84, 396, 401; and RGASPI 558/11/791/33–38.

130. A version of the interview was published in Stalin, *Sochineniia*, vol. 13, 276–81; a fuller record can be found in RGASPI 558/11/374/1–6.

131. RGASPI 558/11/185/126–32.

132. Ken, *Mobilizatsionnoe planirovanie*, 269; Oleg Ken, *Collective Security or Isolation: Soviet Foreign Policy and Poland, 1930–1935* (St. Petersburg, 1996), 121–22, 146–47; S. V. Morozov, *Pol'sko-CHekhoslovatskie otnosheniia, 1933–1939* (Moscow, 2004), 9, 27, 504; *DVP SSSR*, vol. 17, 133–34; *Izvestiia*, 20 April 1934.

133. Haslam, *Soviet Union and Threat from the East*, 43.

134. See Kuusinen's speech to the seventeenth plenum of the Comintern, in *Komintern protiv fashizma*, 313–14; "England and the Anti-Soviet Bloc," *Bol'shevik* 9–10 (1934); D. Z. Manuilskii's speech to the seventeenth party congress. *XVII s"ezd VKP(b): Stenograficheskii otchet* (Moscow, 1934), 305–22. According to Oleg Ken, the British were baffled by the suggestion that they were, as Manuilskii put it, "the real force behind German and Japanese fascism." *Mobilizatsionnoe planirovanie*, 267–68.

135. AVP RF 5/14/101/94/11.

136. RGASPI 558/11/187/28–44.

137. Weygand was one of the few French senior army officers who favored some kind of military relationship with the Soviets. While neither he nor Tardieu was especially well disposed toward the USSR more generally, they were also hostile to Nazi Germany, making any alliance improbable. And though the Germans were courting the Poles, the latter remained convinced that the only way to protect Polish sovereignty was to avoid taking sides with either Germany or the USSR. See, for example, Anthony Adamthwaite, *Grandeur and Misery: France's Bid for Power in Europe, 1914–1940* (London, 1995) ch. 11; S. Demski "Pol'sko-sovetskie otnosheniia v otsenkakh Berlina B 30-e gody: Nekotorye voprosy," in I. I. Kostiushko, P. N. Olshanskii, and I. A. Khrenov, eds., *Sovetsko-polskie otnosheniia, 1918–1945: Sbornik statei* (Moscow, 1974), 191–218; Graham Ross, *The Great Powers and the Decline of the European States System, 1914–1945* (Harlow, England, 1990), 5.

138. RGASPI 558/11/187/81, 111–17.

139. AVP RF 05/14/101/93/23, 05/12/86/64/12.

140. *Lubianka: Stalin* (5 March 1934), 501–5, 517–18, 520–21; RGASPI 558/11/186/118–27; 558/11/ 187/62–79.

141. See chapter 2 in this volume, and William Chase, *Enemies within the Gates? The Comintern and the Stalinist Repression, 1934–1939* (New Haven, 2001) ch. 3.

142. *Politbiuro VKP(b), Komintern i Iaponiia*, 131–38, 143, 159–60; Khlevniuk et al., *Stalin i Kaganovich*, 448, 470, 506, 517; *DVP SSSR*, vol. 17, 562–70, 624–28, 815–17.

143. RGASPI 17/162/17/54; 558/11/87/20–30; 558/11/51/37–38, 43.

144. See, for example, RGASPI 17/162/17/47. In late September 1933, Stalin instructed Litvinov not to rush to sign an eastern pact that did not include Poland and Germany. The two had formally rejected the French offer of a pact only two weeks before, but that did not put an end to efforts to negotiate one.

145. Morozov, *Pol'sko-CHekhoslovatskie otnosheniia*, 165.

146. This constituted approval for a rearmament that was already in progress. RGASPI 558/11/187/120–23; Morozov, *Pol'sko-CHekhoslovatskie otnosheniia*, 179.

147. RGASPI 558/11/188/31–51. For Soviet ambassador Ivan Maiskii's report of his conversation with Sir John Simon and Anthony Eden, see AVP RF 010/10/48/8/30–38. On Goering's meeting with Beck, see AVP RF 05/15/109/67/5.

148. RGASPI 558/11/188/55–56; 558/11/446/130–44. The Soviet estimates of the size of the German army contained in this document were for public consumption.

149. AVP RF 010/10/48/8/10–11. Maiskii nevertheless observed that rumors of an end to hostilities were premature, and indeed, the Americans continued the arms trade with the Nationalists.

150. *Lubianka: Stalin*, 594–97, 661–62.

151. AVP RF 05/14/101/94/12.

152. Together with the Germans. AVP RF 05/14/101/93/34.

153. AVP RF 05/15/109/67/5/6.

154. In the spring of 1936, the Germans proposed a nonaggression pact with France and Belgium, but the French were still publicly expressing an interest in broader arrangements for guaranteeing peace in Europe. For an expression of Soviet skepticism that the French and others would resist such deals, see, for example, A.E., "Diplomatiia voiny," *Bol'shevik*, 10 (1935), 3–90.

155. AVP RF 05/16/115/6/16.

156. *Lubianka: Stalin*, 671–72, 679–81, 693–98, 705–10, 712–14, 735.

157. See chapter 2 of this volume; Chase, *Enemies within the Gates?* 163–74; *Lubianka: Stalin*, 738–41.

158. Karl Radek in *Izvestiia*, 1 August 1936. The text was approved by Stalin.

159. See I. Stalin, *Sochineniia*, vol. 14 (Moscow, 2008), 328–35.

160. The detailed analysis of the intelligence in this chapter ends in 1936 because the late 1930s, wartime, and late Stalin periods are well covered elsewhere. See, for example, Pons, *Stalin and the Inevitable War;* V. P. Iampolskii et al., eds., *Organy Gosudarstvenniy Bezopasnosti SSSR v Velikoi Otechestvennoi Voine*, 5 vols. (Moscow, 1995–2000); V. K. Vinogradov et al., eds., *Sekrety Gitlera na stole u Stalina* (Moscow, 1995); Albert Weeks, *Stalin's Other War: Soviet Grand Strategy* (London, 2002); David E. Murphy, *What Stalin Knew: The Enigma of Barbarossa* (New Haven, 2005); Geoffrey Roberts, *Stalin's War: From World War to Cold War, 1939–1953* (New Haven, 2006).

161. Christopher Andrew and Julie Elkner did anticipate the centrality of this issue in their "Stalin and Foreign Intelligence," *Totalitarian Movements and Political Religions* 4, no. 1 (2003), 69–94, though the article was written just as the intelligence material was being released.

162. See, for example, Michal Reiman, *The Birth of Stalinism: The USSR on the Eve of the "Second Revolution"* (Bloomington, Ind., 1987); Oleg Khlevniuk, "The Objectives of the Great Terror, 1936–1938," in Julian Cooper, Maureen Perrie, and E. A. Rees, eds., *Soviet History, 1917–53: Essays in Honour of R. W. Davies* (Basingstoke, England, 1995).

163. Leonid Nezhinskii has argued that because there was no danger of war in the late 1920s and early 1930s, Stalin must have invented the threat for his cynical political

ends. Nezhinskii, "Byla li voennaia ugroza v kontse 20-kh–nachale 30-kh godov?" *Istoriia SSSR* 6 (1990).

Chapter 4.   The Leader Cult

1. Jan Plamper summarizes some of the arguments in "Introduction: Modern Personality Cults," in Klaus Heller and Jan Plamper, eds., *Personality Cults in Stalinism* (Göttingen, 2004), 19–22.

2. See, for example, Roy Medvedev, *Let History Judge* (Oxford, 1989), 313–19.

3. Robert Tucker, *Stalin in Power: The Revolution from Above, 1928–1941* (New York, 1990), 3. See also his *Stalin as Revolutionary, 1879–1929* (New York, 1973), 421–87; and his "The Rise of Stalin's Personality Cult," *American Historical Review* 2 (1979), 347–66.

4. David Brandenberger, "Stalin as Symbol: A Case Study of the Personality Cult and Its Construction," in Sarah Davies and James Harris, eds., *Stalin: A New History* (Cambridge, England, 2005); David Brandenberger *National Bolshevism: Stalinist Mass Culture and the Formation of Modern Russian Identity, 1931–1956* (Cambridge, Mass., 2002)

5. Erik Van Ree, *The Political Thought of Joseph Stalin* (London, 2002), 161–68.

6. Albert Resis, ed., *Molotov Remembers: Inside Kremlin Politics—Conversations with Felix Chuev* (Chicago, 1993), 166, 181.

7. Anastas Mikoian, *Tak bylo* (Moscow, 1999), 318.

8. D. M. Stickle, ed., *The Beria Affair* (New York, 1992), 111.

9. Sergei Khrushchev, ed., *Memoirs of Nikita Khrushchev*, vol. 1–3 (University Park, Pa., 2004–6), vol. 1, 99; vol. 2, 161–62.

10. Strobe Talbott, ed., *Khrushchev Remembers* (London, 1971), 605.

11. N. Kovaleva et al., eds., *Molotov, Malenkov, Kaganovich, 1957* (Moscow, 1998), 490, 546.

12. "Survivor's Tales," *The Guardian*, 5 March 2003.

13. Simon Sebag Montefiore, *Stalin: The Court of the Red Tsar* (London, 2003), 4.

14. Jan Plamper, *The Stalin Cult* (New Haven, 2012), 123–24.

15. Arfon Rees, "Leader Cults: Varieties, Preconditions and Functions," in Balazs Apor, Jan C. Behrends, Polly Jones, and E. A. Rees, eds., *The Leader Cult in Communist Dictatorships: Stalin and the Eastern Bloc* (Basingstoke, England, 2004), 16.

16. Plamper, "Introduction: Modern Personality Cults," 24–25.

17. G. Plekhanov, *Selected Philosophical Works* (Moscow, 1976), vol. 2, 283–315.

18. Ibid., 314.

19. Tucker, *Stalin as Revolutionary*, 24–32; V. I. Lenin, *Selected Works* (Moscow, 1970), vol. 1, 203.

20. Plamper, "Introduction: Modern Personality Cults," 24–25.

21. Among the scholars, Robert Tucker is particularly insistent that "the first and most enduring of communism's leader cults owed nothing to a desire of the leader himself for personal glory": *Stalin as Revolutionary*, 288. Tucker in many ways echoes Khrushchev, who argued in the "Secret Speech" that "while ascribing great importance

to the role of leaders and organizers of the masses, Lenin at the same time mercilessly stigmatized every manifestation of the cult of the individual, inexorably combated the foreign-to-Marxism views about a 'hero' and a 'crowd' and countered all efforts to oppose a 'hero' to the masses and to the people." Talbott, *Khrushchev Remembers*, 560.

22. Nina Tumarkin, *Lenin Lives! The Lenin Cult in Soviet Russia* (Cambridge, Mass., 1997), 90.

23. Tucker, *Stalin as Revolutionary*, 57–59; Tumarkin, *Lenin Lives!* 96–107. A problem with the conventional view of Lenin's attitude is that it is based on far-from-impartial memoir sources.

24. These initiatives are discussed in Tumarkin, *Lenin Lives!*

25. I. Stalin, *Sochineniia*, vols. 1–13 (Moscow, 1946–51) and vols. 1–3/vols. 14–16 (Stanford, Calif., 1967), vol. 8, 173–75. On the importance of "teacher" imagery, see Barbara Walker, "Iosif Stalin 'Our Teacher Dear': Mentorship, Social Transformation, and the Russian Intelligentsia Personality Cult," in Heller and Plamper, *Personality Cults in Stalinism*, 45–59.

26. RGASPI 558/11/773/83–85ob. Mekhlis cited the note at the February–March 1937 plenum and forwarded it to Poskrebyshev, explaining that it had been sent in 1930.

27. Stalin, *Sochineniia*, vol. 9, 152. On the Ksenofontov-Stalin relationship, see Tucker, *Stalin as Revolutionary*, 324–29, 356.

28. RGASPI 558/11/755/95–100.

29. RGASPI 558/11/830/64–77; Stalin, *Sochineniia*, vol. 13, 17–19.

30. Tucker, *Stalin as Revolutionary*, 438; Medvedev, *Let History Judge*, 28.

31. RGASPI 558/11/800/78–80; 558/11/717/31–320b.

32. Talbott, *Khrushchev Remembers*, 608, 616–17. See also Khrushchev, *Memoirs of Nikita Khrushchev*, vol. 1, 76.

33. At the June 1957 plenum he implied that the practice had arisen only after Lenin's death. Kovaleva, *Molotov, Malenkov, Kaganovich: 1957*, 498, 551. On the naming of *people*, see Boris Kolonitskii, " 'Revolutionary Names': Russian Personal Names and Political Consciousness in the 1920s and 1930s," *Revolutionary Russia*, 2 (1993), 210–28.

34. Graeme Gill, "Changing Symbols: The Renovation of Moscow Place Names," *Russian Review* 3 (2005), 480–82.

35. Orlando Figes and Boris Kolonitskii, *Interpreting the Russian Revolution* (New Haven, 1999), 57.

36. John Murray, *Politics and Place Names: Changing Names in the Late Soviet Period* (Birmingham, England, 2000), 129–32, 167; Tumarkin, *Lenin Lives!* 105, 131.

37. Murray, *Politics and Place Names*, 132–33.

38. Tumarkin, *Lenin Lives!* 151; Richard Stites, *Revolutionary Dreams* (Oxford, 1989), 66. Apparently Iuzovka was actually called Trotsk for several months in 1923. Theodore Friedgut, *Iuzovka and Revolution* (Princeton, 1994), vol. 2, 456.

39. Khrushchev, *Memoirs of Nikita Khrushchev*, vol. 1, 18. Khrushchev dates this incident to 1926 or 1927.

40. RGASPI 558/11/1472/1–32; 558/11/786/106.

41. RGASPI 558/11/831/44, 55–56.

42. Benno Ennker, " 'Struggling for Stalin's Soul': The Leader Cult and the Balance of Social Power in Stalin's Inner Circle," in Heller and Plamper, *Personality Cults in Stalinism*, 164.

43. Grame Gill, *The Origins of the Stalinist Political System* (Cambridge, England, 1990), 242–44.

44. Ennker, " 'Struggling for Stalin's Soul,' " 165–67; Tucker, *Stalin in Power*, 148. For systematic analyses of the evolution of the cult, see Jeffrey Brooks, *Thank You, Comrade Stalin!* (Princeton, 1999); and Plamper, *Stalin Cult*, ch. 2.

45. Tucker, "Rise of Stalin's Personality Cult," 363. For a slightly different interpretation, see John Barber, "Stalin's Letter to the Editors of Proletarskaya Revolyutsiya," *Soviet Studies* 1 (1976), 21–41.

46. Benno Ennker, "The Stalin Cult, Bolshevik Rule, and Kremlin Interaction in the 1930s," in Apor et al., *Leader Cult in Communist Dictatorships*, 89.

47. See various speeches at the January 1933 plenum in J. Arch Getty and Oleg Naumov eds., *The Road to Terror: Stalin and the Self-Destruction of the Bolsheviks, 1932–1939* (New Haven, 1999), 76–101; Medvedev, *Let History Judge*, 315. On Mikoian, see the beginning of chapter 4 in this volume.

48. Stalin, *Sochineniia*, vol. 13, 105–6.

49. "Materialy fevral'sko-martovskogo plenuma TsK VKP(b), 1937 goda," *Voprosy istorii* 3 (1995), 9.

50. "Materialy fevral'sko-martovskogo plenuma TsK VKP(b), 1937 goda," *Voprosy istorii*, 7 (1995), 11–13.

51. M. A. Svanidze, "'Iosif beskonechno dobr . . . ,'" *Istochnik* 1 (1993), 18–20.

52. Evgenii Gromov, *Stalin: Vlast' i iskusstvo* (Moscow, 1998), 144.

53. RGASPI 558/11/1120/8–10.

54. Karl Schlögel, *Terror und Traum: Moskau 1937* (Munich, 2008), 121–25; Lion Feuchtwanger, *Moscow 1937* (London, 1937), 85–87, 93–95; Dmitri Volkogonov, *Stalin: Triumph and Tragedy* (London, 1991), 238.

55. Balazs Apor, "Leader in the Making: The Role of Biographies in Constructing the Cult of Matyas Rakosi," in Apor et al., *Leader Cult in Communist Dictatorships*, 63; Kevin Morgan, "Harry Pollitt, Maurice Thorez, and the Writing of Exemplary Communist Lives," in Julie Gottlieb and Richard Toye, eds., *Making Reputations: Power, Persuasion, and the Individual in British Politics* (London, 2005).

56. Simonetta Falasca-Zamponi, "Mussolini and the Cinematic Imagination," in Heller and Plamper, *Personality Cults in Stalinism*, 96.

57. Brandenberger, "Stalin as Symbol," 253; Katerina Clark, *The Soviet Novel: History as Ritual* (Chicago, 1985), 118–20.

58. A. V. Kvashonkin, L. P. Kosheleva, L. A. Rogovaia, and O. V. Khlevniuk, eds., *Sovetskoe rukovodstvo: Perepiska, 1928–1941 gg.* (Moscow, 1999), 234–35.

59. Clark, *Soviet Novel*, 122–24.

60. Robert Service, *Stalin: A Biography* (Basingstoke, England, 2004), 361.

61. Brandenberger, "Stalin as Symbol," 252; I. Tovstukha, *Iosif Vissarionovich Stalin: Kratkaia biografiia* (Moscow, 1927). A sympathetic biography by Henri Barbusse was published in the West in 1935, and a Russian version of this, edited by Stetskii, appeared in the USSR in 1936. For Stetskii's criticisms of Barbusse's manuscript, see L. V. Maksimenkov, *Bol'shaia tsenzura: Pisateli i zhurnalisty v strane sovetov, 1917–1956* (Moscow, 2005), 342–46. Stetskii objected to several features: the portrayal of the Stalin-Trotsky conflict as a clash of personalities; the emphasis on Stalin as a practical politician rather than a great theoretician; the insufficiently critical depiction of Trotsky; and the inadequate portrayal of Stalin the man, "his style of work, his style of speech," the masses' love for him.

62. Kol'tsov's manuscript is in RGASPI 558/11/1493.

63. K. Chukovskii, *Dnevnik 1930–1969* (Moscow, 1995), 38–39.

64. RGASPI 558/11/842/11–12.

65. RGASPI 558/1/4572/1; 558/11/1493/147; 558/11/1494/78–86. In 1934 he also decreed that the proposed "Stalin Institute" in Tiflis be turned instead into a branch of IMEL and banned any public celebrations of his fifty-fifth birthday. Among the advocates of a public celebration was Barbusse, who had written in *Le monde* of 6 December that the birthday should be celebrated with full ceremony to show the love of millions in the USSR for Stalin. RGASPI 17/163/1020/12; 17/163/1048/26; 558/11/1353/1–7.

66. On the making of this "classic," see S. V. Sukharev, "Litsedeistvo na poprishche istorii," *Voprosy istorii KPSS* 3 (1990), 102–18. See also Amy Knight, *Beria: Stalin's First Lieutenant* (Princeton, N.J., 1993), 57–62. Knight suggests that Stalin may have sought to distance himself from the book shortly after its publication by instigating the Politburo decree that forbade the Transcaucasian party committee from reprinting his works without his permission. The decree is at RGASPI 17/3/970/50.

67. L. V. Maksimenkov, "Kul't: Zametki o slovakh-simvolakh v sovetskoi politicheskoi kul'ture," *Svobodnaia mysl'* 11 (1993), 28–29.

68. RGASPI 558/1/3087/30; 558/1/3118.

69. Van Ree, *Political Thought of Joseph Stalin*, 164; Maksimenkov, "Kul't," 28–29.

70. Ethan Pollock, *Stalin and the Soviet Science Wars* (Princeton, N.J., 2006).

71. On the *Short Course*, see N. Maslov, " 'Kratkii kurs istorii VKP(b)'—entsiklopediia kul'ta lichnosti Stalina," *Voprosy istorii KPSS* 11 (1988), 51–67; David Brandenberger, *Propaganda State in Crisis: Soviet Ideology, Indoctrination, and Terror under Stalin, 1927–1941* (New Haven, 2011), 198–215.

72. Talbott, *Khrushchev Remembers*, 607–8.

73. M. Zelenov, "I. V. Stalin v rabote nad 'Kratkim kursom istorii VKP(b),' " *Voprosy istorii* 11 (2002), 6, 25–27.

74. Ibid., *Voprosy istorii* 12 (2002), 3, 6, 10–11. For many other similar changes made by Stalin, see the forthcoming critical edition of the *Short Course* edited by David Brandenberger and Mikhail Zelenov. We are very grateful to the authors for allowing us to see a version of this.

75. Ibid., *Voprosy istorii* 3 (2003), 4–6.

76. See chapter 5 of this volume.

77. RGASPI 558/11/1122/3–4.

78. L. P. Kosheleva, L. A. Rogovaia, and O. V. Khlevniuk, eds., *Stenogrammy zasedanii Politburo TsK RKP(b)-VKP(b), 1923–1938 gg.* (Moscow, 2007), vol. 3, 693.

79. RGASPI 558/11/1509/82–84.

80. RGASPI 558/11/842/35–44.

81. *Iosif Vissarionovich Stalin: Kratkaia biografiia* (Moscow, 1939).

82. RGASPI 558/1/3226/1.

83. Maksimenkov, *Bol'shaia tsenzura*, 577–78; R. Kosolapov, *Slovo tovarishchu Stalinu* (Moscow, 2002), 468–72. Kosolapov's approach to Stalin is highly polemical; however, the memoirs of Mochalov in his volume are corroborated by other sources.

84. Khrushchev described it as "one of the most characteristic examples of Stalin's self-glorification and of his lack of even elementary modesty." Talbott, *Khrushchev Remembers*, 605.

85. Kosolapov, *Slovo*, 469; Maksimenkov, *Bol'shaia tsenzura*, 577.

86. Kosolapov, *Slovo*, 471–72; Maksimenkov, *Bol'shaia tsenzura*, 577–78.

87. V. A. Belianov, "I. V. Stalin sam o sebe: Redaktsionnaia pravka sobstvennoi biografii," *Izvestiia TsK KPSS* 9 (1990), 115, 117–18, 121–23, 125.

88. Ibid., 115–16.

89. Ibid., 117–18, 127.

90. Ibid., 117, 120, 122–23, 125–26.

91. Brooks, *Thank You, Comrade Stalin!* 25, 93.

92. The translation is taken from the English version: *Joseph Stalin: A Short Biography* (London, 1940).

93. For the cult directed at children, see Catriona Kelly, "Grandpa Lenin and Uncle Stalin: Soviet Leader Cults for Little Children," in Apor et al., *Leader Cult in Communist Dictatorships.*

94. RGASPI 558/11/1496/60–61.

95. Miklos Kun, *Stalin: An Unknown Portrait* (Budapest, 2003), 3–4.

96. RGASPI 558/11/1495/113; *Rasskazy starykh rabochikh o velikom vozhde* (Tbilisi, 1937). See also *Rasskazy starykh rabochikh Zakavkaz'ia o velikom Staline* (Moscow, 1937); V. Kaminskii and I. Vereshchagin, eds., "Detstvo i iunost' vozhdia," *Molodaia gvardiia* 12 (1939), 22–101. Brandenberger notes that print-runs for Iaroslavskii's volume never exceeded 200,000 compared with an initial print-run of 1.2 million copies of the *Short Biography*. Brandenberger, "Stalin as Symbol," 262–63.

97. RGASPI 558/11/1499/39–54.

98. RGASPI 558/11/1495/113.

99. Kun, *Stalin*, 7; Gromov, *Stalin*, 22–23.

100. RGASPI 558/11/1121/24. This document was first published in *Voprosy istorii* 11 (1953).

101. RGASPI 558/11/787/1–2.

102. RGASPI 558/11/1494/6–10.

103. G. El'-Registan, "Neobychainoe puteshestvie," *Molodaia gvardiia* 10–12 (1935); RGASPI 558/11/1494/121–25.

104. Olga Velikanova, *The Public Perception of the Cult of Lenin Based on Archival Materials* (London, 2002), 63–64.

105. RGASPI 558/11/1473/60–68. In January 1939 the secretary of Smolensk obkom wrote to Stalin again to ask whether he had changed his mind, but it is unclear what Stalin's response was on this occasion.

106. RGASPI 558/11/1473/81–82, 92–93, 98; 558/11/207/22–23.

107. This strategy clearly had some success: at the time of Stalin's wife's death, the young diarist Nina Lugovskaya wrote: "Actually it's strange to learn that Stalin has a son and that he had a wife. I never tried to imagine his private life or his family relations." Nina Lugovskaya, *The Diary of a Soviet Schoolgirl, 1932–1937* (Chicago, 2003), 25.

108. RGASPI 558/11/92/22–23.

109. RGASPI 558/11/92/81.

110. *Pravda* only once included a photo of Stalin with a child of his own (Svetlana, in August 1935). Plamper, *Stalin Cult*, 44.

111. RGASPI 558/11/781/126.

112. Kun, *Stalin*, 316.

113. Apor, "Leader in the Making," 77. See also Service, *Stalin*, 357–66.

114. Christel Lane, *The Rites of Rulers* (Cambridge, England, 1981); Stites, *Revolutionary Dreams;* James von Geldern, *Bolshevik Festivals, 1917–1920* (Berkeley, 1993); Karen Petrone, *Life Has Become More Joyous, Comrades: Celebrations in the Time of Stalin* (Bloomington, Ind., 2000); Malte Rolf, *Sovetskie massovye prazdniki* (Moscow, 2009).

115. Ennker, " 'Struggling for Stalin's Soul,' " 169.

116. Stalin, *Sochineniia*, vol. 10, 332–33.

117. RGASPI 558/11/1115/9.

118. RGASPI 558/11/1116/34–42.

119. RGASPI 558/11/1118/1–2.

120. RGASPI 558/11/1118/42.

121. RGASPI 558/11/1122/1.

122. Dmitrii Shepilov, *The Kremlin's Scholar* (New Haven, 2007), 232. Simonov also recalls this episode, although his version is slightly different: Konstantin Simonov, *Glazami cheloveka moego pokoloeniia* (Moscow, 1989), 239.

123. On the subject of Kremlin receptions, see V. A. Nevezhin, *Zastol'nye rechi Stalina* (Moscow, 2003), 3–26.

124. This period coincided with the apogee of the Stakhanovite movement.

125. RGASPI 558/11/720/107.

126. RGASPI 17/163/1091/144–45. On Bolshevik fears of *samotek* (drift, spontaneity), see Malte Rolf, "The Leader's Many Bodies: Leader Cults and Mass Festivals in Voronezh, Novosibirsk, and Kemerovo in the 1930s," in Heller and Plamper, *Personality Cults in Stalinism*, 201–2.

127. RGASPI 17/163/1127/150–51.

128. For examples, see Nevezhin, *Zastol'nye rechi*.

129. Stalin, *Sochineniia*, vol. 13, 255.

130. Nevezhin, *Zastol'nye rechi*, 55.

131. Stalin, *Sochineniia*, vol. 1/14, 56, 62.

132. Ibid., 253–54. For other versions of this speech, see Nevezhin, *Zastol'nye rechi*, 123–33.

133. RGASPI 558/11/1122/158–74. Robert Tucker paraphrases the speech quite faithfully, asserting (not entirely plausibly) that Stalin was modeling himself on Ivan Groznyi. Tucker, *Stalin in Power*, 482–86. Dimitrov's record of the speech is reproduced in *The Diary of Georgi Dimitrov, 1933–1949*, ed. Ivo Banac (New Haven, 2003), 65–67.

134. Diary of Lazar Brontman, http://zhurnal.lib.ru/r/ryndin_s_r/dnevnik1.shtml, entry for 21 January 1935 (accessed 29 January 2011).

135. RGASPI 558/11/1117/49–500b; *Pravda*, 23 November 1933.

136. RGASPI 558/11/1479/23–24; *Pravda*, 28 December 1935.

137. RGASPI 558/11/1479/34–35; *Pravda*, 8 January 1936. A photo of all three leaders accompanies the text.

138. RGASPI 558/11/1479/54–56; *Pravda*, 4 May 1937.

139. RGASPI 558/11/1086/37–52; *Pravda*, 31 October 1937.

140. RGASPI 558/11/1077/67–69; Nevezhin, *Zastol'nye rechi*, 94–110; *Pravda*, 2 August 1935.

141. Nevezhin, *Zastol'nye rechi*, 113.

142. Lane, *Rites of Rulers*, ch. 10; Petrone, *Life Has Become More Joyous, Comrades*.

143. Sergius Yakobson and H. D. Lasswell, "May Day Slogans in Soviet Russia, 1918–1943," in Harold D. Laswell and Nathan Leites, eds., *Language of Politics* (Cambridge, Mass., 1965), 284.

144. V. I. Lenin, "K lozungam," *Polnoe sobranie sochinenii*, 5th ed. (Moscow, 1981), vol. 34, 10–17.

145. Stalin, *Sochineniia*, vol. 5, 171–73. For further reflections, see ibid., vol. 12, 65–66. Lars Lih notes Stalin's intense interest in the correct formulation of slogans: in February 1930, in connection with collectivization, he expressed concern to Molotov that the correct slogan "For the collective farms!" risked being overshadowed by the "artificial" slogan "For the settlement associations!" Lars Lih, Oleg V. Naumov, and Oleg V. Khlevniuk, eds., *Stalin's Letters to Molotov, 1925–1936* (New Haven, 1995), 41.

146. O. V. Khlevniuk, R. W. Davies, L. P. Kosheleva, E. A. Rees, and L. A. Rogovaia, eds., *Stalin i Kaganovich: Perepiska, 1931–1936 gg.* (Moscow, 2001), 515. For Stalin's revisions in October 1933, see ibid., 407–8.

147. RGASPI 17/163/778/210b.

148. RGASPI 17/163/829/101.

149. RGASPI 17/163/854/1250b–126; 17/163/914/78–79. It was the CC, rather than the party, that was described as "Leninist" in November 1931.

150. RGASPI 17/163/939/59.

151. RGASPI 17/163/914/83; 17/163/939/58.

152. RGASPI 17/163/939/50; 17/163/962/84.

153. RGASPI 17/163/962/87. Stalin did not appear to object to the inclusion in the November 1932 slogans of his words "With the banner of Lenin we were victorious in the battles for the October revolution . . . Long live Leninism!" RGASPI 17/163/962/94.

154. RGASPI 17/163/980/97, 99; Khlevniuk et al., *Stalin i Kaganovich*, 408.

155. RGASPI 17/163/994/244.

156. Brandenberger, *National Bolshevism*, 32–36; Clark, *Soviet Novel*, 118–24.

157. RGASPI 17/163/1020/63.

158. RGASPI 17/163/1044/79–80.

159. RGASPI 17/163/1060/88–89.

160. Petrone, *Life Has Become More Joyous, Comrades*, 151, 160–68.

161. RGASPI 17/163/1473/76–79.

162. RGASPI 17/163/1191/28; 17/163/1203/91.

163. *Diary of Georgi Dimitrov*, 104.

164. RGASPI 17/163/1223/115.

165. *Diary of Georgi Dimitrov*, 105.

166. RGASPI 17/163/1257/137.

167. RGASPI 17/163/1323/172; Stalin, *Sochineniia*, vol. 2/15, 10.

168. Interestingly, the draft slogans issued for the twenty-fourth anniversary of the Red Army in 1942 contained a much more pronounced focus on Stalin (and Lenin). The second slogan read "The spirit of Lenin and his victorious banner inspires us for the Patriotic war. Under the banner of Lenin-Stalin, forward to victory!" Stalin did not change this, but did eliminate "for the great Stalin" from the fourth slogan: "For the Soviet fatherland, for the great Stalin the sons of all the people of the Soviet Union go into battle." He left the phrases "party of Lenin-Stalin" and "banner of Lenin-Stalin" in the concluding section, but deleted the two final slogans: "Under the leadership of the great general, the *vozhd'* of the Red Army, and the people, comrade Stalin—forward to victory over the enemy," and "Long live the great *vozhd'* of the Red Army and the people—comrade Stalin." RGASPI 17/163/1331/87–91.

169. RGASPI 82/2/170/25.

170. RGASPI 17/163/1482/82; 17/163/1491/185; 17/163/1505/101–3.

171. From October 1948, his name also featured in a new slogan addressed to the "Leninist-Stalinist Komsomol." RGASPI 17/163/1517/9.

172. *Pravda*, 30 October 1952.

173. Talbott, *Khrushchev Remembers*, 70; Rolf, "Leader's Many Bodies," 205.

174. B. Starkov, "Kak Moskva chut' ne stala Stalinodarom," *Izvestiia TsK KPSS* 12 (1990), 126–27. Molotov recalls that a similar proposal by Kaganovich angered Stalin. Resis, *Molotov Remembers*, 176.

175. RGASPI 17/3/955; 17/163/1049/38; Robert McNeal, *Stalin: Man and Ruler* (London, 1988), 169.

176. RGASPI 17/163/1061/163–64.

177. Throughout the Stalin era, Kirov's name was assigned more frequently to large and small towns than were Lenin's and Stalin's. Murray, *Politics and Place Names*, 51.

178. RGASPI 17/163/1084/119.

179. RGASPI 17/163/1082/56; 17/163/1081/94. For another example, see 17/163/1128/118.

180. RGASPI 558/11/1472/34–36. The Politburo decree to rename it after Kaganovich was taken on 11 May 1935. For an earlier example, see Plamper, *Stalin Cult*, 134.

181. RGASPI 17/163/1081/24.

182. RGASPI 17/163/1084/56.

183. RGASPI 17/163/1099/155–56; 17/163/1106/7–8, 117, 138; 17/163/1107/64; 17/163/1108/43; 17/163/1103/152.

184. RGASPI 17/163/1101/137–38.

185. RGASPI 17/163/1105/58–59.

186. RGASPI 17/163/1125/64–65; 17/163/1127/26; 17/163/1127/53–54. The last two decisions were marked "not for publication."

187. V. Soima, *Zapreshchennyi Stalin* (Moscow, 2005), 27–28. This was the very same Ryndin who was indirectly accused of fostering his own cult at the February–March (1937) plenum.

188. RGASPI 17/163/1118/71–72. For a similar objection by Ordzhonikidze, see RGASPI 17/163/1115/72. Compare his objections to Beria's proposed volume in honor of his birthday. A. V. Kvashonkin, A. V. Lishvin, and O. V. Khlevniuk, eds., *Stalinskoe politbiuro v 30-e gody* (Moscow, 1995), 336.

189. RGASPI 17/163/1111/1–2.

190. RGASPI 17/163/1127/116.

191. RGASPI 17/114/952/37–39. For further examples, see RGASPI 17/114/952/65–66; 145–48; 193.

192. RGASPI 17/163/1128/116; 17/163/1172. For another example, see V. Khaustov, V. P. Naumov, and N. S. Plotnikova, eds., *Lubianka: Stalin i glavnoe upravlenie gosbezopasnosti NKVD, 1937–1938* (Moscow, 2004), 283.

193. RGASPI 17/163/1142/51–52.

194. RGASPI 17/163/1249.

195. Belianov, "I. V. Stalin sam o sebe," 118.

196. The contrast with Hitler's cult in this respect is instructive. See Ian Kershaw, " 'Working Towards the Führer': Reflections on the Nature of the Hitler Dictatorship," in Ian Kershaw and Moshe Lewin, eds., *Stalinism and Nazism: Dictatorships in Comparison* (Cambridge, England, 1997), 94–98.

Chapter 5. The Working Class

1. We will generally use the terms interchangeably, as did many Bolsheviks, especially in the 1920s. See, for example, Stalin's usage in 1926: "It is, secondly, the heterogeneity of the working class . . . I think that the proletariat, as a class, can be divided

into three strata." I. Stalin, *Sochineniia*, vols. 1–13 (Moscow, 1946–51) and vols. 1–3/ vols. 14–16 (Stanford, Calif., 1967), vol. 9, 10.

2. Sheila Fitzpatrick, "The Bolsheviks' Dilemma: Class, Culture, and Politics in the Early Soviet Years," *Slavic Review* 4 (1988), 599–613; Fitzpatrick, "Ascribing Class: The Construction of Social Identity in Soviet Russia," *Journal of Modern History* 4 (1993), 745–70; Fitzpatrick, "The Problem of Class Identity in NEP Society," in Sheila Fitzpatrick et al., eds., *Russia in the Era of NEP* (Bloomington, Ind., 1991); Fitzpatrick, *Tear Off the Masks* (Princeton, N.J., 2005); Igal Halfin, *From Darkness to Light: Class, Consciousness and Salvation in Revolutionary Russia* (Pittsburgh, 2000); Victoria Bonnell, *Iconography of Power: Soviet Political Posters under Lenin and Stalin* (Berkeley, 1997), 21–34.

3. Reginald Zelnik, "Worry about Workers: Concerns of the Russian Intelligentsia from the 1870s to *What Is to Be Done?*" in Marsha Siefert, ed., *Extending the Borders of Russian History* (New York, 2003), 206–26; Halfin *From Darkness to Light.*

4. V. I. Lenin, *Selected Works* (Moscow, 1970), vol. 2, 663; David Priestland, *Stalinism and the Politics of Mobilization: Ideas, Power, and Terror in Inter-war Russia* (Oxford, 2007), 160.

5. Halfin, *From Darkness to Light*, 120; Kendall Bailes, *Technology and Society under Lenin and Stalin* (Princeton, N.J., 1978).

6. F. Chuev *Tak Govoril Kaganovich. Ispoved' Stalinskogo Apostola* (Moscow, 1992), 31. Khrushchev confirms that he was promoted by Kaganovich because the latter felt there were not enough people with working-class backgrounds in the Ukrainian CC. " 'We need to proletarianize our apparatus,' he said." Sergei Khrushchev, ed., *Memoirs of Nikita Khrushchev* (University Park, Pa., 2004), vol. 1, 25. Malyshev describes a session of the Defense Committee (KO) in September 1939 at which Stalin rebuked Kaganovich for promoting Stakhanovites to senior management jobs for which they were not properly qualified. V. A. Malyshev, "Dnevnik Narkoma," *Istochnik* 5 (1997), 108 (entry for 13 September 1939). Kaganovich himself clearly remained deeply attached to his own worker identity. Molotov recalls him saying, " 'For you it's easy, you are an intellectual, but I am from a worker's family.' Even now he says things like this." Albert Resis, ed., *Molotov Remembers: Inside Kremlin Politics—Conversations with Felix Chuev* (Chicago, 1993), 229.

7. Priestland, *Stalinism.*

8. Moshe Lewin, *The Making of the Soviet System: Essays in the Social History of Interwar Russia* (New York, 1985), 254–56.

9. On the Bolshevik approach to eugenics, see Mark Adams, "Eugenics in Russia 1900–1940," in *The Wellborn Science: Eugenics in Germany, France, Brazil, and Russia* (Oxford, 1990), 153–216; Loren Graham, "Science and Values: The Eugenics Movement in Germany and Russia in the 1920s," *American Historical Review* 5 (1977), 1133–64.

10. Fitzpatrick, *Tear Off the Masks*, 31; Sheila Fitzpatrick, *The Cultural Front* (Ithaca, N.Y., 1992), 31.

11. *XI s"ezd RKP(b): Stenograficheskii otchet* (Moscow, 1922), 32.

12. Ibid., 92–93.

13. Ibid., 347–48.

14. Zinoviev reported to the twelfth party congress in 1923 that the declassing of the proletariat had now ceased. *XII s"ezd RKP(b): Stenograficheskii otchet* (Moscow, 1923), 32–33.

15. John Hatch, "The 'Lenin Levy' and the Social Origins of Stalinism: Workers and the Communist Party in Moscow, 1921–28," *Slavic Review* 4 (1989), 558–77; Halfin *From Darkness to Light*, 266–67.

16. *XIV s"ezd VKP(b): Stenograficheskii otchet* (Moscow, 1925), 725–26.

17. Ibid., 126, 164, 446–47.

18. Stalin, *Sochineniia*, vol. 7, 321; vol. 8, 137; vol. 10, 113.

19. Ibid., vol. 9, 10–11.

20. J.-P. Depretto, *Les Ouvriers en U.R.S.S., 1928–1941* (Paris, 1997), 35–36.

21. Stalin, *Sochineniia*, vol. 5, 206; vol. 6, 314; vol. 7, 170, 209–10, 213–14; RGASPI 558/11/1110/49–55. Various measures were subsequently put in place in an attempt to meet workers' demands, including a reduction in wage differentials between skilled and unskilled workers and the introduction of a seven-hour working day. Stalin endorsed the seven-hour day in a letter to Voroshilov, who had argued that introducing it would be "a great stupidity at this time." Stalin countered that what mattered was that all seven hours were used for productive work, noting that the legislation would also serve as useful international propaganda. Priestland, *Stalinism*, 185–86; RGASPI 74/2/38/10.

22. Sheila Fitzpatrick, "Cultural Revolution as Class War," in Fitzpatrick, ed., *Cultural Revolution in Russia, 1928–1931* (Bloomington, Ind., 1978).

23. Priestland, *Stalinism*, 72–73, 170, 183–88.

24. RGASPI 558/11/1111/16; V. P. Danilov, O. V. Khlevniuk, and A. Iu. Vatlin, eds., *Kak lomali NEP: Stenogrammy plenumov TsK VKP(b), 1928–1929* (Moscow, 2000), vol. 1, 239.

25. Stalin, *Sochineniia*, vol. 11, 61.

26. The stenogram of the Politburo session is in L. P. Kosheleva, L. A. Rogovaia, and O. V. Khlevniuk, eds., *Stenogrammy zasedanii Politbiuro TsK RKP(b)-VKP(b), 1923–1938 gg.* (2007), vol. 3, 25–75.

27. RGASPI 558/11/1112/303–4.

28. RGASPI 558/11/1112/22–24.

29. Stalin, *Sochineniia*, vol. 9, 21.

30. Danilov, Khlevniuk, and Vatlin, *Kak lomali NEP*, vol. 3, 249.

31. Ibid., vol. 2, 397.

32. Ibid., vol. 3, 451.

33. Hiroaki Kuromiya, *Stalin's Industrial Revolution* (Cambridge, England, 1988), 84.

34. Danilov, Khlevniuk, and Vatlin, *Kak lomali NEP*, vol. 2, 416.

35. Ibid., 425.

36. According to Rittersporn, "about 68% of all workers and employees came from the villages in 1928–1932." Gabor Rittersporn, "From Working Class to Urban Laboring

Mass: On Politics and Social Categories in the Formative Years of the Soviet System," in Lewis Siegelbaum and Ronald Suny, eds., *Making Workers Soviet: Power, Class, and Identity* (Ithaca, N.Y., 1994), 256. See also Kenneth Straus, *Factory and Community in Stalin's Russia* (Pittsburgh, 1997), 77.

37. Andrea Graziosi, "Stalin's Antiworker 'Workerism,' 1924–1931," *International Review of Social History* 40 (1995), 229; Kuromiya, *Stalin's Industrial Revolution*, 108–9.

38. RGASPI 17/163/754/91–910b.

39. Lars Lih, Oleg V. Naumov, and Oleg V. Khlevniuk, eds., *Stalin's Letters to Molotov, 1925–1936* (New Haven, 1995), 219. See also Kaganovich's words at a meeting of local party officials convened by the CC on 13 January 1930: "At present the position is that a small group of shock workers is carrying on an heroic struggle, is working stubbornly and tensely, while a considerable part, and perhaps the majority, of workers is working the old way." R. W. Davies, *The Soviet Economy in Turmoil, 1929–1930* (Basingstoke, England, 1998), 258.

40. RGASPI 558/11/1112/307.

41. David Hoffmann, *Peasant Metropolis: Social Identities in Moscow, 1929–1941* (Ithaca, N.Y., 1994), 207; Graziosi "Stalin's Anti-Worker 'Workerism,' " 236.

42. Kuromiya, *Stalin's Industrial Revolution*, 200; Hoffmann, *Peasant Metropolis*, 208.

43. Hoffmann, *Peasant Metropolis*, 36; Davies, *Soviet Economy in Turmoil*, 360–61; Kuromiya, *Stalin's Industrial Revolution*, 206.

44. Lih, Naumov, and Khlevniuk, *Stalin's Letters to Molotov*, 215. On the crisis of the third quarter of 1930, see Davies, *Soviet Economy in Turmoil*, 346–77.

45. RGASPI 558/11/1114/49–51; Kosheleva, Rogovaia, and Khlevniuk, *Stenogrammy zasedanii Politbiuro TsK RKP(b)-VKP(b)*, vol. 3, 179–80 (corrected version), 317–18 (uncorrected version).

46. RGASPI 558/11/1115/2–5. This argument was echoed in his "New Conditions, New Tasks" speech, in which he called for mechanization and an organized approach to labor recruitment since the spontaneous influx of peasants had ceased thanks to better conditions in the countryside. Stalin, *Sochineniia*, vol. 13, 52–55.

47. RGASPI 558/11/1115/21–22. This was evidently a high priority for Stalin—in a letter to Kaganovich written before 6 August 1931 he stressed that "the resolution on cooperation is a very important matter." O. V. Khlevniuk, R. W. Davies, L. P. Kosheleva, E. A. Rees, and L. A. Rogovaia, eds., *Stalin i Kaganovich: Perepiska, 1931–1936 gg.* (Moscow, 2001), 37.

48. Matthew Payne, *Stalin's Railroad: Turksib and the Building of Socialism* (Pittsburgh, 2001), 242.

49. RGASPI 17/2/555/74.

50. RGASPI 17/2/557/128–29.

51. RGASPI 17/2/555/110. In a corrected version of the transcript the number of Stakhanovites was adjusted to "a couple of hundred." RGASPI 17/2/561/76.

52. RGASPI 558/11/1078/76–78.

53. RGASPI 558/11/1078/78–83; Stalin, *Sochineniia*, vol. 1/14, 95–96.

54. Graziosi, "Stalin's Antiworker 'Workerism,' " 223–24.

55. Ibid., 253–54.

56. Stalin, *Sochineniia*, vol. 12, 173–74.

57. RGASPI 558/11/1114/1–12.

58. RGASPI 558/11/1115/5–6.

59. Bonnell, *Iconography*, 36.

60. Stalin, *Sochineniia*, vol. 13, 23–27. Just over a year before, the term *oblomovsh-china* featured in an officially sanctioned CC October anniversary slogan: "Against a slavelike work tempo. Against *oblomovshchina*, lethargy, sloppiness, and sluggishness. At a revolutionary tempo forward on the whole front of construction." *Pravda*, 2 November 1929. Stalin adopted similarly patriotic language in a letter he wrote to Gorky at this time, declaring, "Socialism is victorious. '*Wretched*' Russia will be no more. Of course! There will be a powerful and rich *advanced* Russia." A. Artizov and O. Naumov, eds., *Vlast' i khudozhestvennaia intelligentsia* (Moscow, 1999), 138.

61. Stalin, *Sochineniia*, vol. 13, 110–11, 262–65. On Soviet objections to the Nazi "biological" model, see Peter Holquist, "State Violence as Technique: The Logic of Violence in Soviet Totalitarianism," in Amir Weiner, ed., *Landscaping the Human Garden* (Stanford, Calif., 2003), 40.

62. Khlevniuk et al., *Stalin i Kaganovich*, 431, 437.

63. Stalin, *Sochineniia*, vol. 12, 315.

64. Lih, Naumov, and Khlevniuk, *Stalin's Letters to Molotov*, 219; Stalin, *Sochineniia*, vol. 13, 59–60.

65. Lih, Naumov, and Khlevniuk, *Stalin's Letters to Molotov*, 219–20.

66. Stalin, *Sochineniia*, vol. 13, 59–60; Straus, *Factory and Community*, 98–99.

67. On the association between consumption and *kul'turnost'*, see Sheila Fitzpatrick, *Everyday Stalinism: Ordinary Life in Extraordinary Times—Soviet Russia in the 1930s* (Oxford, 1999), 89–114.

68. RGASPI 558/11/1115/21–28.

69. RGASPI 558/11/1118/56–60.

70. Stalin, *Sochineniia*, vol. 1/14, 80, 84; RGASPI 558/11/1078/77 (uncorrected version).

71. T. H. Rigby, *Communist Party Membership in the USSR, 1917–1967* (Princeton, N.Y., 1968), 116.

72. Stalin, *Sochineniia*, vol. 12, 189.

73. Stalin's response to Kin was returned by the postal services, prompting Tovstukha to inquire into the identity of "Kin." RGASPI 558/11/753/114–23.

74. Jeffrey Rossman *Worker Resistance under Stalin: Class and Revolution on the Shop Floor* (Cambridge, Mass., 2005). Stalin made every effort to suppress any public discussion of these events. Khlevniuk et al., *Stalin i Kaganovich*, 139.

75. Sheila Fitzpatrick "The Great Departure: Rural-Urban Migration in the Soviet Union," in William Rosenberg and Lewis Siegelbaum, eds., *Social Dimensions of Soviet Industrialization* (Bloomington, Ind., 1993), 30; RGASPI 81/3/246/720b.

76. RGASPI 558/11/1116/143. For the rather different uncorrected version of the speech, see Kosheleva, Rogovaia, and Khlevniuk, *Stenogrammy zasedanii Politbiuro TsK RKP(b)-VKP(b)*, vol. 3, 652–59, especially 657–58.

77. Stalin, *Sochineniia*, vol. 13, 207.

78. Khlevniuk et al., *Stalin i Kaganovich*, 179; RGASPI 558/11/46/109.

79. *Izvestiia TsK KPSS* 8 (1989), 97; J. A. Getty and V. Naumov, eds., *The Road to Terror: Stalin and the Self-Destruction of the Bolsheviks* (New Haven, 1999), 201.

80. Igal Halfin, *Terror in My Soul* (Cambridge, Mass., 2003), 25.

81. *Pravda*, 2 December 1935; Priestland, *Stalinism*, 282, 326.

82. RGASPI 17/165/64/12–13. Compare Molotov's comments to the June 1937 CC plenum, cited in Priestland, *Stalinism*, 384.

83. " 'Nevol'niki v rukakh Germanskogo Reikhsvera': Rech' I. V, Stalina v Narkomate oborony," *Istochnik* 3 (1994), 73–74; Holquist, "State Violence," 40–41.

84. RGASPI 558/11/1121/48–50.

85. Fitzpatrick, *Tear Off the Masks*, 49.

86. Priestland, *Stalinism*, 324–29, 379–88; Sarah Davies, *Popular Opinion in Stalin's Russia: Terror, Propaganda and Dissent, 1934–1941* (Cambridge, England, 1997).

87. Stalin continued to invoke biographical criteria when it suited him. For example, at a special military meeting probably held in late 1937 or early 1938 (the source is undated), he suggested that A. Egorov was less deserving of the title "Marshal of the Soviet Union" than were Voroshilov, Budennyi, and Bliukher, since he came from an officer's family, while the others were all "sons of the people." The use of the word "people" here rather than "proletariat" or "working class" was more typical of his approach at this time. RGASPI 58/11/1120/104–5.

88. For more on this, see chapter 6 in this volume.

89. *Kinovedcheskie zapiski* 20 (1993/94), 106.

90. *The Diary of Georgi Dimitrov, 1933–1949*, ed. Ivo Banac (New Haven, 2003), 132–34. Dimitrov observed that Voroshilov was clearly upset by this scolding.

91. Malyshev, "Dnevnik Narkoma," 111 (entry for 26 May).

92. Fitzpatrick, *Tear Off the Masks*, 44.

93. See note 6 above.

94. Fitzpatrick, *Tear Off the Masks*, 39.

95. RGASPI 558/11/1118/49–54.

96. The quota system for higher technical education introduced in July 1928 had already been modified in 1932 to give greater weight to academic performance. See Bailes, *Technology and Society*, 169, 178.

97. RGASPI 71/10/130/84–86. The Bolshevik Party itself also underwent similar changes. In 1937 it was directed to recruit simply "the best people" rather than give preference to the proletariat. Fitzpatrick, *Tear Off the Masks*, 41.

98. Stalin, *Sochineniia*, vol. 1/14, 142–45. But note that in his conversation with Roy Howard in March 1936, Stalin had described workers, peasants, and intelligentsia as strata (*prosloiki*). Ibid., 129.

99. Ibid., 142–43.

100. Priestland, *Stalinism*, 288; Stalin, *Sochineniia*, vol. 1/14, 152.

101. RGASPI 17/163/669/65.

102. RGASPI 17/163/778/200b, 21.

103. RGASPI 17/163/811/122.

104. RGASPI 17/163/876/156–57.

105. RGASPI 17/163/1044/76.

106. RGASPI 17/163/1044/72; 17/163/1083/141; 17/163/1127/88; 17/163/1146/134; *Pravda*, 29 October 1936. It is possible that he simply did not make any revisions to the 1935 November slogans—there is no evidence of his editing in the archives, and he was in Sochi at this time. Stalin could be very sensitive about the language used to describe the revolution: when it was described as the "Great October socialist revolution" in the draft November 1938 slogans, Stalin for some reason deleted "Great." RGASPI 17/163/1203/84.

107. RGASPI 17/163/939/57; 17/163/1044/77.

108. RGASPI 17/163/1146/133; 17/163/1473/75.

109. RGASPI 17/163/1191/26; 17/163/1203/85. However, as both Priestland and Van Ree note, the terms "dictatorship of the proletariat" and "dictatorship of the working class" continued to be in use at the eighteenth party congress in 1939. Priestland, *Stalinism*, 397; Erik Van Ree, *The Political Thought of Joseph Stalin* (London, 2002), 141.

110. RGASPI 17/163/1223/115; 17/163/1238/197–98; 17/163/1257/137; 17/163/1284/134. Stalin also changed "socialist intelligentsia" to "Soviet intelligentsia" in the November 1940 slogan.

111. RGASPI 17/163/1404/28.

112. RGASPI 17/163/1404/34.

113. RGASPI 17/163/1423/155–66.

114. Lewin, *Making*, 234.

115. Stuart Finkel, *On the Ideological Front: The Russian Intelligentsia and the Making of the Soviet Public Sphere* (New Haven, 2007), 5–7; L. G. Churchward, *The Soviet Intelligentsia* (London, 1973), 3–9; Richard Pipes, ed., *The Russian Intelligentsia* (New York, 1961).

116. Halfin, *From Darkness to Light*, 149–71.

117. Fitzpatrick, *Cultural Front*, 26.

118. Bailes, *Technology and Society*, 47–48; Priestland, *Stalinism*, 90.

119. Erik Van Ree "The Stalinist Self: The Case of Ioseb Jughashvili (1898–1907)," *Kritika* 2 (2010), 257–82.

120. The quotation is from a letter to Lenin of 3 October 1918 in A. V. Kvashonkin, O. V. Khlevniuk, L. P. Kosheleva, and L. A. Rogovaia, eds., *Bol'shevistskoe rukovodstvo. Perepiska 1912–1927* (Moscow, 1996), 52. For similar derogatory comments about military specialists, see the letter to Lenin of 7 July 1918 in Stalin, *Sochineniia*, vol. 4, 118. For his preference for new "red officers," see ibid., 147, 150; Bailes, *Technology and Society*, 72–73.

121. Stalin, *Sochineniia*, vol. 1/14, 30–32.

122. *Diary of Georgi Dimitrov*, 132.

123. In 1920 he compared such *intelligenty* favorably with the "counter-revolutionary military specialists" who were subsequently Sovietized, arguing that it was unlikely that the former were less reliable than the latter. Stalin, *Sochineniia*, vol. 4, 360–61. See also his comments at the CC meeting with representatives from the national republics and oblasts in 1923. Ibid., vol. 5, 294, 320.

124. L. V. Maksimenkov, *Bol'shaia tsenzura: Pisateli i zhurnalisty v strane sovetov, 1917–1956* (Moscow, 2005), 98.

125. Stalin, *Sochineniia*, vol. 5, 107–8; Edward Acton, ed., *The Soviet Union: A Documentary History* (Exeter, 2005), vol. 1, 238.

126. Halfin, *From Darkness to Light*, 203.

127. On the importance of kinship imagery more generally in the thirties, see Katerina Clark, *The Soviet Novel: History as Ritual* (Chicago, 1985), 114–35.

128. RGASPI 558/11/1104/43–46. For a similar expression of support for creation of their own new "*komsostav*," see Stalin, *Sochineniia*, vol. 7, 85–89.

129. Stalin, *Sochineniia*, vol. 8, 138–39.

130. Ibid., vol. 10, 318–19.

131. Ibid., vol. 10, 322–23; vol. 11, 53–60; Fitzpatrick, "Cultural Revolution as Class War."

132. The term "showcase proletarian" is taken from Miklos Kun, *Stalin: An Unknown Portrait* (Budapest, 2003), 283; Danilov, Khlevniuk, and Vatlin, *Kak lomali NEP*, vol. 1, 262–63.

133. Stalin, *Sochineniia*, vol. 11, 76.

134. Oleg Khlevniuk, *Master of the House: Stalin and His Inner Circle* (New Haven, 2009), 60.

135. RGASPI 558/11/1115/6–8.

136. Stalin, *Sochineniia*, vol. 13, 65–73. Stalin subsequently limited the OGPU's powers to arrest industrial specialists. Khlevniuk, *Master*, 62.

137. RGASPI 17/2/504/219–21 (uncorrected stenogram); 17/2/514/26.

138. RGASPI 17/163/980/98.

139. RGASPI 17/163/1020/59–60, 62.

140. RGASPI 17/163/1060/88.

141. Stalin, *Sochineniia*, vol. 1/14, 62. It was boosted too by his support for the portrayal of members of the intelligentsia as positive heroes in works of art. In November 1935, for example, the head of GUKF, B. Shumiatskii, recorded Stalin's approving remark that the protagonist of a new film about geological expeditions in the Pamir, *Lunnyi kamen'*, was "*intelligentnyi*." See K. M. Anderson, L. V. Maksimenkov, L. P. Kosheleva, and L. A. Rogovaia, eds., *Kremlevskii kinoteatr, 1928–1953* (Moscow, 2005), 1029. Whereas only twelve films produced between 1933 and 1939 focused on industrial workers, twenty dealt with heroic members of the intelligentsia. Peter Kenez, *Cinema and Soviet Society, 1917–1953* (Cambridge, England, 1992), 161–64.

142. Stalin, *Sochineniia*, vol. 1/14, 145.

143. Ibid., 169.

144. For more on this conversation, see chapter 4.

145. RGASPI 558/11/1120/2–4.

146. Bailes, *Technology and Society*, 285.

147. RGASPI 558/11/1120/89–90.

148. Davies, *Popular Opinion*, ch. 8; Priestland, *Stalinism*, 369–73.

149. For more on this work, see chapter 4 of this volume.

150. RGASPI 558/1122/1–18. The speech is marked "27 September" in this archival file, but Maslov dates the meeting to 28 September–1 October. On 1 October, Stalin made a further speech at this meeting. See N. Maslov, ed., "I. V. Stalin o 'Kratkom Kurse Istorii VKP(b)': Stenogramma vystupleniia na soveshchanii propagandistov Moskvy i Leningrada. 1938 g.," *Istoricheskii arkhiv* 5 (1994), 4.

151. Stalin, *Sochineniia*, vol. 13, 38–39.

152. RGASPI 558/11/1122/1–18.

153. For a similar analysis, see Kosior's comments to the February–March 1937 plenum about the party's failure to engage *sluzhashchie* with propaganda campaigns: "*Sluzhashchie* are considered second-class people here." *Voprosy istorii* 6 (1993), 7.

154. In his October 1 speech, he picked on M. Shkiriatov in a similar fashion. Maslov, "I. V. Stalin," 28.

155. RGASPI 558/11/1122/143–55.

156. http://zhurnal.lib.ru/r//ryndin_s_r/dnevnik6.shtml, entry for 20 September 1938 (accessed 29 January 2011). At the Politburo meeting on 11 October, Zhdanov also criticized the press for ignoring *sluzhashchie*, teachers, doctors, and students. Zhdanov's line on the intelligentsia in many ways simply paraphrased the words of Stalin's speech of 27 September. Kosheleva, Rogovaia, and Khlevniuk, *Stenogrammy zasedanii Politbiuro TsK RKP(b)-VKP(b)*, vol. 3, 680–81.

157. RGASPI 17/163/1203/88–89.

158. RGASPI 17/163/1223/112; 17/163/1238/201.

159. Stalin, *Sochineniia*, vol. 1/14, 366.

160. Ibid., 366, 395–99.

161. Lih, Naumov, and Khlevniuk, *Stalin's Letters to Molotov*, 168; Stalin, *Sochineniia*, vol. 2/15, 34.

162. On this process, see Vera Dunham, *In Stalin's Time: Middleclass Values in Soviet Fiction* (Durham, N.C., 1990).

163. Filtzer, *Soviet Workers*, 128.

164. Ibid., 233–53.

165. B. L. Vannikov, "Zapiski narkoma," *Znamia* 2 (1998), 148–49; O. Khlevniuk, "26 iiunia 1940 goda: Illiuzii i real'nosti administrirovaniia," *Kommunist* 9 (1989), 88.

166. Malyshev, "Dnevnik Narkoma," 112 (entry for 19 June); Khlevniuk, "26 iiunia 1940 goda," 89.

167. Malyshev, "Dnevnik Narkoma," 112 (entry for 23 July). At this meeting Stalin agreed to lengthen the working day of sixteen- to eighteen-year olds from six to eight hours.

168. See, for example, Filtzer, *Soviet Workers*, 233–53; Khlevniuk, "26 iunia 1940 goda." For the decree of the plenum of 31 July 1940, see *Izvestiia TsK KPSS* 2 (1990), 186–50.

169. RGASPI 17/2/673/77–79.

170. RGASPI 558/11/1124/46–47.

171. Joan Neuberger, *Hooliganism: Crime, Culture and Power in St. Petersburg, 1900–1914* (Berkeley, 1993), 1–8; Diane Koenker, *Republic of Labor: Russian Printers and Soviet Socialism, 1918–1930* (Ithaca, N.Y., 2005), 283–85.

172. The plenum sanctioned a change to the criminal code: a minimum penalty of one year's imprisonment for hooliganism and petty theft at work was introduced. Peter Solomon, *Soviet Criminal Justice under Stalin* (Cambridge, England, 1996), 308, 311, 327–34; *Izvestiia TsK KPSS* 2 (1990), 189.

173. Neuberger, *Hooliganism*, 60; Koenker, *Republic of Labor*, 284. Solomon, *Soviet Criminal Justice*, 199, 224. Solomon confirms that the majority of those prosecuted under the 26 June edict were in fact young. Ibid., 322.

174. Khlevniuk, "26 iiunia 1940 goda," 89.

175. Lewin, *Making*, 250.

176. Anna Krylova, "Identity , Agency, and the 'First Soviet Generation,' " in Stephen Lovell, ed., *Generations in Twentieth-Century Europe* (Basingstoke, England, 2007), 110.

177. RGASPI 558/11/1124/47–52.

178. RGASPI 558/11/1124/50–52, 56. Oleg Khlevniuk, *The History of the Gulag: From Collectivization to the Great Terror* (New Haven, 2004), 244. Khlevniuk notes that Stalin's words had no serious consequences.

179. For similar concerns about the supply of labor, see his speech at a CC meeting on collectivization in July 1934 in V. Danilov, V. Vinogradov, L. Viola, L. Dvoinikh, N. Ivnitskii, S. Krasil'nikov, R. Manning, O. Naumov, E. Tiurina, and Khan Chzhong Suk (Hahn Jeong-Sook), eds., *Tragediia sovetskoi derevni: Dokumenty i materialy v 5 tomakh, 1927–1939* (Moscow, 1999–2006), vol. 4, 188.

180. RGASPI 558/11/1124/51–53.

181. RGASPI 558/11/1124/54–56.

182. RGASPI 558/11/1123/29.

183. RGASPI 558/11/1124/55–57.

184. Malyshev "Dnevnik Narkoma," 113 (entry for 26 September).

185. "This attitude toward labor as a cheap and formless *rabsila* is one of the key features of industrialization in the Stalin era." Moshe Lewin, *Russia/USSR/Russia* (New York, 1995), 126.

186. Artizov and Naumov, *Vlast'*, 583–84.

187. Defined by Dunham as a "middle class." Dunham, *In Stalin's Time*, 104–9; Clark, *Soviet Novel*, 191–209; Ethan Pollock, *Stalin and the Soviet Science Wars* (Princeton, N.J., 2006).

188. Amir Weiner, "The Empires Pay a Visit: Gulag Returnees, East European Rebellions, and Soviet Frontier Politics," *Journal of Modern History* 2 (2006), 374.

Chapter 6.   Soviet Culture

1. E. J. Brown, *The Proletarian Episode in Russian Literature, 1928–1932* (New York, 1971), 7.

2. V. I. Lenin, "Party Organisation and Party Literature," *Collected Works* (Moscow, 1965), vol. 10, 44–49.

3. Brown, *Proletarian Episode*, 6–10; Christopher Read, *Culture and Power in Revolutionary Russia* (New York, 1990), 203–8; Lynn Mally, *Culture of the Future: The Proletcult Movement in Revolutionary Russia* (Berkeley, 1990); Joseph Schull, "The Ideological Origins of 'Stalinism' in Soviet Literature," *Slavic Review* 3 (1992), 468–84.

4. See, for example, Max Hayward's dismissive comment in Max Hayward and Leopold Labedz, eds., *Literature and Revolution in Soviet Russia, 1917–1962* (London, 1963), xvi.

5. A. Kemp-Welch, *Stalin and the Literary Intelligentsia, 1928–1939* (Basingstoke, England, 1991); Evgenii Gromov, *Stalin: Vlast' i iskusstvo* (Moscow, 1998); L. V. Maksimenkov, "Ocherki nomenklaturnoi istorii sovetskoi literatury (1932–1946). Stalin, Bukharin, Zhdanov, Shcherbakov i drugie," *Voprosy literatury* 4 (2003), 212–58; 5 (2003), 241–97.

6. Hans Gunther, ed., *The Culture of the Stalin Period* (New York, 1989); Boris Groys, *The Total Art of Stalinism* (Princeton, N.J., 1992); Evgenii Dobrenko, "The Disaster of Middlebrow Taste, or: Who Invented Socialist Realism?" in Thomas Lahusen and Evgenii Dobrenko, eds., *Socialist Realism without Shores* (Durham, N.C., 1997); Dobrenko, *The Making of the State Reader* (Stanford, Calif., 1997); Dobrenko, *The Making of the State Writer* (Stanford, Calif., 2001); Dobrenko and Eric Naiman, eds., *The Landscape of Stalinism* (Seattle, 2003).

7. Gromov, *Stalin*, 407.

8. Katerina Clark and Evgenii Dobrenko, eds., *Soviet Culture and Power* (New Haven, 2007), xiv, 139–40.

9. Robert Maguire, *Red Virgin Soil* (Princeton, N.J., 1968), 159–63, 191.

10. Ibid., 226. *Krasnaia nov'* was set up in 1921 with party backing.

11. Sheila Fitzpatrick, *The Cultural Front* (Ithaca, N.Y., 1992), 91–95.

12. Read, *Culture and Power*, 208–12; Brown, *Proletarian Episode*, 35–40.

13. L. Trotsky, *Literature and Revolution* (New York, 1925), 218.

14. L. V. Maksimenkov, ed., *Bol'shaia tsenzura: Pisateli i zhurnalisty v strane sovetov 1917–1956* (Moscow, 2005), 73–74.

15. Kemp-Welch, *Stalin and the Literary Intelligentsia*, 32–33; *Voprosy kul'tury pri diktature proletariata* (Moscow, 1925), 83.

16. Other members of the Politburo commission involved in drawing up the resolution were I. Vareikis, Lunacharsky, F. Raskol'nikov, and G. Lelevich. A. Artizov and O. Naumov, eds., *Vlast' i khudozhestvennaia intelligentsia* (Moscow, 1999), 53–57.

17. For the former, see, for example, Herman Ermolaev, *Soviet Literary Theories, 1917–1934* (Berkeley, 1963), 3, 48; Maguire, *Red Virgin Soil*, 170. For the latter, see Gleb Struve, *Russian Literature under Lenin and Stalin, 1917–1953* (Norman, Okla., 1971), 91; Clark and Dobrenko, *Soviet Culture and Power*, 5, 40–45.

18. Artizov and Naumov, *Vlast'*, 57. On this point, see Schull, "Ideological Origins," 478–83.

19. "History has apparently failed to record Stalin's views on this problem," asserts Struve in his *Russian Literature under Lenin and Stalin*, 82. See also Fitzpatrick, *Cultural Front*, 113; Kemp-Welch, *Stalin and the Literary Intelligentsia*, 45; Brown, *Proletarian Episode*, 35.

20. RGASPI 558/11/760/146–48.

21. Sheila Fitzpatrick, *The Commissariat of the Enlightenment* (Cambridge, England, 1970), 262–65; Stuart Finkel, *On the Ideological Front: The Russian Intelligentsia and the Making of the Soviet Public Sphere* (New Haven, 2007), 98–99, 115–50.

22. Maksimenkov, *Bol'shaia tsenzura*, 50.

23. Artizov and Naumov, *Vlast'*, 36–37.

24. Ibid., 38.

25. Ibid., 39–40; Kemp-Welch, *Stalin and the Literary Intelligentsia*, 26. The All-Russian Union of Writers had been set up by a small group of non-communist writers and scholars in 1919. Finkel, *On the Ideological Front*, 94–95.

26. Finkel, *On the Ideological Front*, 98–99. On *Smena vekh*, see Jane Burbank, *Intelligentsia and Revolution* (New York, 1986), 222–37.

27. Artizov and Naumov, *Vlast'*, 40–42.

28. Schull, "Ideological Origins," 475.

29. Maksimenkov, *Bol'shaia tsenzura*, 126; Artizov and Naumov, *Vlast'*, 84. On FOSP, see Amanda Metcalf "The Foundation of the Federation of Soviet Writers: The Forgotten Factor in Soviet Literature of the Late Twenties," *Slavonic and East European Review*, 4 (1987), 609–16.

30. Kemp-Welch, *Stalin and the Literary Intelligentsia*, 45.

31. Maksimenkov, *Bol'shaia tsenzura*, 79–89, 100–110, 113–19, 129–33, 140–43; R. Horvath, "The Poet of Terror: Dem'ian Bednyi and Stalinist Culture," *Russian Review* 1 (2006), 58–59.

32. RGASPI 558/11/717/11; Gromov, *Stalin*, 72–73. It seems likely that the "conference" was the meeting referred to in an Orgburo resolution of 3 November 1924. The Orgburo, while rejecting a full-scale congress, chose not to object to a "small meeting of proletarian writers connected with the *October* group." This conference took place in January 1925. Artizov and Naumov, *Vlast'*, 49; Brown, *Proletarian Episode*, 29.

33. Gromov, *Stalin*, 75; Artizov and Naumov, *Vlast'*, 688. He also received Voronskii in February 1925.

34. Artizov and Naumov, *Vlast'*, 82, 742 n. 2.

35. RAPP's all-union equivalent was VOAPP.

36. Artizov and Naumov, *Vlast'*, 77, 741 n. 91; Brown, *Proletarian Episode*, 53–54.

37. Artizov and Naumov, *Vlast'*, 88–90.

38. *Pravda*, 18 April 1931.

39. Fitzpatrick, *Cultural Front*, 145.

40. Dobrenko, *Making of the State Writer*, 225.

41. E. J. Brown makes this important point: "Writers embroiled in controversy sought to use Stalin against their adversaries and were therefore themselves to some extent responsible for establishing the pattern of authoritarian control." Brown, "The Year of Acquiescence," in Hayward and Labedz, *Literature and Revolution*, 57.

42. Cf. his October 1932 speech (in the text below). Later he was more excited by the possibilities of cinema.

43. Artizov and Naumov, *Vlast'*, 68, 82, 742 n. 2.

44. Gorky and A. Sviderskii (Narkompros) had backed the play at a session of the artistic council of MKhAT in October 1928. Sviderskii commented, "If the play is artistic, then we, as Marxists, should consider it Soviet. The term 'Soviet' and 'anti-Soviet' play should be abandoned." Following a denunciation of Sviderskii to the CC by the head of Glavrepertkom, Sviderskii accused Glavrepertkom of categorizing "Soviet" and "non-Soviet" plays on the basis of very crude criteria. V. Losev, ed., *Mikhail Bulgakov. Dnevnik. Pis'ma. 1914–1940* (Moscow, 1997), 190.

45. Artizov and Naumov, *Vlast'*, 86–88.

46. P. Kerzhentsev, deputy head of Agitprop, had produced a scathing report about *Flight*, which argued that staging it at MKhAT "would be a victory for the most reactionary and right-wing factions inside Soviet theater." A commission consisting of Voroshilov, Kaganovich, Tomskii, and A. Smirnov considered the play and recommended that it be withdrawn. Artizov and Naumov, *Vlast'*, 91–6, 98–100, 744 n. 14.

47. Ibid., 100–101; I. Stalin, *Sochineniia*, vols. 1–13 (Moscow, 1946–51) and vols. 1–3/vols. 14–16 (Stanford, Calif., 1967), vol. 11, 326–29.

48. Gromov, *Stalin*, 113.

49. Artizov and Naumov, *Vlast'*, 113.

50. *Pravda*, 9 February 1929.

51. The author of an article that cited Stalin's speech was reprimanded. Artizov and Naumov, *Vlast'*, 745 n. 17; RGASPI 558/11/88/21–23.

52. Artizov and Naumov, *Vlast'*, 102–7; RGASPI 558/11/1113/12–43 (uncorrected version).

53. The revival was doubtless partly attributable to the intercession of Gorky: see his letter of 12 November 1931 in " 'Zhmu vashu ruku, dorogoi tovarishch': Perepiska Maksima Gor'kogo i Iosifa Stalina," *Novyi Mir* 9 (1997), 188–89.

54. Gromov, *Stalin*, 114–16.

55. M. Nike, "I. V. Stalin. Otvet pisateliam-kommunistam iz RAPPa (28.02.1929). K istorii rospuska RAPPa," *Minuvshee* 12 (1993), 362–76; Maksimenkov, *Bol'shaia tsenzura*, 135–39.

56. Maksimenkov, *Bol'shaia tsenzura*, 139.

57. Artizov and Naumov, *Vlast'*, 109–12.

58. " 'Zhmu vashu ruku, dorogoi tovarishch,' " 169; Artizov and Naumov, *Vlast'*, 125; Stalin, *Sochineniia*, vol. 12, 177.

59. Kemp-Welch, *Stalin and the Literary Intelligentsia*, 82–86; Brown, *Proletarian Episode*, 150–71.

60. Maksimenkov, *Bol'shaia tsenzura*, 180–81.

61. Stalin, *Sochineniia*, vol. 12, 200–201. He adopted a similarly measured tone in relation to Mikhail Sholokhov's *Quiet Flows the Don* in 1929, arguing that although the writer had made a number of very serious mistakes, this did not mean the work should be banned. Ibid., 112.

62. *XVI s"ezd VKP(b): Stenograficheskii otchet* (Moscow, 1930), 393–96; Kemp-Welch, *Stalin and the Literary Intelligentsia*, 85–86.

63. Artizov and Naumov, *Vlast'*, 147.

64. Ibid., 157–59. Rehearsals for this play were terminated in May 1932, however. Gromov, *Stalin*, 135–36.

65. Artizov and Naumov, *Vlast'*, 139–41; Fitzpatrick, *Cultural Front*, 243–44.

66. Artizov and Naumov, *Vlast'*, 170–71. The OGPU report also contained some more critical comments.

67. R. W. Davies, *Crisis and Progress in the Soviet Economy, 1931–1933* (Basingstoke, England, 1996), 133–41, 209–15.

68. Artizov and Naumov, *Vlast'*, 168.

69. Ibid., 172–73.

70. Kemp-Welch, *Stalin and the Literary Intelligentsia*, 115; V. Ia. Kirpotin, *Rovesnik zheleznogo veka* (Moscow, 2006), 156–57.

71. Kirpotin, *Rovesnik*, 177.

72. Maksimenkov, "Ocherki," 221–24; Maksimenkov, *Bol'shaia tsenzura*, 521; RGASPI 558/11/1116/28.

73. RGASPI 558/11/1116/20–27.

74. RGASPI 558/11/1116/29–30.

75. Artizov and Naumov, *Vlast'*, 131–37; Stalin, *Sochineniia*, vol. 13, 23–27; A. Dubrovsky, "Chronicle of a Poet's Downfall," in Kevin Platt and David Brandenberger, eds., *Epic Revisionism: Russian History and Literature as Stalinist Propaganda* (Madison, Wis., 2006), 79–84.

76. Artizov and Naumov, *Vlast'*, 192; O. V. Khlevniuk, R. W. Davies, L. P. Kosheleva, E. A. Rees, and L. A. Rogovaia, eds., *Stalin i Kaganovich: Perepiska, 1931–1936 gg.* (Moscow, 2001), 323–24. In November 1933, Stalin informed Afinogenov that he considered the second version unsuccessful. For more on this episode, see Jochen Hellbeck, *Revolution on My Mind* (Cambridge, Mass., 2006), 293–94.

77. Khlevniuk et al., *Stalin i Kaganovich*, 431, 437–38.

78. Fitzpatrick, *Cultural Front*, 243.

79. For an example of one their petitions, see A. Fadeev's letter of 10 May to Kaganovich in Artizov and Naumov, *Vlast'*, 176–77.

80. Stalin's visitors' book records a meeting with Gronskii, Kirshon, Fadeev, and Averbakh on 11 May 1932. Artizov and Naumov, *Vlast'*, 689.

81. I. Gronskii, *Iz proshlogo* (Moscow, 1991), 334–36; Kemp-Welch, *Stalin and the Literary Intelligentsia*, 132.

82. RGASPI 558/11/1116/32.

83. Stalin made similar comments about plays at the 26 October meeting. On 23 October the Politburo issued a decree banning theaters from monopolizing certain

plays, and ordering that the most popular plays be staged simultaneously in several theaters. Artizov and Naumov, *Vlast'*, 185.

84. RGASPI 558/11/1116/21–23.

85. RGASPI 558/11/1116/25–27.

86. Gronskii, *Iz proshlogo*, 340–44, 349–54.

87. Kirpotin, *Rovesnik*, 155. Compare the use of a similar image of an unfinished building in Lunacharsky's speech on socialist realism at the second plenum of the Orgkomitet in February 1933. Kemp-Welch, *Stalin and the Literary Intelligentsia*, 143.

88. *Sovetskaia literatura na novom etape* (Moscow, 1933); Kemp-Welch, *Stalin and the Literary Intelligentsia*, 143–45.

89. Ilya Ehrenburg, *Men, Years—Life* (Moscow, 1962–66), vol. 4, 40; Regine Robin, *Socialist Realism: An Impossible Aesthetic* (Stanford, Calif., 1992), 9–36.

90. See Gorky's letter in which he asks Stalin to check and amend his report to the congress: Artizov and Naumov, *Vlast'*, 220; For correspondence with Kaganovich, see Khlevniuk et al., *Stalin i Kaganovich*, 436–37, 441, 447, 449–53, 462–66; and with Zhdanov, see Artizov and Naumov, *Vlast'*, 230–31.

91. *Pervyi vsesoiuznyi s"ezd sovetskikh pisatelei: Stenograficheskii otchet* (Moscow, 1934), 5; Kemp-Welch *Stalin and the Literary Intelligentsia*, 177.

92. Kirpotin, *Rovesnik*, 266–69; Ermolaev, *Soviet Literary Theories*, 197–200.

93. *Pervyi vsesoiuznyi s"ezd*, 490–502, 671. The "Statutes" of the Union also referred to the need for the "creative competition of writers." Ibid., 712.

94. RGASPI 558/11/709/169; 558/11/730/18–20. Gronskii recalls Stalin telling him that Bukharin's and Radek's speeches had only been allowed because of pressure from Gorky: "Gorky raped us." Gronskii himself boycotted the congress because of these speeches. Gronskii, *Iz proshlogo*, 154.

95. *Pervyi vsesoiuznyi s"ezd*, 16–17.

96. Ibid., 272.

97. Ibid., 183–84.

98. Ibid., 466.

99. Robin, *Socialist Realism*, 74.

100. Gromov, *Stalin*, 277–81; Maksimenkov, *Bol'shaia tsenzura*, 326.

101. Artizov and Naumov, *Vlast'*, 279, 409.

102. K. M. Anderson, L. V. Maksimenkov, L. P. Kosheleva, and L. A. Rogovaia, eds., *Kremlevskii kinoteatr, 1928–1953* (Moscow, 2005), 596–97.

103. Ibid., 587–92.

104. Highly publicized meetings between Stalin and leading foreign writers sympathetic to the Soviet cause were a common occurrence in the 1930s. Stalin met with H. G. Wells, H. Barbusse, and R. Rolland, among others, in his efforts to present a positive image to the West. See Michael David-Fox, "The 'Heretic Life' of a Friend of Stalin: Romain Rolland and Soviet Culture," *Slavonica* 1 (2005), 3-29.

105. RGASPI 558/11/1120/1–7.

106. Alexei Yurchak, *Everything Was Forever, Until It Was No More* (Princeton, N.J., 2006), 10–14.

107. It is customary to cite Pasternak's assessment: "And when the war broke out, its real horrors, its real dangers, its menace of real death were a blessing compared to the inhuman reign of the lie, and they broke relief because they broke the spell of the dead letter." Jeffrey Brooks, *Thank You, Comrade Stalin!* (Princeton, N.J., 2000), 173–75; Richard Stites, ed., *Culture and Entertainment in Wartime Russia* (Bloomington, Ind., 1995), 5. Clark and Dobrenko argue a rather different line in their *Soviet Culture and Power*, 348–49. Stalin himself was clearly preoccupied during the war and had somewhat less time to spend on cultural matters.

108. D. Babichenko, ed., *Pisateli i tsenzory* (Moscow, 1994), 112–13.

109. Maksimenkov, *Bol'shaia tsenzura*, 558.

110. F. Panferov, "O cherepkakh i cherepushkakh," *Oktiabr'* 5 (1946), 151–62.

111. *Pravda*, 24 June 1946; Babichenko, *Pisateli*, 115.

112. Maksimenkov, *Bol'shaia tsenzura*, 573–76; Artizov and Naumov, *Vlast'*, 581–84.

113. Konstantin Simonov, *Glazami cheloveka moego pokoleniia* (Moscow, 1989), 128. Simonov's fascinating firsthand account appears quite convincing, although it is inevitably somewhat colored by his own attachment to Stalin, which was shaken but never completely destroyed, and by his desire to justify his conduct in the Stalin era. See Orlando Figes, *The Whisperers* (London, 2007), 615–29.

114. Dmitrii Shepilov, *The Kremlin's Scholar* (New Haven, 2007), 106. Although Shepilov clearly had an interest in defending Stalin's reputation, his attitude to the *vozhd'* was not uncritical.

115. Harold Swayze, *Political Control of Literature in the USSR, 1946–1959* (Cambridge, Mass., 1962), 64–82.

116. See, for example, the MGB report on the Union in Maksimenkov, *Bol'shaia tsenzura*, 606–8.

117. Stalin, *Sochineniia*, vol. 11, 326–29.

118. On Stalin Prizes, see Oliver Johnson, "The Stalin Prize and the Soviet Artist: Status Symbol or Stigma?" *Slavic Review* 4 (2011), 819–43.

119. Simonov, *Glazami*, 200; A. Belik, "O nekotorykh oshibkakh v literaturovedenii," *Oktiabr'* 2 (1950), 150–64.

120. Simonov, *Glazami*, 200–201.

121. *Pravda*, 30 March 1950.

122. Gromov, *Stalin*, 440. Swayze views the Belik episode as a means of introducing moderate change in the prevailing atmosphere. *Political Control of Literature*, 67–71, 82.

123. Ethan Pollock, *Stalin and the Soviet Science Wars* (Princeton, N.J., 2006), 104, 129. See also Yurchak, *Everything Was Forever*, 44–47; Swayze, *Political Control*, 70–71; Katerina Clark, *The Soviet Novel: History as Ritual* (Chicago, 1985), 214.

124. *Pervyi vsesoiuznyi s"ezd*, 712.

125. Maksimenkov, *Bol'shaia tsenzura*, 559.

126. Clark and Dobrenko, *Soviet Culture and Power*, 140.

127. On the reliability of Shumiatskii's notes, see Leonid Maksimenkov's observations in his introduction to Anderson et al., *Kremlevskii kinoteatr*, 75–77.

128. Shepilov, *Kremlin's Scholar*, 105–6. *Makar Dubrava* was awarded a second-class prize.

129. Simonov, *Glazami*, 166–67, 182–83.

130. RGASPI 558/11/202/45–46.

131. RGASPI 558/11/702/101.

132. Maksimenkov, *Bol'shaia tsenzura*, 258–59.

133. Simonov, *Glazami*, 185–86; A. Latynina , "The Stalin Prizes for Literature as the Quintessence of Socialist Realism," in H. Chung, ed., *In the Party Spirit: Socialist Realism and Literary Practice in the Soviet Union, East Germany and China* (Amsterdam, 1996), 116.

134. Artizov and Naumov, *Vlast'*, 675–81.

135. Gromov, *Stalin*, 449–51.

136. RGASPI 558/11/205/129–37.

137. Simonov, *Glazami*, 205–6.

138. Ibid., 206–7.

139. Katerina Clark, "Little Heroes and Big Deeds: Literature Responds to the First Five-Year Plan," in Sheila Fitzpatrick, ed., *Cultural Revolution in Russia, 1928–1931* (Bloomington, Ind., 1984).

140. G. Mar'iamov, *Kremlevskii tsenzor. Stalin smotrit kino* (Moscow, 1992).

141. RGASPI 558/11/828/32–34.

142. RGASPI 558/11/828/27–29.

143. RGASPI 558/11/828/53, 74.

144. RGASPI 558/11/828/48, 51–52; G. Aleksandrov, *Epokha i kino* (Moscow, 1976), 184.

145. For example, it was criticized at the Writers' Congress, where A. Surkov referred disparagingly to its "lemonade ideology." *Pervyi vsesoiuznyi s"ezd*, 515.

146. RGASPI 558/11/828/54.

147. RGASPI 558/11/828/56, 76; 558/11/829/63; 558/11/829/37–39; 58/11/829/45.

148. RGASPI 558/11/828/79–80; 558/11/829/61.

149. RGASPI 558/11/829/5.

150. Stalin had praised his 1928 film, *Arsenal*, which he described as having "real revolutionary romanticism." Gromov, *Stalin*, 189; RGASPI 558/11/828/64.

151. RGASPI 558/11/829/57.

152. RGASPI 558/11/829/64.

153. *Pravda*, 28 January 1936; Leonid Maksimenkov, *Sumbur vmesto muzyki* (Moscow, 1997), 88–112; Fitzpatrick, *Cultural Front*, 187; Elizabeth Wilson, *Shostakovich: A Life Remembered* (London, 1994), 109.

154. RGASPI 558/11/829/69–72.

155. Of course, Stalin also insisted that historical events and figures be presented "truthfully": just one of many examples is in his discussion of Eisenstein's *Ivan Groznyi*. Artizov and Naumov, *Vlast'*, 614–15.

156. Later, Stalin also commended Wassilewska for her "truthful" depiction of "gray" people. Ibid., 450–53.

157. RGASPI 558/11/828/39; 558/11/829/3.

158. Anderson et al., *Kremlevskii kinoteatr*, 579–80.

159. Ibid., 759–61.

160. Artizov and Naumov, *Vlast'*, 573. For more on this episode, see Ethan Pollock, "'Real Men Go the Bania': Postwar Soviet Masculinities and the Bathhouse," *Kritika* 1 (2010), 47–76.

161. RGASPI 558/11/828/53.

162. RGASPI 558/11/828/27–29, 31.

163. RGASPI 558/11/829/7–8 .

164. RGASPI 558/11/829/11, 16–18.

165. Artizov and Naumov, *Vlast'*, 479, 781 n. 4. Werth argues that Stalin had actually suggested the theme to Korneichuk. Certainly Stalin had previously been very complimentary about earlier work by Korneichuk, He subsequently edited a draft of an anonymous review of *The Front* that explained the significance of the play. Alexander Werth, *Russia at War* (London, 1964), 423; Artizov and Naumov, *Vlast'*, 466; Maksimenkov, *Bol'shaia tsenzura*, 531–32. For Amir Weiner's interpretation of the play, see his *Making Sense of War* (Princeton, N.J., 2001), 43–46.

166. Simonov, *Glazami*, 110.

167. Ibid., 162–63; Ilya Ehrenburg, *Men, Years—Life*, vol. 6, 45–46.

168. Clark, *Soviet Novel*, 204.

169. Struve, *Russian Literature under Lenin and Stalin*, 383.

170. Simonov, *Glazami*, 165. Shepilov recounts a similar version of this episode in *Kremlin's Scholar*, 107.

171. Gromov, *Stalin*, 441; Simonov, *Glazami*, 195.

172. Simonov, *Glazami*, 212.

173. Ibid., 204. It was awarded a third prize.

174. Ibid., 233–34.

175. Walter Vickery, "Zhdanovism," in Hayward and Labedz, *Literature and Revolution in Soviet Russia*, 118–20; *Pravda*, 6 October 1952.

Conclusion

1. J. Arch Getty "The Politics of Stalinism," in Alec Nove, ed., *The Stalin Phenomenon* (London, 1993), 101.

2. For example, Robert H. McNeal, *Stalin: Man and Ruler* (New York, 1988), xi.

3. These include Evgenii Gromov, *Stalin: Vlast' i iskusstvo* (Moscow, 1998); Erik Van Ree, *The Political Thought of Joseph Stalin* (London, 2002); Simon Sebag Montefiore, *Stalin: The Court of the Red Tsar* (London, 2003); Yoram Gorlizki and Oleg Khlevniuk, *Cold Peace: Stalin and the Ruling Circle* (Oxford, 2004); Robert Service, *Stalin: A Biography* (2004); Hiroaki Kuromiya, *Stalin: Profiles in Power* (Harlow, England, 2005); Sarah Davies and James Harris, eds., *Stalin: A New History* (Cambridge, England, 2005); Oleg Khlevniuk, *Master of the House: Stalin and His Inner Circle* (New Haven, 2008).

4. For example, Jorg Baberowski, *Der rote Terror: Die Geschichte des Stalinismus* (Munich, 2004), 12. For a contrasting view, see Kuromiya, *Stalin*, 208.

5. David Priestland, *Stalinism and the Politics of Mobilization: Ideas, Power and Terror in Inter-war Russia* (Oxford, 2007).

6. Variations on this view can be found in Bertram D. Wolfe, *An Ideology in Power: Reflections on the Russian Revolution* (New York, 1969); Leszek Kolakowski, "Marxist Roots of Stalinism," in Robert C. Tucker, ed., *Stalinism: Essays in Historical Interpretation* (New York, 1977); Martin Malia, *The Soviet Tragedy: A History of Socialism in Russia, 1917–1991* (New York, 1995).

7. For example, Moshe Lewin, *The Making of the Soviet System: Essays in the Social History of Interwar Russia* (New York, 1985); Ken Jowitt, "Soviet Neo-Traditionalism: The Political Corruption of a Leninist Regime," *Soviet Studies* 3 (1983), 275–97; J. Arch Getty, *Practicing Stalinism: Bolsheviks, Boyars, and the Persistence of Tradition* (New Haven, 2013); David Hoffmann, "European Modernity and Soviet Socialism," in David Hoffmann and Yanni Kotsonis, *Russian Modernity: Politics, Knowledge, Practices* (New York, 2000); Peter Holquist, "To Count, to Extract, and to Exterminate: Population Statistics and Population Politics in Late Imperial and Soviet Russia," in Ronald Suny and Terry Martin, eds., *A State of Nations: Empire and Nation-Making in the Age of Lenin and Stalin* (New York, 2001).

INDEX

Trotsk (Gatchina), 142

Trotsky, L., 57, 69, 143, 166, 203–4; on
    Bolshevik leadership, 22, 24, 31; and
    capitalist encirclement, 92, 98, 102;
    on culture, 233–37, 240; expulsion
    and exile of, 31, 37, 80–81, 83–89, 91;
    as head of Red Army, 23; on
    intelligentsia, 212; on Kirov
    assassination, 84–85; and Shakhty
    affair, 74; on Stalin as bureaucrat, 7,
    26, 28, 58; and succession to Lenin,
    22–24, 167; and Trotskyism, 45, 57,
    86–89, 106, 169, 174, 193, 201, 221;
    on working class, 183

Tsaritsyn, 142–44, 176

Tucker, R., 133

Tukhachevskii, M., 115, 202

Tumarkin, N., 138

Turgenev, I., 259

Turkey, 66, 97–98, 110, 113

Tychina, P., 254

Uchida, Y., 123

Ukraine, 50, 177; and capitalist
    encirclement, 100, 103, 112, 117–19;
    crop failures in, 30, 117; and spies,
    64–65, 87

United Kingdom. See Britain

United Opposition, 29, 31, 37, 102, 106

United States, 106, 110, 117, 119, 123, 127

Utesov, L., 265

Van Ree, E., 134

Vannikov, B., 223

Vardin, I., 234, 238

Veger, E., 180

Versailles Treaty, 127

Vishnevskii, Vs., 268

Voikov, P., 105

Voitinskaia, O., 254

Volin, B., 148

Volkogonov, D., 147

Voronskii, A., 233–34, 238

Voroshilov, K., 67, 93, 105, 109, 114–15,
    119, 214; and cult of Stalin, 135, 153,
    165–67; and culture, 269; and place
    names, 177–79; and slogans, 172, 210

Vorovskii, V., 98

Wasilewska, W., 255

Weiner, A., 230

Wells, H., 212

Weygand, M., General, 97, 124, 302 n.
    137

workers, working class, 2, 6, 15, 64, 276;
    as "advanced," 191, 196, 198; as
    "backward," 191–95, 199–200, 225,
    229, 276–77; dilution of, 186–88,
    190–92; and foreign policy, 93–95,
    107, 130; and Great Terror, 201–4,
    223; as heroic figures, 183–84, 186,
    188–91, 197–98, 228; and Labor
    Reserve scheme, 227–28; language for,
    206–10, 225–26, 229; and legislation
    of 1940, 223–24, 228; low productivity
    of, 223–28; and NEP, 185, 187;
    "Organization Report" of, 24; as party
    members, 184, 186–87, 199, 213; and
    Rabkrin, 21–23; Stakhanovite
    movement, 56, 164–65, 168–69, 191,
    194–95, 198–99; standard of living of,
    59, 69, 193–94, 206–7, 227; and
    strikes, 59, 185, 187, 189, 200

wrecking, 8–9, 30, 42, 46, 53, 55, 57,
    199–200, 202–3; and capitalist
    powers, 48, 75, 89, 169; and Shakhty
    affair, 74–75, 188

Yakobson, S., 170

Yugoslavia, 126

Yurchak, A., 11, 256

Zamiatin, E., 245

Zarkhi, N., 253

Zhdanov, A., 202, 252–54, 257, 272;
    and cult of Stalin, 159, 163